PHILOSOPHY IN
MULTIPLE VOICES

PHILOSOPHY IN MULTIPLE VOICES

GEORGE YANCY

ROWMAN & LITTLEFIELD PUBLISHERS, INC.
Lanham • Boulder • New York • Toronto • Plymouth, UK

ROWMAN & LITTLEFIELD PUBLISHERS, INC.

Published in the United States of America
by Rowman & Littlefield Publishers, Inc.
A wholly owned subsidiary of The Rowman & Littlefield Publishing Group, Inc.
4501 Forbes Boulevard, Suite 200, Lanham, Maryland 20706
www.rowmanlittlefield.com

Estover Road
Plymouth PL6 7PY
United Kingdom

British Library Cataloguing in Publication Information Available

Library of Congress Cataloging-in-Publication Data:
Philosophy in multiple voices / edited by George Yancy.
    p. cm.
  Includes bibliographical references.
  ISBN-13: 978-0-7425-4954-8 (cloth : alk. paper)
  ISBN-10: 0-7425-4954-2 (cloth : alk. paper)
  ISBN-13: 978-0-7425-4955-5 (pbk. : alk. paper)
  ISBN-10: 0-7425-4955-0 (pbk. : alk. paper)
  1. Philosophy—Introductions. I. Yancy, George.
  BD21.P476 2007
  108—dc22
                                        2007008389

Printed in the United States of America

♾™ The paper used in this publication meets the minimum requirements of American
National Standard for Information Sciences—Permanence of Paper for Printed Library
Materials, ANSI/NISO Z39.48-1992.

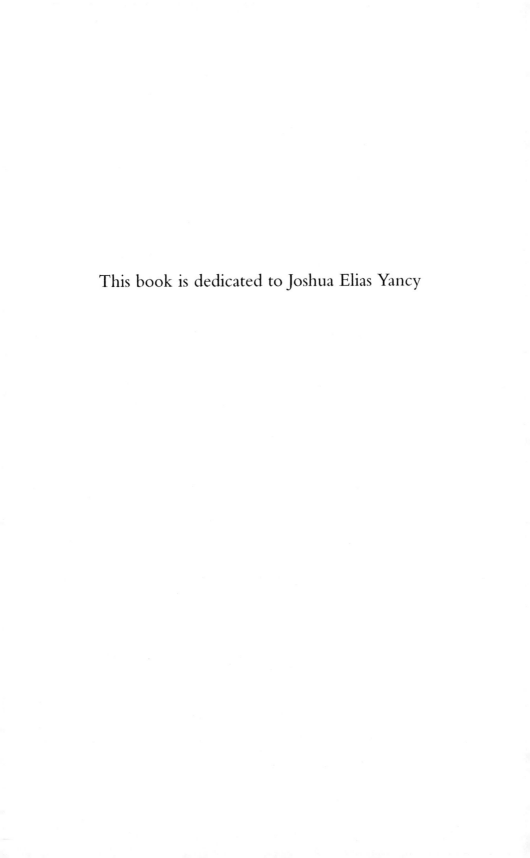

This book is dedicated to Joshua Elias Yancy

CONTENTS

Acknowledgments

I WOULD LIKE TO THANK Dr. Ross H. Miller, currently senior editor at Rowman & Littlefield, for his patience, enthusiastic encouragement, candidness, and dedication to the fruition of this project. Eve DeVaro Fowler, former philosophy editor at Rowman & Littlefield, is thanked for her conversations and enthusiasm for this text. As an editor, she was always engaged and passionate about new ideas and how such ideas might contribute to the growth of knowledge. She knew how to make authors and editors feel strong and hopeful. I would also like to thank Emily W. Ross for her spiritedness, understanding, and cordiality. Ruth Gilbert, editorial assistant, is thanked for her professionalism and organizational skills. I would like to say thanks to Katherine Macdonald, Associate Production Editor, specifically in terms of her appreciation for detail and for moving this project along within a timely fashion. I would especially like to thank Terry Fischer, Managing Editor, for his indispensable assistance in the final stages of this project. I would like to thank all of the contributors for their enthusiasm and willingness to give of their time to produce such excellent contributions. I would especially like to thank Randall Halle for deciding to contribute to this project on such short notice. Thanks for your dedication and alacrity. Monique Roelofs's assistance and critical insights were invaluable. Jim Swindal, colleague and chairperson of the philosophy department, and Francesco C. Cesareo, dean of the McAnulty College and Graduate School of Liberal Arts, are thanked for their continual interest in and support of my scholarly work. I would like to thank Fred Evans for his critical philosophical insights, friendship, and shared sense of political justice. Our work has philosophical overlap and key points of family resemblance. John McClendon's advice, friendship, and scholarship speak for themselves. James Spady, as always, is thanked for his support and prescience regarding the importance of my own philosophical voice. I would like to extend a special thanks to Fred Evans, John Lachs, and Clevis Headley for the time they took to comment upon the introduction to this text. My mother, Ruth, Artrice, Carson, and Brother El are thanked for their support and love. My in-laws are thanked for their long-distance support, fun and extremely helpful visits, and abundant love for the Yancy boys. My family, Susan, Adrian, Gabriel, Elijah, and Joshua, the littlest one to whom this book is dedicated, are all thanked for their patience and persistence at *dispelling the illusion* that to be a productive philosopher one must remain secluded within the private domain of reflective thought.

Introduction:
No Philosophical Oracle Voices

GEORGE YANCY

> *There are no transcendental rules a priori that are the essential,*
> *thus defining, feature of "philosophy."*
>
> —LUCIUS OUTLAW

> *Hey, don't be fooled. Where we live philosophy is white. . . .*
> *White men, white marble, white hair, white shirts under blue*
> *blazers and red ties.*
>
> —CHRIS J. CUOMO

I HAD THE RARE and philosophically stimulating opportunity to engage in an extensive conversation with American philosopher Paul Weiss two months before his death.[1] In fact, our discussion took place just two weeks before he turned 101. At 100, Weiss was sharp, engaging, and remembered details from his past with tremendous clarity. We discussed his personal encounters with Bertrand Russell and Alfred North Whitehead, and his thoughts on Martin Heidegger, death, what makes a creative philosopher, the meaning of life, why he founded the *Review of Metaphysics* and the Metaphysical Society of America, both of which he started as a direct response to logical positivism, and so much more. I was struck by his philosophical vivacity. I was particularly moved by his conception of the philosopher as one who looks for trouble. This fascinating conception of the philosopher as a "troublemaker" resonated with my own philosophical proclivities and tenacity, and spoke to aspects of my experiences, though in ways that Weiss may not have intended the term to be used. On one occasion, for example, a white philosopher-mentor of mine told me not to become pegged a philosopher who does African American philosophy. The subtext of his "advice" cautioned me against being *marked*, as it were, as someone who has somehow moved outside the "legitimate" bounds of philosophy. The fact of the matter is that he, however, had been marked; he had been interpellated by normative assumptions governing the nature of "legitimate" philosophical inquiry. His unquestioned assumptions insulated him from examining his own blinkers, effectively insuring a level of opacity regarding how he was implicated in larger, specifically Western, systemic historical and institutional forces and epistemic orders, which helped to form his philosophical identity, and in various value-laden suppositions regarding philosophy, its content, and its aims.[2]

Had I desired and taken steps to become a Kantian scholar, I am sure that he would not have cautioned me against spending my philosophical energies exploring Kant's *Critique of Pure Reason* or his deontological ethics. Had I desired to specialize in the area of philosophy of religion, such themes as God's existence, theodicy, the problem of religious language, or the problem of God's foreknowledge and human freedom would have no doubt been granted philosophical legitimacy without question. In short, I would not have been pegged, but encouraged to specialize. His advice that I not become pegged functioned as an instantiation of a regulatory norm that had already shaped his philosophical formation. As philosopher Lisa Heldke notes, "Understandings developed from positions of privilege require their holders to ignore or conceal too much about how the world is understood from other standpoints; in being responsible to such a position, one must be irresponsible to too many others."[3] I was in the process of being groomed to become one of the "philosophical we," those who have accepted what constitutes the discursive parameters of "genuine" philosophical problems without critically "asking who is this 'we' whose problems these are, out of whose experiences do they arise, and from whose perspective are they salient?"[4] It is important, however, that we never forget the processes of "domination and exclusion which are implicated in an abstract appeal to the 'we' who *share*."[5] It might be argued that my white philosopher-mentor did not act "objectively" (that is, he was not less partial) toward my interests. His own unreflective stance vis-à-vis his privileged position as a white male within a white male dominant elitist profession like philosophy created a form of systematic ignorance about the way that power shaped, in this case, his understanding of the distinction between "legitimate" philosophy and "illegitimate" philosophy. "Acting objectively (responsibly) requires understanding oneself and one's connections with others, in order to make reasoned and reasonable assessments about how to respond to others' needs, desires, and interests, stated and unstated."[6] Within this context, his "advice" did not take into consideration my own philosophical needs, but excluded me as an active participant in my own philosophical formation and also excluded an entire field of philosophical inquiry. On this score, African American philosophy was deemed ersatz philosophy and unworthy of intellectual commitment.

Instead of following his advice, however, I caused trouble. I refused his hailing and thus challenged those philosophical areas of inquiry that have traditionally refused to take seriously the philosophical significance of the Black experience and the philosophical knowledge productions characteristic of a people who have struggled to articulate their own sociopolitical praxes and historical journey. I troubled his unstated assumption that African American philosophy was too marginal, too insignificant, by making this a primary area of philosophical concern, thus nurturing a philosophical subjectivity grounded within the historical struggle of Black people in America, a struggle that has, among others, epistemological and social ontological resources. On another occasion, a teacher in high school once said to me: "Major in philosophy? You have to be wealthy to pursue philosophy." Again, I opted to cause trouble. Given the reality that most of my early childhood and teenage years were spent living in Richard Allen Homes, a low-income housing project in North Philadelphia, the prospect of pursuing something as "impractical" as philosophy seemed to ring with some truth. However, as a young teenager, self-sequestered in my room, I spent long days and long nights reading as much philosophy as I could find at the local neighborhood library and at my school's library. Reading Plato, Aristotle, and Spinoza in the hood was already a site of troublemaking, though not from the perspective of those already in the hood, but from the perspective of those who viewed/view Black people within ghetto lifeworlds as nihilistic, hopeless, uneducable, and pathological. To have a voracious desire to read at all created trouble for those who could only envision Blacks in the ghetto as mediocre and anti-intellectual.

Reading the works of Plato, Aristotle, and Spinoza was completely off the map of expectation, even for many of my teachers. My early adventures into the thoughts and works of these philosophers troubled the statistics, assumptions, and theories of those who were/are procrustean in their understanding of Black people. In fact, many of the philosophers that I read at the time had already theorized my incapacity for doing philosophy and, by implication, narrated the inevitable trajectory of my shallow or even nonexistent intellectual life. After all, Hume said that any intelligent philosophical words that came from my mouth indicated nothing more than that I was a good "parrot who speaks a few words plainly";[7] Kant said that my being Black was clear *proof* that anything that I said was stupid;[8] Hegel said that I was incapable of any level of abstract critical reflection because "the Negro is an example of animal man in all his savagery and lawlessness."[9] Doing philosophy in Black skin is always already a site of troublemaking; it is to trouble the mythos of white superiority. Doing philosophy, then, came with a peculiar disjunctive bind. Either I was to settle for what nature itself forbade or I was to challenge the laws of nature, as it were, do philosophy in Black skin, and thereby become an anomaly. I troubled both, refusing the view that my personal intellectual narrative had been foreclosed by ineluctable laws of nature, on the one hand, and refusing the role of a philosopher-freak, a monstrosity, on the other.

Of course, this theme of biology as destiny also negatively implicated white women. For example, Aristotle thought that a woman was a "misbegotten male." Tertullian described women as "the devil's gateway," Schopenhauer thought that women were "big children their whole life long,"[10] and Kant observed that a woman's "philosophy is not to reason, but to sense."[11] So, even white women, though not because of their whiteness, trouble the waters as they continue to define themselves and self-ascribe as philosophers within academic spaces that question a priori the legitimacy of their insights and reflections. In short, in philosophy, despite the assumption that many philosophers hold that the body is simply accidental to philosophical engagement, bodies do matter. White male bodies can do philosophy along a continuum from brilliantly to poorly, but they are still capable of doing philosophy. There is nothing about doing philosophy that belies their nature. Within a phallocentric philosophical universe of discourse, women's knowledge productions are rendered "soft" and thereby not philosophical. On this score, the term "soft" has a family resemblance to such expressions as mild, sentimental, deficient, feeble, illogical, intuitive, dependent, passive, and unmanly.

Women of color in the field of philosophy, however, are deemed walking, talking "bushes,"[12] an explicit reference to the specific area of the genitalia; they are stereotyped as maids and prostitutes.[13] The point here is that passivity and dependency are descriptor terms, for the most part, that have historically been applied to *white* women. For example, while it is true that women of color are also deemed intellectually deficient, it is important to note that Black women have had to fight against images of themselves as matriarchs and whores.[14] In other words, Black women are deemed "hard," independent, sexually voracious and assertive—not innocent, fragile creatures deserving to be placed upon a pedestal. Regarding the image of the stereotypically Black maid, African American philosopher Anita Allen disclosed that a white male philosopher once placed the palms of his hands very gently around her face and said, "You look like a maid my family once had."[15] Allen, in effect, became the embodied Mammy figure for this white male philosopher. The dominant Mammy stereotype rendered Allen both invisible in terms of her critical philosophical acumen and hypervisible in terms of the historical distortion and caricature of Black women as protective of white children who were often cared for at the expense of Black children. Allen became someone whose job it was to nurture the white male philosopher without any hint of bitterness. It was not her philosophical brilliance that mattered, but her caretaking abilities, her role as servant, her being as a site of white pleasure and security. It is no easy task for Black women philosophers *to be* philosophers within such white male spaces of phantasmagoria. Indeed, within these spaces, women of color also become sexually exotic others, deemed always already sexually available, and objects of white male desire and transference. This is not to deny that white women have suffered sexual harassment from male philosophers or have suffered the sting of degrading reductions and name-calling, but it is important not to flatten the differential oppressive histories that were/are operative in the lives of white women and women of color.

As women of color trouble the field of philosophy, not only through the sheer fact of their embodied presence, but through the insights that they bring to bear upon such areas as ethics, epistemology, political philosophy, issues of social justice, critical theory, standpoint theory, and the like, they continue to be stereotyped as Mammies and Jezebels. Within the context of an anti-Black racist world, Frantz Fanon notes, "[W]hen I was present, it [reason] was not; when it [reason] was there, I was no longer."[16] Indeed, when reason and philosophy become collapsed as the sine qua non of what it means to be human, the ability or lack of ability to do philosophy gets raised to the level of philosophical anthropology. On this score, philosophical reflection is inextricably linked to the question of the *anthropos*, the very meaning of the human.

The philosopher as troublemaker, inflected through my own current philosophical projects and sense of mission, suggests one who is *not* content with the philosophical status quo, the strict policing of philosophical borders, the rigidity of historical and philosophical nostalgia, the encouragement of curricular calcification through the stipulation of myopic criteria for what constitutes philosophy and who its key players are, the illusion of politically and contextually neutral philosophical discourse, and the belief that one's philosophical assumptions are completely unrelated to one's identity as raced, gendered, sexed, and classed.[17] I would like to think that I have *not* settled for the often superficial, greater than thou, self-adulation of so many philosophers that I have encountered. Of course, even as I write and continue to publish, paradoxically I stand on the precipice of taking myself too seriously, forgetting that the practice of philosophy is contingent upon values that are founded by finite persons trying to make sense of a very small part of reality.

Philosophy as practiced in many universities and colleges in America is ripe to have its inertial tendencies troubled and shaken. There was a time when I lived under the illusion that philosophers were above petty bickering, backstabbing, name calling, punitive retribution at the level of blocking the advancement of another member in the department, racism, sexism, jealousy, propitiating those in positions of academic power for personal gain, and sycophantic worship. On this score, the professional practice of philosophy (the quotidian activities of publishing or perishing, writing furiously to complete that one book that will presumably secure tenure, participation at conferences where you make sure to shine before your colleagues, even if it means trashing another philosopher's work, the political hiring and firing of philosophers, etc.) can be extremely disillusioning. As philosopher Adrian M. S. Piper says, "It's not only that you yourself have to be subject to these power plays, Machiavellian schemes of one-upmanship, back stabbing . . . but it really destroys your ability to believe that the field is about what it says it's about."[18]

One form of troublemaking in the field of philosophy involves removing the veneer that departments of philosophy are these respectful, engaging sites free of deep political and personal fights. What passes as elenchus is often perfunctory self-aggrandizement that aims at devouring one's interlocutor, demanding recognition for one's "superior" philosophical talents, and showcasing one's "brilliance" through the enumeration of one's long list of publications. Within this context, a philosopher's racism, sexism, myopia, and xenophobia often go overlooked and unchallenged, while academia continues to run smoothly, producing functionary gatekeepers who insure that critical thought has its limits and that what is "philosophically significant" remains defined by certain tunnel-vision norms of selectivity. Within such a context, the stakes are very high. Philosophical standards are established, the philosophical canon is deemed sacrosanct, the discursive lines are drawn, and the battle begins. Many philosophical voices are marginalized and deemed ersatz vis-à-vis the dominant philosophical voice. Within the context of this dominant philosophical voice, careers are shaped, and some philosophers even move completely outside the confines of philosophy departments in order to engage in activities of knowledge production that are deemed extraneous to those "genuine" philosophical problems and themes dominant within those very departments.

The philosophical gatekeepers exert their influences, and through an act of prestidigitation, as it were, certain philosophical discourses, philosophical problems, assumptions, and distinctions, indeed, intelligibility itself, are deemed *given* and unconditioned. Their genesis is obfuscated through processes of normalization. This normalizing process—through canonical repetition, the crafting of syllabi, funding, socially constituted valorizations, and other institutionalizing processes—attempts to blur the reality that philosophizing is immanent and grounded within social and historical practices as opposed to founded upon a transcendental basis. In fact, there is often a sense that some philosophers are on a philosophical crusade to banish forms of philosophy, forms of discourse, and forms of embodiment that belie the philosopher as a pure knowing subject, one who lives the life of the mind free from the contingencies of history, context, and place. Needless to say, many of these philosopher-crusaders are very sincere, but sincerity can also function as bad faith, a form of being-in-the-world where philosophical hegemony is seen as *necessary* to the project of keeping philosophy qua philosophy pure, unsullied by the particularistic interests of those discourses that are best left outside the proper domain of "real" philosophy.

Being "outside" suggests spatiality vis-à-vis the "inside." The insiders, those who regulate and police both physical and discursive spaces, are those who see themselves as protecting the "purity" of philosophical borders, those who protect, through "imperial" superimposition, a certain conception of philosophy, those who sustain and reinforce familiar ways of understanding philosophical problems, defining philosophical problems, and approaching and addressing them. Even a certain style of discourse is deemed the only medium through which philosophical problems and their solutions can be articulated. The insiders function as what Fred Evans calls "oracles," voices that are deemed "absolute," "non-revisable," "complete," and "homogenous."[19] Indeed, the philosophical oracle voice feels threatened by those philosophically heterogeneous voices that compete for audibility, even as they attempt to be heard from sidelines to which they have been relegated and prejudged philosophically nugatory. The philosophical oracle voice speaks from an identity that is narrow and fixed, unreceptive to different philosophical voices/identities that emerge from different ways of engaging the world, understanding the world, and being-in-the-world.

The oracle voice is godlike, supposedly surveying the world from the aspect of eternity. The oracle voice is presumed self-grounded and unconditioned; it speaks and sees the world from nowhere, because it is deemed outside the flux of history, context, multiplicity, and heteroglossia. The philosophical oracle voice is deemed above the complex web of contestatory voices; it is unmoved by the play of multiple voices and the diversity of rich forms of life. It functions as Aristotle's unmoved mover. In other words, the philosophical oracle voice determines what counts as philosophy without its own voice being shaped by anything like the multiplicity of other voices entailed in the tradition, that is, by that which is anterior to its emergence. In fact, the philosophical oracle voice is deemed *causi sui*. This raises the issue of perspective and embodiment. After all, the philosophical oracle voice presumes to speak from nowhere. Hence, it functions as if disembodied. But this already renders its voice problematic. Its voice is already suspect, because in presuming to speak from nowhere it undermines its ability to speak at all. Engaging in a form of philosophical reflection that deems itself metacorporeal, or at least completely unencumbered by the body, the philosophical oracle voice has no point of view at all; for it is as embodied that a voice has a perspective, articulates a view. Hence, the philosophical oracle voice is specious; it, as I have implied, elides its historicity, dutifully covering over its ideology of domination, power-lust, value-laden interests, and forms of institutional behavior that give material support to the perpetuation of the notion that what constitutes philosophy is determined by transcendental rules a priori. In short, the philosophical oracle voice is predicated upon a lie and logically undermines its self-ascriptive, oracular standing while simultaneously revealing precisely what it attempts to hide.

From this perspective, the oracle voice assigns other contesting voices to their "natural" place within a hierarchy. It can do this because of its presumed synoptic vision, its grasp of totality. Contestatory voices are appropriated, consumed, and explained away within the "natural" unfolding of the philosophical oracle voice's historical telos. Such contestatory voices are then deemed anthropologically interesting only and lacking in sophistication and rigor. V. F. Cordova argues that questions posed by Native American students in philosophy, who are grounded within a different "spiritual wealth," are typically regarded as questions befitting an anthropologist. Within this context, anthropology, as Cordova maintains, becomes that site for "exploring the esoteric and barely humanoid existence and thought patterns of non-Western peoples."[20] In other words, within the exclusive logic[21] of the oracle voice's self-identity, other voices are negated through being "pliable, foldable, file-awayable, classifiable."[22] In short, while there is de facto diversity of philosophical voices, it can be argued that the oracle philosophical voice silences these other voices through its assimilative logic or simply remains "indifferent to, and set above in the implied particularism"[23] of such discursive fields as feminist philosophy, African American philosophy, Afro-Caribbean philosophy, Native American philosophy, Asian American philosophy, Latin American philosophy, and lesbian and queer philosophy. Of course, more is at stake here than the *descriptive*. The issue of philosophical heterogeneity must be raised to the level of the *axiological*, where the diversity of philosophical voices is actually valued and encouraged, and where diversity is not predicated upon the superficial recognition of differences for the sake of drawing the circle tighter around the borders of what constitutes "real" philosophy.

The point here is that the philosophical oracle voice can continue to maintain hegemony through the recognition of de facto diversity. Recognition of plurality and curricular diversification is not sufficient to challenge the power of the oracular policing of philosophical borders. After all, African American, Latin American, and Native American voices, for example, can be recognized and included within courses in philosophy, but their recognition and inclusion need not dialectically challenge and actually shape or transform the conceptual and normative spaces that have been configured by the philosophical oracle voice, a voice that reinforces its power precisely through a form of hierarchical juxtaposition. Being "included" connotes a sense of being allowed, as if having a favor extended. In this way, inclusion is still governed by the oracle voice that decides whether *to include* and decides the terms of the inclusion. On this score, Native American philosophical thought, where "philosophical," according to the philosophical oracle voice, remains dubious, is consumed and dabbled with in order to spice up the oracular core of influence within the profession of philosophy without effectively threatening its existing absolutism, rigidity, and hierarchy.[24] The complexity and possibilities of Native American philosophical thought are erased and rendered invisible precisely through its "inclusion." The oracle voice can engage in discourses that celebrate forms of pluralism and diversity that further obfuscate its maintenance of power. Part of the process of this obfuscation is that the securing of the oracle voice's power through its treatment of other philosophical voices as mired in cultural forces and matrixes that render them inferior. The oracle voice, then, is able to remain hermetically sealed within its self-ascribed "universality" and clean abstraction; its so-called univocal purity deemed free from such heteronomous, accidental influences as prejudice and various other historical, cultural, political, gendered, and "racial" forces. Within the framework of the argument that is being advanced here, "philosophical pluralism" is a coded expression that strengthens the neutrality of the oracle philosophical voice, the neutral benchmark in terms of which those "other," plural philosophical voices are judged. Indeed, some philosophy departments attempt to remedy this problem by offering "nonmainstream" philosophy courses. Even here, however, the oracular center continues to hold. Again, these "alternative philosophies" are "allowed" to speak. In this way, gatekeepers feel less guilty when faced with issues of encouraging multiplicity, diversity, and pluralism. With a false sense of accomplishment they exclaim, "We encourage alternative philosophical voices!" But instead of challenging the philosophical status quo, such alternative philosophical voices are treated as sideshow performances in philosophical exotica, mere ineffectual sound bytes, pseudophilosophical chatter, and false starts. This simply reinforces the centrality of the master narrative of "true" philosophy. Indeed, "it nourishes philosophers who believe there are two kinds of philosophy—one's own philosophy and philosophies that are wrong."[25]

As a site of power, the philosophical oracle voice resists seeing itself as *different* and *particularistic*. Indeed, it is "strongly invested in not knowing much about" its presumptions, narrow-mindedness, historical genesis, "racial" and cultural investments, and prejudicial underpinnings.[26] One might say that the philosophical oracle voice is an instantiation of what María Lugones terms "arrogant perception."[27] Within the context of this text, the oracle voice as a form of arrogant perception involves the classification of African American philosophy, Afro-Caribbean philosophy, Native American philosophy, Asian American philosophy, Latin American philosophy, feminist philosophy, and lesbian and queer philosophy as peripheral, secondary "philosophical" voices. Such arrogant perception is actually *productive* of a form of ignorance vis-à-vis the philosophical fecundity, challenging insights, and uniqueness of other equally legitimate philosophical voices.[28] Moreover, the arrogant field of vision of the philosophical oracle voice not only relegates the discursive dimensions of these "intruder voices" to subphilosophical domains, but what might be called "intruder bodies" (Black bodies, Latina bodies, Native Nation bodies, queer bodies, and others) are seen as outsiders, "philosophical imitators," inferior, and are thereby ostracized, to the extent to which this is possible, from the various physical sites where certain privileged bodies (the majority of which are white male heterosexist bodies) exercise their "superiority" and engage in philosophical forms of voicing that are presumed to have transhistorical implications and significance. At American Philosophical Association conferences I have often felt this sense of bodily invisibility and ostracization, as if I were suddenly thrown into an unfamiliar world. "So, there may be 'worlds' that construct me in ways that I do not even understand or I may not accept the construction as an account of myself, a construction of myself."[29]

The oracle voice speaks as if it has gotten hold of an *essence*, that is, that which is the sine qua non of what constitutes philosophy. In other words, the oracle voice claims to have the absolute truth, the unchanging and timeless nature, regarding the meaning, content, and aims of philosophy. Philosophy, on this score, becomes a *universal substantive*, unaffected by context, history, language, custom, sentiment, prejudice, geography, and so on. The latter, as argued above, are deemed accidents, mere contingent factors to which the oracle voice is impervious. On the view developed here, philosophy, in terms of its meaning, content, and aims, is fundamentally indexed to place, time, geography, cultural context, gender, and the like. Hence, within the context of the aims of this text, particularly in terms of challenging the philosophical oracle voice, I am disinclined to ask, what is the *nature* of philosophy? As philosopher John J. Stuhr argues, "Efforts to genuinely re-vision philosophy are distinct from enterprises aimed at finally revealing the so-called 'nature of philosophy' to the clear-eyed and clear-minded (who usually are simply the like-minded)." This revisioning, rather, is characteristic of a *process*, something unfinished and messy. In attempting to understand the so-called *what* of philosophy, I am not looking for a singular, self-identical substantive. As Stuhr concludes, "A re-vision [of philosophy] must be an affair of multiple re-visions; and philosophy must be an affair of multiple, philosoph*ies*."[30]

Instead of excluding other philosophical voices ex cathedra, there is an emphasis placed upon the necessity and significance of telling a richer and thicker narrative regarding the sociological, historical, and material conditions that impact the emergence of styles of reflective thought, the centrality of specific over-beliefs, the metaphors and tropes that inform reflective thought, the content of reflective thought, and what is deemed relevant to reflective thought. This does not mean that one cannot engage in descriptive processes of making sense of the various ways in which the world is differentially and pluralistically engaged philosophically. There is nothing inherently problematic about *describing* activities of philosophical world-making. The philosophical oracle voice, however, instead of operating upon the assumption that "philosophizing is inherently grounded in socially shared practices"[31] and accepting that this assumption also applies to its own philosophical voice, elides its own discursive historicity and normative structural practices, and argues for its own philosophical purity as if from a priori criteria. Describing, then, the socially shared, though not univocal, configuration of Africana philosophy, for example, points to a sensibility that requires one to *look*, to explore, to trace the diachronic permutations and relatively stable practices that form the ways in which flesh-and-blood thinkers attempt to fashion a world out of various socially inherited intellectual and existential strategies. "If the epistemic correlate of essence is conceptualization," as Lewis Gordon argues, "then the theoretical or conceptual domain is always situated on what can be called the reflective level."[32] The philosophical oracle voice presumes to engage in reflection *sub species aeternitatis*. However, the conceptual domain is linked to reflective thought in terms of its positional, situated, and contextual modalities. Hence, the reflective aspects of our lives as situated "always brings in an element of concrete embodiment of relevance. What this means is that theory, any theory, gains its sustenance from that which it offers *for* and *through* the lived-reality of those who are expected to formulate it."[33]

Within this framework, the meaning of philosophy implicates existential and ontological vectors. For the human, *to exist* and *to be* is to do philosophy, is to be tied to particular historical lifeworlds of particular "racial," gendered, ethnic, and geographical groups that engage in forms of reflection/world-making that are shaped by various socially negotiated norms.[34] As negotiated, these norms are not *transcendental,* though tracing the genesis of certain norms may remain relatively obscured due to complex historical confluence. Devoid of a transcendental basis does not mean that philosophical practices are not predicated upon consensus formations and rule-following. Indeed, "since a discipline is an inherently *social* enterprise in which some degree of consensus—at the very least—is necessary, that in itself requires rules."[35] Moreover, in the absence of epistemic *foundations* this does not mean that various philosophical lifeworlds are bereft of arguments, rhetorical strategies, self-corrective strategies, and persuasive maneuvers that insure the avoidance of conclusions reached willy-nilly. It is also important to acknowledge that "it is possible to have norms that transcend particular groups such that they cover the 'intellectual' and 'social' life-praxes of different groups in ways, even, that make it *possible* to resolve what otherwise might be 'fundamental' disagreements."[36] On this score, the location of our historical and cultural existence and being "give our philosophizings their prismatic character."[37] To argue that there is an *essence* that defines all practices of philosophizing, as the philosophical oracle voice presumes to do, can deteriorate into forms of "cleansing," which can have deleterious implications for those that I have designated "outsiders."

A few years ago, I recall a philosophy student once telling me that she and other students at her university were discouraged from examining the work of Kant through the prism of gender or race. The critical works and insights of feminist philosophers and philosophers who explore issues of race, in short, were being excluded, treated as outsiders, "cleansed" from the classroom. It was as if the professor actually held in contempt these "outside" voices; it was not simply a question of philosophical disagreement. These "outsider" interpretations of Kant were treated as inconsequential, sociological gibberish. After all, or so the oracle voice would claim, philosophers who do feminism and those who do philosophy of race do so for purely ideological reasons. For the oracle voice, such approaches are grounded in the mire of a form of self-serving identity politics that has absolutely nothing to do with either philosophy qua philosophy or Kant's pristine philosophical disinterestedness. Within the context of this particular classroom, the pristine knowing subject that is Kant and the "generic" knowing subject of traditional epistemology were both deemed transcendent and beyond the interstices of socially and historically embodied subjectivity, which is mediated by gender and race. Instead of encouraging a broad, critical subjectivity within the context of a course on Kant's philosophy, the oracle voice policed the borders of what doing "proper" Kantian scholarship is all about, thus foreclosing an appreciation for the possibilities inherent in philosophy as an open engagement with ideas that may very well challenge one's own. "If a professor's pedagogy is not liberatory," as bell hooks notes, "then students will probably not compete for value and voice in the classroom."[38] This raises the larger issue regarding the expectations that philosophers bring to the educational ethos of classrooms and what they desire for their students. Do we want to encourage students to play it safe, fanatically abide by party lines, stand in fear of having their disciplinary borders breached by outside "contaminants," or do we want to encourage students of philosophy to become future philosophers who are open to appreciate and take seriously multiple voices and who believe that "there is no fundamentalist love of empire in honest love of wisdom"?[39] It is my sense that students of philosophy should be encouraged to cultivate philosophical "identities rooted in understandings of themselves and their relations to others that increase their ability to be responsible participants in inquiry."[40] This suggestion admits of fallibilism. While intended to be persuasive, it does not pretend to *police*; it is not a question of possessing absolute truth but encouraging a sense of responsibility.

In an effort to keep plural philosophical voices alive within my introductory philosophy courses, I expressly make it a point to emphasize the specifically *Western* and *white male* philosophical works that will be explored. While it is true that introductory philosophy courses are typically introduced to students through various philosophical works written by "dead white men," it is not enough to note that they are *dead* white men. I point out to my students, the majority of whom are white, that philosophy is still dominated by white men and that most of these white men engage in dialogical exchanges with other white men. My larger aim is to instill a sense of uneasiness among my students. I do this by also pointing out that many of these same white men advanced arguments to the effect that white women were incapable of doing philosophy. After pointing this out, I often receive a heightened look of interest from my white female students. At times, I challenge all of the students to provide the name of a single (dead or alive) white female philosopher. The silence is typically deafening. I also make a point of stating that while we will explore the works of the specifically *Western* philosophical tradition, there are non-Western philosophical traditions that are equally significant. In this way, I make the point that Descartes, for example, inhabited a conceptual world where so-called universal, generic, self-evident philosophical problems were not shared by those living in Africa in 1619. The objective is to make broad connections between geography, experience, and a particular philosophical ethos. My aim is to get students to think about the possibility that Western philosophy embodies a form of philosophical chauvinism, a form of myopia that often fails to see beyond its own historical assumptions. Later in the course, I typically introduce various philosophical themes neglected within introductory courses in philosophy. For example, I turn to those experiential and existential points of embarkation from which African American/Africana philosophical voices evolve. During the transition, I get the sense that my students feel as if we have just made a significant leap from philosophy "proper" to this other, nonphilosophical and messy area called race. *Naming* is a powerful tool. I make it clear to them that *whiteness* is inextricably linked to the invisible normative core of modernity and that race was always already present as an institutional and material force during this period. I make it clear that many of the so-called major Anglo-American and European contributors to Western philosophy, like the "founding fathers" of America, were white males, steeped in white political and institutional power, whose philosophical livelihood was often at the expense of those bodies that were Black and deemed subhuman.

This way of teaching philosophy, particularly to white undergraduates, creates trouble for them.[41] It is a form of troublemaking that is designed to get them to engage in practices of intellectual freedom, to encourage them to de-mask their felt sense of superiority and risk the possibility of radically rethinking *what* and *how* they have been taught. If I am successful, they get a sense of themselves as deeply historical and contingent, and they begin to see themselves partly as the product and confluence of powerful norms and metaphors mobilized for their comfort and privilege, and begin to see that the determination of knowledge and the acquisition of knowledge are dynamic processes. As for philosophy, they come to appreciate the perspective that philosophizing is inextricably linked to those problems and conundrums that have been historically inherited and that the determination of the nature of a philosophical problem is not given a priori; rather, it is tied to and evolves out of a lived historical tradition. And Western philosophy is specifically understood as always already situated within a historical context of relevance, interests, purposes, and normative aims. It is within a lived context of concern that philosophical thought evolves and takes shape. Within this context, the questions "Whose knowledge?" and "Which tradition?" presuppose a nonhegemonic, nonuniversal conception of all philosophizing. This understanding contributes to the formation of the important sensibility that I referenced earlier, that is, where acting objectively (responsibly) necessitates understanding oneself and one's links with others, for the purpose of making reasoned and reasonable judgments about how to act in response to the needs of others, their desires, and interests. This approach, as I have argued, is diametrically opposed to the arrogant perceptual proclivities of the oracle philosophical voice that grasps "at the confirmation of its supremacy through defeating or imposing its existence on others."[42]

This text was conceived in the spirit of what María Lugones refers to as world traveling.[43] The concept here is used to denote the sense in which the various multiple philosophical voices within this text constitute spaces of philosophical invitation to those who are willing to travel (nonarrogantly) to different sites of critical philosophical constellations of meaning construction. The text is for those who are willing to explore different ideas regarding philosophical identity, particularly identity questions that are not captured by traditional white male constructions of what it means to be a self, to know, to be; to explore how various philosophical spaces are shaped through liberation discourses, how radically different philosophical agendas are shaped through the existential and experientially informed praxes of different groups, how indigeneity mediates what is deemed philosophically relevant, how the revision of heteronormative knowledge is linked to liberation efforts on the part of those who are deemed "outsiders"; and to explore the relationship between issues of ethnicity, group formation, historical context and canonicity, issues of philosophical knowledge production vis-à-vis the lens of race and gender. Each of these spaces continues to grapple with complex issues of its own constructive and reconstructive philosophical histories, conceptual frames of reference, philosophical identity, aims, assumptions, historicity, and tradition and canonical formation, within institutional contexts that are agonistic and hostile.

This text serves both a pedagogical and a discursive function. Pedagogically, it is an effective ready-to-hand text that will provide scholars and students with a collection of multiple philosophical voices and perspectives that will expose them to important philosophical problematics, traditions, and concerns that are still underrepresented within the institutional confines of philosophy. The text is also designed to broaden my own sense of philosophical formation in terms of what it means to identify with a particular philosophical "we," a critical collective that is not stultified through arrogant perception. This is linked to the discursive importance of the text. The text functions as a particular challenge to the agonistic philosopher-traveler qua conqueror and imperialist.[44] The text, as I have suggested, is invitational; it does not attempt to exclude but invites transactional dialogue, critical imagination, and the desire to travel, to enter those spaces and discursive worlds where the love of wisdom gets inflected through its lived embodiment.

Notes

1. See George Yancy, "Paul Weiss: Addressing Persistent Root Questions until the Very End," *Review of Metaphysics* 56, no. 1 (September 2002): 123–55.

2. Nancy Tuana notes that feminist philosophical thought is Western philosophy's most recent tradition (see her chapter within this text). While locating feminist philosophy within the context of Western philosophy, however, she points out that feminist philosophy moves from the core assumption that gender is a significant "lens for philosophical analysis that transforms both the content and at times even the methods of philosophical research." The point here is that feminist philosophy, at least within its specifically *Western* instantiation, is still critical of the formation of the oracle, characterologically, white male hegemonic philosophical voice.

3. Lisa Heldke, "On Being a Responsible Traitor, *A Primer*," in *Daring to Be Good: Essays in Feminist Ethico-Politics*, ed. Bat-Ami Bar On and Ann Ferfuson (New York: Routledge, 1998), 96.

4. For an intriguing discussion of the masculine implications of the "philosophical we," see Naomi Scheman's *Engenderings: Constructions of Knowledge, Authority, and Privilege* (New York: Routledge, 1993), esp. 1–8.

5. Drucilla Cornell, *The Philosophy of the Limit* (New York: Routledge, 1992), 35.

6. Heldke, "On Being a Responsible Traitor," 87.

7. David Hume, "Of National Characters," in *Race and the Enlightenment: A Reader*, ed. Emmanuel Eze (Malden, MA: Blackwell, 1997), 33.

8. Immanuel Kant, "On National Characteristics," in *Race and the Enlightenment*, 57.

9. Georg Wilhelm Friedrich Hegel, "Geographical Basis of World History," in *Race and the Enlightenment*, 127.

10. Beverly Clack, *Misogyny in the Western Philosophical Tradition: A Reader* (New York: Routledge, 1999), 1.

11. Clack, *Misogyny in the Western Philosophical Tradition*, 148

12. Linda Martín Alcoff, "Of Philosophy and Guerilla Wars," in *The Philosophical i: Personal Reflections on Life in Philosophy*, ed. George Yancy (Lanham, MD: Rowman & Littlefield, 2002), 185.

13. George Yancy, "Interview with Adrian Piper," in *African American Philosophers, 17 Conversations* (New York: Routledge, 1998), 59.

14. Elizabeth V. Spelman, "Theories of Race and Gender: The Erasure of Black Women," *Quest: A Feminist Quarterly* 5, no. 4 1982: 39.

15. Anita Allen, personal correspondence, November, 25, 2006.

16. Frantz Fanon, *Black Skin, White Masks*, trans. Charles Lam Markmann (New York: Grove Press, 1967), 119–20.

17. Of course, it is important to note that American philosophy in the form of pragmatism was itself insistent upon fallibilism and the significance of the social situatedness and broadly contextual nature of our philosophical claims and various knowledge productions.

18. Yancy, "Interview with Adrian Piper," 59.

19. I would like to thank philosopher Fred Evans for how he has developed the concept of "oracle," specifically its discursive, political, and philosophical importance. See, for example, the characterization of "oracle" in his articles, "Multi-Voiced Society: Philosophical Nuances on Salman Rushdie's *Midnight's Children*," *Florida Journal of International Law* 16, no. 3 (2004): 727–41, and "Voices of Chiapas: The Zapatistas, Bakhtin, and Human Rights," *Philosophy Today* 42 (2000): 196–210.

20. V. F. Cordova, "Native American Philosopher," *American Philosophical Association Newsletter on American Indians in Philosophy*, no. 2 (Spring 2001): 5.

21. Cornell, *Philosophy of the Limit*, 24.

22. María Lugones, "Playfulness, 'World'-Travelling, and Loving Perception," in *Making Face, Making Soul/Haciendo Caras: Creative and Critical Perspectives by Feminists of Color*, ed. Gloria Anzaldua (San Fransisco: Aunt Lute Books, 1990), 402.

23. John P. Pittman, "Introduction," in *African-American Perspectives and Philosophical Traditions*, ed. John P. Pittman (New York: Routledge, 1997), 7.

24. Philosopher Shannon Sullivan employs this reasoning effectively through her discussion of multicultural pluralism and the power of whiteness to maintain hegemony precisely through its call for greater diversity. See her book, *Revealing Whiteness: The Unconscious Habits of Racial Privilege* (Bloomington: Indiana University Press, 2006), 126.

25. John J. Stuhr, *Genealogical Pragmatism: Philosophy, Experience, and Community* (Albany: State University of New York Press, 1997), 80.

26. Sullivan, *Revealing Whiteness*, 128.

27. Lugones makes it clear that she gets this term from philosopher Marilyn Frye, "Playfulness, 'World'-Travelling, and Loving Perception," 390.

28. In a personal correspondence (January 5, 2007), John Lachs provides the insight that while he suspects that some such voices were/are arrogant indeed, other such voices simply live in ignorance and "mean" no harm. They may have caused harm, but more than a few of them shrink back in horror when this is pointed out to them.

29. Lugones, "Playfulness, 'World'-Travelling, and Loving Perception," 395–96.

30. Stuhr, *Genealogical Pragmatism*, 49.

31. Lucius Outlaw Jr., "African, African American, Africana Philosophy," in *African-American Perspectives and Philosophical Traditions*, ed. John P. Pittman (New York: Routledge, 1997), 73.

32. Lewis Gordon, *Existence in Black: An Anthology of Black Existential Philosophy* (New York: Routledge, 1997), 4.

33. Gordon, *Existence in Black*, 4.

34. Outlaw, "African, African American, Africana Philosophy," 84.

35. Outlaw, "African, African American, Africana Philosophy," 84.

36. Outlaw, "African, African American, Africana Philosophy," 84.

37. Lucius T. Outlaw Jr., *On Race and Philosophy* (New York: Routledge, 1996), 73.

38. bell hooks, *Teaching to Transgress: Education as the Practice of Freedom* (New York: Routledge, 1994), 85.

39. Stuhr, *Genealogical Pragmatism*, 84.

40. Heldke, "On Being a Responsible Traitor," 90.

41. When teaching primary texts of Hume, Kant, and Hegel on the subject of race, I have had philosophy graduate students requestion and reassess previous methodological approaches to their texts. Indeed, I have had some graduate students tell me that they feel cheated as a result of having not been taught what these seminal thinkers thought about people of African descent and women, for example.

42. Paget Henry, "Whiteness and Africana Phenomenology," in *What White Looks Like: African American Philosophers on the Whiteness Question*, ed. George Yancy (New York: Routledge, 2004), 208.

43. Lugones, "Playfulness, 'World'-Travelling, and Loving Perception," 395–96.

44. Lugones, "Playfulness, 'World'-Travelling, and Loving Perception," 400.

What Is Feminist Philosophy? 1

NANCY TUANA

Penn State University

F EMINIST PHILOSOPHY is Western philosophy's most recent tradition. While feminist perspectives have not been absent from contemporary non-Western philosophical traditions, within the Western philosophical traditions feminist philosophy has impacted every philosophical approach and all of the areas of philosophy. The "difference" of the feminist philosophical tradition proceeds not from a unique method but from the premise that gender is a crucial lens for philosophical analysis that transforms both the content and at times even the methods of philosophical research.

Feminist attention to gender has resulted in an approach to philosophy that provides new insights in all areas of philosophical scholarship: history of philosophy, ethics, epistemology, philosophy of science, aesthetics, social and political philosophy, metaphysics, logic, philosophy of language, and so on. It is a tradition that works within and very frequently across all of the mainstream traditions within Western philosophy, including the Continental, analytic, and American traditions.

Feminist philosophical scholarship emerges out of and responds to the lives of women and women's aspirations for freedom, but it is also attentive to the ways in which gender structures oppress men and impact human-nature interactions. As feminist philosophical scholarship emerged, it became increasingly attentive to the fact that gender cannot be adequately understood apart from other often intersecting locations including economic status, ability, race/ethnicity, and sexuality. Because of this, feminist philosophical scholarship often overlaps with many of the other philosophical approaches detailed in this volume.

Feminist philosophical scholarship begins with attention to women, to their roles and locations. What activities are women engaged in? How do their activities compare to those of men? What social roles or political activities are women part of or excluded from? What do women's roles and locations allow or preclude? How have their roles been valued or devalued? How do the complexities of a woman's situatedness, including her class, race, ability, and sexuality, impact her locations? In addition to this set of questions, feminist philosophical approaches also include attention to the experiences and concerns of women. Have any of women's experiences or problems been ignored or undervalued? How might attention to these experiences transform our current methods or values? And from here feminist philosophers move to the realm of the symbolic. How is the feminine instantiated and constructed within the texts of philosophy? What role does the feminine play in forming, either through its absence or its presence, the central concepts of philosophy? How do conceptions of the feminine or concepts marked by gendered associations circulate in the larger social realm?

Contemporary feminist philosophical scholarship emerged out of the experiences and concerns of the women's movement. Philosophers who were themselves feminists and living in those regions where the women's rights movement had a strong impact—in particular, North America, Europe, and Australia—began in the early 1970s to grapple with the issues that emerged as a result of this movement. While women had come close to achieving legal parity with men (the right to vote, to own property, etc.) in most countries by the early decades of the twentieth century, they remained seriously disadvantaged in the areas of economic and social parity. The goal of the women's movement during this period was to eradicate any remaining legal restrictions on women's freedom (e.g., inequitable marriage contracts or employment discrimination) as well as to identify and remove any institutional or social sources of gender inequity. Contemporary feminist philosophical scholarship in its first decade (1970–1980) focused on the topics central to the women's rights movement including the identification of the practices and institutions responsible for women's oppression, the examination of how to best obtain equity for women (e.g., equal rights within the current political and social structure vs. revolutionary changes of that structure), and ethical analyses of reproductive freedom.

As feminist philosophical scholarship developed, some feminist philosophers began to consider the ways in which the history of philosophy might provide a resource for understanding contemporary views of women's nature or abilities. Feminist philosophers began to investigate how canonical philosophers dealt with the question of women, both to determine if their views might provide resources for addressing contemporary issues and whether the sexism of their theories continued to pervade contemporary philosophical and, perhaps, even social and political practices.

As feminist philosophical scholarship began to gain a foothold and professional organizations like the Society for Women in Philosophy (SWIP) and scholarly journals devoted to feminist philosophy, like *Hypatia: A Journal of Feminist Philosophy,* began to emerge, feminist philosophical scholarship increasingly focused on the more "traditional" philosophical issues, such as the nature of truth, the basis for ethical action, the nature of scientific research, and so on. While attention to gender as a crucial lens of analysis was central to the work of feminist philosophers, most feminist philosophers also employed (and sometimes transformed), for feminist purposes, the philosophical tools they had been trained to use. As a result, feminist philosophy began to emerge from all the prevalent traditions of Western philosophy, including analytic, Continental, and classical American philosophy, and, with time, the thematic focus of feminist work was also impacted by the particular topics and questions highlighted by these traditions.

When I speak of feminist philosophical scholarship as a tradition, I do not intend to imply that it is homogeneous either in its methods or in its conclusions. Furthermore, while feminist philosophers have embraced approaches from the various traditions within philosophy, they have also argued for the reconfiguration of the accepted structures and problematics of philosophy. For example, feminists have not only rejected the privileging of epistemological concerns over ethical concerns common to much of analytic philosophy, they have argued that these two areas of concern are inextricably intertwined. This has often led to feminists using methods and approaches from more than one philosophical tradition.

While it is impossible in a chapter this brief to describe the richness of feminist philosophical thought, I will offer an overview of feminist approaches to a series of philosophical topics to provide a glimpse of the breadth and depth of this tradition. I urge the reader, however, to understand that what I can offer is only a sketch of a profoundly complex tradition, and one that is a living tradition that is fluid and emergent. This chapter, then, is best seen as an invitation to enter into an important philosophical dialogue.

History of Philosophy[1]

Feminist attention to gender in the history of philosophy has led to numerous vectors of analysis. Two of the central foci are (a) attention to women and (b) investigation of the symbolic imaginary relating to the feminine and the masculine.

Attention to Women

Feminist attention to women in the history of philosophy is bifurcated between, on the one hand, examining the views of canonical philosophers about women's nature and proper roles, and, on the other hand, recovering women philosophers. I will begin with the latter. As feminist philosophers began to research women philosophers from earlier centuries, it became increasingly clear that the *absence* of women philosophers was a relatively recent phenomenon. As Eileen O'Neill documents in her essay "Disappearing Ink: Early Modern Women Philosophers and Their Fate in History," there is a robust inclusion of women philosophers in standard seventeenth-century histories of philosophy. However, by the nineteenth century this list has been narrowed down to a small handful, and then in early twentieth-century histories disappears altogether.

O'Neill argues that there are four factors that contributed to this phenomenon. The first factor is the "purification" of philosophy. "By allying philosophy motivated by religious concerns with an unreflective mysticism, eighteenth-century historians excised whole philosophical schools, and the work of many women, from philosophy proper."[2] Second, the work of other women, such as Anna Maria van Schurman and Anne Finch, Viscountess Conway, disappeared because their ideas or worldview did not "win out." Third, O'Neill notes that philosophy that becomes "unfashionable" is often characterized as feminine and thus worthy of forgetting. "The alignment of the feminine gender with the issues, methods, and styles that 'lost out,' together with a good deal of slippage between gender and sex, and the scholarly practice of anonymous authorship for women, led to the almost complete disappearance of women from the history of early modern philosophy."[3] Finally, O'Neill argues that to explain the striking absence of women's philosophical contributions in the nineteenth century we must look outside of philosophy to the aftermath of the French Revolution and anxieties about how to maintain a system of male rule predicated on sexual difference in the context of ideals of a common humanity and an egalitarian social order.

As a result of studies like this, issues of canon formation became a central concern of feminist approaches to the history of philosophy.[4] Documenting the values that provide the foundation for canon selection and are used to determine which questions and styles count as philosophical and whose voices are sufficiently influential to be chronicled became a focus of feminist historical scholarship. If, for example, we limit our definition of philosophy to that work done in the academy and seminary as opposed to in the convent or salon, or insist on the treatise over and above the letter or the novel as the rhetorical vehicle for the work of philosophy, then we will exclude those locations and styles that are most common for women in particular historical periods.[5] Armed with this insight, feminist philosophers of history began to contest the standard "great men" model of history and the values that underlie it and argued for the importance of retaining the thought and impact of women philosophers such as Elisabeth of the Palatine, Jane Addams, Mary Astell, Anne Finch, Sor Juana Inés de la Cruz, Jacqueline Pascal, Anna Maria van Schurman, and Mary Wollstonecraft, to name just a few.

Another set of themes emerged from efforts to attend to what canonical philosophers had to say about gender. Feminist philosophers documented that a common thread of most canonical texts in the history of philosophy is the view of women as inferior to men. Feminists have documented that the Aristotelian conception of women as lesser or misbegotten men has had a profound structuring impact on the history of philosophical conceptions of men as the true form and women as inferior.[6] Luce Irigaray has argued that women have been defined not in terms of true difference from men, but in terms of lack according to an A (male) −A (female) logic, a logic well illustrated by Hegel's claim that women, while educable, are not capable of activities like science or philosophy that demand a universal faculty.[7] In such a schema, women are merely an inferior version of the masculine.

Feminist analyses of philosophers' views of women identified a cluster of related views about women's nature that were common to canonical philosophical views. The view of woman as less perfect or less developed than man, whether due to divine design or evolution, translated for many canonical philosophers into the belief that women possess inferior rational capacities in comparison to men, the view that women had a less sophisticated moral sense than men, and a commonly found view that due to women's nature, in particular more limited moral and rational capacities, they were less able than men to govern themselves or society wisely. It is important to mention that while these tenets were common themes in the history of philosophy, they were not embraced in the same way by all philosophers. Many philosophers modified their view by attending to classes or, in later periods, races of people, arguing that the capacities of women from the higher classes or races were indeed superior to those of men from the lower. However, even within these philosophical frameworks, women from those groups identified as "superior" were seen as less capable than men from these groups.

A common conclusion derived from this view of women was the belief that women's abilities were best suited for the private realm where a woman's desires and capacities could be both directed toward the welfare of her family and governed by her husband. While many philosophical accounts lauded the importance of the private realm and the suitability of women to the important tasks of raising children, the private realm of family was consistently viewed as requiring less-developed rational capacities than the public realm.

While it might be tempting to view these remarks as simply reflective of the societal biases of the time, feminist philosophers have demonstrated that this response is inadequate. It assumes that such sexism is limited to a philosopher's views of women and has not been inscribed on the central categories of philosophical theories—what it is to be rational, to be moral, to be a political agent. As feminist philosophers began to pay attention to canonical philosophers' views on women, we discovered that the sexism ran far deeper than false beliefs about women. These investigations have led to the realization that the very concepts of philosophy—reason, justice, virtue—have themselves been inscribed by this conception of man and thereby by the masculine as the true form.

Philosophical Imaginary

Feminist attention to gender has revealed that many of the central categories of philosophy are formed through the exclusion of the feminine. An early example of such an analysis is Genevieve Lloyd's *The Man of Reason: "Male" and "Female" in Western Philosophy.* Lloyd demonstrates that "rationality has been conceived as the transcendence of the feminine; and the 'feminine' itself has been partly constituted by its occurrence within this structure."[8] To the extent that the central categories of philosophy have been inscribed by gendered conceptions, that is, defined in terms of traits historically associated with masculinity and requiring control or transcendence of those traits historically associated with the feminine (the body, the emotions, and the passions), then sexist bias cannot be trivialized or seen as philosophically insignificant. As Michèle Le Dœuff has argued, this philosophical imaginary of gender is inscribed onto dominant conceptions of reason and thus is not an instance of sexism that can be ignored or excised, for it is at the core of the values from which the category of reason emerges.[9] It is rather one of the ways that philosophical theorizing is complicit in a social organization that impoverishes the lives of women as well as men.

This realization has led to feminist efforts to identify and refigure the role of "the feminine" in the texts of canonized philosophers and to examine the specifically feminine sites of philosophy. In this fashion, feminist historians of philosophy have begun to identify resources for engendering the central concepts of philosophy in ways not predicated on an imaginary that views the feminine as inferior. There are various strategies for doing so. Some, like Annette Baier's work on Hume or Barbara Herman's analysis of Kant, return to the canonical texts to tease out new or overlooked resources for revaluing the role of embodiment, imagination, and the affective life.[10] Others turn to the work of "recovered" women philosophers to trace alternatives to dominant models of philosophy. Catherine Villanueva Gardner, for example, argues that a complex notion of sensibility and a rhetorical style that exemplifies sensibility can be found in the work of women philosophers such as Mary Wollstonecraft, Catharine Macaulay, Christine De Pisan, George Eliot, and Mechthild of Magdeburg.[11] Gardner argues that the work of these uncanonized philosophers provides a rich conception of the role the passions play in moral philosophy. Another reading strategy is to provide correctives to histories of philosophy that have ignored topics like the emotions or the imagination, such as Susan James's account of the passions in seventeenth-century philosophy.[12] Yet another style of feminist reading can be found in the work of Luce Irigaray, who focuses on the contradictory movement and unstable logic of the exclusion of sexual difference in the history of philosophy.[13] It is her goal to open the historical texts of philosophy to contemporary feminist concerns not simply to confront what has been repressed, but to rethink it.

Feminist attention to the philosophical imaginary and the lessons learned from the canonization of particular philosophical styles has led to sensitivity to the rhetorical dimensions of philosophical writings, as well as to an appreciation of their affective dimensions. Mainstream efforts to excise the figural in order to uncover the literal truth of canonical texts give way in feminist rereadings to an appreciation of the role of imagination in philosophy and better understanding of how reason, imagination, and emotion are interwoven in the practice of philosophy. This attention to rhetoric and affect can be seen as an aspect of the philosophical imaginary common to many feminist historians of philosophy who reject the division between reason and passion.

Ethics and Social Theory

Contemporary feminist philosophical scholarship has also enriched and arguably transformed the field of ethics. Feminist perspectives on ethics developed in response to the ways in which sexism impacted traditional Western ethics and has focused on three interrelated biases. The first, as mentioned above, is the view of women's moral capacities as less developed than those of men. The second bias is that accounts of moral capacities have privileged traits historically identified as masculine, such as reason, autonomy, and independence, over traits identified as feminine, such as caring, community, and interconnection, and that moral theories have similarly emphasized reason, principles, and impartiality over emotion, situatedness, and relationships, again reinforcing the primacy of the culturally masculine. The third bias is the fact that the majority of moral theorizing has focused on the public realm, with primary attention to men's interests, and has neglected moral concerns arising in the private realm, as well as often overlooking women's rights and interests in the public realm.

The Virtues of Women

Attending to the gendering of moral capacities and virtues has a long history. The tenet that women's virtues differed from those of men was canonized in Aristotelian philosophy. Based on the commonly held belief in women's relative physical weakness and rational inadequacies in comparison to men, Aristotle argued that the virtues of women would be different than those of free men. While free men were charged with developing such virtues as courage, temperance, honesty, and justice, women's virtues were viewed as those that would best suit their domestic role and rational capacities, for example, industry and self-command.

The question of women's specific virtues or moral abilities was an often-debated tenet in the history of philosophy. While many nonfeminist philosophers continued to insist upon women's inferior moral abilities, many philosophers whose works can be seen as concerned with women's rights questioned both the alleged difference in moral virtues and the imputed inferiority. Mary Wollstonecraft (1759–1797) and John Stuart Mill (1806–1873), for example, argued that there were no fundamental differences between women's and men's moral capacities. But many others argued that while there was a difference in the virtues of women and men, this difference did not imply that women's moral capacities were inferior to those of men. A few such theorists, however, like Elizabeth Cady Stanton (1815–

1902), reversed the traditional position by arguing that women's morality was both different than and superior to that of men.

Few contemporary philosophers hold the type of gender essentialism that had been the basis in the past for viewing morality as gendered. However, an attention to gendered differences in moral reasoning and habits once again became popular with the work of Carol Gilligan. In her widely read *In a Different Voice: Psychological Theory and Women's Development*, Gilligan critiqued Lawrence Kohlberg's widely used model of moral development as privileging masculine approaches to moral reasoning, and, in particular, privileging universal principles such as justice and ignoring more typically feminine concerns with relationships, caring, and responsibilities that are richly situated and not amenable to formulation through universal rules. Gilligan argued that the empirical finding that women typically did not develop to the higher stages of Kohlberg's scale of moral development (often only achieving the third stage of his six-stage process, while men often reached stages four and five) was a reflection not of women's moral inadequacy but of a biased methodology.

While some have interpreted Gilligan's work as supporting the view that women's morality is different in kind than that of men, the most significant impact of her work has been to turn scholarly attention to an analysis of moral frameworks that includes attention to care, community, and relationships—analyses previously inhibited by accounts of moral capacities that privileged traits historically identified as masculine.

An Ethics of Care

Gilligan's emphasis on an ethics rooted in relationships was the catalyst for a profound rethinking of ethics within feminist philosophy. The ethics of care is seen by many as either an alternative to or a complement to principle-based universalistic ethical theories. Unlike universal rules, which require that behavior be impartial and the same for everyone in like circumstances, an ethics of care is a richly situated ethics that sees each caring relationship as unique. Rather than the rational and emotional detachment predicated by Kantian or utilitarian moral theories, care ethicists argue that ethical practice includes the emotions as well as reason.

A feminist ethics of care has been developed by a number of theorists including Virginia Held, Eva Kittay, Nel Noddings, Sara Ruddick, and Joan Tronto.[14] While care ethicists do not all share the same definition of care, there are areas of agreement amongst them. A caring relationship is seen as one in which an individual is both attentive to the specific needs and interests of another, as well as acts to advance those needs and interests. Hence, care involves both knowledge and motivation. It is also seen as an interactive relationship in which the one caring must be attentive to the responses of the one cared for and modifies her or his efforts to care based on how the other responds to her or his actions. Care ethicists have noted that many of our relationships are not between equals but rather between individuals in very different positions—parent/child, doctor/patient, teacher/student. Based on this, care ethicists have argued that our moral theories would be best constructed not from contract models that often assume relatively equally positioned individuals but rather from models that recognize the range of relationships possible between what Nel Noddings calls the "one-caring" and the "cared-for."[15]

One relationship feminist care ethicists often turn to is that of parenting and, more specifically, mothering. Sara Ruddick focused on "maternal practice" as a form of thinking that, while traditionally overlooked by moral theorists, provides an excellent model of relationships that strive to foster the goals of preservation, growth, and social acceptability.[16] Ruddick argues that the virtue of "attentive love" involves both reason and emotion and is key to good maternal practice. Ruddick does not limit what she calls maternal practice to women or even to parents, but rather argues that maternal practice should extend to the public world; she contends that the skills of maternal thinking will enable society to move toward a politics of peaceful cooperation.

Eva Kittay extends such insights to consider the situation of long-term care of those who are too young or too ill or impaired to take care of themselves.[17] She argues for the need for what she calls a globally pertinent ethics of long-term care. Kittay, like other care theorists, argues that much of traditional ethical theorizing, as well as liberal political theory with its distinction between public and private, gains legitimacy only through a deep denial of the inevitability of human dependency. Our conceptions of justice and much of our social policy is structured around the myth of the able-bodied, independent individual. Acknowledging the centrality and ever-changing nature of dependency to human life, then, demands a reassessment of issues of equity and justice that takes both dependency and the complex natures of care relationships seriously.

Critics of feminist ethics of care worry that care relationships have been "gendered" feminine in such a way that the traits privileged in caring relationships are and will continue to be seen as less valued than the traits of independent agents and will result in women continuing to be seen as "naturally" more fit for such labors and thereby trapped in low-paid service occupations. Clearly, a transformation of ethics that takes seriously the centrality of relationships must go hand-in-hand with social reorganization that recognizes and supports the value of caring labor.

Attention to Women's Concerns

Virginia Held has argued that dominant moral theories and the specific issues that have been at the heart of contemporary Western ethical analyses and the focus of contemporary social theory have privileged men's experiences and have focused far more on the public realm than the private.[18] Through their attention to the concerns of women, feminist ethicists and social theorists have introduced new issues to these realms of philosophy such as affirmative action, sexual harassment and sexual violence, and comparable worth, and have brought new insights to more traditional issues, for example, discussions of reproductive rights and technologies, understandings of power, the institutions of marriage, sexuality, and love, as well as caring labor.

Many identify Simone de Beauvoir's *The Second Sex* as the catalyst for contemporary feminist philosophical work. *The Second Sex* provides one of the first sustained analyses of the lived experience of "becoming woman." Beauvoir examines the institutions and practices that lead to women internalizing a sense of inferiority to men, that is, women as Other. Beauvoir's philosophical insights are contained in her now famous phrase, "one is not born a woman: one becomes one." In this she presages feminist distinctions between sex and gender, and the ways in which women are "produced" through complex disciplinary practices such as marriage, motherhood, and sexuality.[19]

Feminist social theory that emerged after Beauvoir's *The Second Sex* was influenced by her view that there is nothing natural or inevitable about inequalities between women and men. Rather, she argues that inequalities are created and sustained by various social institutions and ideologies that result in power imbalances between women and men. A dominant focus of feminist social theory has been to identify the causes of deeply entrenched inequalities between men and women and, in particular, to consider alternative social, political, and economic arrangements that would better ensure equity for all. Alison Jaggar's 1983 *Feminist Politics and Human Nature* provided an influential discussion of the various political theories feminists employed in efforts to argue for more equitable social arrangements. Jaggar delineated four primary frameworks: liberal feminism, which focuses on rights and equal access and argues that the primary cause of women's oppression is laws and rules that limit women's equal access to educational, economic, and political institutions; Marxist feminism, which argues that at the root of sexist oppression is class oppression; radical feminism, which identifies patriarchy and male control over women's bodies, including sexuality and reproduction, as the cause of sexual subordination; and socialist feminism, which views economic and social institutions as interdependent and thus attempts to incorporate the insights of the class analysis of Marxism with the radical feminist critique of patriarchal social organizations.

Feminist philosophers have also argued that attending to economic or social institutions that impact gendered relations cannot be done in isolation from other axes of oppression such as sexuality, race, ability, or class. The work of feminist philosophers such as Linda Martín Alcoff, Claudia Card, Nancy Fraser, Marilyn Frye, Sarah Lucia Hoagland, Eva Kittay, María Lugones, Anita Silvers, Elizabeth Spelman, Iris Marion Young, and Naomi Zack reveal the importance of analyses that identify the structure and consequences of the interaction between different forms of discrimination or subordination.[20]

Some of the most systematic work on intersectionality has been done by African American feminist scholars who have referred to their approach as womanist. Alice Walker helped to define the conception of womanist in relation to feminist in her collection of essays, *In Search of our Mother's Gardens*. According to Walker, "a Womanist is to feminist as purple is to lavender," and she later elaborates that a womanist is one who is "committed to survival and wholeness of entire people, male and female."[21] The term was developed as a way to weave together African American women's simultaneous commitment to feminism as well as to the history, culture, and religion of the African American community. A womanist perspective, whether it be in ethics, sociology, philosophy, history, or religious studies, employs as its lens for analysis the *intersections* between race, class, and gender. According to Patricia Hill Collins, womanist thought and practice provide a resource for knowledge, a standpoint consisting of "the experiences and ideas shared by [Black] women that provide a unique angle of vision on self, community, and society."[22] The philosopher Angela Davis and the political philosopher Joy James have both contributed to this interdisciplinary field, which includes theorists such as Katie Cannon, Patricia Hill Collins, bell hooks, and Delores Williams.[23]

Philosophy of Science and Epistemology

Feminist philosophers have also made significant contributions to the philosophy of science and to epistemology. Feminist scientists and philosophers of science, in analyzing the impact of gender bias on scientific theorizing, uncovered numerous examples, particularly in the biological and medical sciences, where scientific practice was either androcentric, that is, focused on male interests or male lives, or sexist, that is, the result of the biased perception that women and/or their roles are inferior to those of males.

Gender Bias in Science

One classic example of gender bias in science emerged out of feminist investigations of theories of human evolution. Feminists argued that theories of evolution, in providing accounts of the origin of the family and of the sexes and their roles, turned on widely accepted biases about sexual difference. "Man, the hunter" theories of human evolution were analyzed and critiqued not only for focusing primarily on the activities of males but for the assumption that only male activities were significant to evolution. Hunting behavior alone was posited as the rudimentary beginning of social and political organization, and only males were presumed to be hunters. Language, intellect, interests, emotions, tool use, and basic social life were portrayed as evolutionary products of the success of the hunting adaptation of males. In this evolutionary account, females were portrayed as following nature's dictates in caring for hearth and home, and only male activities were depicted as skilled or socially oriented.

Feminist primatologists, among them Linda Marie Fedigan, Sarah Blaffer Hrdy, Nancy Tanner, and Adrienne Zihlman, would not only expose the gender bias of "man, the hunter" theories, their research led to an alternative account of evolution now accepted as more accurate. By questioning the assumption that women's actions were instinctual and thus of little evolutionary importance, these scientists began to examine the impact of women's activities, in particular, the evolutionary significance of food gathering. From this focus of attention, an alternative account of evolution emerged that posited food-gathering activities, now of both women and men, as responsible for increased cooperation among individuals, which resulted in enhanced social skills as well as the development of language and the development of tools.[24]

Examples of androcentrism or sexism in science are numerous and are frequently shown to result in poor science and, in many cases, ethically problematic beliefs or practices. Here are just a few of the examples identified by feminists: the exclusion of women in clinical drug trials, attributions of gendered cognitive differences where female differences are posited to be derivations from the norm, the imposition of a male model of the sexual response cycle on women, and the lack of attention to male contraceptive technologies.[25]

The Issue of Objectivity and Situated Knowledges

Feminist attention to gender bias in science and technology led to an appreciation of the role of values in knowledge practices. Feminist theorists such as Donna Haraway, Sandra Harding, and Helen Longino argued that nonfeminist accounts of scientific objectivity were inadequate in that they provide no method for identifying values and interests that are unquestioningly embraced by the scientific community and that impact theoretical assumptions or the design of research projects. Careful analysis of the history of science documented systematic assumptions of women's biological, intellectual, and moral inferiority that were not the idiosyncratically held beliefs of individual scientists but were widely held beliefs imbedded in social, political, and economic institutions, as well as scientific theories and practices.[26] Given this, no account or practice of scientific objectivity that does not control for community-wide biases and values could be epistemically responsible.

Feminist philosophers of science thus argue for what Sandra Harding labeled "strengthened objectivity" by developing methods for uncovering the values and interests that constitute scientific projects, particularly those common to communities of scientists, and developing a method for accessing the impact of those values and interests.[27] In developing such an account, feminists gave up the dream of a "view from nowhere" account of objectivity with its axiom that all knowledge, and in particular scientific knowledge, could only be obtained using methods that strip away all subjective components such as values and interests. Feminists, rather, argued that all knowledge is "situated," that is, it emerges from particular social, economic, political locations. Strengthened objectivity requires attention to particularity and to partiality, with the goal not to strip all bias from knowledge but to assess the impacts of "beginning knowledge from different locations."[28] On this account, human knowledge is inherently social and engaged. The goal, then, of any quest for objectivity is to examine how values and interests can either limit or enlarge our knowledge practices.

As just one of many examples analyzed by feminists, consider the current emphasis on recombinant DNA technologies that have been proposed as a unifying principle for molecular biology.[29] Feminists have argued that rather than the lauded neutrality and objectivity, this position reflects numerous values and interests. Recombinant DNA technologies emphasize the centrality of DNA as a "master molecule" that controls life, and they ignore or view as of less importance the organism's environment or the organism's history.[30] In this way, such an allegedly neutral technology actively frames a sharp division between genetic and nongenetic factors, trivializes the role of environments, and reinforces biological determinism. Feminists have argued that efforts to cement molecular genetics as the foundation of the science of biology lead to an interpretation of life, including behavior and social structures, as "gene products."

This situated knowledge practice of contemporary molecular biology is clearly linked to the emergence of "big science" as well as venture capital. Funding for the Human Genome Project has emphasized a hierarchical, centralized organization of scientific research. And venture capital, following the promise of marketable discoveries in biomedical research, has similarly fueled the growth of such science.

As molecular genetics becomes the focus of biology, it carries with it embedded ideologies concerning the functions and significances of genes and environments, ideologies that in turn carry with them a renewed emphasis on genetic factors in disease. For example, although the vast majority of all cancers, including breast cancer, are attributable to environmental factors, there is an increasing emphasis in scientific research and medical practice on genetic factors, a move that has been sharply criticized by feminists.[31] Another concern of feminists and race theorists is that this "geneticization" of human health has also led to a renewed interest in biological difference between groups, which is reinscribing a biological basis to racial classifications.[32] These shifts in research focus can have dramatic effects on resource allocations. We know that occupational hazards and environmental carcinogens are clearly implicated in cancer rates, and the effects of environmental racism on the health of minorities have been well documented. Yet funding for research and "clean-up" for modifiable environmental factors is shifting to research on genetic inheritance.

Given feminist attention to the interaction between biology and environment in the constitution of sex (as well as gender) and sexual identity, this reemergence of biological determinism is in conflict with feminist values and interests. Strengthened objectivity, thus, urges an attention to the different values and interests guiding both types of research and their role in contributing to more effective and liberatory practices of science and technology.

Situating knowledge and strengthening objectivity also focused attention on the importance of ensuring that there are a diversity of knowers and knowledge projects, for difference is a potential epistemic resource. Including those working from different perspectives and with different methods helps to ensure an identification of the role of values in the production of knowledge and provides a means to assess which values provide the most reliable knowledge—both in terms of empirical adequacy and in terms of addressing the needs and concerns of a wider spectrum of society. In the hands of feminist philosophers of science and epistemologists, attention to diversity was transformed from a concern about equity to an issue of more adequate knowledge practices.

Feminist Epistemology

Feminist scholarship in the area of philosophy of science, particularly the view of knowledge as situated, intersects with issues feminist epistemologists have raised. One central tenet of feminist epistemological analyses is a critique of traditional "S knows that p" models of knowledge.[33] Many feminist epistemologists have argued that the traditional view of the knowing subject as distinct but not distinctive is inadequate in that it obscures the ways in which human knowledge practices emerge out of and are influenced by social structures, including those of gender. Genevieve Lloyd's insights about the gendering of reason led to additional feminist analyses of the allegedly "generic" knowing subject. Feminists have argued that the knowing subject, as well as epistemic traits such as epistemic authority, testimony, and judgments of warrantability, as they have been constructed within modern philosophy, have manifested traits and characteristics associated with privileged males, namely, white, propertied, Christian, heterosexual, and able-bodied.[34] Feminist epistemologists have concluded that the goal of a generic knower is misguided in that subjectivity is always at least partially socially constituted. On this position, none of us, regardless of gender, race, class, or ability, are generic subjects.

This rejection of knowers as generic led to feminist investigations of the epistemic significance of subjectivity. Feminist epistemologists identified how numerous factors play a constitutive role in the construction of knowledge, including one's historical and cultural location; the worldview and values one inherits in being raised in a particular culture; one's various social locations, including class, race, gender, religion, and other identifications; and the cognitive role of emotions. This attention to subjectivity gave rise to an appreciation of the role of affective dimensions of cognition in the knowledge process: the role of emotion, imagination, empathy, and values.[35] Such attention to subjectivity also emphasizes attention to whose values and whose imaginings are taken as credible, and whose stories are silenced.

Feminist epistemologists thus moved from the simple query "How do we know?" to issues of cognitive authority, namely, "Which individuals are authorized as knowers and by which means?" and "Which methods are deemed epistemically valuable?" And these questions began to reveal the complex relationships between power and knowledge: "Who benefits from or is disadvantaged by what we know?" "Who benefits from or is disadvantaged by what we don't know?" "Who benefits from or is disadvantaged by having only certain methodologies accepted as legitimate?" In other words, an adequate epistemology is one that includes an analysis of the structures of cognitive authority and maps the complex links between issues of power, privilege, and knowledge.

An additional aspect of the knowing subject that some feminists take to be epistemically significant is the fact and nature of our embodiment. The model of the generic knower has traditionally ignored or minimized the epistemic role of embodiment and has rejected the epistemic relevance of our bodily differences. Attention to the body calls attention to the specificities and partiality of human knowledge, as well as reminds us of the importance of acknowledging the role of materiality, including the relations between human materiality and the materiality of the more-than-human world, in the knowledge process. But once we admit the body into our theories of knowledge, feminists argue that we must also recognize its variations; we must, for example, examine the ways in which bodies are "sexed" or "raced" or differently "abled." Linda Alcoff, to give just one example, argues that racial and sexual difference is manifest in bodily comportment, habit, feeling, and perceptual orientation.[36] The move to include "knowing how" as an important source of knowledge also brings up the significance of "bodily" knowledge, that is, skills or habits that are a blend of bodily and cognitive practices.[37]

Another concern of "S knows that p" models of knowledge raised by some feminists is that they posit an individual knowing subject. Lynn Hankinson Nelson has argued that the knowing subject is the community, not the individual.[38] Others, like Helen Longino, have offered a modified position that embraces the individual as the holder of knowledge but rejects an individualist account of knowing by arguing that knowledge is so held only by persons who are part of complex social communities where both the knower and what is known are marked by that relationship.[39] It should be noted, however, that some feminist epistemologists, for example Louise

Antony, have argued that nonmodified individualist accounts are adequate to feminist epistemological concerns.[40]

Naomi Scheman has argued that one central theme of nonindividualist accounts of knowledge that has been overlooked by mainstream epistemological accounts is a realization of the epistemic significance of the fact of human interdependence and the epistemic centrality of trust.[41] On this model, knowledge practices are social and our epistemic dependency on others is pervasive; thus, the social institutions and practices that permit or limit such interactions become epistemically significant and must be subject to epistemological investigation. She argues that an adequate epistemology requires attention to forms of social organization to determine how social, political, or economic injustices may impact who is deemed worthy of trust and whose experiences and interests are and are not treated as epistemically significant.

Feminist epistemologists are concerned not only with descriptive analyses of our current knowledge practices, they are also committed to developing accounts of how our knowledge practices can be improved. Given that many feminist epistemologists hold that knowledge and justification involves trust, dependency, values and interests, community, power, and privilege, feminist normative accounts of knowledge often employ notions of epistemic responsibility, that is, the belief that we have a responsibility to consider both how social structures impact the generation of knowledge as well as the complex effects of knowledge projects upon the lives of other men and women as well as upon the more-than-human world.[42] Notions of epistemic responsibility mark the belief of many feminist epistemologists that we as individuals and members of social orders must take responsibility for how cognitive authority is established, for the values that knowledge practices embrace, and for those values that are rejected or rendered invisible. In this sense, the goal of developing better methods for gaining knowledge and the goals of creating a just society and more equitable human–nature interactions go hand in hand.

Conclusion: Feminist Philosophy as Liberatory Philosophy[43]

Feminist philosophy, like other feminist scholarly and activist practices, is one of a number of liberatory theories. Liberatory theorists are those who are committed to using the skills they have, whether they be philosophical, literary, scientific, sociological, and the like, to identify and address contemporary sources of injustice and attempt to overturn oppressive practices.[44] Given our awareness of oppression and our commitment to developing theories and methods that will serve to remove such injustices, feminist philosophers are committed to developing analyses that contribute to the goal of building a more just social order. In this way, feminist philosophy is not a luxury, but a necessity.

Notes

1. Some parts of this section were published in "The Forgetting of Gender and the New Histories of Philosophy," Conference Proceedings, in *Teaching the New Histories of Philosophy*, ed. J. B. Schneedwind. University Center for Human Values, Princeton University, 2004.

2. Eileen O'Neill, "Disappearing Ink: Early Modern Women Philosophers and Their Fate in History," in *Philosophy in a Feminist Voice: Critiques and Reconstructions*, ed. Janet A Kourany (Princeton: Princeton University Press, 1998), 34.

3. O'Neill, "Disappearing Ink," 36.

4. See, for example, Gardner (2000); Dykeman (1999); Susan James, *Passions and Action: The Emotions in Seventeenth-Century Philosophy* (Oxford: Clarendon Press, 1997); John J. Conley, *The Suspicion of Virtue: Women Philosophers in Neoclassical France* (Ithaca: Cornell University Press, 2002); Waithe (1987, 1989, 1991); Cecile T. Tougas and Sara Ebenrick, eds., *Presenting Women Philosophers* (Philadelphia: Temple University Press, 2000).

5. As just one example, see Rooksby's "Moral Theory in the Fiction of Isabelle de Charriere."

6. Nancy Tuana, *The Less Noble Sex: Scientific, Religious, and Philosophical Conceptions of Woman's Nature* (Bloomington: Indiana University Press, 1993).

7. Luce Irigaray, *Speculum of the Other Woman*, trans. Gillian C. Gill (Ithaca: Cornell University Press, 1985). G. W. F. Hegel, *The Philosophy of Right*, trans. T. M. Knox (New York: Oxford University Press, 1973), 8.

8. Genevieve Lloyd, *The Man of Reason: "Male" and "Female" in Western Philosophy* (Minneapolis: University of Minnesota Press, 1984), 104.

9. Michèle Le Dœuff, *The Philosophical Imaginary*, trans. C. Gordon (Stanford: Stanford University Press, 1989).

10. Annette Baier, *A Progress of Sentiments: Reflections on Hume's Treatise* (Cambridge: Harvard University Press, 1991); Barbara Herman, *The Practice of Moral Judgment* (Cambridge: Harvard University Press, 1993).

11. Catherine Villanueva Gardner, *Rediscovering Women Philosophers: Philosophical Genre and the Boundaries of Philosophy* (Boulder, CO: Westview Press, 2000).

12. James, *Passions and Action*.

13. Irigary, *Speculum of the Other Woman*.

14. Virginia Held, *Feminist Morality: Transforming Culture, Society, and Politics* (Chicago: University of Chicago Press, 1993); Eva Kittay, *Love's Labor: Essays on Women, Equality, and Dependency* (New York: Routledge, 1999); Nel Noddings,

Caring: A Feminine Approach to Ethics and Moral Education (Berkeley: University of California Press, 1984); Sara Ruddick, *Maternal Thinking: Towards a Politics of Peace* (Boston: Beacon Press, 1989); and Joan Tronto, *Moral Boundaries: A Political Argument for an Ethic of Care* (New York: Routledge, 1993).

15. Noddings, *Caring*.

16. Ruddick, *Maternal Thinking*.

17. Kittay, *Love's Labor*.

18. Held, *Feminist Morality*.

19. The reception of Beauvoir's philosophical work illustrates the very types of exclusions feminists are critiquing in the history of philosophy. Her writings were, until recently, often relegated to asides or footnotes and typically treated as derivative of the philosophy of Sartre. The 1967 *The Encyclopedia of Philosophy*, to cite just one representative example, only refers to Beauvoir in two entries, one on Sartre where we are told that she is one of the founders of *Les Temps Modernes* and another on existentialism where we are told that she employed some of Sartre's analyses in her writings. Contemporary feminist philosophical scholarship on Beauvoir has transformed her position in the philosophical canon by demonstrating the significant impact of Beauvoir's ideas on Sartre's philosophy and by locating her work within the phenomenological tradition. See, for example, Simons, *Feminist Interpretations of Simone de Beauvoir*.

20. Linda Martín Alcoff, *Visible Identities: Race, Gender, and the Self* (New York: Oxford University Press, 2006); Claudia Card, *Lesbian Choices* (New York: Columbia University Press, 1995); Nancy Fraser, *Unruly Practices: Power, Discourse, and Gender in Contemporary Social Theory* (Minneapolis: University of Minnesota Press, 1989); Marilyn Frye, *The Politics of Reality: Essays in Feminist Theory* (Trumansburg, NY: Crossing Press, 1983); Sarah Lucia Hoagland, *Lesbian Ethics: Toward New Value* (Palo Alto, CA: Institute of Lesbian Studies, 1988); Kittay, *Love's Labor*; María Lugones, *Pilgrimages/Peregrinajes: Theorizing Coalition against Multiple Oppressions* (Lanham, MD: Rowman & Littlefield, 2003); Anita Silvers, et al., eds., *Disability, Difference, Discrimination: Perspectives on Justice in Bioethics and Public Policy* (Lanham, MD: Rowman & Littlefield, 1998); Elizabeth Spelman, *Inessential Woman: Problems of Exclusion in Feminist Thought* (Boston: Beacon Press, 1988); Iris Marion Young, *Justice and the Politics of Difference* (Princeton: Princeton University Press, 1990); and Naomi Zack, *Race and Mixed Race* (Philadelphia: Temple University Press, 1993).

21. Alice Walker, *In Search of our Mother's Gardens: Womanist Prose* (New York: Harcourt Brace Jovanovich, 1983), xi–xii.

22. Patricia Hill Collins, *Black Feminist Thought: Knowledge, Consciousness, and the Politics of Empowerment*, 2nd ed. (New York: Routledge, 1991), 22.

23. Katie Cannon, *Black Womanist Ethics* (Atlanta: Scholars Press, 1988); Hill Collins, *Black Feminist Thought*; bell hooks, *Ain't I a Woman?: Black Women and Feminism* (Boston: South End Press, 1981); hooks, *Feminist Theory from Margin to Center* (Boston: South End Press, 1984); hooks, *Talking Back, Thinking Feminist,*

Thinking Black (Boston: South End Press, 1989); Delores Williams, *Sisters in the Wilderness: The Challenge of Womanist God-Talk* (Maryknoll, NY: Orbis Books, 1993).

24. Donna Haraway, *Primate Visions: Gender, Race, and Nature in the World of Modern Science* (New York: Routledge, 1989).

25. Debra A. DeBruin, "Justice and the Inclusion of Women in Clinical Studies: An Argument for Further Reform," *Kennedy Institute of Ethics Journal* 4 (1994): 117–46; Carol Gilligan, *In a Different Voice: Psychological Theory and Women's Development* (Cambridge: Harvard University Press, 1982); Elizabeth A. Lloyd, *The Case of the Female Orgasm: Bias in the Science of Evolution* (Cambridge: Harvard University Press, 2005); Nelly Oudshoorn, *The Male Pill: A Biography of a Technology in the Making* (Durham, NC: Duke University Press, 2003).

26. Londa L. Schiebinger, *The Mind Has No Sex? Women in the Origins of Modern Science* (Cambridge: Harvard University Press, 1989); Tuana, *The Less Noble Sex*.

27. Sandra Harding, *Whose Science? Whose Knowledge?* (Ithaca: Cornell University Press, 1991).

28. Sandra Harding, *Is Science Multi-cultural? Postcolonialisms, Feminisms, and Epistemologies* (Bloomington: Indiana University Press, 1998).

29. James Darnell, Harvey Lodish, and David Baltimore, *Molecular Cell Biology*, 2nd ed. (New York: Scientific American Books, 1990).

30. Evelyn Fox Keller, *Refiguring Life: Metaphors of Twentieth Century Biology* (New York: Columbia University Press, 1995); Donna Haraway, *Modest_Witness @Second_Millennium. FemaleMan©_Meets_ OncoMouse™: Feminism and Technoscience* (New York: Routledge, 1997).

31. Zillah Eisenstein, *Manmade Breast Cancers* (Ithaca: Cornell University Press, 2001).

32. Haraway, *Modest_Witness*.

33. Lorraine Code, *What Can She Know? Feminist Theory and the Construction of Knowledge* (Ithaca: Cornell University Press, 1991); Lynn Hankinson Nelson, *Who Knows: From Quine to a Feminist Empiricism* (Philadelphia: Temple University Press, 1990).

34. Addelson 1983; Code, *What Can She Know?*; Naomi Scheman, *Engenderings: Constructions of Knowledge, Authority, and Privilege* (New York: Routledge, 1993).

35. Susan E. Babbitt, *Impossible Dreams: Rationality, Integrity, and Moral Imagination* (Boulder, CO: Westview Press, 1996); Lorraine Code, *Rhetorical Spaces: Essays on Gendered Locations* (New York: Routledge, 1995); Helen Longino, *Science as Social Knowledge* (Princeton: Princeton University Press, 1990); and Alison Wylie, *Thinking from Things: Essays in the Philosophy of Archaeology* (Berkeley and Los Angeles: California University Press, 2002).

36. Linda Martín Alcoff, "On Judging Epistemic Credibility: Is Social Identity Relevant?" in *Engendering Rationalities*, ed. Nancy Tuana and Sandra Morgen (Albany: State University of New York Press, 2001).

37. Susan Bordo "The Cartesian Masculinization of Thought," *Signs* 11 (1988): 619–29; Rosi Braidotti, *Nomatic Subjects: Embodiment and Sexual Difference in Contemporary Feminist Theory* (New York: Columbia University Press, 1994); Patricia Hill Collins, *Black Feminist Thought: Knowledge, Consciousness, and the Politics of Empowerment* (New York: Routledge, 1990); Elizabeth Grosz, *Volatile Bodies* (Bloomington: Indiana University Press, 1994); Sonia Kruks, *Retrieving Experience: Subjectivity and Recognition in Feminist Politics* (Ithaca: Cornell University Press, 2001); Lugones, *Pilgrimages/Peregrinajes*; Ladelle McWhorter, *Bodies and Pleasures: Foucault and the Politics of Sexual Normalization* (Bloomington: Indiana University Press, 1999); Gail Weiss, *Body Images: Embodiment as Intercorporeality* (New York: Routledge, 1999).

38. Nelson, *Who Knows*.

39. Helen Longino 1993.

40. Louise Antony, "Is Psychological Individualism a Piece of Ideology?" *Hypatia* 10, no. 3 (1995): 157–74.

41. Scheman, *Engenderings*.

42. The concept of epistemic responsibility was first developed by Lorraine Code (*Epistemic Responsibility* [Hanover: University of New England Press, 1987]) and has been developed by her and others since then.

43. Given the brevity of this chapter, I focused on three central areas of feminist philosophical scholarship: history of philosophy, ethics and social theory, and philosophy of science and epistemology. However, feminist philosophical scholarship is making an impact in other areas of philosophy such as metaphysics (Battersby, Frye, Haslanger, Witt), aesthetics (Brand, Freeland), and the philosophy of religion (Anderson, Armour, Jantzen).

44. In this group I include those working in areas such as race theory, queer theory, liberation theology, materialism, disability studies, as well as the various areas of study included within multicultural studies.

Bibliography

History of Philosophy

Beauvoir, Simone de. *The Second Sex*. New York: Knopf, 1953.

Baier, Annette. *A Progress of Sentiments: Reflections on Hume's Treatise*. Cambridge: Harvard University Press, 1991.

Conley, John J. *The Suspicion of Virtue: Women Philosophers in Neoclassical France*. Ithaca: Cornell University Press, 2002.

Deutscher, Penelope. *Yielding Gender: Feminism, Deconstructionism, and the History of Philosophy*. London: Routledge, 1997.

Dykeman, Therese Boos, ed. *The Neglected Canon: Nine Women Philosophers First to the Twentieth Century*. Dordrecht: Kluwer Academic, 1999.

Gardner, Catherine Villanueva. *Rediscovering Women Philosophers: Philosophical Genre and the Boundaries of Philosophy*. Boulder, CO: Westview Press, 2000.

Herman, Barbara. *The Practice of Moral Judgment*. Cambridge: Harvard University Press, 1993.

Irigaray, Luce. *Speculum of the Other Woman*. Trans. Gillian C. Gill. Ithaca: Cornell University Press, 1985.

James, Susan. *Passions and Action: The Emotions in Seventeenth-Century Philosophy*. Oxford: Clarendon Press, 1997.

Kofman, Sarah. *Socrates: Fictions of a Philosopher*. Trans. Catherine Porter. Ithaca: Cornell University Press, 1998.

Le Dœuff, Michèle. *The Philosophical Imaginary*. Trans. C. Gordon. Stanford: Stanford University Press, 1989.

Lloyd, Genevieve. *Feminism and the History of Philosophy*. New York: Oxford University Press, 2002.

———. *The Man of Reason: "Male" and "Female" in Western Philosophy*. Minneapolis: University of Minnesota Press, 1984.

O'Neill, Eileen. "Disappearing Ink: Early Modern Women Philosophers and Their Fate in History." In *Philosophy in a Feminist Voice: Critiques and Reconstructions*, ed. Janet A Kourany. Princeton: Princeton University Press, 1998.

Rooksby, Emma. "Moral Theory in the Fiction of Isabelle de Charriere: The Case of Three Women." *Hypatia* 20, no. 1 (2005): 1–20.

Shapiro, Linda. "Princess Elisabeth and Descartes: The Union of Soul and Body and the Practice of Philosophy." *British Journal for the History of Philosophy* 7, no. 3 (1999): 503–20.

Tougas, Cecile T., and Sara Ebenrick, eds. *Presenting Women Philosophers*. Philadelphia: Temple University Press, 2000.

Tuana, Nancy. *The Less Noble Sex: Scientific, Religious, and Philosophical Conceptions of Woman's Nature*. Bloomington: Indiana University Press, 1993.

———. *Woman and the History of Philosophy*. New York: Paragon Press, 1992.

Waithe, Mary Ellen, ed. *Ancient Women Philosophers, 600 B.C.–500 A.D.* Dordrecht, The Netherlands: M. Nijhoff Publishers, 1987.

———. *A History of Women Philosophers*. Vol. 3: *Modern Women Philosophers, 1600–1900*. Dordrecht: Kluwer Academic Publishers, 1991.

———. *Medieval, Renaissance, and Enlightenment Women Philosophers, A.D. 500–1600*. Dordrecht: Kluwer Academic Publishers, 1989.

Ethics and Social Theory

Alcoff, Linda Martín. *Visible Identities: Race, Gender, and the Self*. New York: Oxford University Press, 2006.

Baier, Annette. *A Progress of Sentiments: Reflections on Hume's Treatise*. Cambridge: Harvard University Press, 1991.

Beauvoir, Simone de. *The Second Sex*. New York: Knopf, 1953.

Benhabib, Seyla. *Situating the Self: Gender, Community, and Postmodernism in Contemporary Ethics*. New York: Routledge, 1997.

Cannon, Katie G. *Black Womanist Ethics*. Atlanta: Scholars Press, 1988.

Card, Claudia. *Lesbian Choices*. New York: Columbia University Press, 1995.

Card, Claudia, ed. *Feminist Ethics*. Lawrence: University Press of Kansas, 1991.

Clement, Grace. *Care, Autonomy, and Justice: Feminism and the Ethic of Care*. Boulder, CO: Westview Press, 1996.

Collins, Patricia Hill. *Black Feminist Thought: Knowledge, Consciousness, and the Politics of Empowerment*. 2nd ed. New York: Routledge, 1991.

Combahee River Collective Staff. The Combahee River Collective Statement: Black Feminist Organizing in the Seventies and Eighties. Brooklyn: Kitchen Table/Women of Color Press, 1986.

Davis, Angela Y. *If They Come in the Morning: Voices of Resistance*. New York: Third World Press, 1971.

———. *Women, Culture, and Politics*. New York: Random House, 1989.

———. *Women, Race, and Class*. New York: Random House, 1981.

Frye, Marilyn. *The Politics of Reality: Essays in Feminist Theory*. Trumansburg, NY: Crossing Press, 1983.

Fraser, Nancy. *Unruly Practices: Power, Discourse, and Gender in Contemporary Social Theory*. Minneapolis: University of Minnesota Press, 1989.

Gilligan, Carol. *In a Different Voice: Psychological Theory and Women's Development*. Cambridge: Harvard University Press, 1982.

Hamington, Maurice. *Embodied Care: Jane Addams, Maurice Merleau-Ponty, and Feminist Ethics*. Urbana: University of Illinois Press, 2004.

Hekman, Susan. *Moral Voices, Moral Selves: Carol Gilligan and Feminist Moral Theory*. Philadelphia: Pennsylvania State Press, 1995.

Held, Virginia. *Feminist Morality: Transforming Culture, Society, and Politics*. Chicago: University of Chicago Press, 1993.

Herman, Barbara. *The Practice of Moral Judgment*. Cambridge: Harvard University Press, 1993.

Hoagland, Sarah Lucia. *Lesbian Ethics: Toward New Value*. Palo Alto, CA: Institute of Lesbian Studies, 1988.

hooks, bell. *Ain't I a Woman?: Black Women and Feminism*. Boston: South End Press, 1981.

———. *Feminist Theory from Margin to Center*. Boston: South End Press, 1984.

———. *Talking Back, Thinking Feminist, Thinking Black*. Boston: South End Press, 1989.

Jaggar, Alison. *Feminist Politics and Human Nature*. Totowa, NJ: Rowman & Allanheld, 1983.

James, Joy. *Resisting State Violence: Gender, Race, and Radicalism in U.S. Culture*. Minneapolis: University of Minnesota Press, 1996.

———. *Shadowboxing: Representations of Black Feminist Politics*. New York: St. Martin's, 1999.

———. *Transcending the Talented Tenth: Black Leaders and American Intellectuals*. New York: Routledge, 1997.

Kittay, Eva. *Love's Labor: Essays on Women, Equality, and Dependency.* New York: Routledge, 1999.

Lugones, María. *Pilgrimages/Peregrinajes: Theorizing Coalition against Multiple Oppressions.* Lanham, MD: Rowman & Littlefield, 2003.

Manning, Rita. *Speaking from the Heart: A Feminist Perspective on Ethics.* Lanham, MD: Rowman & Littlefield, 1992.

Noddings, Nel. *Caring: A Feminine Approach to Ethics and Moral Education.* Berkeley: University of California Press, 1984.

Nussbaum, Martha C. *Sex and Social Justice.* New York: Oxford University Press, 1999.

Ruddick, Sara. *Maternal Thinking: Towards a Politics of Peace.* Boston: Beacon Press, 1989.

Silvers, Anita, David Wasserman, and Mary B. Mahowald, eds. *Disability, Difference, Discrimination: Perspectives on Justice in Bioethics and Public Policy.* Lanham, MD: Rowman & Littlefield, 1998.

Simons, Margaret. *Feminist Interpretations of Simone de Beauvoir.* University Park: Penn State Press, 1995.

Spelman, Elizabeth. *Inessential Woman: Problems of Exclusion in Feminist Thought.* Boston: Beacon Press, 1988.

Tong, Rosemarie. *Feminine and Feminist Ethics.* Belmont, CA: Wadsworth, 1993.

Tronto, Joan. *Moral Boundaries: A Political Argument for an Ethic of Care.* New York: Routledge, 1993.

Walker, Alice. *In Search of our Mother's Gardens: Womanist Prose.* New York: Harcourt Brace Jovanovich, 1983.

Walker, Margaret Urban. *Moral Understandings: A Feminist Study in Ethics.* New York: Routledge, 1998.

Williams, Delores. *Sisters in the Wilderness: The Challenge of Womanist God-Talk.* Maryknoll, NY: Orbis Books, 1993.

Young, Iris Marion. *Justice and the Politics of Difference.* Princeton: Princeton University Press, 1990.

Zack, Naomi. *Race and Mixed Race.* Philadelphia: Temple University Press, 1993.

Philosophy of Science and Epistemology

Addelson, Kathryn Pyne. "The Man of Professional Wisdom." In *Discovering Reality: Feminist Perspectives on Epistemology, Metaphysics, Methodology, and the Philosophy of Science,* ed. Sandra Harding and Merrill Hintikka. Dordrecht: D. Reidel, 1983.

———. "Sublets, Power and Knowledge: Description and Prescription in Feminist Philosophies of Science." In *Feminist Epistemologies,* ed. Linda Martin Alcoff and Elizabeth Potter. New York: Routledge.

Alcoff, Linda Martín."On Judging Epistemic Credibility: Is Social Identity Relevant?" In *Engendering Rationalities,* ed. Nancy Tuana and Sandra Morgen, Albany: State University of New York Press, 2001.

———. *Visible Identities: Race, Gender, and the Self.* Oxford University Press, 2006.

Alcoff, Linda, and Elizabeth Potter, eds. *Feminist Epistemologies.* New York: Routledge, 1993.

Antony, Louise. "Is Psychological Individualism a Piece of Ideology?" *Hypatia* 10, no. 3 (1995): 157–74.

Antony, Louise M., and Charlotte Witt, eds. *A Mind of One's Own: Feminist Essays on Reason and Objectivity.* Boulder, CO: Westview Press, 1993.

Babbitt, Susan E. *Impossible Dreams: Rationality, Integrity, and Moral Imagination.* Boulder, CO: Westview Press, 1996.

Birke, Lynda, and Ruth Hubbard. *Reinventing Biology: Respect for Life and the Creation of Knowledge.* Bloomington: Indiana University Press, 1995.

Bordo, Susan. "The Cartesian Masculinization of Thought." *Signs* 11 (1988): 619–29.

———. *Unbearable Weight: Feminism, Western Culture, and the Body.* Berkeley: University of California Press, 1993.

Braidotti, Rosi. *Nomatic Subjects: Embodiment and Sexual Difference in Contemporary Feminist Theory.* New York: Columbia University Press, 1994.

Code, Lorraine. *Epistemic Responsibility.* Hanover: University of New England Press, 1987.

———. *Rhetorical Spaces: Essays on Gendered Locations.* New York: Routledge, 1995.

———. *What Can She Know? Feminist Theory and the Construction of Knowledge.* Ithaca: Cornell University Press, 1991.

Collins, Patricia Hill. *Black Feminist Thought: Knowledge, Consciousness, and the Politics of Empowerment.* New York: Routledge, 1990.

Creager, Angela N., Elizabeth Lunbeck, and Londa Schiebinger. *Feminism in Twentieth-Century Science, Technology, and Medicine.* Chicago: University of Chicago Press, 2001.

Darnell, James, Harvey Lodish, and David Baltimore. *Molecular Cell Biology,* 2nd ed. New York: Scientific American Books, 1990.

DeBruin, Debra A. "Justice and the Inclusion of Women in Clinical Studies: An Argument for Further Reform." *Kennedy Institute of Ethics Journal* 4 (1994): 117–46.

Eisenstein, Zillah. *Manmade Breast Cancers.* Ithaca: Cornell University Press, 2001.

Fausto-Sterling, Anne. *Sexing the Body: Gender Politics and the Construction of Sexuality.* New York: Basic Books, 2000.

Gilligan, Carol. *In a Different Voice: Psychological Theory and Women's Development.* Cambridge: Harvard University Press, 1982.

Grosz, Elizabeth. *Volatile Bodies.* Bloomington: Indiana University Press, 1994.

Haraway, Donna. *Modest_Witness@Second_Millennium. FemaleMan©_Meets_OncoMouse™: Feminism and Technoscience.* New York: Routledge, 1997.

———. *Primate Visions: Gender, Race, and Nature in the World of Modern Science.* New York: Routledge, 1989.

Harding, Sandra. *Is Science Multi-cultural? Postcolonialisms, Feminisms, and Epistemologies*. Bloomington: Indiana University Press, 1998.

———. *Whose Science? Whose Knowledge?* Ithaca: Cornell University Press, 1991.

Hekman, Susan. *Gender and Knowledge: Elements of a Postmodern Feminism*. Boston: Northeastern University Press, 1987.

Keller, Evelyn Fox. *Refiguring Life: Metaphors of Twentieth Century Biology*. New York: Columbia University Press, 1995.

———. *The Century of the Gene*. Cambridge: Harvard University Press, 2002.

Kruks, Sonia. *Retrieving Experience: Subjectivity and Recognition in Feminist Politics*. Ithaca: Cornell University Press, 2001.

Lloyd, Elizabeth A. *The Case of the Female Orgasm: Bias in the Science of Evolution*. Cambridge: Harvard University Press, 2005.

Lloyd, Genevieve. *The Man of Reason: "Male" and "Female" in Western Philosphy*. Minneapolis: University of Minnesota Press, 1984.

Longino, Helen. *Science as Social Knowledge*. Princeton: Princeton University Press, 1990.

———. "Subjects, Power and Knowledge: Description and Prescription in Feminist Philosophies of Science." In *Feminist Epistemologies*, ed. Linda Martín Alcoff and Elizabeth Potter. New York: Routledge, 1993.

Lugones, María. *Pilgrimages/Peregrinajes: Theorizing Coalition against Multiple Oppressions*. Lanham, MD: Rowman & Littlefield, 2003.

McWhorter, Ladelle. *Bodies and Pleasures: Foucault and the Politics of Sexual Normalization*. Bloomington: Indiana University Press, 1999.

Nelson, Lynn Hankinson. *Who Knows: From Quine to a Feminist Empiricism*. Philadelphia: Temple University Press, 1990.

Oudshoorn, Nelly. *The Male Pill: A Biography of a Technology in the Making*. Durham, NC: Duke University Press, 2003.

Potter, Elizabeth. *Gender and Boyle's Law of Gases*. Bloomington: Indiana University Press, 2001.

Scheman, Naomi. *Engenderings: Constructions of Knowledge, Authority, and Privilege*. New York: Routledge, 1993.

Schiebinger, Londa L. *The Mind Has No Sex? Women in the Origins of Modern Science*. Cambridge: Harvard University Press, 1989.

Shiva, Vandana. *Biopiracy: The Plunder of Nature and Knowledge*. Boston: South End Press, 1997.

Weiss, Gail. *Body Images: Embodiment as Intercorporeality*. New York: Routledge, 1999.

Wylie, Alison. *Thinking from Things: Essays in the Philosophy of Archaeology*. Berkeley and Los Angeles: California University Press, 2002.

Metaphysics, Aesthetics, Philosophy of Religion

Anderson, Pamela Sue. *A Feminist Philosophy of Religion: The Rationality and Myths of Religious Belief*. Oxford: Blackwell, 1998.

Armour, Ellen T. *Deconstruction, Feminist Theology, and the Problem of Difference: Subverting the Race/Gender Divide*. Chicago: University of Chicago Press, 1999.

Battersby, Christine. *The Phenomenal Woman: Feminist Metaphysics and the Patterns of Identity*. New York: Routledge, 1998.

Brand, Peg, and Mary Devereaux, eds. *Women, Art, and Aesthetics. Hypatia: A Journal of Feminist Philosophy* 18, no. 4 (2003).

Freeland, Cynthia. *But Is It Art?* Oxford: Oxford University Press, 2001.

Frye, Marilyn. *The Politics of Reality: Essays in Feminist Theory*. Trumansburg, NY: Crossing Press, 1983.

Haslanger, Sally. "Feminism and Metaphysics: Negotiating the Natural." In *Cambridge Companion to Feminism in Philosophy*, ed. Miranda Fricker and Jennifer Hornsby. Cambridge: Cambridge University Press, 2000.

Jantzen, Gail. *Becoming Divine: Towards a Feminist Philosophy of Religion*. Manchester: Manchester University Press, 1998.

Tuana, Nancy. "Material Locations: An Interactionist Alternative to Realism/Social Constructivism." In *Engendering Rationalities*, ed. Nancy Tuana and Sandra Morgen. Albany: State University of New York Press, 2001.

Witt, Charlotte. "Feminist Metaphysics." In *A Mind Of One's Own*, ed. Louise Antony and Charlotte Witt. Boulder, CO: Westview Press, 1993.

What Is Lesbian Philosophy? (A Misleading Question)

2

SARAH LUCIA HOAGLAND
Northeastern Illinois University

I. Complicating Relationality

"Lesbians are not women."

> *The place—a Modern Languages Association meeting, again, in a room packed with lesbians. The atmosphere—an electric excitement that comes when community dykes who are pushing theory and academic dykes who are activists gather, driven by a quest for making meaning of and for our lives. A sentence spoken . . . astounded gasps, tears, rage, and sheer joy.*

"LESBIANS ARE NOT women" and similarly "we are not born but rather become women" address the economy of gender, the management of social relations in the French society their authors inhabited and elsewhere in the Anglo-European world. These statements—the second by Simone de Beauvoir in the 1950s and the first by Monique Wittig in the 1980s—astounded their audiences not because they voiced an essence about a component but because they articulated the texture of a network, the weave of a social fabric, the relationality of engagement. Lesbian be-ing is about relationality.

Central to Monique Wittig's position are the material conditions of the man/woman distinction: Men arrogate women economically, sexually, and politically. "Lesbianism is the only concept I know of which is beyond the categories of sex (woman and man), because the designated subject (lesbian) is *not* a woman, either economically, or politically, or ideologically. For what makes a woman is a specific social relation to a man."[1] "Lesbians are not women" challenges the material and social fabric—the place women, as providers of services, hold in relation to men so that men can claim, oxymoronically, autonomy.

49

As Marilyn Frye writes, women's

> function is the service of men and men's interests as men define them. . . .
> Whether in lower, middle or upper-class home or work situations,
> women's service work always includes providing or being responsible for
> ensuring personal service (the work of maids, butlers, cooks, personal sec-
> retaries), sexual service (including provision for his genital sexual needs and
> bearing his children, but also including "being nice," "being attractive for
> him," etc.), and ego service (encouragement, support, praise, attention).[2]

Lesbians as a group do not provide this function in society, though some
lesbians actually do these things, either for pay or in passing or both.

> Lesbian. One of the people of the Isle of Lesbos. . . . The use of the word
> "lesbian" to name us is a quadrifold evasion, a laminated euphemism. To
> name us, one goes by way of a reference to the island of Lesbos, which in
> turn is an indirect reference to the poet Sappho (who used to live there,
> they say), which in turn is itself an indirect reference to what fragments of
> her poetry have survived a few millennia of patriarchy, and this in turn (if
> we have not lost you by now) is a prophylactic avoidance of direct men-
> tion of the sort of creature who would write such poems or to whom such
> poems would be written . . . assuming you happen to know what is in
> those poems written in a dialect of Greek over two thousand five hundred
> years ago on some small island somewhere in the wine dark Aegean Sea.
>   This is a truly remarkable feat of silence. (Marilyn Frye, 1983, 160)

Even today, my spellcheck has *Sapphic,* but not *Sappho.*

> Those of us who stand outside the circle of this society's definition of ac-
> ceptable women; those of us who have been forged in crucibles of differ-
> ence—those of us who are poor, who are lesbians, who are Black, who are
> older—know that survival is not an academic skill. (Audre Lorde, 1984, 112)

The word *lesbian.* Lesbian. The word that makes them panic, makes them
afraid, makes them destroy children. The word that dares them. Lesbian. *I
am one.* Even for Patricia, even for her, *I will not cease to be!* As I kneel amid
the colorful scraps, Raggedy Anns smiling up at me, my chest gives a sigh.
My heart slows to its normal speech. I feel the blood pumping outward to
my veins, carrying nourishment and life. (Beth Brant, 1985, 85)

Lesbians are outside the conceptual scheme, and this is something done,
not just the way things are. One can begin to see that lesbians are excluded
by the scheme, and that this is *motivated,* when one begins to see what purpose the exclusion might serve in connection with keeping women gen-

erally in their metaphysical place. It is also true that lesbians are in a position to see things that cannot be seen from within the system. What lesbians see is what makes them lesbians and their seeing is why they have to be excluded. Lesbians are woman-seers. When one is suspected of seeing women, one is spat summarily out of reality, through the cognitive gap and into negative semantic space. If you ask what became of such a woman, you may be told she became a lesbian, and if you try to find out what a lesbian is, you will be told there is no such thing.

But there is. (Marilyn Frye, 1983, 173)

I sit here naked in the sun, typewriter against my knee trying to visualize you. Black woman huddles over a desk in the fifth floor of some New York tenement. Sitting on a porch in south Texas, a Chicana fanning away mosquitos and the hot air, trying to arouse the smouldering embers of writing. Indian woman walking to school or work lamenting the lack of time to weave writing into your life. Asian American, lesbian, single mother, tugged in all directions by children, lover or ex-husband, and the writing. (Gloria Anzaldúa, 1981, 165)

This struggle is not about essence, but about an identity legislated through institutions and challenged as relation by practice, enactment, engagement . . . reconfiguring textures of the weave. "Lesbian" is not a natural category.

Lesbianing is be-ing-in-relationship. You cannot be a lesbian and not be in relation, though you may not have a lover. Some people imagine themselves Man, autonomously, a-relationally; lesbian be-ing is about being with others in various permutations of friend, lover, and stranger relationships, in collectives, in the street, on the baseball field; it is about seeking out, querying, and acknowledging one another all in a glance or a nod. Speaking in code. Speaking in tongues.[3] Being lesbians is about there being others, without whom one isn't, in a world that hides, erases, destroys.

Gestures of recognition, re-cognition, preexist appeals to originary legitimacy or skepticism about other minds, including "I thought I was the only one," because there is first a needing to know what so fiercely declares itself by engaging others: "I was walking around in little pieces, and I never even knew, that the way back home to me is the road I took to you."[4] The possibility of meaning making, particularly against-the-grain of meaning making, arises not as an individual decision but as collective process. Lesbian Connection.

Being at a concert, Meg Christian singing, "She was a big tough woman, the first to come along, that showed me being female meant you still could be strong. . . ."[5] Sharing—a moment, in this moment in time, we recognized,

even if we had not such a gym teacher, or even gym. More than recognize
. . . rec-ognize, because someone gave voice to something not yet articulated,
gave voice to an ache that burst out in sheer joy at that moment, in this particular place and time. A moment that will not be replicated; today there are
other possibilities. This is not about sameness of individuals, nor sameness of
experience, nor individualized-collective-self-interest. It is about moments
shared and possibilities conspired, spirits animated.

> I was born here
> Second row third seat from the left
> listening to icon women
> who had helped create a dynasty
> for all us young artist wanna be's and
> in that moment
> the spirit of women's work washed over me and
> respect for women's space became my belief
> I was born into womanry
> Birthed by three midwives
> who didn't smack me into screams
> but dared me to speak and
> those three became my surrogates
> . . .
> Cause they were the three that birthed me
> And this is the house that raised me
> And you are the women that watched over me
> And that's why I'm the woman that I turned out to be.
>   C. C. Carter on the closing of Mountain Moving
>   Coffeehouse, December 10, 2005, Chicago

Yet with possibility, there is failure:

Latina/Lesbian is an oxymoron, an absence of relation. Latina/Lesbian
lacks a hyphen. The territoriality of the movement erases the hyphen.
Latina/Lesbian necessarily speaks with a bifid tongue. ¿Cómo podría saber
the tones of a hyphenated, hybrid, tongue when she is committed and
confined to a negation? The Latina/Lesbian is a critic in the Movement.
The Movement can only hear her speak when it sheds the purity that per-
meates its domain, its geography.

The movement of the tortillera into the Lesbian Movement is a fantastic
flight because as she flees the confines of nation in search of substance, range

and voice she becomes an oxymoron, the Latina/Lesbian: two terms in extreme tension. No hyphen: no hybridization. (María Lugones, 2003, 175)

The place—a Midwest Society for Women in Philosophy gathering. The atmosphere— casual and relaxed, but excited, anticipating the presentation . . . then shock, what did she say? tears, a timid, "If this is so, then I am not lesbian." Frustrated demands for explanation. Then on to lunch.

II. Lesbian Engaging, Becoming Self-conscious Critical Practitioners of Culture

Modern Western ethical theories espousing impartiality presuppose existing social institutions, such as colonialism, the family, private property, and the state, and ignore or dismiss relations of power and oppression and hence resistance. Beginning at the periphery and taking up relations of power, noting that impartiality stabilizes unequal power relations, Latin American philosophers of liberation take the side of the oppressed and respond to their cry (following Levinas). But the significant argument, the capacity to hear that "whisper amidst the noise," focuses primarily on agents acting on behalf of the oppressed.[6] Simone de Beauvoir's argument provides an answer to Nietzsche's distain of slave morality: Those whose freedom is cut off have no option but to begin with a no-saying; then amidst ambiguity, move on to assume responsibility for their choices and will an open future.[7] Nevertheless, rather than taking up the subjectivity of the oppressed, her argument is about the oppressed from the vantage point and agency of someone presumably not oppressed.

Lesbian ethics takes up agency under oppression and involves becoming critical practitioners of our culture. It is an ethics of resistance. And creation. Katie Cannon's Black womanist ethics situates itself similarly in relation to slave women and women under segregation. "Black women's analysis and appraisal of what is right or wrong and good or bad develops out of the various coping mechanisms related to the condition of their own cultural circumstances. In the face of this, Black women have justly regarded survival against tyrannical systems of triple oppression as a true sphere of moral life."[8]

For to survive in the mouth of this dragon we call america, [Black women] have had to learn this first and most vital lesson—that we were never meant to survive. Not as humanbeings. (Audre Lorde, 1984, 42)

One message of Anglo-European ethics is that either we have free will—we are autonomous and in control and capable of being responsible for all that goes on—or we are helpless victims and hence not moral agents.

Any such theory is of no use to marginalized peoples (although it is quite useful to those working to maintain the status quo). We are neither in control nor are we helpless victims. *It is not because we are free and moral agents that we make moral choices; rather it is because we make choices, acting within limits, that we declare ourselves to be moral beings.*[9]

Lesbian ethics is not a set of rules of right behavior or injunctions of duty or determinations of obligation, nor an inward-looking focus on good character, though all of these productions affect lesbians' efforts. Modern ethical concepts, designed to coerce "consensus," undermine lesbian connection and community.[10] "For the master's tools will never dismantle the master's house."[11] Approaching responsibility not as the *obligation* but as the *ability* to respond, we evaluated conditions of oppression that undermine our ability to respond as well as our ability to re-cognize resistance in others: conditions that de-moralize us.[12]

Beginning with a background understanding that the oppressed develop skills such as lying in resistance to coercion, Adrienne Rich raised the question of lying among women, challenging us to address ways we treat each other: "There is a danger run by all powerless people that we forget we are lying, or that lying becomes a weapon we carry over into relationships with people who do not have power over us." A lie is "a shortcut through another's personality."[13]

Addressing lesbian battering and stalking, Claudia Card argues that the terror of intimate invasion robs you of agency, holding you captive through fear. To protect against this, she advocates institutionalizing friendship, formalizing boundaries, borders, even roles. She argues that what distinguishes a true friend may be character, that possibly one can ground a friendship without knowing much of the other's history or likes and dislikes.[14] However, the extremely difficult task of developing the ability to respond to abuse, as is true of the complex ability to practice friendship, is not separable from the larger context or those embedded in it.

What promotes a fertile ground for violence and for the internalization of violence? Anannya Bhattacharjee argues that the individualism behind relying on enforcing institutions puts a survivor at odds with and undermines collective resistance to intimate abuse.[15] Anne Leighton argues that there are multiple audiences for sexual and racial violence, many of them institutionalized, including, as Judith Butler argues, the juridical system. What are the audiences' varied relationships to the violence? Many women of color articulate interdependencies of domestic, state, and global violence.[16]

Talking of a Pan-African lesbian feminism, M. Jacqui Alexander writes,

> Part of our own unfinished work, therefore, is remembering the objective fact of these power systems and their ability to graft themselves onto the very minute interstices of our daily lives. We are all defined in some relationship to hierarchy. Neither complicity (usually cathected unto someone else) nor vigilance (usually reserved for ourselves) is given to any of us *before* the fact of our living. They are learned in this complicated process of determining who we are and whom we wish to become. The far more difficult question we must collectively engage concerns the political positions (in the widest sense) we come to practice, and not merely espouse, the mutual frameworks we adopt, as we live (both consciously and unconsciously) our daily lives.[17]

This is where work of challenging juridical constructions (Judith Butler) and of being disloyal to masculinity, to whiteness, to heterosexuality comes in for those so constituted, the work of being a race traitor (Minnie Bruce Pratt), disloyal to civilization (Adrienne Rich), rejecting the boundary formation of the proper.[18]

Lesbian ethics is a quest, given lesbian lives, for new value, a moral revolution. In the United States, emerging from the Women's Liberation Movement, lesbian ethics challenges the concept of female agency prescribed by the Western feminine construction of masculine discourse. Its theorists consider questions of liberatory praxis, addressing various consequences of oppression among lesbians both as victims and as perpetrators of oppression, and have produced significant conceptual shifts in addressing our interactions.

Highlighting the framework of patriarchy, Mary Daly challenges female agency promoted through patriarchal myth, including the heteropatriarchal category of "good" woman, which animates neither female power (powerful women are evil) nor female bonding. She invokes ontological courage: to be outrageous, to be other; and epistemic courage: to become disillusioned; and moral courage: to Sin Big, to re-member the Goddess, to refuse to collaborate in her murder both mythically and existentially.[19]

As we engaged each other from concrete locations, one central issue developed: the question of difference. One example: While Mary Daly draws on many traditions to show that patriarchy and women's victimization are global, Audre Lorde notes that she summons only European goddesses in resistance, leaving the message that European tradition is the source of liberatory possibility. Because such an overarching analysis does not re-cognize either women of non-Western cultures or women of color within the West as having sources of integrity and female power arising out of their particular cultural grounding, it can not provide a means for retrieving their erased subjectivity and agency. Hence it unwittingly reifies the colonial project.

Raising postcolonial questions, Rey Chow asks how Chinese women would be recognized beyond victim status.[20] Gloria Anzaldúa, for example, heralded Coatlicué and Tonantzin who were similarly suppressed in the case of Guadalupe, the Spanish Catholic attempt to construct a Mexican Virgin Mary (Anzaldúa, 1987).

Universalizing erases the active subjectivity of most of those struggling with oppression; as Barbara Smith points out, those who are most privileged within a given category come to represent it—white Women, Black men. In much feminist work, white middle-class women's experiences and situations, while particular, are used as the standard of resistance—assertiveness training and mediation *as* feminist praxis, the right to obtain an abortion *as* freedom of choice. Other contexts and other women are appropriated, disappeared, colonized—that is, understood only through the logic of the norming context. "As white women ignore their built-in privilege of whiteness and define *woman* in terms of their own experience alone, then women of Color become 'other,' the outsider whose experience and tradition is too 'alien' to comprehend."[21]

As a result of challenges from women of color and community struggle, the groundbreaking conceptual shift in lesbian ethics has been retheorizing difference, and it began with Audre Lorde in the 1970s. Rejecting the Western European construction of difference, which has meant that one of us must be inferior, she argues that the concept of difference is the source of new value. If we bonded or united, found common cause with, only on the basis of sameness, then we would be fragmenting ourselves, leaving behind those parts we don't share, which is to say conditions we face, struggles we have (or have not) engaged in, what we have learned in this complicated process of negotiating structures of power:

> So, when the black woman and the white woman become lovers, we bring that history and all those questions to the relationship as well as other people's problems with the relationships. (Cheryl Clarke, 1981, 36)

Community for lesbians has held possibilities for new value, not as a state or formal institution but as a context emerging from collective engagement. And since "we are everywhere," we have ready-made reasons for understanding difference in ways distinct from Anglo-European culture driven by the Hegelian construction of difference: In a Hegelian one-on-one antagonistic relationship, either the other's understanding or mine must prevail and thus difference is capable of annihilating me—another central message of modern Anglo-European ethics.

However, we lesbians exist one among many, autokoenously, as selves in community.[22] "[The source of the metaphysics of political struggle] is the deep knowing that we are in fact interdependent, neither separate nor autonomous." "As we moved to unite these powerful forces of sex and spirit," writes M. Jacqui Alexander, "it requires the work of each and every one, to unearth this desire to belong to the self *in* community as part of a radical project—not to be confused with the self-preoccupation on which individualism thrives. Self-determination is both an individual and collective project."[23]

As I meet you, you make me self-conscious of being other than I think of myself. But our engagement is not a solitary one-on-one encounter, it is always already an encounter amid others, both other encounters and others witnessing this encounter. As we are multiply mirrored in community (both oppressively and liberatorily), no one gaze annihilates us; we become refracted and complex and so can develop critical skills, access and assess mirrors, gain vital information, considering what we will resist and what we will develop in relation with others.[24]

"It is not our differences which separate women, but our reluctance to recognize those differences and to deal effectively with the distortions which have resulted from the ignoring and misnaming of those differences."[25] Difference is not only not a threat, it is a source of knowledge at the core of community survival and development. "Difference must not merely be tolerated, but seen as a fund of necessary polarities between which our creativity can spark like a dialectic."[26]

Marilyn Frye analyzes the arrogant eye that disappears or appropriates difference in the norming context of Western ideology—everything is organized with reference to himself—a process practiced in terms of gender, ethnicity, even species. One example she develops connects the arrogant eye to the concept of love as promoted in heterosexual romance—everything is either for him or against him. The arrogant perceiver's expectation creates an environment into which the other must fit; she becomes someone interested in serving him. If she does not, something is (morally) wrong with her. In contrast, Marilyn Frye argues, the mark of a voluntary association is that one can survive displeasing the other. The one who loves is not selfless; she knows and has her own desire. But she perceives the other without the presupposition that the other poses a constant threat or exists for her service. The loving eye knows the independence of the other, knows her complexly.[27]

María Lugones takes up the question of arrogant perception, but rather than stressing the independence of the other, she argues, "I am profoundly dependent on others without having to be their subordinate, their slave, their servant." She focuses on the failure to identify with the other, as whites fail to identify with people of color. She names this a failure of love, a failure to love cross-racially and cross-culturally. She notes how often white women "ignore, ostracize, stereotype, tokenize or render women of color invisible," even while women of color are physically present. "The more independent I am, the more independent I am left to be. Their world and their integrity do not require me at all."[28]

Editing the groundbreaking anthology, *This Bridge Called My Back,* Cherrie Moraga and Gloria Anzaldúa pushed radical women of color, many lesbian, to give voice to radically distinct experiences in combining "the search for beauty with the struggle for social justice."[29] One theme concerns having learned to live with contradictions, especially the contradiction of the pressure to fit into a dominant white culture while realizing that success would lead to self-annihilation. A second theme concerns how white women use race privilege at the expense of women of color, for example using something a woman of color has said when it supports the white woman's theory but otherwise ignoring it, as if she has nothing to learn from women of color, certainly nothing that might challenge her own theory. A third theme is that one can be both an oppressor and a victim. Subsequently, Michelle Cliff takes up "an identity they taught me to despise." Cherrie Moraga and Norma Alarcón and other Chicanas take up the construction of La Malinche, exploring the internalization of relations between two oppressed peoples, raising the possibility of exploring how folks can contain within themselves both the conqueror and the conquered.

In the middle of all this work, Gloria Anzaldúa initiated a second groundbreaking conceptual shift in value with her work on borderlands, developing the concept of "la mestiza," the border-dweller. While borders are dividing lines between nations, groups, defining places "safe" and "unsafe," distinguishing "us" from "them," the borderlands is the place between cultures where reside those who inhabit both but fit nowhere and who thus become adept at switching modes. They are the queer, the half-breed, la mestiza. By straddling two or more cultures and being caught where beliefs are not constructed and there are no definitions, la mestiza experiences a loss of meaning and sense of agency; she enters a state of intimate terror.[30]

By calling on Coatlicué, and finding the strength of the resistor who refuses to accept outside authority, la mestiza can create a new consciousness and develop new abilities. But she must give up all pretense to safety, for the borders that supposedly keep undesirable ideas out are our entrenched habits and patterns of behavior. La mestiza makes herself vulnerable to foreign ways of seeing and thinking, strengthening her tolerance for ambiguity and her flexibility, because rigidity means death. The work of la mestiza is to break down the subject-object duality and create another culture, a new mythos, particularly new ways of relating to each other for, as Gloria Anzaldúa argues, our desire is relational.

> We are not born women of color. We become women of color. To *become* women of color, we would need to become fluent in each other's histories, to resist and unlearn an impulse to claim most-devastating, one-of-a-kind, defying-comparison oppression; to unlearn an impulse allowing mythologies to replace *knowing* about one another; to cultivate a way of knowing in which we direct our social, cultural, psychic, and spiritually-marked attention upon each other. We cannot afford to cease yearning for each other's company. (M. Jacqui Alexander, 2002, 91)

Certainly lesbian ethics is about finding ways to recognize and not replicate oppressive values. But if part of lesbian strength lies in resisting the proper, how do we challenge or move each other to address social injustice in all its forms without taming spirit?

María Lugones and Gloria Anzaldúa explore the subjectivity and strategies of resistance of she who is oppressed. One strategy María Lugones takes up involves the skills of the trickster. One can play the fool, playing on others' ignorances/privileges by playing with structures. She notes that she can play the Latin American as gringos construct her—stereotypically intense—or she can play the real thing. An Angla who knows nothing of playful world-travel, or knows only agonistic world-travel, will not notice the difference. The trickster, the clown, is crucial for dismantling the seriousness of tyranny and the power of privilege, marking one a fool if she persists in a state of ignoring.[31]

Years earlier, taking up a flexibility learned of necessity by people of color in dealing with white/Anglo organization of life in the United States, María Lugones developed the notion of "playful world-travel," traveling between worlds, the work of la mestiza. Playful world-traveling involves going into the world of another and, in the process, shifting from being one person to being a different person. This is distinct from men's idea of play developed in terms of winning and losing, competition, rules, and battles. By traveling to the world of another who is quite different from me without trying to destroy it or them, I can work to "understand *what it is to be them and what it is to be [me] in their eyes."*[32] It involves finding oneself to be another person there, embracing ambiguity, being open to uncertainty and surprise—what Gloria Anzaldúa calls *atravesando fronteras*—avoiding the "seriousness" that honors only one set of meanings. It involves understanding what it is to be the other, and what it is to be ourselves in their eyes.[33]

> Anyone who is not self-deceiving about racist ethnocentrism can begin to see [women of color] unbroken through engaged thinking that takes seriously her own participation in an ethnocentric culture in a racial state. Such thinking requires that she become and think as a self-conscious critical practitioner of her culture and a self-conscious and critical member of the racial state. Furthermore, such thinking is possible because she is a participant in both. (María Lugones, 2003, 43)

Analyzing an essay by Minnie Bruce Pratt, a white U.S. southern-raised lesbian, who simultaneously challenged racism and homophobia, Biddie Martin and Chandra Mohanty argue that the apparent solidity of white identity, of a white "we" in the United States, is derived from marginalization of difference, supported by "exclusion of specific histories of oppression and resistance, the repression of differences even within oneself." They show how "home" is an illusion of coherence and safety that is based on suppression of "others," secured by men's terror, and built on women's surrendering responsibility, in particular white women not noticing the Othering of others in the name of our alleged protection.[34]

Significantly, the one unifying element for Minnie Bruce Pratt as she crossed borders, gaining perspective on her "we" and her home, is her lesbianism, her love of women, which takes her traveling to worlds other than her own. "A careful reading of the narrative demonstrates the complexity of lesbianism which is constructed as an effect, as well as a source, of her political and familial positions. Its significance, that is, rather than assumed as an essential determinant," is demonstrated in relation to other experiences—textures of the weave. "What lesbianism becomes as the narrative unfolds is that which makes 'home' impossible." Community is the product of work and struggle, it must be constantly reinterpreted and revalued, and it is inherently unstable and contextual.[35]

One becomes a self-conscious critical practitioner of her culture by embracing difference, crossing borders to meet others, developing her skills as she risks that engagement, embracing our interdependency, struggling to create community.

III. Against-the-Grain Engaging and Resistant Negotiation

What I most regretted were my silences. Of what had I *ever* been afraid? . . . My silences had not protected me. Your silence will not protect you. But for every real word spoken, for every attempt I had ever made to speak those truths for which I am still seeking, I had made contact with other women while we examined the words to fit a world in which we all believed, bridging our differences. (Audre Lorde, 1984, 41)

The place—the MLA, early 1980s, the room huge and packed, women sitting everywhere—the next to last time Mary Daly and Audre Lorde were together in a room. The energy—electric, riveted, hungry

Modern Western epistemological methodology animates an isolated, disengaged, cognitive practice of abstract purification that grasps a singular world and erases or dismisses relations of power and oppression and hence resistance. All our emotions and our cognitive skills that engage us relationally, such as caring, are dismissed, as are our material and cultural groundings. Paradigm theory articulates the embeddedness of our cognitive skills, that our capacity to see things is related to our theoretical understanding (How is it that lesbians see women?), but nevertheless dismisses relations of power. Beginning with material location, standpoint epistemology takes up matters of power and exposes distinct conceptual frameworks. It articulates the means by which dominant ideology mystifies and obscures its power, normalizing relations of exploitation (peasant exploitation *as* free trade); indeed, those at the center lack epistemic privilege. But because of the use of concepts such as "mystification" or "authenticity," understanding is still framed as objective and hence not relational.

Lesbian praxis involves developing the necessary epistemic skills to go against the grain and engage others outside dominant framing.

From oppression, whereby one is designated nonexistent as lesbian while simultaneously encoded subordinate as woman, one resists being (only) the self constituted there. The skills, the virtues, include what W. E. B. DuBois calls double consciousness and can involve, for example, rejecting or destabilizing a particular relationality even while playing into it, maintaining the ignorance of those who dominate. Or one may choose to challenge hegemonic logic on its own terms, to resist within the public transcript. There are also strategic resistant practices of ignoring the public transcript, of not responding on its terms, of enacting hidden transcripts.

> Silences: attentive silences, refusal to speak silences, tongue cut out silences, provocative silences, refusal to listen silences, intimate silences. (María Lugones, 2003, 167)

Indeed, as lesbians come out, to ourselves, to each other, to family, to the press, to our spiritual communities, to our doctors (The X-ray litany: "Yes, I am sexually active; no, I don't take birth control; yes, I'm sure I'm not pregnant. What? No, no possibility of mistake."), we are epistemically positioned to challenge hegemony: As the framework does not countenance lesbians, we have come to assert something that does not exist. It is a skill to fly in the face of reality, to go against the grain. Sinister Wisdom.

However, becoming critical practitioners of our culture(s), developing skills of against-the-grain negotiation, and engaging each other includes more than the skills of coming out. Those working to preserve the sense of a dominant paradigm employ an impressive array of strategies to appropriate, co-opt, assimilate, annihilate distinct worlds of sense.

To directly counter hegemonic discourse, one must enter its logic, accept its parameters, travel with the grain and meet others on its terms. Coercive consensus. For example, within the United States, feminists were forced to defend (not just demand), that is explain and justify, acknowledge doubts, and develop "reasonable" arguments in favor of equal rights for women. *Ipso facto* these feminists were enacting the structural relation they worked to destabilize, for they were "agreeing" (not disagreeing) at a deeper level that women's (but not men's) rights are debatable in a democracy, that such a debate makes sense, is meaningful.

To go against the grain involves being able to see each other, to see women, not what reasonable people consider women, to see beyond the dominant constructions as well as the reconstructions designed to undermine our gains as activists, to engage resistors.

As feminists demanded acknowledgment of violence against women (undermining the "boys will be boys" rhetoric of legitimation), critical shifts to maintain hegemony ensued. For example, Julia Penelope details a transformation from the active voice, "John beat Mary," to the passive voice: "Mary was beaten by John," to "Mary was beaten," and on through linguistic transformations to the nominalized passive, "Mary is a battered woman." As feminists forced public acknowledgment of rape and domestic beating as violence, something he did to her becomes something that happened to her which comes to be understood as part of her character while John disappears. Studies spring up to investigate the peculiar nature of women to whom these things happen, animating the understanding that something about the "feminine character" invokes men's abuse. Knowledge as enactment, portrayed as representation.

Following Mary Daly, Catharine MacKinnon analyzes reversals, for example, how women's testimony of sexual abuse has been turned against us: that which is offered as proof of sexual torture becomes instead proof of woman's nature. A videotape of a woman being raped becomes proof not of a woman being raped, but of the rape-able nature of women. Analyzing what happened to Anita Hill's testimony before the Senate confirmation hearing, Catharine MacKinnon points out that a woman testifying to her abuse became instead pornography to those witnesses reasoning through hegemonic logic.

A related reversal occurs in the United States regarding race. Many have long complained against police brutality of blacks, particularly black men. Then one day, the unexpected happened, and someone videotaped an actual incident of cops beating an unarmed black man and gave it to the press—indisputable proof to the world of what many had been saying for a long time. But instead of being indisputable proof of police brutality, that very videotape, the videotape of the L.A. police beating Rodney King, became in the court system proof of the dangerous nature of black men—cops have to resort to that much force.

Hegemony maintains itself by denying epistemic credibility to those who do not practice its logic. It maintains itself by dismissing attempts to speak truths and the resistant practices that challenge it, framing them not as false (because to do so is nevertheless to admit that they are meaningful—possibly true even if false) but as meaningless, nonsense, "abnormal," "perverse," "not serious," "terrorist," "crazy," "stupid," "unnatural," "insane," "criminal," and so on. For example, white privileged men disappear the social contradictions that protectors are predators and that to maintain a masculine identity of protector men need women to be in danger, by institutionally designating particular groups of men as predators—most notably in the United States, black men.

To venture forth into this discomforting world, Western epistemological praxis wants to always already know, to greatly reduce the work it must do, to protect itself from a con while simultaneously asking for one, to avoid responsibility, respons-ability, the ability to respond. The perfect john. And as johns are incompetent lovers, so such a methodology prepares us to be incompetent knowers, particularly in our inability to engage, to enter the story and meet others.[36]

Acknowledging partial, locatable, critical knowledges is a problem only to the hegemonic fiction of the isolated, contextless Cartesian perceiver who can reasonably doubt that anyone else even exists. Such knowing requires no agency of or engagement with the other. A located and limited self is terrifying only if one imagines oneself alone.

Descartes's legacy primes us to dismiss that which and those who undermine our certainty. So when working to understand resistant communities not our own, such a methodology leaves us striving to be right rather than working to engage—the desire to stay in control, the desire to avoid making mistakes, unwilling to risk crossing hegemonic barriers. Disbelief is a cognitive practice that dismisses that which does not present itself to be understood within the dominant conceptual framework—practices of the arrogant perceiver.

Resisting rationalities involve moving toward uncertainty, suspending not necessarily beliefs but disbelief, and re-cognizing distinct worlds of sense, distinct logics. I have framed this as conceptual separatism, that which makes possible the collective formation of other contexts of sense-making such that one's cognitive abilities are not limited to challenging or defending oneself against arrogating hegemonic constructions.

While other worlds of sense are not completely separate from the dominant frame of meaning, they don't need to be. Debates about whether there are any points of contact or similarity miss the point. Certainly the scientific revolution had points of contact with the religious paradigm: To the scholar of the dominant naming of women throughout the twenty-five-hundred or so year tradition that flows from ancient Greece through Christianity, colonial conquest, science, and capitalism, no significant change in that naming, either evolutionary or revolutionary, leaps to mind. Nevertheless, with the Copernican revolution, the promotion of the mechanistic metaphor, the construction of inner/outer, the shift from knowers as participators to knowers as spectators, the shift from having a place to being located in space . . . all of these changes yield a distinct logic that drove the direction of Western philosophical imagination and creativity. And a collective shift in logic is what's critical in animating distinct paradigms, frameworks of meaning.

Critical epistemic work, becoming critical practitioners of culture, involves undermining the hegemony of dominant discourses by re-cognizing and engaging counterdiscourses, thereby shifting the ground of epistemic sense. But the central ability for lesbian engaging involves being able to see each other across borders in active subjectivity outside hegemonic interpellations.

Meaning and understanding revolve around what we focus on, try to make sense of, acknowledge, take up, argue about, which is to say that shifting the ground of epistemic sense is also to shift the center of our attention, those to whom we try to appear reasonable, those with whom we are open to dialogue, conversation. Meaning-making is a collective process. The Cartesian imaginary suppresses altogether the located and intersubjective dimension in the production of knowledge.[37]

Here is a tension within lesbian communities—when wanting visibility, if a friend insists on imagining only with hegemonic meaning, she insists on others meeting her there, undermining the possibility of community.

An example among feminists: While much criticism of white feminism concerns exclusionary tendencies in feminist theory and practice, Anannya Bhattacharjee argues that the growing tension between women of color and the mainstream (white) movement to stop violence against women is not a question of who is "included" in the movement but rather reflects contradictory understandings of the impact of collaboration with the state.[38] Most white feminists and lesbians, despite having negotiated considerable conceptual coercion, have come to rely on the state and negotiate meaning through it, particularly as a legitimacy-granting institution. And, as Judith Butler argues, "juridical systems of power *produce* the subjects they subsequently come to represent."[39] As a result, white feminists, lesbian and straight, are not *seeing* women and/or lesbians of color—not as political companions—are not women-of-color-seers, and hence choke the possibility sustaining community.[40]

Significantly, the understanding I struggle to articulate with the idea of conceptual separatism is at home in María Lugones's work on ontological pluralism, insisting on many logics, which any lover of purity seeks to erase. The maintenance and development of those logics, just as much as dominant logic, are collective endeavors.

The idea is to start with resistance, even when it is not liberatory, to be able to see the active subjectivity, the agency, of those who are oppressed, not only those of our own groupings, however determined, but others also marginalized by hegemony, to see in its opacity what is dismissed by dominant logic as nonsense, insane, insignificant, criminal, learning to see through different logics. Seeing resistances gives us an understanding of structures of power. But more significantly, as María Lugones writes, from within those embedded locations one can see deeply into the social, a praxis that involves streetwalker theorizing.[41] Understanding is not a ritual of abstract withdrawal and study or achieved from the managerial, bird's-eye stance.

In rage and frustration one day, I wrote out what I really cared about, why epistemology has mattered to me. Questions included: What do you do when everyone around you thinks in terms of ideas you know to be bullshit? Or when you are feeling insane because everyone around you acts as if nothing is wrong? How do you counter foreclosure of meaning, conceptual coercion? How do you resist being gaslighted, maintain the confidence of your perceptions? Do you worry about being mistaken? That is, if you find out that you have been mistaken about something, does that make you feel like you can't go on? What do you do when your understanding is dismissed? (Does it matter who is dismissing it? Do you use different strategies depending on who?) There were other questions. I presented them to my circles of lesbian interlocutors and received intense, thoughtful, and engaged responses.

Among other things, I discovered that none were concerned with certainty; making mistakes was welcomed as part of the process of learning. Moreover, Jackie Anderson argued, "I struggle more with anger and rage at not having my thoughts respected." The denial of epistemic credibility. On whose ground are we willing to meet?

She went on, "I do feel that there are things transparent to me that I don't understand why they aren't transparent to others. *Not because I think I'm right, but because I can't engage when they don't get it.*" In thinking about her response and understandings she's offered over time in our relationship, I realized that I had made a(nother) solipsistic move. Certainly the thing that was bothering me, bullshit all around, is of major concern in an imperial culture. But the critical move is not turning inward. My question, How do you maintain the confidence of your perceptions?, encourages an inward turning, a closing off from others, a disengagement not just from the bullshit but from others also struggling. Thinking about her response, my question is now: How do you reach around the bullshit, the dominant logic, to find others? And who are you animating as you attempt to do so?

Our critical epistemic skills are not about being right, they are about being able to engage. While our abilities of understanding have been compromised in key ways due to modern Western epistemic practice, our possibilities of connection, of engaging, exist in embedded locations, both ours and others'. Embedded, embodied knowing involves working in relation to others, making contact with other women.

The groundbreaking epistemic shift introduced by Gloria Anzaldúa is the possibility of border thinking: transgressing, moving across borders, surrendering the familiar. A celebration of an other logic. Border thinking focuses on the "hostilities, discontinuities and possibilities of connection and sense-making among las/los atravezados/os—those who cross over, pass over, or go through the confines of the normal."[42] Border thinking is a form of life possible in the fractures of hegemonic control of meaning; it takes up practices of knowing arising from the skills of shifting between conceptual frameworks, of meeting others outside the dominant logic.

Lesbian epistemic praxis, becoming critical practitioners of culture, involves becoming subjects to each other, involves finding each other outside hegemonic logic, involves an interactive knowing, a relational knowing, a participatory knowing, the skills of border epistemic praxis. It involves not being focused on being right but being focused on engaging, a listening with the expectation that others will speak back, and not necessarily animating dominant conceptual boundaries. Another border theorist, a Caribbean theorist, Édouard Glissant, offers the idea of understanding not as (Western) grasping, but as *donner avec,* what Betsy Wing takes up in English as "gives-on-and-with." We talked once of hearing each other into speech.[44] Conversations in struggle, challenges—are you listening?! Struggles to bridge seemingly fixed barriers, negotiating collective agendas, going for complex communication which recognizes opacity and resists liberal transparency[54] . . . collectively animating against-the-grain improper.

IV. Multiplicity and Relationality

In challenging Mary Daly, Audre Lorde was not demanding a change in or improvement of theory, it's not about getting it "right." Nor is her work a rejection of radical feminism, since she, along with Gloria Anzaldúa and Paula Gunn Allen, is a radical feminist. From Pat Parker: "I am a feminist. I am neither white nor middle class. And the women that I've worked with were like me."[45] Audre Lorde's challenge, as Amber Katherine points out, is an interactive demand. The critical question, raised by lesbians and women of color to white lesbians and white feminists, over and over, is one of relationality and of becoming subjects to each other through resistant negotiation. White heteropatriarchy constructs and reconstructs barriers, borders, walls, making lesbian political companionship, lesbian connection, difficult to sustain and easy to let slide away.

> When you're white, you don't have to think about your presence when I'm not around. You don't interrogate my absence. You take the absence as a real absence and that it is your choice to include me. But I'm not an addition. I'm always there. (Jackie Anderson)

There are different kinds of walls between Latina and African American lesbians, between South Asian and African American lesbians, for example, and many others, within white supremacist United States. Writing to women of color, María Lugones argues:

> To the extent that Women of Color names a coalition, it is a coalition in formation against significant and complex odds that, though familiar, keep standing in our way. . . . To the extent that we are "created different" by the logic of domination, the techniques of producing difference include divide and conquer, segregation, fragmentation, instilling mistrust toward each other for having been pitted against each other by economies of domination, instilling in us the distinction between the real and the fake.[46]

Challenging the move to purity, fixed borders, and tests of authenticity in resistant communities, María Lugones takes up the distrust of bicultural people, those who are neither fully here nor there. Addressing horizontal hostility, she articulates a paradox: "[T]hose who cultivate resistant perception with respect to each other in their 'home' place nevertheless often internalize oppressive perception of those outside their circle." There is more than one resisting logic. The spaces we travel daily are resistantly animated and complicated.[47]

Ontological pluralism is familiar to many of us, for example, as Marxist-feminist standpoint theory illuminates or radical feminist work articulates; there is more than one reality functioning. But too many of us do not take the ontological implications seriously nor explore the possibilities, for it means we are different selves within these realities. Much oppression theory acknowledges different realities in one way or another, but one reality will be deemed authentic, or we understand ourselves to be our real self in only one of those (essentialism). Hence, many activists reach for utopian vision where we imagine our "true" potential can emerge.

María Lugones rejects this move:

> If we think of people who are oppressed as not consumed or exhausted by oppression, but also as resisting, or sabotaging a system aimed at molding, reducing, violating, erasing them, then we also see at least two realities: one of them has the logic of resistance and transformation; the other has the logic of oppression. But indeed these two logics multiply and they encounter each other over and over in many guises.[48]

We form and are formed by our relations and engagements, which is to say if we inhabit more than one world, we are multiply formed and forming. We are both subordinate and resistant, *really*. This is not the fragmentation that presupposes a unified self, this is about multiple selves: We are, *really,* subordinated women. And we are, *really,* lesbians resisting. The woman is both a fluffy-headed housewife *and* a saboteur.[49]

Directing our attention to intersections of language, territoriality and sociality, María Lugones takes up Mary Daly's *Wickedary* as an explicit performance of linguistic resistance and transgression together with another text of linguistic resistance, *El Libro de Caló,* a dictionary of Pachuco slang, which contests territory and disrupts Anglicity, destabilizing colonial relations. Inhabiting both dictionaries, María Lugones rejects a bilingual's temptation to translate. Seeking, instead, unmediated communication, conversation that speakers must struggle for, fashioned through lived connections, she laments the impossibility of a "wicked caló." Because the *Wickedary* does not take to the streets but stakes its domain in the Background, *Wickedary* gossips have no way of meeting Caló marimachas who, while needing to contest the limits of *Caló,* nevertheless must take up its spatial emphasis. And so she reaches for an everyday vocabulary that simultaneously contests patriarchies and colonialism, a territory where marimachas and gossips meet and converse.[50]

As Amber Katherine writes, "[S]uch a politic is not born out of a particular theoretical framework but rather through complex communication fueled by a desire to make connections under complex systems of oppression, the desire to show you hear."[51] Indeed, it is the possibility of such connections that motivates María Lugones's refusal to translate for gossips and marimachas. Our subjectivity changes as we become subject to local jurisdiction, to the practices and understanding of nonmainstream collectivities in concrete contexts.

Certainly one is interpellated within the dominant logic. But one is not *only* constituted by it. The possibility of sense making or of resistance is not located solely within the dominant logic. To say one is subordinated, indeed to say one is silenced, is not to say one is passive and unable to respond. *One can be both subordinated and resistant. One can be both silenced and speaking.* That one cannot get outside discourse, outside of sociality, does not mean one cannot move outside the dominant logic. But this is not a matter of a purist transcending, quitting the field altogether. It's a matter of meeting others and refusing transparency, of traveling in more than one world, of multiple consciousness, of collective epistemic shifts, and discovering oneself to be multiply constituted.

V. Resituating, Reassessing, "Lesbian"

Lesbian philosophy emerges from activism; all the theoretical developments have come from engaged practice. However, the sense of community that grounded and drove *Lesbian Ethics,* contexts in which we risk and try out ways of relating and doing things differently, no longer exists. While of course there are enclaves of lesbians in many, many places, the coming together in collective work to develop communities that undermine oppression has dissipated. So it is time to come back, once again, to the claim "lesbians are not women." It is time to ask again, who are understood to be the women that lesbians are not?

Elsa Barkley Brown argues that "[w]e still have to recognize that being a woman is, in fact, not extractable from the context in which one is a woman—race, class, time, and place. That is as true for white women as it is for African American, Latina, Asian, and Indian women. We have still to recognize that *all women do not have the same gender.*"[52] At the time that Harriet Taylor and John Stuart Mill were promoting the enfranchisement of women, John Stuart Mill was an official in the British East India Company. Apparently, they felt no sense of contradiction; apparently for them and within the dominant logic, Indian women were not women. Anne McClintock argues that as the Victorian middle class distinguished itself from the working class over labor, the model of a woman as someone who does not work, does not involve herself with dirt, disappeared working-class women. That is to say, working class women also were not women, or had a different gender than white middle-class women.

Miriam Ching Louie argues that the gendering of women has to do with functionality for the state. White middle-class U.S. women are used to maintain the white race. Mexican women, on the other hand, are also used to maintain the white race but in a considerably different capacity. Along with Mexican men, Mexican women serve "as a giant labor reserve and shock absorber for the bumps and potholes of U.S. economic development."[53] Slaves had a sex, were raped and bred as animals were, but had no gender in the dominant logic; that is, they were not understood by whites to be women and men.

So what is being rejected in rejecting "woman"? Attending to (white) men's domination of (white) women is not enough because those men and women are not the only men and women needed to maintain the social order. Indeed, that idealized relationship is constructed in part to maintain and be maintained by other relationships including slavery and colonialism. "Lesbians are not women" does not emerge from the same economy that women of color face. Hence, the rejection of that model may be celebratory for white lesbians yet something else altogether for lesbians and women of color.[54]

Women of color have been denied that notion of womanhood, having first had a much stronger one eradicated through Christian colonialism and capitalism. As María Lugones argues, bringing indigenous women into the

(Western) category "human" was a step down. Anglo-European culture deemed "barbarian" those peoples who were communal and in which females had authority, and Western cultural practitioners have worked to eradicate these barbarisms. Both communality and female authority have been (and still are) critical markers that Western culture uses to distinguish "primitive" from "civilized."[55]

Analyzing what she calls the modern colonial gender system, María Lugones points out that there is a light and dark side. The gender binary is part of the light side of the modern colonial structure and is strictly enforced to the point of coercive surgery, altering anyone who is intersex, born not anatomically "male" or "female" according to designated criteria. In the dark side, however, this strict enforcement of the gender binary does not exist. Indeed, Oyèrónké Oyěwùmí argues that in Yoruban culture, prior to colonization, there were no gender categories.[56]

As María Lugones continues, "Historically, the characterization of white European women as fragile and sexually passive opposed them to non-white, colonized women, including women slaves, who were characterized along a gamut of sexual aggression and perversion, and as strong enough to do any sort of labor."[57] Sojourner Truth's demand, "Ain't I a woman?" was not a call for inclusion but for revaluation and realignment—the textures of the weave. Speaking about many native societies, Paula Gunn Allen argues, "Feminists too often believe that no one has ever experienced the kind of society that empowered women and made that empowerment the basis of its rules of civilization."[58] That is, while white women have a particular history of struggle against gender imposition connected to the claim that lesbians are not women, women of color do not have that same history, or rather, have the same history but have been and continue to be constituted differently by it.

This history has brought us to this place now. And so asks María Lugones,

> If you bracket the meaning of lesbian that emerges from the light side of the binary, the sense of agency that comes from rejecting the ideal of "woman" which gives you a sense of possibility within the binary, and then look for what it is about lesbian that is not tied to the dominant notion of woman, what is there? What do you find in lesbian that is meaningful but not overdetermined by the binary? (María Lugones, conversation)

Taking risks has made us lesbians, risks of desire, of engagement. It's about learning to speak languages under the radar of the official language and resisting monolingual and monocultural pressures. And for this we embrace ambiguity, contradiction, paradox. It's about creating, not presuming, connections, and, for that, resisting translation. It is about recognizing that community must be constantly struggled for, that it is fragile and unstable and must be constantly reinterpreted and revalued. Meeting each other, first meetings, coming out, and sustaining our connections has never been safe.

The lesbian spaces eked out in the United States in the 1970s were driven primarily by working-class lesbians, white, Black, Latina, Native American and Asian-Pacific American, Jewish, disabled, ablebodied, deaf, old, young, healthy and chronically ill, middle- and upper-class lesbian activists through work and struggle and desire. And this work has been taking place in other countries as well, including (but not limited to) Argentina, England, France, Belgium, Germany, Italy, Australia, New Zealand, Aotearoa, Canada, Quebec, Montreal, Spain, Holland, Japan, India, Mexico, Nicaragua, Poland, Israel, Switzerland, South Africa, Philippines, Malaysia, Thailand, Peru, Yugoslavia, East Germany, Ireland, China, Cuba, Venezuela, Algeria, Surinam, Sweden, Hungary, Indonesia, Colombia, El Salvador, Brazil, Namibia, Costa Rica, and Chile. (From my travels, correspondence, and collection of 1980s lesbian journals.) That we spoke and speak different languages, different cultures, didn't mean we couldn't communicate, it meant we struggled with communication, took the risks of communication, driven by a desire for community.

But the structures and barriers between us set us up to keep from connecting across class and culture and race and nationality—white lesbians with black lesbians but also black lesbians with Latinas, for example. And at some point the risks became too great; the complicated and difficult work of building community, of making connections across barriers, have been left behind by too many.

The work ahead for lesbian philosophy is seeing "lesbian" in relation to "others" and how our histories continue to affect our subjectivities today, the textures of the weave. We can trouble the category "lesbian," the identity, the designation, but not the process of struggling against hegemonic identity designation. The work ahead is struggling across barriers to meet each other outside the proper without abstraction or translation, taking up the concrete imprint of the proper on each of us and embracing opacity. "This allows the perceiver to face those outside shared values and shared community with a willingness to ask the question of identity anew, with the curiosity of someone who is looking for companions in the formation of a larger resistant subjectivity. Who are you? Who are we? become different questions when asked anew, without presupposing the real/fake dichotomy."[59]

The interactive demand from women of color is a demand for resisting translation. Transparency is a modern Western philosophical goal, a colonial move—to insist that all can be brought into the proper or the rational as if there were only one. We have the right to opacity (Glissant), to the recognition that two spirits and marimachas and tortilleras and jotas and bulldaggers and khushs and desi dykes and resubians and daikus and jamis are not translatable into lesbians. Not seeking or presuming translation. For example, at a Heterosexism and Empire workshop at the 2005 INCITE conference, a Vietnamese participant questioned, given the history of gendering in her country, what it would mean for her to talk about being masculine or feminine. It is not about the components, it is about the textures of the weaves.

VI. Final Thoughts

No matter how this project is framed in opposition to or as distinct from Western philosophy, it is still a Western philosophical project, and I want to make that clear in a particular way, otherwise it becomes a colonizing project. Although "we are everywhere" as goes the slogan, two-spirit people, for example, in, say, the Iroquois tradition, are not translatable into lesbians and gay men. Ditto marimachas and jotos in Latin America or in the United States. Acknowledging this also makes articulating something called "lesbian philosophy" misleading.

On the other hand, the work that is being done by lesbians, dykes, jotas, bulldykes, desi dykes also offers a mirror through which Western philosophy, modernism and postmodernism, can see itself for its particularity and concreteness that it denies through strategies of universalizing. (Meaning making occurs in contexts; when abstractions make sense to anyone, it is because an unacknowledged context is implicitly referred to.) Such reflection also promotes self-reflection as well as recognition of how other worlds of sense are disappeared. The philosophy and theorizing emerging from jotas and zamis and desi dykes located complexly contributes to understanding philosophy as contextualized and multicentered.

It is critical to understand Western philosophy as one voice among many, as a cultural production rather than the arbiter of all that is true and reasonable, and to understand its own resistance to that acknowledgment. Philosophy is a living practice.

Indeed, modern Western philosophy's penchant for universalizing, for appropriative translation, for understanding everything only within its parameters and as translatable into them, for elevating itself to the status of arbiter of all it surveys . . . this is the violence that is the other side of the freedom of Enlightenment liberal praxis: totalitarian generalization.[60] Anglo-European civilization is enforced as the meaning of reality and everything else is made to be the same (and hence inferior) or other (and hence a threat), or made nonsense, erased, annihilated. Universalized Western philosophical frameworks carry the markers of a way of living, a form of life.

So, what does it mean to be writing consciously from a concrete place? Édouard Glissant writes Caribbean theory not as a description of what those from Martinique or the Caribbean think, but as a practice emerging from that place as the place which gives him his possibilities. Writing consciously from a concrete place, the place of our possibilities, allows us to become subjects, to engage by resisting translation.

And so, I write for my life. And I write this to you. Words, ideas, thoughts, conceptual shifts, are central to my work. And they keep betraying me, or I betray them and then they betray others. I am telling you this to say that if, at the end of this reading you are doing, you think you have grasped, captured lesbian philosophy, then you missed the point of this project. The point is to invite you to locate yourself and enter the fray without translation. Who are you coming to this place? Where do you come from? What and who do you bring? And how are you willing to engage?

We are searching for new meaning. This is a time when philosophers need desperately to be working against the grain. Those interested in the projects in this volume . . . we need to be talking to each other without going through the normalizing function of the Western canon, need to welcome the tensions that emerge as we speak from these different places, and we need to approach each other with generosity.

We cannot afford to cease yearning for each other's company. (M. Jacqui Alexander)

Notes

1. Monique Wittig, *The Straight Mind* (Boston: Beacon, 1992), 20.

2. Marilyn Frye, *The Politics of Reality: Essays in Feminist Theory* (Trumansburg, NY: Crossing Press, 1983), 9.

3. Anzaldúa, "Speaking in Tongues."

4. Meg Christian, "The Road I Took To You," *Face the Music* (Oakland, California: Olivia Records, 1977).

5. Meg Christian, "Ode to a Gym Teacher," *I Know You Know* (Oakland, California: Olivia Records, 1975).

6. Enrique Dussel, *Philosophy of Liberation*. Translated from the Spanish by Aquilina Martinez and Christine Morlcovsky. (Maryknoll, N.Y.: Orbis Books, 1975).

7. Simone de Beauvior, *The Ethics of Ambiguity,* trans. Bernard Frechtman (Secaucus, NJ: Citadel Press, 1980).

8. Katie Cannon, *Black Womanist Ethics* (Atlanta: Scholars Press, 1988), 4.

9. Sarah Lucia Hoagland, *Lesbian Ethics: Toward New Value* (Chicago: Institute of Lesbian Studies, 1988).

10. Hoagland, *Lesbian Ethics*.

11. Lorde, *Sister Outsider*.

12. Hoagland, *Lesbian Ethics*.

13. Adrienne Rich, *Women and Honor: Notes on Lying* (Pittsburgh: Motherroot Publications/Pittsburgh Women Writers, 1977. Reprinted in *On Lies, Secrets, and Silence*. New York: Norton, 1979).

14. Claudia Card, *Lesbian Choices* (New York: Columbia University Press, 1994), chs. 5 and 6.

15. Anannya Bhattacharjee, "A Slippery Path: Organizing Resistance to Violence against Women," in *Dragon Ladies: Asian American Feminists Breathe Fire*, ed. Sonia Shah (Boston: South End Press, 1997).

16. For instance, Jael Silliman and Anannya Bhattacharjee, eds., *Policing the National Body: Race, Gender, and Criminalization* (Cambridge, MA: South End Press, 2002).

17. M. Jacqui Alexander, "Remembering *This Bridge,* Remembering Ourselves: Yearning, Memory, and Desire," in *This Bridge We Call Home,* ed. Gloria E. Anzaldúa and Analouise Keating (New York: Routledge, 2002), 92.

18. See Judith Butler 1997; Minnie Bruce Pratt, "Identity: Skin Blood Heart," in *Yours in Struggle: Three Feminist Perspectives on Anti-Semitism and Racism,* by Elly Bulkin, Minnie Bruce Pratt, and Barbara Smith (Ithaca, NY: Firebrand, 1984); Adrienne Rich, "Disloyal to Civilization," in *Lies, Secrets and Silence* (New York: Norton, 1979).

19. Mary Daly, *Gyn/Ecology* (Boston: Beacon Press, 1978); and Daly, *Webster's New Intergalactic Wickedary of the English Language* (Boston: Beacon Press, 1987).

20. Rey Chow, "Violence in the Other Country: China as Crisis, Spectacle, and Woman," in *Third World Women and the Politics of Feminism*, ed. Chandra Talpade Mohanty et al. (Bloomington: Indiana University Press, 1991), 93.

21. Lorde, *Sister Outsider*, 117.

22. Hoagland, *Lesbian Ethics*.

23. Alexander, "Remembering *This Bridge,*" 98–99.

24. Hoagland, *Lesbian Ethics*.

25. Lorde, *Sister Outsider*, 122.

26. Lorde, *Sister Outsider*, 111.

27. Frye, *Politics of Reality*, ch. 3.

28. Lugones, *Pilgrimages/Peregrinajes,* ch. 4.

29. Alexander, "Remembering *This Bridge,*" 82.

30. Gloria Anzaldúa, *Borderlands*.

31. María Lugones, *Pilgrimages/Peregrinajes*.

32. Lugones 2003, 97.

33. Lugones 2003, *Pilgrimages/Peregrinajes,* ch. 4.

34. Biddie Martin and Chandra Mohanty, "Feminist Politics: What's Home Got to Do with It?" in *Feminist Studies/Critical Studies,* ed. Teresa de Laurentis (Bloomington: Indiana University Press, 1986), 193–98.

35. Martin and Mohanty, "Feminist Politics," 202, 210.

36. Hoagland 2003.

37. Anibel Quijano, "Coloniality of Power Eurocentrism, and Latin America," *Neplanta: Views from the South* 1.3 (2000), cited by Walter Mignolo, *Local Histories/Global Designs* (Princeton: Princeton University Press 2000).

38. Anannya Bhattacharjee, "Private Fists and Public Force: Race, Gender, and Surveillance," in Silliman and Bhattacharjee, eds., *Policing the National Body,* 2002.

39. Judith Butler, *Gender Trouble: Feminism and the Subversion of Identity* (New York: Routledge, 1990), 2.

40. Sarah Lucia Hoagland, "Heterosexualism and White Supremacy," Mypathia. 22.1. (2007).

41. Lugones, *Pilgrimages/Peregrinajes,* ch. 10.

42. Anzaldúa 1987, 3.

43. Nellie Morton, *The Journey Is Home* (Boston: Beacon Press, 1985), ch. 8.

44. María Lugones, "On Complex Communication," *Hypatia* 21(3), (2006).

45. Pat Parker, "Revolution: It's Not Neat or Pretty or Quick," in Moraga and Anzaldúa, eds., *This Bridge Called My Back,* 241.

46. Lugones 2003, 84.

47. Lugones, *Pilgrimages/Peregrinajes,* ch. 7.

48. Lugones 2003, 12.

49. Sarah Lucia Hoagland, *Lesbian Ethics: Toward New Value* (Chicago: Institute of Lesbian Studies, 1988, 40).

50. María Lugones, "Wicked Caló: A Matter of the Authority of Improper Words," in *Feminist Interpretations of Mary Daly*, ed. Sarah Lucia Hoagland and Marilyn Frye (University Park: Penn State University Press, 2000).

51. Amber Katherine, "'A Too Early Morning': Audre Lorde's 'An Open Letter to Mary Daly' and Daly's Decision Not to Respond in Kind," in *Feminist Interpretations of Mary Daly,* 294.

52. Elsa Barkley Brown, "Polyrhythms and Improvisation: Lessons for Women's History," *History Workshop Journal* 31 (Spring, 1991).

53. Miriam Ching Yoon Louie, *Sweatshop Warriors: Immigrant Women Workers Take on the Global Factory* (Cambridge, MA: South End Press, 2001), 64.

54. Conversation, Maria Lugones.

55. Enrique Dussel, *The Invention of the Americas: Eclipse of "the Other" and the Myth of Modernity,* trans. Michael D. Barber (New York: Continuum, 1995); Ronald Takaki, *In a Different Mirror: A History of Multicultural America* (Boston: Little, Brown, and Co., 1993).

56. Oyèrónké Oyewùmí. *The Invention of Women: Making an African Sense of Western Gender Discourses* (Minneapolis: University of Minnesota Press, 1997).

57. María Lugones, "Heterosexualism and the Colonial/Modern, Gender System," *Hypathia.* 22. 1 (2007).

58. Paula Gunn Allen, *The Sacred Hoop: Recovering the Feminine in American Indian Traditions* (Boston: Beacon Press, 1986), 213.

59. Lugones, *Pilgrimages/Peregrinajes*, ch. 7.

60. Dussel, *Invention of the Americas*; Anibal Quijano, "Coloniality of Power, Eurocentrism, and Latin America," *Neplanta: Views from South* 1, no. 3 (2000); Walter D. Mignolo, *The Darker Side of the Renaissance* (Ann Arbor: University of Michigan Press, 1995).

Bibliography

Alarcón, Norma. *Chicana Critical Studies*. Berkeley, CA: Third Woman Press. 1993.

Alexander, M. Jacqui. "Remembering *This Bridge*, Remembering Ourselves: Yearning, Memory, and Desire." In *This Bridge We Call Home*, ed. Gloria E. Anzaldúa and Analouise Keating. New York: Routledge, 2002.

Allen, Paula Gunn. *The Sacred Hoop: Recovering the Feminine in American Indian Traditions*. Boston: Beacon Press, 1986.

Anzaldúa, Gloria. *Borderlands/La Frontera: The New Mestiza*. San Francisco: Spinsters/Aunt Lute, 1987.

———. "Speaking in Tongues: A Letter to 3rd World Women Writers." In *This Bridge Called My Back: Writings by Radical Women of Color*, ed. Cherríe Moraga and Gloria Anzaldúa. New York: Kitchen Table, Women of Color, 1981.

Beauvoir, Simone de. *The Ethics of Ambiguity*. Trans. Bernard Frechtman. Secaucus, NJ: Citadel Press, 1980.

———. *The Second Sex*. New York: Vintage, 1952.

Bhattacharjee, Anannya. "Private Fists and Public Force: Race, Gender, and Surveillance." In *Policing the National Body: Race, Gender, and Criminalization*, ed. Jael Silliman and Anannya Bhattacharjee. Cambridge, MA: South End Press, 2002.

———. "A Slippery Path: Organizing Resistance to Violence against Women." In *Dragon Ladies: Asian American Feminists Breathe Fire*, ed. Sonia Shah. Boston: South End Press, 1997.

Brant, Beth. *Mohawk Trail*. Ithaca, NY: Firebrand Books, 1985.

Brown, Elsa Barkley. 1991. "Polyrhythms and Improvisation: Lessons for Women's History." In *History Workshop Journal* 31 (Spring): 85–90.

Butler, Judith. *Excitable Speech: A Politics of the Performative*. New York: Routledge, 1997.

———. *Gender Trouble: Feminism and the Subversion of Identity*. New York: Routledge, 1990.

Cannon, Katie. *Black Womanist Ethics*. Atlanta: Scholars Press, 1988.

Card, Claudia. *Lesbian Choices*. New York: Columbia University Press, 1994.

Card, Claudia, ed. *Adventures in Lesbian Philosophy*. Bloomington: Indiana University Press, 1994.

Carter, C. C. "Tribute to Mountain Moving." *Identity, glbti, race, gender, culture* 10, no. 12 (2006): 16.

Christian, Meg. *Face the Music*. Oakland, CA: Olivia Records, 1977.

———. *I Know You Know*. Oakland, CA: Olivia Records, 1975.

Chow, Rey. "Violence in the Other Country: China as Crisis, Spectacle, and Woman." In *Third World Women and the Politics of Feminism*, ed. Chandra Talpade Mohanty et al. Bloomington: Indiana University Press, 1991.

Clarke, Cheryl. "Lesbianism: an Act of Resistance." In *This Bridge Called My Back: Writings by Radical Women of Color*, ed. Cherríe Moraga and Gloria Anzaldúa. New York: Kitchen Table, Women of Color, 1981.

Cliff, Michelle. *Claiming an Identity They Taught Me to Despise*. Watertown, Massachusetts: Persephone Press, 1980.

Combahee River Collective. 1981. "A Black Feminism Statement." In Moraga and Anzaldúa.

Crenshaw, Kimberlé Williams. "Beyond Racism and Misogyny: Black Feminism and 2 Live Crew." In *Words that Wound: Critical Race Theory, Assaultive Speech, and the First Amendment*, ed. Mari J. Matsuda, Charles R. Lawrence III, Richard Delgado, and Kimberlé Crenshaw. Boulder, CO: Westview Press, 1993.

———. "Whose Story Is It, Anyway? Feminist and Antiracist Appropriations of Anita Hill." In *Race-ing Justice, En-gender-ing Power*, ed. Toni Morrison. New York: Pantheon Books, 1992.

Daly, Mary. *Gyn/Ecology*. Boston: Beacon Press, 1978.

———. *Webster's New Intergalactic Wickedary of the English Language*. Boston: Beacon Press, 1987.

Descartes, René. *Meditations on First Philosophy*. Trans. Donald A. Gress. Hackett Publishing Co., 1979.

DuBois, W.E.B. *The Souls of Black Folk*. In *Three Negro Classics* ed. James Weldon Johnson. N.Y.: Avon Books, 1965.

Dussel, Enrique. *The Invention of the Americas: Eclipse of "the Other" and the Myth of Modernity*. Trans. Michael D. Barber. New York: Continuum, 1995.

———. *Philosophy of Liberation*. Translated from the Spanish by Aquilina Martinez and Christine Morkovsky. Maryknoll, NY: Orbis Books, 1985.

Frye, Marilyn. "The Necessity of Differences: Constructing a Positive Category of Women." *SIGNS: Journal of Women in Culture and Society* 21, no. 3 (1996).

———. *The Politics of Reality: Essays in Feminist Theory*. Trumansburg, NY: Crossing Press, 1983.

Glissant, Édouard. *Poetics of Relation*. Trans. Betsy Wing. Ann Arbor: University of Michigan Press, [1981] 1989.

Grahn, Judy. *Another Mother Tongue*. Boston: Beacon Press, 1984.

Hoagland, Sarah Lucia. "Heterosexualism and White Supremacy." *Hypatia* 22.1 (2007).

———. "Lesbian Ethics," a review essay. In *A Companion to Feminist Philosophy*, ed. Alison Jaggar and Iris Young NY: Blackwell, 1998.

———. *Lesbian Ethics: Toward New Value*. Chicago: Institute of Lesbian Studies, 1988.

———. "Practices of Knowing: Transcendence and Denial of Epistemic Credibility, or Engagement and Transformation." *International Studies in Philosophy* 35, no. 2 (2003).

Hoagland, Sarah Lucia, and Marilyn Frye, eds. *Feminist Interpretations of Mary Daly.* University Park: Penn State University Press, 2000.

Katherine, Amber. "'A Too Early Morning': Audre Lorde's 'An Open Letter to Mary Daly' and Daly's Decision Not to Respond in Kind." In *Feminist Interpretations of Mary Daly*, ed. Sarah Lucia Hoagland and Marilyn Frye. University Park: Penn State University Press, 2000.

Kuhn, Thomas. *The Structure of Scientific Revolution*, 2nd ed. Chicago: University of Chicago Press, 1970.

Kusch, Rodolfo. *Indigenous and Popular Thought in América.* Trans. María Lugones and Joshua Price. Draft. N.d. Originally published as *El Pensamiento Indigena y Popular en América.*

Lorde, Audre. *Sister Outsider.* Freedom, CA: Crossing, 1984.

Louie, Miriam Ching Yoon. *Sweatshop Warriors: Immigrant Women Workers Take on the Global Factory.* Cambridge, MA: South End Press, 2001.

Lugones, María. "Heterosexualism and the Colonial/Modern, Gender System." *Hypatia.* 22.1 (2007).

———. "On Complex Communication," *Hypatia* 21(3) (2006).

———. *Pilgrimages/Peregrinajes: Theorizing Coalition Against Multiple Oppressions.* NY: Rowman & Littlefield, 2003.

———. "Wicked Caló: A Matter of the Authority of Improper Words." In *Feminist Interpretations of Mary Daly*, ed. Sarah Lucia Hoagland and Marilyn Frye. University Park: Penn State University Press, 2000.

MacKinnon, Catharine A. *Only Words.* Cambridge: Harvard University Press, 1993.

Martin, Biddie, and Chandra Mohanty. "Feminist Politics: What's Home Got to Do with It?" In *Feminist Studies/Critical Studies,* ed. Teresa de Laurentis. Bloomington: Indiana University Press, 1986.

McClintock, Anne. *Imperial Leather: Race, Gender, and Sexuality in the Colonial Contest.* New York: Routledge, 1995.

Mignolo, Walter D. *The Darker Side of the Renaissance.* Ann Arbor: University of Michigan Press, 1995.

———. *Local Histories/Global Designs.* Princeton, NJ: Princeton University Press, 2000.

Mohanty, Chandra Talpade. "Under Western Eyes: Feminist Scholarship and Colonial Discourses." In *Third World Women and the Politics of Feminism*, ed. Chandra Talpade Mohanty et al. Bloomington: Indiana University Press, 1991.

Mohanty, Chandra Talpade, et al., eds. *Third World Women and the Politics of Feminism.* Bloomington: Indiana University Press, 1991.

Moraga, Cherríe. *Loving in the War Years.* Cambridge, Massachusetts: South End Press, 2000

Moraga, Cherríe, and Anzaldúa, Gloria, eds. *This Bridge Called My Back: Writings by Radical Women of Color.* New York: Kitchen Table, Women of Color, 1981.

Morton, Nellie. *The Journey Is Home.* Boston: Beacon Press, 1985.

Nietzsche, Friedrich. *Beyond Good and Evil.* Chicago: Henry Regnery Co., 1995.

Oyĕwùmí, Oyèrónké. *The Invention of Women: Making an African Sense of Western Gender Discourses.* Minneapolis: University of Minnesota Press, 1997.

Parker, Pat. "Revolution: It's Not Neat or Pretty or Quick." In *This Bridge Called My Back: Writings by Radical Women of Color,* ed. Cherríe Moraga and Gloria Anzaldúa. New York: Kitchen Table, Women of Color, 1981.

Penelope, Julia. *Speaking Freely: Unlearning the Lies of the Father's Tongues.* New York: Pergamon Press, 1990.

Perdue, Theda. "Cherokee Women and the Trail of Tears." In *Unequal Sisters: A Multicultural Reader in U.S. Women's History,* ed. Vicki L. Ruiz and Ellen Carol DuBois. New York: Routledge, 2000.

Pratt, Minnie Bruce. "Identity: Skin Blood Heart." In *Yours in Struggle: Three Feminist Perspectives on Anti-Semitism and Racism,* by Elly Bulkin, Minnie Bruce Pratt, and Barbara Smith. Ithaca, NY: Firebrand, 1984.

Quijano, Anibal. "Coloniality of Power, Eurocentrism, and Latin America." *Neplanta: Views from South* 1, no. 3 (2000).

Reinfelder, Monika. *Amazon to Zami: Towards A Global Lesbian Feminism.* London: Cassell, 1996.

Rich, Adrienne. "Disloyal to Civilization." In *Lies, Secrets and Silence.* New York: Norton, 1979.

———. *Women and Honor: Notes on Lying.* Pittsburgh: Motherroot Publications/Pittsburgh Women Writers, 1977. Reprinted in *On Lies, Secrets, and Silence.* New York: Norton, 1979.

Silliman, Jael, and Anannya Bhattacharjee, eds., *Policing the National Body: Race, Gender, and Criminalization.* Cambridge, MA: South End Press, 2002.

Takaki, Ronald. *In a Different Mirror: A History of Multicultural America.* Boston: Little, Brown, and Co., 1993.

Wittig, Monique. *The Straight Mind.* Boston: Beacon, 1992.

What Is Queer Philosophy?

RANDALL HALLE
University of Pittsburgh

QUEER PHILOSOPHY IS an emergent project. Neither a fully elaborated philosophy of queerness nor a queer philosophy as such yet exists. Queer philosophy should not be confused with a celebration of deviances or perversion, although queer studies of gays and lesbians, the transgendered, the intersexed, the members of fetish communities, and so on have given important momentum to the project. The knowledge held by those outside normative exclusions does prove of particular significance to queer analysis. Queerness, as will be discussed here, is not a question of the marginal or excluded as such, but rather of a *universal dynamic*. I suggest here that queer philosophy develops out of the realization that queerness constitutes a universal experience of being, although at the moment it may only be recognized as an experience and knowledge proper to a limited number of people.[1] In a sense, queer philosophy emerges as a philosophical attention to queerness.

In the following, I will begin with a historical survey of the emergence of queer theory (to be distinguished from queer philosophy) and a brief discussion of its domain of analysis. Queer theory, like other critical theories, developed in a particular relationship to material conditions and the strivings of liberation movements. After the introduction, I will attend to a "querying" of the work of Kant as an example of a queer theoretical engagement with the Western philosophical tradition. The discussion will then seek to distinguish the potentials of queer theory from queer philosophy where the latter moves into a second order of abstraction, investigating the universality of queerness rather than focusing on particular manifestations. In what follows, I want to be clear that in my distinguishing queer philosophy from queer studies in particular and from queer theory's general commitment to gay and lesbian specificity, I am not trying to say that gay studies, trans-studies, and so on are not important. They should be done. However, I would contend that at this point an orientation toward universality and abstraction can actually create a situation in which we can better understand the specific and limited. As when critical race studies began to attend to non-U.S. constructions of race, the second-order orientation of the questions posed obviate residual essentialisms. Queer theory/philosophy both derive from the antiessentialist impetus that developed out of social constructionism and performativity.

Queer philosophy follows this trajectory one step further. Because the comparison of queer theory and philosophy I undertake is akin to a neo-Hegelian position—queer philosophy as deriving from the history of queer thought—the discussion here will then give way to a focus on Hegelian philosophy, in particular the question of alterity. Finally, the chapter will turn to a reflection on the possibilities of queer knowing.

The Emergence of Queer Theory out of the Spirit of Gay Liberation

The quest by gays and lesbians for civil rights gained momentum in the 1960s. Sparked by the energy of the Stonewall rebellion in New York (June 27–31, 1969), a new militant movement emerged and spread rapidly beyond the United States. The struggle for gay liberation flourished in the 1970s. As a movement, it became radicalized through the AIDS crisis in the 1980s and infused majoritarian national political debates in the 1990s. And since sexual orientation has expanded into the discourse on human rights, it has also come to have an impact on geopolitics. This movement emancipated a new positive subject from long years of pathologization and criminalization. In spite of the mountain of prejudicial evidence serving as foundation to legal, medical, religious, and educational institutions, the women and men of the early movement took a brave stance to insist on the equality and rationality of their lives and aspirations. The quest for liberation undertaken by gays and lesbians thus required not only a form of direct political engagement and community organization but an extensive revision of heteronormative knowledge. Gay liberation thereby compelled the emergence of gay and lesbian studies as a means not only to counter prejudice but also to promote an appreciation of the cultural production of gays and lesbians. Just as gay and lesbian studies had a clear relationship to the gay and lesbian liberation movements, it mirrored the dynamic that developed also with other directions in the new social movements of the sixties and seventies, for instance the relationship between the women's movement and the simultaneously developing area of women's studies.

Gay and lesbian studies thus started primarily as descriptive studies by and for participants in the era's movement. Lesbians and gays sought first to produce new positive knowledge for themselves and then secondly to develop a critical position from which they could respond to the overwhelmingly negative discourse of homosexuality. Lesbian and gay studies became established within academic settings. Across disciplines, quantitative sociological analysis, psychological studies, literary and historical studies all entered into new terrain to comprehend the lifeworld of the emancipated homosexual. In culturally and historically comparative research gay activist scholars begin to seek their counterparts across time.[2] And in this quest for knowledge an interesting break began to emerge.

Certainly it was clear that the era after the Stonewall rebellion differed significantly from other eras. However, the work of historians like Mary Macintosh, Michel Foucault, and Jeffrey Weeks proved especially significant in revealing how the subject emancipated by gay liberation differed in its social construction from other historical subjects.[3] Same-sex desire might be a historical constant but its particular expression from epoch to epoch, place to place, differed dramatically. Thus, they suggested, there were no gays among the participants in the early Christian church; there was no direct line of thought from Plato to Oscar Wilde to Andy Warhol. Compelled in part by virtue of such studies, the recognition that the era of gay liberation was not a culmination of a transhistorical logic, that it itself might give way to a new and hitherto unexplored era, opened up the possibility for gay and lesbian studies to enter into a level of abstraction in thinking about sexuality and desire as such. This recognition, and the debates it unleashed, made possible a significant move from descriptive studies to descriptive theory, a point I want to underscore and to which I will return.

The complex consideration of sexuality and desire, however, opened up the possibility of exploring other forms of sexuality beyond a singular focus on a homosexual/heterosexual divide. This new attention also corresponded to the emergence of new sexual liberation movements in the 1980s. Considerations of bisexuality, S–M, and transgendered experiences expanded the perspective of research to a broader set of identities and fostered the development of the term "queer studies" as a collective designation.[4] Queer studies remained, at its core, identity and community based. Within it, identitarian studies like lesbian studies or transgendered studies explore the exclusion of particular groups of people, particular types, particular behaviors, striving variously for inclusion or transformation of the existing system. "Queer" as a term in queer studies, however, served not so much to designate an identity position, rather it pointed to an interest in a further move toward abstraction. "Queer" then served as a *placeholder* for specific identities, for the sake of propelling them into a first-order abstraction. It did not signify the meaning of these identities.

We can thus distinguish two directions here from each other: queer studies from queer theory. Queer studies emerged in the 1990s in direct relation to political and social movements and communities, while queer theory developed at the same time following more abstract interests.[5] To be sure, at this time queer theory still had a close relationship with the sexual liberation movements now expanded and radicalized under the pressure of the AIDS crisis. However, I would suggest that queer theory, drawing from insights offered by various materialist, feminist, structuralist, and poststructuralist discourses, continued into a second order of abstraction. Queer did not serve as an umbrella designation for specific sexed and gendered communities; rather, it emerged as a radical critique of gender and sexual essentialism, heteronormativity, and dominant subjectivity in general.[6] Leo Bersani, Judith Butler, Sue-Ellen Case, Joan Copjec, Douglas Crimp, John D'Emilio, Lee Edelman, Anne Fausto-Sterling, Michel Foucault, Elizabeth Grosz, David Halperin, Donna Harraway, Gert Hekma, Teresa de Lauritis, D. A. Miller, Michael Moon, Harry Oosterhuis, Gayle Rubin, Joan Scott, Eve Kosofsky Sedgwick, James Steakley, and Michael Warner, among others, offered significant contributions to the development of queer theory. To be sure, because their work attended to specific questions of gender and sexuality, their work certainly overlaps with queer studies. Yet their work established queer theory as a significant direction in cultural analysis appropriating a variety of productive critical tools: for instance, social constructionism, the concept of homosociality, antiessentialism, antinormativity, heterogeneity, fluidity, and performativity, among others.

The terms of critical analysis queer theorists developed do engage with material lived experience, but they also open up a metacritical discussion that often seems distant from the streets. Indeed, aspects of the work of queer theory have complicated the presumptions of identity- and community-based politics. Leading figures in the development of queer theory like Judith Butler have repeatedly experienced attacks for a distance from "real-world politics."[7] These types of attacks indicate that queer theory has moved away from the position occupied by lesbian and gay studies. There can be no doubt that queer theory has developed as a descriptive theory addressing a spectrum of lived human experiences that exceeds such pairs as heterosexuality/homosexuality, female/male, and femininity/masculinity. And inasmuch as lived material experience evidences a great deal of complexity, we must also expect a similar complexity from our descriptive apparatus. In this regard, queer theory proves more capable of apprehending the world in its complexity and totality than gay and lesbian studies does. At the same time, queer theory has also moved increasingly into a level of abstraction that derives not from what is given in a particular moment in the material world but rather from questioning what possibilities might be there that transcend the apparent limits of a particular moment.

I would like to focus then on this question: What kind of relationship can we recognize developing between philosophy and queer theory? We might posit it as a move into increasing levels of abstraction, although increasing abstraction does not mean distance from social-material concerns. Abstraction does not mean queer philosophy would strive for complexity as such but rather that queer philosophical abstraction affords a cohesion in perspective; it increases clarity. Furthermore, we could consider the development I am describing of queer studies into queer theory into queer philosophy as some process of supercession. However, each move does not replace the other. The information offered by gay studies allowed the debates around the social construction of sexuality to arise. The information transgendered studies afforded about the expression of gender allowed for the discussion of performativity to arise. Social constructionism and performativity in turn not only compelled the development of queer theory but had a significant effect on research in gay, lesbian, bisexual, or transgendered histories.[8]

Queer philosophy emerges in its own right first as queer theoretical tools are used for a sustained critique of the discipline of philosophy. Such queer critique can develop in a number of ways. Queer theorists can seek to rewrite the history of philosophy, by discovering lost or silenced texts and philosophers, by countering heterosexist presumptions with evidence of other economies of desire inscribed in philosophical texts. For instance, we could foreground Plato's relationship to παιεδεραστεί (pæderasty) or the Marquis de Sade's relationship to Enlightenment thought. Queer as an umbrella designation of various identities can search through the history of philosophy to find and counter negative images of same-sex desire, of bisexual desire, of transgendered experience, and so on. In following these directions queer theory would not undertake analyses that distinguish themselves significantly from gay, lesbian, transgendered studies. In the 1970s and 1980s, especially gay and lesbian studies sought to accomplish such revisions of the literary and cultural canon. They strove for positive images, forgotten histories, and sought to formulate critical responses to the biases that led to exclusion. Or queer theoretical critique can "query" particular aspects of philosophical discourse to develop the term "queer" in itself.

The Critique of Willed Reason

Let me offer a brief digression as exploration of some possible ways that queer critique of philosophy can open up the work of, for example, Kant. Turing our attention to Kant here begins our specific exploration of queer philosophy as a neo–Hegelian exploration, beginning via a queer history of philosophy. Contemporary philosophers often make a distinction between Kant's pure philosophical writings, namely the three critiques of reason and judgment, and his more political and anthropological writings.[9] They variously dismiss or marginalize Kant's writing about life on other planets or about the causes of differences in skin pigment. Or they ascribe to a different category his reflections on how to achieve perpetual peace or how to promote enlightenment. For queer theory, this division becomes significant because it has the effect of separating Kant's work on gender and sexuality as anthropological from his critical consideration. The "pure" philosophical writings thereby undergo a form of extraction from the overall oeuvre, a distinction that Kant himself certainly did not make. In this case, a queer critical approach reveals how a philosophy of human rationality and subjectivity takes shape *on the basis of* a particular perspective on gender and sexuality. It reveals how modern philosophy is grounded on a certain vision of human intimacy and that later commentators ignored or overlooked the presumptions having developed as "common sense."

After the discussion of *The Critique of Pure Reason* (1781) with its concentration on the abstract and transcendent qualities of pure reason, Kant then addressed the role of reason in the objective world through his discussion of *The Critique of Practical Reason* (1788). He focused on the means whereby the subject described in the earlier critique came to express itself and have effect on the objective world: through *the will* as determining force exercised on the objective world. The will provided the bridge between pure and practical reason. Kant wrote on this point, arguing:

> For here reason can at least attain so far as to determine the will, and, in so far as it is a question of volition only, reason does always have objective reality. This is, then, the first question: Is pure reason sufficient of itself to

determine the will, or is it only as empirically conditioned that it can do so? (Prac R, 15)

Such theorizing certainly appears abstract. However, his discussion of the will did not debut in *The Critique of Practical Reason*. Rather, it was in *The Groundwork to a Metaphysics of Morals* (1785), written shortly before *Practical Reason*, that Kant set forth the basis of the terms through which the will operated.

> The dependence of the faculty of desire upon feelings is called inclination, and this accordingly always indicates a *need*. The dependence of a contingently determinable will on principles of reason, however, is called an *interest*. This, accordingly, is present only in the case of a dependent will, which is not of itself always in conformity with reason; in the case of the divine will we cannot think of any interest. But even the human will can *take an interest* in something without therefore *acting from interest*. The first signifies *practical* interest in the action, the second, *pathological* interest in the object of the action. The former indicates only dependence of the will upon principles of reason *in themselves*; the second, dependence upon principles of reason for the sake of inclination, namely where reason supplies only the practical rule as to how to remedy the need of inclination. (414)

In this discussion, Kant defines will through a series of distinctions that set apart desire, feeling, inclination, and need; moreover, he distinguishes types of will motivated by pathological dependencies and interests. He relegates therewith a whole plethora of forces that motivate human actions outside *willed reason* to the realm of the irrational and immoral. Kant thus establishes a position of a rational moral subject and an antipodal immoral desiring individual.

The discussion remains perhaps abstracted unless the critical investigation attends to how such a distinction comes to affect Kant's understanding of social organization. We can intuit that the presumed immorality of this desiring individual stands in for precisely the host of subjects that may be designated as queer. I would suggest that this *desiring individual* actually identifies the fundamental position of the queer subject in modern Western philosophy. Remaining specifically focused on Kant's work, however, we can recognize how this desiring individual comes to define and position whole classes of people.

In his later moral work, after articulating the necessity of willed reason's independence from any determining irrational force, for example, lust or desire, we can find how he asserts an interconnection between marriage and pure reason. He writes:

> Even if it is supposed that their end is the pleasure of using each other's sexual attributes, the marriage contract is not up to their discretion but is a contract that is necessary by the principle of humanity, that is, if a man and a woman want to enjoy each other's sexual attributes, they *must* necessarily marry, and this is necessary in accordance with pure reason's principles of Right. (*Metaphysics of Morals*, § 24)

Marriage offers a necessary contract whereby two parties can enter into sexual union rationally. They thus must not fear that their lust has debased them by taking control of their will. Kant, restricting marriage to a heterosexual union, thereby relegates all other forms of affective sexual relations to a place outside Right, outside justice, outside morality, outside rationality, and ultimately outside the state.

In his *Anthropology* (1798), through the dictum that "the woman should reign and the man should rule, because inclination reigns and reason rules," Kant then established a condition whereby all women became aligned with inclination (*Anthro*, 309 303.17).[10] This alignment positioned women precariously outside reason. It had significant ramifications for their role in the household and ultimately the state. Distinct from rationality, he established a loose set of autonomous feminine characteristics involving passivity and weakness, which would subordinate women in the household.[11] In *The Metaphysics of Morals* (1797), Kant established a dominance of the husband based "only on the natural superiority of the husband to the wife in his capacity to promote the common interest of the household, and the right to direct that is based on this can be derived from the very duty of unity and equality with respect to the *end*" (*Metaphysics of Morals*, § 26). The household came to define a whole series of dependencies: wives, and children, as well as all the people who worked for the household, whether it be as cook, cleaner, or wood chopper. Kant, in his own words summed it up in this way, "[A]ll women and, in general, anyone whose preservation in existence (his being fed and protected) depends not on his management of his own business but on arrangements made by another (except the state). All these people lack civil personality and their existence is, as it were, only inherence" (*Metaphysics of Morals*, § 46). Because the father-husband disposed over the household, those individuals who depended on the household for their livelihood occupied a heteronomous condition, unable to exercise their reason freely. Contractual heterosexual relations impel the Kantian subject. Furthermore, they establish relations of dependency and sovereignty, thus differentially allocating capacities for reason. This difference begins with gender and desire. Such relations do not only establish a governing imperative over same-sex desire but over all forms of sexuality and all forms of relationships, inasmuch as all relationships are gendered. It just as much governs the relationships of the head of household to his male servant as it does that of the relationship of the husband and wife, or the husband and concubine.

This excursion through the works of Kant could continue much further, but the point was first to draw out the connections between the "abstract philosophical" and the practical writings. We can certainly see that Kant sought out practical relations and applications among the various levels of his works. Then returning to the question of queer theory's engagement with philosophy, we can further see how queer critique opens up new approaches and relations to Kant's work. Some feminist scholars, attending only to the discussions of women's roles in Kant, have sought to enter into a reformist relationship that identifies the anthropological and moral texts as sexist while leaving the critiques as descriptive of a universal subjectivity.[12] Such an approach seeks to hold open the possibility of women simply finding inclusion in Kant's Enlightenment subject. By including assessments of sexual desire, we recognize how willed reason acts as an abjecting mechanism, foreclosing for vast portions of humanity the possibility of participation in the Kantian universal moral subject. In doing so we recognize the important correspondences between gender and sexuality and feminism and queer theory. The definition of the desiring individual does not only have an effect on women but also on members of other categories based on age, sexuality, property position, income dependence, and so on. Moreover, we can begin to recognize how his philosophy, understood as the height of the Enlightenment, establishes preconditions for gendered and sexual domination in the modern era. It proves insufficient to describe Kant simply as influenced by heterosexism. We can see that Kant actually promotes heteronormative structures. His understanding of rationality is compelled by a heterocoital imperative that relegates other economies of desire, and desire as such, outside reason and morality. From a queer critical perspective then, we would insist that "desiring individuals" too have rationales and ethics which Kantian reason cannot contain.

Thus a queer critique, in order to accord rationality to the queer subject, compels a break with this dominant sex-gender paradigm and fundamentally rejects the distinctions by which Kant defined *willed reason*. In order to contain the reason of the "desiring individual," queer critique thus would inspire in a philosophical system a reformulation of reason, will, morality, universality, and so on. If we rely on this recognition to define the direction of queer philosophy, then, I suggest, queer ethics or queer discussions of reason would begin from the point that all rationalities and ethics are situational, negotiable, and not exclusive of some practice or some group. Thus, we follow a move into increasing philosophical abstraction away from the concerns of a gay or feminist movement. Queer theory, as it moves beyond the "umbrella function," enters into a level of significant abstraction (not unlike certain influential strands of feminist theory). It is not only a matter of positive descriptive identity and community studies. Queer critical engagements can, in the overused but important formulation, "query" philosophical texts to arrive at new knowledge. This new knowledge in turn opens up new possibilities of practical activity.[13] Queer philosophy does not reject philosophy as much as works its way *through* it.

Queer Theory Is Not Yet Queer Philosophy

While queer theory marks certain significant developments, still queer theory is not equivalent to queer philosophy or queer science. This distinction might seem odd given, on the one hand, a tendency in literary and cultural studies to collapse theory and philosophy as terms. On the other hand, the quest for queer science might also seem odd given the general abdication of scholars in the humanities from understanding their work as contributing to the *human sciences*. By distinguishing queer theory from queer philosophy, I am certainly not interested in enforcing disciplinary boundaries but rather in thinking about long-range and full possibilities for the term "queer."

In that queer theory developed its tools of analysis out of the legacy of Western philosophy, it is like other contemporary forms of critical theory. The work of Hegel, Marx, Nietzsche, Freud, Heidegger, Saussure, Pierce, Wittgenstein, Derrida, and Deleuze, among others, offered a foundation upon which queer theorists built. However, in contradistinction to gay, lesbian, bisexual, transgendered studies that relied primarily on positivist, sometimes quantitative, and formalist analyses of historical events, communities, and texts, queer theory as critical theory has a distinct ability to engage philosophical discourse as such—like feminist theory and critical race theory. Yet queer theory has not yet developed a sustained critical engagement with its own foundation. In this regard, queer philosophy is an emergent discourse only now coming into its own. For queer theory to develop into queer philosophy, it requires a critique of its own foundation in modern Western philosophy. Only through such a critique can it accomplish the epistemological break that would distinguish it as a self-consistent philosophical discourse. Queer philosophy has a great contribution to make to the study of philosophy as a critical position vis-à-vis the first history philosophy.

In a trajectory in the history of ideas marked by, for instance, Kant, Hegel, and Marx, we would typically recognize significant ruptures and radical critiques. In the common story of developments, Hegel's idealism rejected the Kantian subject, while Marx's materialism put Hegelian philosophy on its head. Hegel broke with Kant, Marx broke in turn with Hegel. Yet precisely in this trajectory we could recognize that as radical as the presumed ruptures are, these three divergent, even antithetical philosophical directions nevertheless share a common root in that each shares a presumption of heterosexuality as the sine qua non of rational social subjects. We saw how in the development of his system, Kant allocated the properties of reason to the male head of the household, leaving de facto all nonsovereign dependents—wives, daughters, servants, and the nonheterosexual—permanently outside reason. Hegel similarly intensified the significance of the hetero-coital imperative, making it the basis of civil society, the resolution of the dialectic, the key to the ethical order. Marx and Engels relied on a natural sexual division of labor, a distinction of reproduction and production, and, inasmuch as they critiqued double standards in bourgeois sexual morality, they still held out heterosexual "sex-love" as the sign of the revolutionary accomplishment of positive proletarian culture. What does this mean for philosophy in general and the development of queer philosophy specifically?

Hegel suggested that philosophy is the history of philosophy. The project he undertook understood itself as the beneficiary of all the knowledge developed before it, all the ideas found in the long recorded history of ideas. Hegel, as is well-known, understood his position as the culmination of a long development that allowed him to recognize objectively the telos of history. While we might easily take exception with Hegel's understanding that the spirit of freedom had found its historical home somewhere outside his window in early nineteenth-century Prussia, nevertheless I would still suggest that the project of an all-inclusive history of philosophy affords us not only a sense of significant knowledge but a hope for real wisdom and even possible insight into how to inhabit the world fully. However, the general project of Western philosophy to which Hegel contributed developed in a manner that made it impossible for philosophy to accomplish its own love of wisdom. It could not fully disclose the world it inhabited to itself because it could not acknowledge the full complexity of the history of philosophy. If, as Hegel suggested, philosophy is the history of philosophy, then the dominant narrative of modern Western philosophy has developed not in simple ignorance of the full range of lived human experiences but through active negation of the complexity of social, sexual, and affective relations. A queer critical engagement with the history of philosophy begins from this point, seeking to reveal that the project of modern Western philosophy is a history determined by a hetero-coital imperative.

We need not look too far to find alternatives to this history; we can easily remain within the Western Eurocentric narrative. Certainly classic Greek and Roman philosophy recognized sexual economies that went beyond reproductive sexual relations. In this regard, *a* history of philosophy can reveal that affective and physical relations had forms quite different from the bourgeois nuclear family of the modern period. Such knowledge was certainly available to the modern period. Yet the modern European philosopher proved discontent to allow the particular economies of gender and sexuality that had developed to stand as one of many possibilities in the world. Nor did a history of sexuality prove sufficient to offer philosophy an awareness of an inherent permutablity of lifeworld relations. Rather, the modern period, infused with a belief in progress and in its own position as vanguard in perfecting the history of the world, emerged not simply as a repudiation of other sexual economies but as a foreclosure of any possible positive effect of their knowledge. This is not to suggest that scholarship does not exist in the modern period that seeks to account for, describe, and represent the real heterogeneity of human physical and emotive relationships. To be sure, traces of actual alternatives to hetero-coital sexuality fill modern philosophy, literature, and the arts. Yet such alternatives were excluded from the dominant mode of philosophy. Indeed, *the* history of philosophy that dominated in the West relied on the reproductive monogamous couple to accomplish its domination.

Recall that from at least the seventheenth century onward, for a host of liberal philosophers like Kant grappling with morality, their discussion of rights did not lead to a general consideration of ownership and private property but to an estimation of a particular form of the household present in the merchant and middle class. In the course of three centuries of philosophical development, the bourgeois nuclear household, as a site of hetero-coital activity, came to define parameters of rationality, naturalness, morality, ethics, citizenship, civil society, sociability, revolutionary subjectivity, and so on. The desiring individual, aberrant from this particular form of heterosexual activity, came to define the irrational, abnormal, inhuman, immoral, unethical, unreasonable, corrupt, selfish, excessive, uncontrolled, wandering, antisocial, seditious, and so on. Deviations from this "ideal" occupied a queer position, and representations that even sought to address the queer as a site of positive potential could easily be positioned into threats against the good as such. From this point a queer critique of modern philosophy begins.

The hetero-coital imperative did not limit only the development of modern German philosophy. In this respect, Kant, Hegel, and Marx do not represent a separate path, a *Sonderweg,* in the modern period; rather, they participate in the objective tendencies of domination within modern philosophy as such. The emergence of queer theory at the end of the twentieth century marked for the first time a possibility within the history of Western philosophy for a break with the hetero-coital imperative. I offer that the break with the hetero-coital imperative, however, is only the starting point of the critical potential of queer theory.

To clarify what must happen to accomplish this transition, I want to reflect for a moment on certain basic terms being used here: theory, knowledge, philosophy, science. Theory certainly informs knowledge. There is no positivist fact bearing truth in itself. There is no theory-free observation, and a Weberian value-free theorizing only accomplishes a foregrounding of how theory makes knowledge possible. Although this position is one shared with many directions in philosophy, it serves as foundational to a queer critique. Theory's root in classical Greek, Θεωρία (*theoria*), meant to look at, view, contemplate. As such it was bound to observation and spectacle. For the Greeks, a theorem was a proposition to be proved to a spectator. Theory in this understanding is not abstract from material conditions; rather, it is part of sense-making in the world. A theory offers a system to account for a set of phenomena, a method for comprehending a cultural artifact, a schema for describing a mode of production.

What does it mean to bring queer and theory together as a designation? The etymology of queer is unclear. Although the etymologists quickly point out that the timeline remains unclear, the OED traces its roots back to the German *quer:* cross, oblique, squint. Queer in its earliest usage describes an experience or a form of apprehension in which something is recognized as strange, other, different, out of the ordinary. Queer does quickly take on a vulgar usage as in "dirty rotten queer" to describe people of nonnormativized gender and sexuality. Its initial contemporary use in queer theory marked a form of reclamation vis-à-vis this vulgar connotation: queer theory as focused study of those people's experiences outside the gender and sexual norm. This reclamation project and a new queer pride, however, continues to meet with opposition from many members of the lesbian and gay liberation movement, who do not find it possible to imbue such a negatively loaded word with a sufficient form of positivity in order to be a vehicle of pride.

What intrigues me to note, though, is that queer as oblique, squint, strange, other, does describe an aspect of theory and theorem that needs to be underscored. Theory differs from awareness of recognition in that it approaches an appearance in the world that does not (yet) make sense. Only that which is out of the ordinary, strange, oblique to understanding requires the regard and contemplation of theory. Only that which is not comprehended must be held up as theorem, to be "squinted" at. Theory proves necessary as the bridge between apprehension and comprehension. Queer proves descriptive of the *fundamental motivation for theory*, to make sense of that which stands outside the understanding.[14] It does not mean that what is queer is unreasonable or irrational but that it is a disruption to accepted rationales and in order to find its reason theory must arise to describe it. In this regard queer theory thus describes a dynamic inherent in and constitutive of the descriptive aspirations of all theorizing. All theorizing is queer theory. Queerness is the "unconscious" of theory.

At this point, however, we want to note that in the history of philosophy a form of theoretical apparatus has arisen, as we discussed above with Kant, that rather than comprehend the compelling quality of queer actually seeks to contain and restrict the impact of its potential by barring it from reason or rationality. Of course, the investigation of how we apprehend in space and time was fundamental to Kant's theoretical apparatus, yet we can also begin to recognize that the overall project, in the approach it took to desire and reason, also sought to establish limits on what we can comprehend. Kant's theorizing, as part of the trajectory of modern Western philosophy, proved unable to develop as queer philosophy.

Queer Philosophy Is Not Queer Science

Stepping back for a moment from queer theory, let us note that descriptive theories are the beginning of philosophy but we might want to distinguish them from philosophy as such. A descriptive theory begins then from observation of (queer) material relations but has arrived at only an initial level of abstraction. Descriptive theory cannot move into philosophy without passing through three transformations. It must first arrive at a level of abstraction that allows it to recognize how history and location determine and specify the observed conditions. Then, second, it must identify what objective tendencies in history transform historically or spatially specific conditions. Finally, it must comprehend what structures transcend one condition into another. This knowledge, deriving from abstracted principles, arrives at the level of science, *scientia*.

Philosophy, *philo Sophia,* Aristotle distinguished from Φρόνησις (*phronesis*), which is the form of philosophical wisdom that motivates just behavior and proper living. It derives from experience of the world. For the post-Aristotelian Stoics and Epicureans, however, the distinction gave way to a focus on philosophy not as a pursuit of divine knowledge but of practical wisdom. From this point onward, there is a circle that arises with theory, science, and philosophy that is fundamentally practical in orientation. I argue here that philosophy distinguishes itself from belief or opinion in that it moves from theoretical knowledge derived by direct acquaintance, through the abstraction of scientific knowledge, back into engagement with the material world. Really, though, wisdom follows theory in that it does not appear in the quotidian; it is only in confrontation with the strange that wisdom must arise and intervene. Only when we have a sense that something does not follow our expectations, is unusual, do we call upon wisdom. Queer philosophy then is that philosophical stance that does not foreclose the possibility of understanding the strange. It acknowledges the extraordinary and accepts the transformative aspect such acknowledgment initiates. Queer philosophy does not reject the strange desire as irrational but rather proves open to extrapolating across rationales in order to expand wisdom. Not all philosophical systems have proven equally able to comprehend the knowledge of the strange. Modern philosophy emerged by delimiting, excluding, setting boundaries between things, notions, people. Queer knowing arises in the transition across such limits. It is the task of queer philosophy to focus on the dynamic of queerness. It can begin this task by reassessing the knowledge of those people excluded as desiring individuals. Inasmuch as queer theory can develop into queer philosophy, a queer way of knowing, there lies a possibility of a radical break in philosophy whereby the history of philosophy is able in its universality to come into its own, finally. It is not within or against, but through and beyond the existing system of Western philosophy that queer philosophy directs its project.

Difference and Queerness

Queer philosophy begins from a recognition of difference as centrally constitutive to knowledge. In its emergence out of gay and lesbian studies, queer philosophy had of course to contend with the systematic exclusion of diverse forms of knowing from dominant philosophical paradigms. Queer philosophy overlaps, thus, to a certain extent with considerations of alterity. Yet, to come into its own queer philosophy cannot simply observe relations of difference; rather, it must also apprehend an effect of *queerness* as such that goes beyond difference. To explain what I mean, I want to focus our attention on alterity, which as a subdomain of philosophy has productively explored for instance how consciousness is constructed in relation to an other.

In this direction of study we understand that the "I" is not alone or, to adopt Rimbaud's more poetic language, "I" is an other. Emmanuel Levinas offered more recent sustained discussions of alterity.[15] But to understand the proposition of consciousness emerging through a relationship of alterity we can turn to Hegel as a foundational statement on the question. We cannot really overestimate the influence of this account of self-consciousness on philosophy, and beyond to psychology, political philosophy, literary studies, cultural studies, and numerous other discourses. It thus merits some attention as it poses, I would suggest, a central notion that queer philosophy must itself supersede.

In *The Phenomenology of Spirit* (1807), Hegel followed a dialectic procedure that allows for an understanding of subjectivity as (antagonistic) pairs forming a unity. Hegel distinguished consciousness from self-consciousness. Consciousness in itself has no phenomenal objects. Consciousness has only certainty, full knowing of the notion. The notion (*Begriff*) of the object vanishes in the conscious experience of it. In certainty consciousness as such is homogeneous, all-encompassing. The truth of the other does not exist—yet. I say yet because self-consciousness does require an other. To be self-aware, Hegel explains, requires a sense of limit established by conflict with an other consciousness. The recognition of an equally independent and self-contained consciousness allows the self to be aware of its actions *for itself.*

We could say that the Hegelian ego is bipartite, like the Kantian, but with Hegel self-consciousness or subjectivity is a relationship with the other and not with a metaphysical condition of reason. When Hegel speaks of self-consciousness as a dialectic, the "I" is bound up with a "Not-I" as the precondition for self-consciousness. The "Not-I" exists as object, as other for the "I" inasmuch as it gives the "I" form. It does not have independence as such, it does not exist for itself; rather, it exists at first as simple determination on self-consciousness. The other develops out of a condition of abstract object for the self only in the unfolding of "Life" (§ 173). We might suggest at this point that alterity tames the effect of the other, presenting it for inspection as constitutive essence. Indeed, in most discussions subsequent to Hegel the character of the other does not draw much attention. For instance, Lacan's other is bound up with the law of the father but does not need to be identified with any particular man or type of father. Generally, the other exists insomuch as it exists for the subject of self-consciousness.

Certainly, we do know from Hegel that self-consciousness enters into a dialectical relationship with the other. The self, having lost the experience of totality that accrued to simple consciousness, enters into conflict with the other. This condition of conflict establishes an "unhappy, inwardly disrupted consciousness" that takes the other as an enemy who must be vanquished (§ 207). To vanquish the other, however, means a loss of self and a reversion to consciousness. The unhappy consciousness thus discovers that it must learn to find the lost universality of consciousness by some other means.

Much attention has been paid to how Hegel offers one solution to this crisis of self-consciousness in labor. Even Judith Butler discussed the unhappy consciousness both in her first book *Subjects of Desire* (1987) and in the more recent *The Psychic Life of Power* (1997), focusing in both studies on the resolution offered by exteriorization in labor. For Hegel, the individual subject turns his desire for universality into a control over a thing, an object of his own production. This marks the emergence of a bourgeois citizen-producer who experiences universality in a marketplace. However, this displacement onto labor and production ultimately remains unhappy because it cannot offer full universality.

I would like to interject two observations about this concentration on unhappy consciousness and labor. First, we can not overestimate how the subject harbors a propensity for violence vis-à-vis the other. This violence is not abstract. For anyone who has ever been attacked because they occupied the position of other to someone's unhappy self-consciousness, the general disregard for the experience of the other indicates that there is a significant lack of knowledge in this approach. The other is not necessarily a docile object in relation to the aggression of the self. However, the power differentials that exist in self-other relations can make the other a constant object of assault and violence. I will return to this point below. Second, and interestingly, what remains overlooked in Hegel's account of

self-consciousness is that he does offer a resolution to the conflict and it is
one that derives from heterosexuality.

Hegel offers love as the resolution to the conflict with the other. In *The
Philosophy of Right* (1821) Hegel wrote: "Love means in general the consciousness of my unity with another, so that I am not isolated on my own
[*für mich*], but gain my self-consciousness only through the renunciation of
my independent existence [*meines Fürsichseins*] and through knowing myself as the unity of myself with another and of the other with me" (§ 158).
Elsewhere in *The Phenomenology* he phrased it thus: "It is the *pure heart*
which *for us* or *in itself* has found itself and is inwardly satiated, for although
for itself in its feeling the essential Being is separated from it, yet this feeling is, in itself, a feeling of *self* " (§ 218). In other words, even though the
subject struggles to establish self-consciousness, love allows it to experience
the universality and unity of being that belonged to the undifferentiated
state of simple consciousness. This love, however, is of course not any love
and not just the love of man and woman but of husband and wife as pro-
genitors of the family.

Like Kant, Hegel denied a solely procreative function to marriage. The
purpose of marriage is primarily to check the natural drives of husband
and wife, *not* to have children. Marriage creates a unity, according to
Hegel, that transcends individual drives and needs for the sake of an all-
encompassing totality. However, Hegel expressed only disdain for Kant's
definition of marriage as a contract for the mutual use of each other's sex
organs.[16] Where Kant began with marriage—not the family—as one form
of contractual law, Hegel began with the entire family as love bond sub-
lated into ethical mores (*Sittlichkeit*). Marriage, "the *union* of the natural
sexes," went beyond this "union" to bring together private property and the
socialization of children into the basis of the ethical realm.

At the heart of Hegel's ethics of the family is a highly elaborated es-
sentialization of gender distinctions, marking two types or characters that
primarily inhabit distinct public and private spheres. Complementary characteristics make logical Hegel's apportionment of the social sphere into two
interrelated spheres: the house as the feminine sphere of activity and the
world outside the house as the masculine. "Man therefore has his actual
substantial life in the state, in learning [*Wissenschaft*], etc., and otherwise in
work and struggle with the external world and himself. . . . Woman, however, has her substantial vocation [*Bestimmung*] in the family, and her ethical disposition consists in this [family] *piety*" (§ 166). In such oppositions
we recognize an intensification and rupture of Kant's characterization of
women and men within the household.

Gender distinctions defined oppositions that were *not* dialectical but natural and essential. Even though they represent positive and negative determinations on individual existence, Hegel did not understand them as contradictions that would drive the dialectic. In the heteronormative husband/wife relationship, Hegel charted out a system whereby the posited natural, essential characteristics of masculinity and femininity complemented each other to give rise to a harmonious social order. Thus we have in this harmony a vision of a perfected dialectic. The heterosexuality of the family suffused the entire social order with ethical form. Defined as essential, the gendered difference gave rise to heterosexuality as one of the first signposts of the ends of history.[17]

It is thus crucial to recognize that *heterosexuality is not simply a preferred form of sexuality*, one among many. Instead, it provided the prototype for the kind of social homogeneity that was at the heart of Hegel's positive social totality. Heterosexuality here is not simply a compulsory form of sexuality. Rather, it ascends to the ethical norm that pervades the entire nation-state. It is the knot that binds the totality together. Without heteronormativity, the Hegelian social structure, a social structure that infuses the philosophy of modernity, falls apart into contingencies, particularities, and accidentalities of desire. This state of diffusion worries the Hegelian system.

Out of this lengthy discussion, I want to highlight three aspects. First, paradigms of alterity tame difference not simply by contending primarily with the subject, but also, as is clear in the Hegelian system, by containing difference to stabilized essences. Gender as natural essential difference provides an inescapable form of determination. Heterosexuality as natural essential final sublation of difference positions *all* other forms of desire as unnatural inessential. A queer critique of the Hegelian system that begins by questioning gender as essence or by rejecting the naturalness of heterosexuality cannot end with a simple attempt at inclusion as different differences. Nonnatural, nonessential difference does not resolve the propensity for violence inherent in self-consciousness.

Second, the critique of the hetero-coital imperative as structuring the logic of the Hegelian system alludes to a queer propensity that exceeds difference. Recall that Derrida similarly underscored in the neologism *différance* the instability of differing and deferring in every system. Queerness, however, is not just the instability of every system, but rather the destabilizing compelled by the systematic exclusion of knowledge. While a system such as the Hegelian can contain difference, queerness compels systematic transformation. Deconstruction recognized the instability of all systems. Queerness works by rupture, revealing partiality of reason and exclusion as a price of systematicity. However, deconstruction affords primarily negative critical knowledge. It is nihilistic in the Nietzschean sense. Queerness propels movement beyond systems but not necessarily because it is itself systematic, nor can one assume that the transformation propelled by it is in any sense systematic. Queer philosophy opens up possibilities of positive knowledge. It is, in the Nietzschean sense, joyful.

Third, queer philosophy, inasmuch as it recognizes both the insufficiency of difference and the destabilizing effect of the queer, can develop by offering new approaches to the presumed violence of self-consciousness. To that end I would like to offer a few brief comments that give direction to a consideration of queer subjectivity and sociablity. If we return to Hegel we can recognize that even in identifying heterosexual difference as resolution of the dialectic, Hegelian self-consciousness does not become a mystical unity of self and other. The family represents for Hegel a limited field of harmony that restores to the self-conscious subject some sense of the universality experienced by simple consciousness. The family, however, precisely in its most "natural" form, is a filiative determination on the child. Without a subsequent rational affiliation akin to the commitment that initially convened the family unit, the child can only experience the modern nuclear family as a totalizing force on its will, not as a field of universality. Without rational affiliation, the Hegelian nuclear family based in "love" threatens to be the antithesis of Hegel's description.

The self-conscious subject appears, however, able to carry out an act of rational affiliation. Recall that even for Hegel, the "Not-I" gives the "I" an understanding of the whole of differentiated being; consciousness arrives at self-consciousness through an awareness of its own thinking as differentiated and finite. The self-awareness of finitude affords also an awareness of the plenitude of the other. We do not even need to know consciously the other to be aware that the other holds open new possibilities of knowing for the self. Really, Hegelian self-awareness is a very curious development when examined closely. We do not even need to know the other for the other to effect a change in consciousness. The inter-subjective experience of the other drives an inner-subjective state in the self. Hegel writes, "Now, it is true that for this self-consciousness the essence is neither an other than itself, nor the pure abstraction of the 'I,' but an 'I' which has the otherness within itself, though in the form of *thought*, so that in its otherness it has directly returned into itself" (*Phenomenology*, § 200). We cannot consciously know an other given the autonomous independence that a priori defines the other, but we can be self-consciously aware of knowledge offered to us by the other.

Queer philosophy need not begin from the presumption that self-consciousness begins as violent. Rather, given the inner-subjective state, we can understand that the subject arrives at self-awareness predisposed to inter-subjective sociability. We rationally can aspire to avail ourselves of the knowledge of the other. In this regard when in *The Phenomenology* Hegel suggests that "self-consciousness is Desire" (§ 174), it is not violent desire. Hegel, compelled by a hetero-coital imperative, can only imagine positive desire between the sexes. For the public realm of civil society and state he can only image a masculine homosocial order of violence barely contained by ethics inculcated through filiative "love." The desire of self-consciousness, freed from distinction as heterosexual desire and filiative love, holds open new vistas for queer philosophical investigation. Self-consciousness as desire for the other seeks its full plenitude in the experiences afforded by others. We can recognize self-differentiation as unleashing a desire that *draws* us to the other. We do not exist as isolated monads; rather, we willingly, freely, desire sociability—that is, to inhabit lifeworlds with others.[18] Ultimately, queer philosophy has the potential to envision a sociable plenitude that radically exceeds the selfish liberation in labor or the limited liberation in the family/nation that Hegel proposes as resolution to the unhappy consciousness.

Gay Science, Queer Knowing

To apprehend the effect of queerness is not simply to observe relations of difference. Nor is it a matter, as in explorations of alterity, to describe the constitutive effect of the other, that is, without object there is no subject, without an other, consciousness cannot become aware of a self, and so forth. Queer philosophy has certain affinities with deconstruction, but queer differs from *différance*. In spite of its critique of logocentrism, deconstruction can find no knowledge outside Western metaphysics. Rather than suggest, as deconstruction does, that to identify something as marginal or outside Western philosophy means that it is actually constitutive of or defining to Western philosophy, queer philosophy begins from the position that the comprehension of excluded or marginal rationales fundamentally transforms the possibilities of (Western) philosophy. Queer philosophy is transformative, not deconstructive.

I have sought here to attend to some of the terms of the critique by which queer philosophy is currently emerging: hetero-coital imperative, heteronormativity, homogenizing, totalizing, universalizing. This list develops inasmuch as queer theory proceeds with the queer critique of its own foundations. As queer theory moves toward a metacritical position, it opens up new discursive possibilities. Queer theory begins to approximate what we might describe as queer philosophy or queer ways of knowing. In this regard it follows the positive route of philosophical engagement charted out by Nietzsche in *The Gay Science*. Nietzsche strove in this text to accomplish a "joyful wisdom," a "gay science" that could overcome nihilistic pessimism. His recognition of antiessentialism as a means of revaluation prefigures the project of queer theory and suggests a method by which descriptive theory is able to bridge abstraction and material engagement.

Only as creators!—This has given me the greatest trouble and still does: to realize that what things *are called* is incomparably more important than what they are. The reputation, name, and appearance, the usual measure and weight of a thing, what it counts for—originally almost always wrong and arbitrary, thrown over things like a dress and altogether foreign to their nature and even to their skin—all this grows from generation unto generation, merely because people believe in it, until it gradually grows to be part of the thing and turns into its very body. What at first was appearance becomes in the end, almost invariably, the essence and is effective as such. How foolish it would be to suppose that one only needs to point out this origin and this misty shroud of delusion in order to *destroy* the world that counts for real, so-called *reality*. We can destroy only as creators. But let us not forget this either: It is enough to create new names and estimations and probabilities in order to create in the long run new "thing.s"[19]

What Nietzsche describes is a form of material engagement, but not the kind that derives from a Marxian materialism. Nietzsche as anti-idealist arrives at materialism by a different route, the full practical implications of which still remain unexplored. Emergent queer philosophy, I would suggest, takes up this direction. It may therefore not prove immediately appropriable for quotidian politics in a manner that some movement activists would like, but that does not mean that it is not practical. Certainly it is not practical. Certainly it is oriented toward engagement with the material world. Queer theory interprets the world, queer philosophy teaches one how to inhabit it *fully*.

Notes

1. This essay thus extends the work begun in Randall Halle, *Queer Social Philosophy: Critical Readings from Kant to Adorno* (Champaign: University of Illinois Press, 2004).

2. See for example Zoachary Quill, *Homosexuality through the Ages* (Los Angeles: Wiz Books, 1969); Kay Tobin and Randy Wicker, *The Gay Crusaders* (New York: Arno Press, 1975); Vern L. Bullough, *Homosexuality, a History* (New York:

New American Library, 1979); John Boswell, *Christianity, Social Tolerance, and Homosexuality: Gay People in Western Europe from the Beginning of the Christian Era to the Fourteenth Century* (Chicago: University of Chicago Press: 1980); Jonathan Katz, *Gay/Lesbian Almanac: A New Documentary in Which Is Contained, in Chronological Order, Evidence of the True and Fantastical History of Those Persons Now Called Lesbians and Gay Men* (New York: Harper & Row, 1983); Jim Kepner, *Becoming a People: A 4,000-Year Gay and Lesbian Chronology* (Hollywood, CA: National Gay Archives, 1983).

3. Mary Macintosch, "The Homosexual Role," in *The Making of the Modern Homosexual*, ed. Kenneth Plummer (London: Hutchinson, 1981); Michel Foucault, *The History of Sexuality*, 3 vols. (New York: Pantheon, 1978–1986); Jeffrey Weeks, *Sex, Politics, and Society: The Regulation of Sexuality since 1800* (New York: Longman, 1981).

4. See, for instance, Brett Beemyn and Mickey Eliason, eds. *Queer Studies: A Lesbian, Gay, Bisexual, and Transgender Anthology* (New York: New York University Press, 1996).

5. One of the first published uses of the term "queer theory" can be traced to "Queer Theory: Lesbian and Gay Sexualities," *Differences: A Journal of Feminist Cultural Studies* 3 (1991), a special issue edited by Teresa de Lauritis.

6. This discussion of "queer" derives from the lengthier analysis undertaken in my book *Queer Social Philosophy: Critical Readings from Kant to Adorno* (Champaign: University of Illinois Press, 2004).

7. For examples of the dilemmas of the period, see discussions in Judith Butler, interview with Peter Osborne and Lynne Segal, "Gender as Performance," *Radical Philosophy* 67 (1994): 32–39; Judith Halberstam, *Female Masculinity* (Durham: Duke University Press, 1998); Lynda Hart, *Between the Body and the Flesh: Performing Sadomasochism* (New York: Columbia University Press, 1998); Sally O"Driscoll, "Outlaw Readings: Beyond Queer Theory," *Signs: Journal of Women in Culture and Society* 22 (1997): 30–55.

8. There are numerous examples. See for example the classic discussion in Edward Stein, ed., *Forms of Desire: Sexual Orientation and the Social Constructionist Controversy* (New York: Routledge, 1992).

9. For a sustained critical discussion of this position see G. Felicitas Munzel, *Kant's Conception of Moral Character: The "Critical" Link of Morality, Anthropology, and Reflective Judgement* (Chicago: University of Chicago Press, 1999).

10. "die Frau soll herrschen und der Mann regieren; denn die Neigung herrscht, und der Verstand regiert."

11. See the chapter in his *Anthropology* on "The Character of Gender."

12. See for instance Susan Mendus, "Kant: An Honest but Narrow-Minded Bourgeois?" in *Women in Western Political Philosophy: Kant to Nietzsche*, ed. Ellen Kennedy and Susan Mendus (New York: St. Martin"s Press, 1987).

13. Queer theory, like similar strands in feminist theory, critical race studies, or Marxian class analysis, often must suffer an indictment that it is distant from real-world

experiences and politics. Such indictments generally do not dismiss the insights offered by these critical directions; rather, they demand a clarity and simplicity of language. While I am sympathetic to a request for jargon-free writing, I would object to the general impetus behind such indictments. We live in a complex and changing world and it proves oddly reductive to expect our theoretical engagments with this world to be less complex and dynamic.

14. Jacques Lacan; Slavoj Zizek.

15. See for instance Emmanuel Levinas, *Alterity and Transcendence* (New York: Columbia University Press, 1999).

16. See § 75 of *The Philosophy of Right*.

17. There have been extensive discussions of essentialism and particularly the significance of Hegel for the proposition of essentialism. For a brief and insightful discussion of Hegel and gender see Seyla Benhabib, "On Hegel, Women and Irony," in *Feminist Interpretations and Political Theory*, Ed. Carole Pateman and Mary Lyndon Shanley (University Park: Pennsylvania State University Press, 1991).

18. Kant's subject got it wrong, it is not rationality and the willingness to limit coercion that establishes sociability. For insightful reflections on the relationship of desire to intersubjective communication and communicability see Slavoj Zizek's reflections on Schelling in "The Abyss of Freedom," in *The Abyss of Freedom/Ages of the World: An Essay by Slavoj Zizek with the Text of Schelling's "Die Weltalter" (Second Draft, 1813) in English Translation by Judith Norman* (Ann Arbor: University of Michigan Press, 1997).

19. Friedrich Nietzsche, *The Gay Science* (New York: Vintage, 1974).

Bibliography

Abelove, Henry, Michele Aina Barale, and David Halperin, eds. *The Lesbian and Gay Studies Reader.* New York: Routledge: 1993.

Altman, Dennis. "Global Queering." *Australian Humanities Review* 2 (1996). http://www.lib.latrobe.edu.au/AHR/archive/Issue-July-1996/altman.html.

———. *Global Sex.* Chicago: University of Chicago Press, 2001.

Bataille, Georges. *Visions of Excess: Selected Writings 1927–1939.* Minneapolis: University of Minnesota Press, 1985.

Baxandall, Rosalyn. "Marxism and Sexuality: The Body as Battleground." In *Marxism in the Postmodern Age: Confronting the New World Order,* ed. Antonio Callari, Stephen Cullenberg, and Carole Biewener. New York: Guilford Press, 1995.

Beemyn, Brett, and Mickey Elianon, eds. *Queer Studies: A Lesbian, Gay, Bisexual, and Transgender Anthology.* New York: New York University Press, 1996.

Berger, Maruice, Brian Wallis, and Simon Watson eds. *Constructing Masculinity.* New York: Routledge, 1995.

Berlant, Lauren. The Queen of America Goes to Washington City: Essays on Sex and Citizenship. Durham: Duke University Press, 1997.

Bersani, Leo. *Homos.* Cambridge: Harvard University Press, 1995.

Blasius, Mark, and Shane Phelan, eds. We Are Everywhere: A Historical Source-book of Gay and Lesbian Politics. New York: Routledge, 1997.

Boswell, John. Christianity, Social Tolerance, and Homosexuality. Chicago: University of Chicago Press, 1980.

Breines, Paul. "Revisiting Marcuse with Foucault: An Essay on Liberation Meets the History of Sexuality." In Marcuse: From the New Left to the Next Left, ed. John Bokina and Timothy J. Lukes. Lawrence: University Press of Kansas, 1994.

Brown, Wendy. States of Injury: Power and Freedom in Late Modernity. Princeton: Princeton University Press, 1995.

Butler, Judith. Antigone's Claim: Kinship between Life and Death. New York: Columbia University Press, 2000.

———. Bodies that Matter: On the Discursive Limits of "Sex." New York: Routledge, 1993.

———. Excitable Speech: A Politics of the Performative. New York: Routledge, 1997.

———. Gender Trouble: Feminism and the Subversion of Identity. New York: Routledge, 1990.

———. "Imitation and Gender Insubordination." In The Lesbian and Gay Studies Reader, ed. Henry Abelove, Michèle Aina Barale, and David M. Halperin, 307–21. New York: Routledge, 1993.

———. The Psychic Life of Power: Theories in Subjection. Stanford: Stanford University Press, 1997.

———. Subjects of Desire: Hegelian Reflections in Twentieth-Century France. New York: Columbia University Press, 1987.

Butler, Judith, Ernesto Laclau, and Slavoj Zizek. Contingency, Hegemony, Universality: Contemporary Dialogues on the Left. London: Verso, 2000.

Butler, Judith, and Joan Wallach, eds. Feminists Theorize the Political. New York: Routledge, 1992.

Cadava, Eduardo, Peter Connor, and Jean-Luc Nancy, eds. Who Comes after the Subject? New York: Routledge, 1991.

Califia, Pat. Sex Changes: The Politics of Transgenderism. San Francisco: Cleis Press, 1997.

Champagne, Rosaria. "Queering the Unconscious." South Atlantic Quarterly 97 (1998): 281–97.

Cheah, Pheng. "Mattering." Review of Bodies that Matter, by Judith Butler, and Volatile Bodies, by Elizabeth Grosz. Diacritics 26 (1996): 108–39.

Clark, Eric O. Virtuous Vice: Homoeroticism in the Public Sphere. Durham: Duke University Press, 2000.

Comstock, Gary David, and Susan E. Henking eds. Que(e)rying Religion: A Critical Anthology. New York: Continuum, 1997.

Copjec, Joan, ed. Supposing the Subject. London: Verso, 1995.

Crimp, Douglas, and Adam Rolston, AIDS Demo Graphics. Seattle: Bay Press, 1990.

David-Menard, Monique, ed. *Feminist Interpretations of Immanuel Kant*. University Park: Pennsylvania State University Press, 1997.

de Lauretis, Teresa. "Queer Theory: Lesbian and Gay Sexualities." *differences: a Journal of Feminist Cultural Studies*. 3, no. 2 (1991): iii–xviii

Deleuze, Gilles, and Félix Guattari. *Anti-Oedipus: Capitalism and Schizophrenia*. Minnesota: University of Minnesota Press, 1983.

———. *A Thousand Plateaus: Capitalism and Schizophrenia*. Minnesota: University of Minnesota Press, 1987.

D'Emilio, John, and Estelle Freedman. *Intimate Matters: A History of Sexuality in America*. New York: Harper & Row, 1988.

———. The World Turned: Essays on Gay History, Politics, and Culture. Durham: Duke University Press, 2002.

Diacritics

differences: a Journal of Feminist Cultural Studies.

DiPiero, Thomas. *White Men Aren't*. Durham: Duke University Press, 2002.

Dollmore, Jonathan. Sexual Dissidence: Ausgutine to Wilde, Freud to Foucault. Oxford: Clarendon, 1991.

Duberman, Martin, ed. *A Queer World: The Center for Lesbian and Gay Studies Reader*. New York: New York University Press, 1997.

Duberman, Martin B., Martha Vincus, and George Chauncey, eds. *Hidden from History*, New York: NAL, 1989.

Duggan, Lisa. "Theory in Practice: The Theory Wars, or, Who's Afraid of Judith Butler?" *Journal of Women's History* 10, no. 1 (1998): 9–19.

Dynes, Wayne, ed. *Encyclopedia of Homosexuality*, 2 vols. Garden City, NY: Garland, 1989.

Dynes, Wayne, and Stephen Donaldson, eds. *History of Homosexuality in Europe and America*. New York: Garland, 1992.

Edelman, Lee. *Homographesis*. New York: Routledge University Press, 1994.

———. "Queer Theory: Unstating Desire." *GLQ: A Journal of Lesbian and Gay Studies* 2, no. 4 (1995): 343–46.

———. "Tearooms and Sympathy, or, The Epistemology of the Water Closet." In *Nationalisms and Sexualities*, eds. Andrew Parker et al., 263–85. New York: Routledge, 1992.

Evans, David T. Sexual Citizenship: The Material Construction of Sexualities. New York: Routledge, 1993.

Faderman, Lilian. Odd Girls and Twilight Lovers: A History of Lesbian Life in Twentieth-Century America. New York: Columbia University Press, 1990.

Faderman, Lilian, and Brigette Erikson. *Lesbian-Feminism in Turn-of-the-Century Germany*. Weatherby Lake, MO Naiad Press, 1980.

Fausto-Sterling, Anne. Myths of Gender: Biological Theories about Women and Men. New York: Basic Books, 1992.

Foucault, Michel. *Ethics: Subjectivity and Truth*. New York: New Press, 1994.

———. *The Foucault Effect: Studies in Governmentality*. Chicago: University of Chicago Press, 1991.

———. *The History of Sexuality.* 3 vols. New York: Vintage Books, 1980.

———. Remarks on Marx: Conversations with Duccio Trombadori. New York: Semiotext(e), 1991.

———. "What is Enlightenment." In *The Foucault Reader,* ed. Paul Rabinow. New York: Pantheon, 1984.

Fout, John C. *A Select Bibliography on the History of Sexuality.* Annandale-on-Hudson, NY: Committee on Lesbian and Gay History, Bard College, 1989.

Fout, John C., ed. Forbidden History: The State, Society, and the Regulation of Sexuality in Modern Europe. Chicago: University of Chicago Press, 1992.

Garber, Marjorie. Vested Interests: Cross-Dressing and Cultural Anxiety. London: Routledge, 1992.

Gerard, Kent, and Gert Hekma, eds. The Pursuit of Sodomy: Male Homosexuality in Renaissance and Enlightenment Europe. New York: Harrington Park Press, 1989.

GLQ

Gluckman, Amy, and Betsy Reed, eds. *Homo Economics: Capitalism, Community and Lesbian and Gay Life.* New York: Routledge, 1997.

Goldberg, Jonathan, ed. *Queering the Renaissance.* Durham: Duke University Press, 1994.

Greenberg, David F. *The Construction of Homosexuality.* Chicago: Chicago University Press, 1988.

Grosz, Elizabeth. Space, Time, and Perversion. Essays on the Politics of Bodies. New York: Routledge, 1995.

———. *Volatile Bodies. Toward a Corporeal Feminism.* Bloomington: Indiana University Press, 1994.

Halle, Randall. *Queer Social Philosophy: Critical Readings from Kant to Adorno.* Champaign: University of Illinois Press, 2004.

Haraway, Donna. Simians, Cyborgs, and Women: The Reinvention of Nature. New York: Routledge, 1991.

Hekma, Gert, Harry Oosterhuis, and James Steakley, eds. *Gay Men and the Sexual History of the Political Left.* Binghamton, NY: Haworth Press, 1995.

Hennessy, Rosemary. "Incorporating Queer Theory on the Left." In *Marxism in the Postmodern Age: Confronting the New World Order,* ed. Antonio Callari, Stephen Cullenberg, and Carole Biewener. New York: Guilford Press, 1995.

Herdt, Gilbert, ed. Third Sex, Third Gender: Beyond Sexual Dimorphism in Culture and History. New York: Zone Books, 1994.

Herzer, Manfred. Bibliographie zur Homosexualitat: Verzeichnis des deutschsprachigen nichtbelletristischen Schrifttums zur weiblichen und mannlichen Homosexualitat: aus den Jahren 1466 bis 1975. Berlin: Winkel, 1982.

Hull, Isabel V. Sexuality, State, and Civil Society in Germany, 1700-1815. Ithaca: Cornell UP, 1996.

Jagose, Annamarie. *Queer Theory: An Introduction.* New York: New York University Press, 1997.

Journal of the History of Sexuality

Journal of Homosexuality

Katz, Jonathan Ned. *The Invention of Heterosexuality*. New York: Dutton, 1995.

Kennedy, Ellen, and Susan Mendus, eds. *Women in Western Political Philosophy: Kant to Nietzsche*. New York: St. Martin's Press, 1987.

Kuzniar, Alice A., ed. *Outing Goethe and His Age*. Stanford: Stanford University Press, 1996.

Lancaster, Roger, and Micaela di Leonardo, eds. *The Gender/Sexuality Reader: Culture, History, Political Economy*. New York: Routledge: 1997.

Phelan, Shane. "The Shape of Queer: Assimilation and Articulation." *Women and Politics* 18, no. 2 (1997): 55–73.

Martin, Carolyn Biddy. Femininity Played Straight: The Significance of Being Lesbian. New York: Routledge, 1996.

Meer, Theo van der, and Anja van Kooten Niekerk, eds. *Homosexuality. Which Homosexuality? International Scientific Conference on Gay and Lesbian Studies*. Amsterdam/London: An Dekker/Gay Men's Press, 1989.

Pateman, Carole, and Mary Lyndon Shanley eds. *Feminist Interpretations and Political Theory*. University Park: Pennsylvania State University Press, 1991.

Plummer, Kenneth, ed. *The Making of the Modern Homosexual*. London: Hutchinson, 1981.

Raffo, Susan, ed. *Queerly Classed*. Boston: South End Press, 1997.

Sedgwick, Eve Kosofsky. *Between Men: English Literature and Male Homosocial Desire*. New York: Columbia University Press, 1985.

———. *Epistemology of the Closet*. Berkeley: University of California Press, 1990.

———. *Performativity and Performance*. New York: Routledge, 1995.

———. *Tendencies*. New York: Routledge, 1994.

Signs

Silverman, Hugh. *Philosophy and Desire*. New York: Routledge, 2000.

Silverman, Kaja. *Male Subjectivity at the Margins*. New York: Routledge, 1992.

Snitow, Ann, Christin Stansell, and Sharon Thompson, eds. *Powers of Desire: The Politics of Sexuality*. New York: New Feminist Library, 1983.

Steakley, James. The Homosexual Emancipation Movement in Germany. New York: Arno, 1975.

Stein, Edward, ed. Forms of Desire: Sexual Orientation and the Social Constructionist Controversy. New York: Routledge, 1992.

Tobin, Robert. *Warm Brothers: Queer Theory and the Age of Goethe*. Philadelphia: University of Pennsylvania Press, 2000.

Warner, Michael, ed. *Fear of a Queer Planet: Queer Politics and Social Theory*. Minneapolis: University of Minnesota Press, 1993.

Weeks, Jeffrey. Coming Out: Homosexual Politics in Britain from the Nineteenth Century to the Present. Rev. ed. New York: Quartet, 1990.

Weeks, Jeffrey. *Sex, Politics, and Society*. London: Longman, 1981.

What Is Africana Philosophy?   4

LUCIUS T. OUTLAW JR.
Vanderbilt University

ODAY THE TERM "Africana philosophy" ("Africana": persons, peoples, and things African and of African descent; by and/or about the same) is increasingly, though still gradually, being used by academic philosophers and other knowledge-workers to identify, characterize, and to legitimate, as academically appropriate instances of philosophical effort, a wide range of endeavors of speaking and writing by persons African and principally of African descent, on the African continent and throughout what is now routinely referred to as the "African diaspora" (constituted by various sites of settlement throughout the world of persons and peoples African and of African descent). The term is used, as well, to establish that the focal concerns of the thoughtful black folks referred to are of philosophical significance and worthy, therefore, of the respectful attention of all who would take philosophizing, professionally and otherwise, and black folks seriously.

These determined efforts, underway for several decades now (though not always under the heading of "Africana philosophy"), particularly when conducted self-consciously and with deliberate collaboration, are resulting in the development of new formations and communities of discourse within and across established disciplines (philosophy and religious studies departments; programs, curricula, and organizations in philosophy and other disciplines) and relatively new interdisciplinary academic enterprises (Black, African American, Africana, diaspora, and ethnic studies programs, departments, centers, and institutes). The pioneers and audiences most invested initially in these developments and their shaping agendas have been folks of African descent primarily, though other folks "of color" and some white folks have been steady supporters.[1] More recently, in the United States of America in particular, an increasing number of white graduate students and junior scholars have been giving close attention to Africana philosophy while joining and adding to discourses with their own significant offerings of questions, analyses, and others contributions in addition to their presence.[2]

In the early course of these developments (during the 1970s in the United States), the predominant professional organizations of philosophers; the academic discipline of philosophy in terms of the institutionalized canonical genealogies of historic figures, issues, and texts; the demography and sociocultural subworlds of the professoriate and of graduate studies—all became the focus of severe critiques by many of the pioneers, and later by many of the more recent contributing discussants, of new discourses about and constituting Africana philosophy. In fact, such critiques have been a major feature of the development of Africana philosophy and were required in order to make space in the discipline and the profession for the intellectual and sociological presence of black folks, for their concerns and intellectual praxes. The requirement was generated by the compelling need to argue strenuously, against a great deal of inertial as well as active resistance, that the absence of persons African and of African descent in the discipline's canons was not evidence of their (racially) inherent lack of capabilities for philosophizing at fairly and properly determined levels of accomplishment comparable to those of the canonic figures all identified as "white."

These early efforts thus took on the related tasks of vindicating black folks against racist constrictions of their humanity, constrictions of the history of their accomplishments as well as of their potentialities and future possibilities, by white racial supremacist denials of their abilities to reason "philosophically" as best modeled, supposedly, by white philosophers. Much effort was expended arguing *against* the racially constrained (and gendered) intellectual and social organization of the discipline of philosophy, and arguing *for* respectful recognition and inclusion of black thinkers and their articulations in the discipline's canons. Such inclusions, however, would require revisions, in some cases rather radical, of how practitioners of professionalized academic philosophy were trained to conceive of the discipline in terms of its subject matters, methods, criteria of veracity, curricula, and origins and histories, and, ultimately, the origins and histories of white peoples and their accomplishments. In turn, it was hoped, these revisions would (or ought to) prompt subsequent revisions to the professional, personal, and social identifications of white folks in the discipline and beyond to the extent that these identifications have rested on or harbored operative, influential, habituated, and thus taken-for-granted "passions, sentiments, and habits" conditioning professional and social convictions and praxes that involve substantial investments in *whiteness*.[3]

Revisions to identifications were already underway for many of the black folks involved in developing Africana philosophy and setting rationales for various agendas. Initial motivations, for many, had come from outside academic philosophy: in developments in the civil rights, Black power-Black consciousness, Black nationalist, and Pan-Africanist movements in the United States of America; in anticolonial, national independence, and Pan-African movements throughout the continent of Africa, the Caribbean, and South America. Within the United States, the "politics of identity and recognition" these movements spawned had significant impacts on several cohorts of persons of African descent pursuing undergraduate and graduate studies at the time, in academic philosophy especially.[4]

One important consequence was the desire, the need felt, to both draw on and contribute to the intellectual resources through which these movements were articulated, their agendas set, strategies and tactics determined and acted on, and various black publics mobilized through persuasive rhetoric ("consciousness raising," "educating the masses") to engage in and carry on the Struggle. For a number of the persons engaged in formal studies of academic philosophy, there was the initial belief that the discipline was a substantial repository of many of the intellectual resources needed to accomplish this transformative work. But, the movements' challenges to self-understandings that were raised by characterizations of a "black" self to be identified with, in contradistinction to a troubled "negro" self long crippled by white racial supremacy, especially through programs fostering the mis-education of black folks, compelled many to undertake strenuous self-critiques and critiques of regimes of white racial supremacy at work in schooling at all levels. The aim and spirit of many of the critique efforts were in service to radical, even revolutionary, reconstructions motivated by passionate commitments to convictions and aspirations grounded in and fueled by notions of *blackness*: ideas and ideals of passions, sentiments, and habits; of culture creation and political work; of the organization of social and economic life in keeping with norms, values, and agendas for life fashioned by and for black people—that is, Africans and peoples of African descent—to structure *their* lifeworlds, *their* histories and futures. Hence, there was the need to fashion distinctive articulations of praxis-guiding understandings by which to shape and guide liberating revisions of more nurturing and sustaining lifeworlds and lives of *black* folks: that is, to engage in the production and articulation of "Black philosophy"!

During these efforts and developments, which took place mostly during the 1970s, the principal media and venues for expressing the articulations calling for and expounding Black philosophy were papers read at conferences and, after a time, at sessions at annual meetings of divisions of the American Philosophical Association (APA) organized by the association's Committee on Blacks in Philosophy. One of the earliest conferences was held at the University of Illinois-Chicago Circle in 1970. During the following years, several conferences were organized and hosted by colleagues in philosophy at Tuskegee Institute (since 1985 Tuskegee University), often under the thematic heading of "Philosophy and the Black Experience." This theme became the title for a special double issue of the *Philosophical Forum* (vol. 9, nos. 2–3, 1977–1978) that was guest-edited by Jesse McDade (at the time a member of the faculty in philosophy at Morgan State University in Baltimore, Maryland) and devoted to papers presented during a 1976 conference at Tuskegee. During that same year, through the efforts of William R. Jones (then on the faculty of the Yale University Divinity School and chairman and founder of the first formal Committee on Blacks in Philosophy of the APA), a small group of black academic philosophers was hosted by the Johnson Foundation at Wingspread, the foundation's headquarters in Racine, Wisconsin, to devote several days to concentrated explorations of what properly could and should be meant by "Black philosophy," and what the agenda should be for further developing the enterprise.[5] Other conferences were hosted at Morgan State University during the decade.

An especially noteworthy feature of virtually all of the pioneering conferences was the prominence of academic and nonacademic intellectuals and scholars working in fields other than philosophy who made presentations and joined in the often intense pioneering discussions, among these such persons as C. L. R. (Cyril Lionel Robert) James and Harold Cruse, both of whom participated in Tuskegee conferences. From the very beginning, then, efforts to forge *black* thought modalities in philosophy were multidisciplinary and decidedly free of the confining (and potentially distorting) intellectual norms and strategies, and of the modes of disciplinary social organization, that prevailed in professionalized academic philosophy.

Furthermore, the multi- and interdisciplinary enrichments that fertilized early endeavors were among some of the more important contributions of the pioneers who were, themselves, persons with formal education and training in academic philosophy and other disciplines on which they drew for their interventions. For example, William R. Jones and Robert C. Williams worked in religion and theology as well as in philosophy; Cornel West began his teaching career at Union Theological Seminary engaging closely with James Cone, one of the pioneers and leading articulators of Black and liberation theologies; and all three enjoyed extensive, fruitful relations with other leading thinkers and scholars producing the groundbreaking works of Black and liberation theologies as well as with a number of the most influential preacher-ministers of the day, such as Reverend Calvin Butts (Abyssinian Baptist Church, New York City) and Reverend Dr. James A. Forbes Jr. (Union Theological Seminary and Riverside Church, New York). Each drew on all of these resources for contributions to efforts to fashion black philosophy. (Williams was himself a minister, serving several years as dean of chapel at Fisk University while a member of the university's faculty in philosophy and religious studies. And Cornel West is hardly shy about standing in pulpits to speak about his prophetic sense of matters having to do with black folks, with other peoples and groupings (class, gender, sexual orientation, etc.), and with the ways of undemocratic, capitalist U.S. America.

During the 1980s, this decidedly U.S. American call to intellectual arms for "black philosophy" gave way to "Africana philosophy" as the covering term for various efforts—among them critique, revision, reconceptualization, and creative imagination—to liberate folks of African descent from the restrictions and entanglements of white racial supremacy, along the way liberating white folks, too, from its distorting effects. In part, the change of terminology was prompted by the need to move beyond agendas and discourses oriented around, and limited by, a term for what, largely, was historically a U.S. American deployment of a color code referenced to skin color that served as a proxy for raciality. In part, the change was prompted by earlier (1960s–1970s) developments in other fields of intellectual endeavor as Pan-African concerns and convictions took hold on more than a few. Prideful regard on the part of a significant number of persons of African descent, both native to the United States and immigrants, for successful and ongoing African movements for independence from European colonial domination and exploitation fueled extensions of racialized historical and cultural identifications to peoples, cultural elements, and political ideas, ideals, and practices on the African continent (even compelling a few to emigrate to several of what were, at the time, the more exciting and promising new African nation-states of

Ghana, Nigeria, and Tanzania, among others). And the successful holding of the Sixth Pan-African Congress in Dar es Salaam, Tanzania, during July 1974 was a potent boost to the value of investments in Pan-African convictions and agendas.[6] More than three hundred official and unofficial delegates, observers, participants, and interested black people from the United States attended the congress.[7] Their doing so reinforced and fueled even more transnational and transcontinental identifications and expressions of solidarity on the part of many of them with all peoples African. ("We are *all* African people!" was a frequently invoked declaration during these decades.)

Such identifications and aspirations were made manifest in the terms chosen to identify and characterize—in some cases to revise the identification and characterization of—the foci and range of coverage (of subject matters and of geography) of many of the emergent and emerging programs, centers, institutes, and departments in colleges and universities devoted to studies of black folks. Whereas "Black" studies had generally been the favored characterizing and identifying term early on (though the Africana Studies and Research Center at Cornell University set a transcontinental, Pan-African agenda when established in 1969), increasingly in later years the term was replaced with "African American," and in other instances with "Africana" studies, in the latter case to set the range of the intellectual (and political) tasks in keeping with the near-global dispersals and living situations of black African and black African–descended peoples.

So, too, with the shift to "Africana" philosophy. For by the mid-1980s, several of the pioneers of the call for and of efforts to give definitive shape and content to discourses of Black philosophy had been influenced significantly by the developments and consequences of what might well be called yet another instance of U.S. American black folks' "turn toward Africa" and toward "things African." Leonard Harris, for example, while earning his PhD in philosophy at Cornell University, pursued studies in Cornell's Africana Studies and Research Center. After completing his studies and while developing his career, Harris also began (and continues) making frequent experiencing and research trips to various African countries (Kenya, Nigeria, Ghana, Ethiopia, Eritrea, South Africa), to the Caribbean, and to countries in South America in which substantial portions of the populations are persons of African descent. These excursions, lived and intellectual, brought him into contact with local African and African-descended intellectuals, academics, and scholars, academic philosophers among them. The same was the case for a number of other black philosophers in the United States. And such excursions—whether as actual journeys or journeys taken vicariously through constructions of the imagination by way of engagements with readings, music, art, dance, languages, clothing, films; through choosing African names for oneself and/or one's children; and through discursive engagements with persons involved in organizational activities on terms that would come to be called "Afrocentric"—would prove to be of major significance to more than a few of these philosophers, personally and professionally.

Similar developments affected African and African-descended intellectuals on the African continent and throughout the African diaspora. For among postcolonial developments in a number of the relatively recently independent African, Caribbean, and South American countries was the emergence of a generation of persons born during the decades just before independence who had successfully completed programs of advanced study in academic philosophy (and in theology, literature, and other disciplines), often in the most elite institutions in the metropoles of the former colonizing countries. After completing their studies, many had returned to their home countries and taken up posts in educational institutions increasingly administered and led by persons African and of African descent. Soon thereafter, much in keeping with agendas to "decolonize the minds" of African students, discussions emerged that took up questions that had been prompted by the publication in 1945 of *Bantu Philosophy* by the Belgian priest Placide Tempels (who had been engaged in missionary work in what then was called the Belgian Congo): namely, whether, in truth, the various African peoples had indigenous philosophies, as Temples had claimed was true of Bantu-speaking Africans; whether Africans were, in fact, even *capable* of producing philosophical articulations of sufficient quality to merit calling them such. The discussions of these issues had been intensified and influenced significantly by the articulations of a cohort of this same generation who, while studying in the capital metropole of France, had taken it upon themselves to identify and characterize the essential character or nature of Negro Africans—their *Négritude*—that distinguished them from white Europeans.[8] The intense debates of these and other issues conditioned substantially notions of what academic philosophy should be in African institutions and of what service it should be to the continuing work of consolidating the independence and modernization of African countries and to the decolonizing rehabilitation of African psyches and communities.

Other African American academic philosophers, including this writer, would undertake similar excursions to those of Harris and make contacts with a significant number of this new generation of African philosophers and other engaged intellectuals, contacts that would lead to very productive cross-fertilizing relationships. In 1981, for example, I ventured to Nairobi, Kenya, to participate in the Second Afro-Asian Philosophy Conference at the University of Nairobi, which featured presentations and discussions by African and other philosophers and intellectuals, a conference sponsored by the professional organization of philosophers in Kenya and the Inter-African Council of Philosophy, the latter an organization whose members were national organizations of professional philosophers and other scholars in various African countries.[9] During the conference I was invited to a meeting of the council's executive committee (among the members present were J. Olubi Sodipo of Nigeria, Kwasi Wiredu of Ghana, Paulin Hountondji of the People's Republic of Benin, and H. Odera Oruka of Kenya, host of the conference) to ask whether the council and the individuals present would accept an invitation to travel to the United States to participate in a transcontinental, international conference of African and African-descended philosophers and other scholars if I were able to raise sufficient funds to host such a gathering. My proposal was warmly received and enthusiastically endorsed by the council's executive committee and by each of the individuals present. After I returned to the United States, with the assistance of several members of the council's executive committee sufficient funds were raised through support from the National Endowment for the Humanities, the Rockefeller Foundation, the Fédération International des Sociétés de Philosophie (International Federation of Philosophical Societies or FISP), and the Social Science Research Council of New York to host the International Conference on Africana Philosophy at Haverford College (Haverford, Pennsylvania) during the summer of 1982. Sodipo, Wiredu, Hountondji, and Oruka were among the many who ventured to Haverford to participate in the historic gathering.

Among the fruitful engagements and experiences I benefited from while at the Nairobi conference and in the city of Nairobi, particularly notable were my discussions with Hountondji, Wiredu, and Oruka regarding the cogency of the idea that among "traditional" African peoples there were, indeed, persons whose reasonings and articulations merited academic philosophers regarding them as worthy instances of philosophizing in keeping with expanded senses and criteria of philosophical effort emerging from respectful, though critical attention to articulations by such persons. At issue were matters of the historical, sociological, and epistemological scope and content of the enterprise being developed that we now term "Africana philosophy," the subfield of African philosophy in particular: namely, whether African philosophy should include the articulations of "traditional" African thinkers (that is, persons who lived prior to the advent of "modern" formal education in Africa and those who, subsequently, were not among the beneficiaries of such schooling). Hountondji was adamant in saying "No!" to such inclusions; Wiredu soft-spoken in his careful, thoughtful deciding in the affirmative; and Oruka passionate in joining Wiredu in concluding "Yes!" (Oruka would go on to produce pioneering field research and publications along precisely this line of inquiry with his studies of "sage philosophy."[10] Wiredu, on his own and while collaborating with his Ghanaian colleague Kwame Gyekye, would go on to produce equally pioneering work on the philosophical articulations and significance of instances of thought by Akan thinkers.[11])

Such discussions did much to reinforce and expand the scope of efforts on my part and others' to contribute to work in the United States to create, sustain, and refine discursive ventures devoted to studies and productions of philosophical articulations by black folks. However, in "turning toward things African" and finding engagements with continental African thinkers to be sources of important learning for our efforts, it became increasingly clear that organizing the scope of our thinking by terms and notions drawn from the racialized contexts of the United States of America was neither sufficient nor appropriate on the whole, though it might be appropriate in some cases—say, where the concern might be with the philosophical articulations of persons of African descent who are natives of or immigrants to the United States.

Still, the question of possible linkages of those articulations to the discursive, political, and other lifeworld endeavors of persons and peoples African and/or of African descent elsewhere has had to be raised and explored in order to have a full and proper account even of U.S.-based developments. For to the extent that notions of "blackness" or "Africanity" were used decisively to demarcate the focal human subjects of philosophical discussion, the inquiries had to grapple with the ways black folks managed to foster the creative adaptations of old modalities of thought and praxis, as well as the creative development and testing of new modalities. These modalities provided a way by which, as oppressed and exploited peoples whose humanity was denied and who were made to live social death, they not only survived in becoming new peoples in new situations but nurtured ways to sustain senses of human propriety toward themselves *and* toward their oppressors, and found ways, even, to flourish.[12] Such developments took place almost by historical necessity, the result of centuries-long creations of colonized continental Africans and of a diaspora of African and African-descended peoples by way of purchase and capture, transport and sale, for enslavement in New Worlds. Recognizing, respecting, and attending critically to these modalities of thought and praxis require a broad—that is to say, transcontinental—scope while taking care to attend to decisive differences as well as to commonalities and similarities. *Africana philosophy* has become the concept of choice through which to map these transcontinental intellectual terrains as well as under which to engage in philosophizing about matters of concern and about persons and peoples African and of African descent.

It must be noted that the discursive quests of the 1970s and after, whether under the heading of "black philosophy" or "Africana philosophy," were never pursued only by folks of African descent native to the United States of America. From the beginning scholarly thinkers with training in academic philosophy who were originally from continental Africa were intimately involved, among the contributing prioneers were Ifeanyi Menkiti (Nigeria), John Murungi (Kenya), and Henry Olela and William Abraham (Ghana). Others came later and continue to enrich the efforts: Kwasi Wiredu (Ghana), Dismas Masolo (Kenya), Segun Gbadegesin (Nigeria), Théophile Obenga (Congo, Equatorial Africa), Tsenay Sereque-berhan (Eritrea), Olúfémi Táíwò (Nigeria), Safro Kwame (Ghana), George Carew (Sierra Leone), Nkiru Nzegwu (Nigeria), Ajume Wingo (Cameroon), Souleymane Bachir Diagne (Senegal), and Kwame Anthony Appiah (Ghana and Great Britain), among many others. And, there are the contributions of scholarly thinkers of African descent working in academic philosophy and other disciplines, and contributing thinkers of significance who were not based in institutions of higher education, from other regions in the African diaspora, the Caribbean and South America in particular: Paget Henry (Antigua); Roy Martinez (Belize); Anthony Bogues, Lewis Gordon, Charles Mills, and Sylvia Wynter (Jamaica); Bernard Boxill (St. Lucia); Kwame Touré, a.k.a. Stokely Carmichael, and C. L. R. James (Trinidad, West Indies); and Walter Rodney (Guyana), among many. Of particular significance, as well, have been the fertilizing and motivating works of such influential figures as Marcus Garvey, Oliver Cromwell Cox, Aimé Césaire, Frantz Fanon, Stuart Hall, Paul Gilroy, and Orlando Patterson; and the works of particularly noteworthy women such as Angela Davis, Joyce Mitchell Cook, Hazel Carby, Patricia Williams, bell hooks, Patricia Hill Collins, and Joy James.

Much more needs to be taken into account about the extent to which what has come to be considered "philosophical" thought by and about folks

African and of African descent was articulated by persons a great many of whom were not associated with academic philosophy yet whose articulations have had and continue to have very substantial influence on many of the persons working in academic philosophy. In the context of the United States, for example, canonical texts by Frederick Douglass (*Narrative of the Life of Frederick Douglass, an American Slave: Written by Himself*, 1845), Anna Julia Cooper (*A Voice From the South*, 1892), Booker T. Washington (*Up from Slavery*, 1901), Alexander Crummell, Ida B. Wells-Barnett (*Crusade for Justice: The Autobiography of Ida B. Wells*), and W. E. B. DuBois (*The Souls of Black Folk*, 1903) are poignant examples among many. So, too, are influential works by creative writers and essayists such as Margaret Walker (*Jubilee*), Richard Wright (*Native Son* and *Black Boy*), Gwendolyn Brooks (*Blacks*), Ralph Ellison (*Invisible Man, Shadow and Act*), James Baldwin (*Another Country, The Fire Next Time*), John Oliver Killens (*And Then We Heard the Thunder, Youngblood*), Sam Greenlee (*The Spook Who Sat by the Door*), Harold Cruse (*The Crisis of the Negro Intellectual, Reform or Revolution?*), and many, many others. In person and/or through their works these intellectuals, aided by the consciousness-raising and self-image transforming work of artists who were the initiators and carriers of the Black Arts Movement (including Nikki Giovanni, Sonia Sanchez, Haki R. Madhubuti, Larry Neal, Gwendolyn Brooks, Amiri Baraka, A. B. Spellman, Jeff Donaldson, Donald L. Graham, and others[13]), helped nurture several generations of Negroes into and through the transformations of consciousness by which we became *Black* folks. Their contributions were enriched by those of a bevy of scholars of an older generation, many of them in colleges and universities founded to serve black folks: historians John Hope Franklin, Benjamin Quarles, William Leo Hansberry, Lerone Bennett, and Vincent Harding; creative writers Arnold Bontemps, Sterling Brown, and James Weldon Johnson; social scientists Charles S. Johnson, E. Franklin Frazier, Ralph Bunche, and Oliver Cox; ethnomusicologist John W. Work; artists Aaron Douglas, Romare Bearden, Jacob Lawrence, and Elizabeth Catlett; musicians John Coltrane, Thelonious Monk, Charles Lloyd, Nina Simone, Miles Davis, Aretha Franklin, Sarah Vaughn, and many others.

In summary: The intellectual and artistic productions from these and others were additions to centuries-long legacies of culture creation that have formed a complex, fecund mix of intellectual, aesthetic, psychological, emotional, and spiritual resources. These were tapped to fuel and to give meaning and direction to efforts to form a distinctive field of discursive endeavors rendered intelligible in new ways and to new ends, intellectual and sociopolitical, by characterizing them as *philosophical* though decidedly about and in service to black folks, folks African and of African descent.

And the results of these decades of effort?

First, several hard-won modes of professional recognition:

- The American Philosophical Association, the largest and predominant organization of professional, academic philosophers in the United States, created and supported a standing Committee on Blacks in Philosophy and newsletter (*Newsletter on Philosophy and the Black Experience*), though recognition had come years earlier from other organizations of professional philosophers, particularly the Radical Philosophers Association, the Society for Phenomenological and Existential Philosophy, and from other organizations of researchers, scholars, and teachers such as the African Studies Association, the Association for the Study of African American Life and History, and the National Council of Black Political Scientists, each of which opened its meetings to advocates of black/Africana philosophy.
- The American Philosophical Association added "Africana philosophy" to its list of recognized fields and subfields and opened its divisional programs to sessions devoted to explorations in Africana philosophy.
- Departments of philosophy in colleges and universities added courses on African American and/or African philosophy to their curricula, and added canonical texts by African-descended activist-intellectuals and more recent texts produced by professional, academic philosophers of African descent to course reading lists.
- Departments of philosophy, and other disciplines, invited practitioners of Africana philosophy to visit classes and to give lectures on subject matters in the emerging field.
- Especially, departments of philosophy conducted searches for and hired, retained, tenured, and promoted persons who have made Africana philosophy their field of specialization or an area of particular competence.
- Recognition is also evident through the support of the research and scholarship of philosophers, African and of African descent especially, who do work in Africana philosophy by foundations and governmental agencies that provide fellowship support to scholars and teachers. Among these foundations and agencies are the American Council of Learned Societies (ACLS), the Rockefeller

Foundation, the National Endowment for the Humanities, the Social Science Research Council, UNESCO (United Nations Education, Scientific and Cultural Organization), Fédération International des Sociétés de Philosophie, the Woodrow Wilson International Center for Scholars, and the Fulbright Programs for U.S. Scholars and for Visiting Scholars administered by the Council for the International Exchange of Scholars.

• After *years* of earlier refusal and resistance, acquisition editors and editorial boards at publishers, and editors of journals in philosophy, have recognized the vitality, importance, and opportunities offered by Africana philosophy as a field of scholarly discourse and an important—and potentially profitable—market with canonical historical figures and important philosophical issues, which for decades a great many (though not all) of them and their predecessors had disparaged, ignored, neglected, or simply not known about. Consequently, what began as provocative presentations of papers at sessions of conferences and professional meetings (the majority of which were never published), and lectures to audiences often well beyond the mainstream of academic philosophy, has gradually evolved into a slowly growing but increasingly more widely recognized and heard number of professional philosophers African and of African descent who are producing a rather steady stream of publications (essays in journals, chapters in anthologies, single-authored essay collections, and monographs on particular topics).

Regarding this last area of recognition: Several publishers and persons are to be noted for their courage and good sense in cutting against the grain of this publishing disdain and ignorance and thus for leading the way in lowering invidious barriers to the publication of works by African and African-descended philosophers. Among publishers to be noted: the Westminster Press, publisher, in 1982, of Cornel West's *Prophesy Deliverance! An Afro-American Revolutionary Christianity*; Kendall/Hunt, publisher of Leonard Harris's 1983 pioneering anthology *Philosophy Born of Struggle: Afro-American Philosophy from 1917*; Indiana University Press, the University of Wisconsin Press, and Temple University Press. Other publishers have followed suit, notably Blackwell, Oxford University Press, Wadsworth, Routledge, and Rowman & Littlefield.

At each of these publishers particular editors made affirmative and affirming judgments regarding manuscripts and submitted proposals by, or requested from, scholars African and of African descent and argued the cases for their publication sufficiently well (often with the assistance of readers of manuscripts who recommended publication) that editorial boards sanctioned publication. Often the works were unorthodox by prevailing criteria governing subject matter and themes of philosophizing and audiences to be served. One such editor is Maureen MacGrogan, formerly acquisition editor for publishers Routledge and Roman & Littlefield.[14] Another is the late Marx Wartofsky, longtime editor of *Philosophical Forum*, who twice devoted the journal to special issues on philosophy and black experiences and in both cases had the special issue guest-edited by knowledgeable and competent philosophers of African descent.

The recognitions, the endeavors recognized, and the growing body of published works by practitioners of Africana philosophy have contributed to substantially increasing and broadening legitimation of, and respect for, the emergent subfields (African philosophy, African American philosophy, Caribbean philosophy) now comprising Africana philosophy as a disciplinary field within academic philosophy and, thus, to greater legitimation of and respect for its practitioners. The same follows, too, for the apprenticing graduate students, course-taking undergraduate and graduate students, interested and contributing colleague teacher–scholars in other disciplines (law, political science, English and literary criticism, African American/ Africana studies, history, religious studies, theology, sociology, music, fine art), and interested persons in various lay publics who engage in reading and drawing on published works of Africana philosophy for their own scholarly purposes and who attend lectures and conferences and discuss focal figures and issues with others.

Furthermore, with more recognition, respect, legitimation, and growing audiences, publishers have been making more investments in the enterprise, including by supporting the publication of major resource collections[15] and the publication of a special-focus series, such as "Africana Thought: The World of Black Philosophy,"[16] launched by Routledge and edited by Lewis R. Gordon (philosophy, Temple University) and Paget Henry (Africana studies and sociology, Brown University). There is now, as well, a seemingly self-sustaining international journal, *Philosophia Africana: Analysis of Philosophy and Issues in Africa and the Black Diaspora*, initiated and edited by Emmanuel Chukwudi Eze (philosophy, DePaul University).

The Companions to Philosophy series volumes, which bring together into one ready-to-hand resource a host of important previously published and new essays and revised conference presentations, along with the

Africana Thought series and the journal, when combined with a sizable stream of articles, book chapters, and books that have been published during the last two decades, make for a now rather respectable body of works in Africana philosophy that have been put out by publishers in English-speaking Europe and North America. However, when the writings on subjects of Africana philosophy by African philosophers and other scholars are taken into account that have been and are published on and distributed within the African continent (Egypt, Kenya, Ethiopia, Nigeria, Senegal, Benin, Eritrea, Ivory Coast, Uganda, Democratic Republic of the Congo, Tanzania), and published in Europe but distributed within Africa and Europe, in English and other languages (Arabic, Amharic, French, German, Cushitic languages), it has to be recognized that the literary resource base of Africana philosophy is now quite substantial and growing. These widely dispersed and varied literary resources make for a compelling need—and opportunity—for the production of tools such as comprehensive annotated bibliographies to support national and international research and scholarship and to enrich understandings of the international reach and dimensions of the enterprise of Africana philosophy.

Even more legitimacy and respect have and will be gained as new cohorts of teacher-scholars have been and are being produced and hired by institutions higher up in the ranking orders of U.S. American colleges and universities wherein they create and publish new works in Africana philosophy while also contributing through teaching, public lectures, conference presentations, professional meetings, and civic engagements. And with the enhanced legitimation and respect that come with publication (of no small significance to teacher-scholars having to face evaluation for retention, tenure, and promotion), and with increased exposure through the creation and nurturing of larger and more diverse audiences (through college and university courses, especially, as well as through lectures and conferences), there will be the reciprocal effects of creating desires and needs for more critically enhanced articulations, the motivations to produce them, and the rewards of producing them.

However, it should be expected that these developments, in the United States in particular, will very likely be complicated by the greater racial and ethnic diversity of practitioners who enter the discursive field of Africana philosophy and make contributions. Moreover, the landscapes of intellectual and academic fields of discourse continue to diversify thematically and methodologically as the sociocultural variety of practitioners becomes more complex as the U.S. American population as a whole becomes more diverse racially and ethnically—and, concomitantly, so does the demography of the faculties and student bodies of the country's colleges and universities. Of course, these developments will generate challenges and changes within Africana philosophy and among practitioners, many of which cannot be anticipated or predicted.

Though some can. Already, increasing numbers of differentiating clusters of efforts are emerging as practitioners continue to forge conceptual movements beyond the high-level gathering power of the foundational ordering and normative notions of *African, African American,* and even *Africana* to lower-level delimiting foci more appropriate for exploring the articulations and related historical and cultural lifeworlds of particular African and/or African-descended peoples within and across particular geographic regions. For example, explorations of the conceptual schemes, articulations, and lifeworld praxes of the Akan people are one contribution to endeavors comprising work in African philosophy where the initial delimiting/organizing geographic focus is continental Africa, but further delimited by attending to a particular ethnic group.[17] It is to be hoped that many more such focused studies of people-groups will be undertaken, in some cases taking up and continuing controversial explorations that were initiated decades ago by ethnographers and anthropologists, as well as later by academic philosophers, that were disparaged by some as "ethnophilosophy" and thus not appropriate instances of academic philosophy.

Another example: explorations of articulations by various persons of African descent native to geopolitical situations in the Caribbean (such as the rather recent founding of the Caribbean Philosophical Association and the hosting of philosophy conferences in the region, such as Conceptualizing Philosophy, Conversations I: Cave Hill Philosophy Symposium [CHIPS] 2005, University of West Indies, Cave Hill Campus, March 31–April 1).[18] It is to be expected that these differentiations of foci by geopolitical, geocultural regions will continue with interesting and fruitful results and challenging consequences. For with differentiations and the highlighting of differences will come tensions and strains.

In the near term one concern will be whether "Africana" will continue to have cogency as a gathering concept—for whom, and to what ends—or whether it will be displaced by similar or decidedly *dis*similar notions. Will there be a compelling *need* to continue to seek the sociopolitical, intellectual, and knowledge-producing consequences of a philosophical anthropology that sees virtue in lifeworlds formed and sustained, in large part, by culture-making descent groupings identified and self-identifying, and valorized, positively and negatively, through complicated notions of geographically inflected raciality and ethnicity? Or, will such concerns become philosophically and politically anachronistic, at best, as attending to the life-worlds of folks African and of African descent devolves to historians while contemporary and future engaged intellectuals and scholars, philosophers among them, focus attention and energies on building and sustaining life-worlds, identities, and futures out of meanings that neither define nor are defined by the geographical origins of people-groupings of races, ethne, nations, and nation-states? Moreover, it should be expected that more critical studies will be produced—new subjects broached, new questions asked—as the aspirations, assumptions, and commitments of previous generations of scholars give way to those of later generations confronting their own historical challenges.

Among the critical issues overdue for attention are those having to do with black women. To date, developments comprising Africana philosophy have involved embarrassingly and irresponsibly little focus on the histories, needs, concerns, and articulations of women of African descent, even though a number of black women have been and are involved as pioneers and as contributors, a significant number of whom have degrees in academic philosophy.[19] Already mentioned: Joyce Mitchell Cook (the first African American woman to receive the PhD in philosophy in the United States and who merits a biographical monograph), Blanche Radford-Curry, Angela Davis, Joy James, Michelle Moody-Adams, and Nkiru Nzegwu. There are others: Anita Allen-Castellitto, Kathryn Gines, Barbara Hall, Devonya Havis, Claudette Jones, Barbara McKenney, Desiree Melton, Adrian Piper (a widely recognized, highly acclaimed artist, as well), Jacqueline Scott, La Verne Shelton, Georgette Sinkler, Jennifer Vest, Yolanda Wilson, and others, with still more in the graduate pipeline. Whether these women, those in positions in departments of philosophy and other units in colleges and universities in particular, will further develop feminist and/or womanist pathways in Africana philosophy remains to be seen.

Angela Davis is already leading the way with her *Women, Race, and Class* (1983), *Women, Culture, and Politics* (1990), and *Blues Legacies and Black Feminism: Gertrude "Ma" Rainey, Bessie Smith, and Billie Holiday* (1999).[20] So, too, Joy James, with her insightful and provocative critical work *Transcending the Talented Tenth: Race Leaders and American Intellectualism* (1996) and her *Shadowboxing: Representations of Black Feminist Politics* (1992), among other important writings, is also leading the way. However, as was noted at the outset, a great many very important articulations construed as philosophical and included in Africana philosophy were produced by persons without degrees in academic philosophy (or with no degrees at all). This includes a number of very important articulations by several black women already mentioned, including bell hooks (*Ain't I a Woman: Black Women and Feminism*, 1999; *Teaching to Transgress*, 1994; and *Feminism is for Everybody: Passionate Politics*, 2000, among many publications); Patricia Hill Collins (*Fighting Words: Black Women and the Search for Justice, Contradictions of Modernity*, 1998; *Black Feminist Thought: Knowledge, Consciousness, and the Politics of Empowerment*, 2000; *Black Sexual Politics: African-Americans, Gender, and the New Racism*, 2005); writings by one of the pioneers of critical race theory in legal studies, Patricia Williams (*Alchemy of Race and Rights*, 1992, and *Seeing a Color-Blind Future: The Paradox of Race*, 1998); writings by Kimberly Crenshaw, another pioneering critical theorist of racial matters in law and jurisprudence who edited the important collection *Critical Race Theory: The Key Writings that Formed the Movement* (1995); work by literary critic Hortense Spillers (*Black, White, and in Color: Essays on American Literature and Culture*, 2003; and *Conjuring: Black Women, Fiction, and Literary Tradition (Everywoman)*, coedited with Marjorie Pryse, 1985).

To be added to these are an abundance of novels and essays by black female creative writers, several of whom have achieved well-deserved critical acclaim: Toni Morrison, obviously, and Alice Walker; the brilliant, poignant, and controversial Zora Neale Hurston (*Their Eyes Were Watching God*); master of science-fiction writing Octavia Butler; and anthologizing and other contributions by womanist scholar Beverly Guy-Sheftall (*Words of Fire: An Anthology of African-American Feminist Thought*, 1995, and, with Johnnetta B. Cole, *Gender Talk: The Struggle for Women's Equality in African American Communities*, 2003).

Also in need of careful consideration by practitioners of Africana philosophy is the emergent work of black female (and male) theologians, especially works of the "womanist" persuasion, such as writings by Katie Cannon (*Katie's Canon: Womanism and the Soul of the Black Community*, 1997); Renita Weems (*Just a Sister Away: Understanding the Timeless Connection between Women of Today and Women in the Bible*, 2005; *Listening for God: A Minister's Journey through Silence and Doubt*, 2000); and Delores Williams (*Sisters in the Wilderness: The Challenge of Womanist God-Talk*, 1995), who is the widow of deceased pioneer of African American/Africana philosophy Robert C. Williams.

All of these and compatriot writings by black women must be taken up and considered carefully and critically by practitioners of Africana philosophy, enhanced by the contributions of black women scholars in complementary disciplines such as the contributions of historians Darlene Clark Hine (*Black Women in America*, 3 vols., 2005), Evelyn Higginbotham (*Righ-

teous Discontent: The Women's Movement in the Black Baptist Church, 1880–1920, 2006 reprint). This should be done for personal edification as well as to enlarge and strengthen shared understandings as philosophers and, thereby, to enlarge, appropriately, the scope and content of the field. For I am firmly convinced that education in academic philosophy, at both undergraduate and graduate levels, is much too impoverished by the lack of studies of women and other long-neglected subjects, but also by the absence of broad and deep, historically informed, complementary groundings in a number of the social sciences (sociology, history, anthropology, political economics), humanities (religion, literature, art), and/or cultural studies more broadly. Giving focal attention to issues and works regarding black women would be a challenging and rewarding way of educating ourselves—those of us with such needs—out of our ignorance and would help prepare us to better educate our students. This is a line of development that *must* be taken up, soon, to give better balance to the future of Africana philosophy.

Yet another concern regarding the future of the enterprise: Will Africana philosophy continue as an enterprise conditioned, even guided, by "Afrocentric" concerns and convictions?

The passionate insistence that knowledge production, validation, and mediation by and about and to black peoples should be epistemologically and politically "Afrocentric"—that is, *centered* in and on as well as *focused* on the values, interests, needs, and agendas of folks African and of African descent—continues to be a definitive position advocated vociferously and worked at continuously by Molefi Kete Asante, one of the most widely recognized and highly productive of proponents of this challenging orientation to knowledge-work.[21] Others, of course, have been, and others continue as, contributors to this multifarious collection of intellectual, academic, cultural, and political aspirations, organizations, movements, and institutions.

Along with Asante, one of the more important of these contributors is Maulana Karenga, who holds terminal degrees (PhD) in both ethics and political science. And while he, more than Asante, has on occasion joined African and African-descended academic philosophers in conference gatherings to debate and otherwise work through challenging ideas and concepts, intellectual and sociopolitical/cultural programs, strategies, and tactics, both Karenga and Asante have pursued their considerably productive and influential knowledge-work and other engagements outside of the associations of academic philosophers. Nonetheless, both of these passionately and continuously engaged and deeply committed activist-researchers, teacher-scholars, and public intellectuals continue to have wide-ranging influence on knowledge-work and cultural life, and not just on black folks. To a large extent, and in many ways, these two are exemplary of activists who came of age (and of black self-consciousness) during the Black Power/cultural nationalist movements of the 1960s to 1980s, and beyond, and remain two of the movements' most articulate and productive scholar-intellectuals. The emergence and evolution of Black philosophy into still-evolving Africana philosophy have not been unaffected by Asante, Karenga, and a number of their compatriots and intellectual-political progeny.

To what extent will this continue to be the case? Will there be, as some of us hope and advocate, much more willful and mutually beneficial cooperative engagements between philosophers African and of African descent in colleges and universities studying and working in departments of philosophy (and in Black/African American/Africana studies programs, departments, centers, and institutes) and philosophizing Afrocentric scholar-intellectuals, some of whom are academics, some not? This remains to be seen. (A place to watch: Temple University in Philadelphia, Pennsylvania, where Asante is based in the Department of African American Studies for which he served for many years as founding chairperson. It was the first such department to offer studies in African American Studies leading to the PhD degree. Lewis Gordon is now based in their philosophy department from which he continues pioneering research, publishing, conference organizing, and organizational development work in Africana philosophy.) More robust and continuous collaboration of this kind is long overdue. Circumstances, I suspect, in addition to the willful decisions of key persons, will force the matter to the fore.

Presently, there is neither a predominant organization of national or international scope that includes most practitioners of Africana philosophy and sets the agenda for the work engaged in, nor no one or two persons whose articulations set the agenda and serve as the authoritative model for Africana philosophy. It remains to be seen whether aspiring academic entrepreneurs of Africana philosophy, of critical studies of women and gender, of raciality and ethnicity, and of Afrocentric knowledge-production, across various fields and disciplines, will be successful in their efforts to position themselves and/or their institutional bases and organizations, their publishing efforts, as de facto and subsequently recognized definitive leaders among participants, sites, and media in these otherwise dispersed and democratic (some more, some less) discursive enterprises or whether there will continue to be multiple sites of production, multiple modes of articulation, multiple agendas, with serious doubts about how well black folks, and others, are served. The history of recently emergent intellectual endeavors sharing the commonalty of motivations and of being guided, more or less, by high-level notions of and investments in "Africana" philosophizing has been characterized, nonetheless, by diversities not yet fully explored (gender, sexual orientation, class differentiations, ethnic nationalisms are some examples). It is to be hoped, then, that the explorations will not only continue but be intensified and expanded through disciplined work, and that the diversities will be appreciated and studied carefully as reservoirs of creative adaptations by folks African and of African descent to the exigencies of getting on in a challenging world of diverse lifeworlds, adaptations infused with thoughtfulness—that is, with philosophizings—of various kinds that are accorded ever more respectful critical study by serious thinkers. It is hoped that this chapter will contribute to just such an unfolding.

Notes

1. The following are but some of the persons of African descent in academic, professional philosophy who have been pioneers of Africana philosophy in the United States: Robert C. Williams, Max Wilson, Broadus N. Butler, and Charles Frye—all deceased; Richard McKinnon, Leonard Harris, Joyce Mitchell Cook, Albert Mosley, Berkeley Eddins, Ifeanyi Menkiti, Laurence M. Thomas, La Verne Shelton, Howard McGary, Lancinay Keita, Bernard Boxill, Blanch Curry, Dwight Murph, William R. Jones, Cornel West, J. Everett Green, Robert Cheemooke, Tommy Lott; joined later by Frank Kirkland, John Pittman, Lewis Gordon, and Paget Henry (the latter crossing over from sociology). Also of decisive significance have been the nurturing, sustaining, "midwifery" contributions of Alfred Prettyman.

2. Anna Stubblefield and Judith Green are two of several white philosophers making Africana philosophy an area of focus of their work. See, for example, Stubblefield's *Ethics along the Color Line* (Ithaca, NY: Cornell University Press, 2005).

3. For Alexis de Tocqueville's discussion of what I term the "social causality" of Anglo-Americans' passions, habits, and sentiments, important constitutive elements of what he termed Anglo-Americans' "social state," see chapter 3, "Social State of the Anglo-Americans," in his *Democracy in America*, trans. Harvey C. Mansfield and Delba Winthrop (Chicago: University of Chicago Press, 2000): "The social state is ordinarily the product of a fact, sometimes of laws, most often of these two causes united; but once it exists, one can consider it as the first cause of most of the laws, customs, and ideas that regulate the conduct of nations; what it does not produce, it modifies" (45). For an insightful and critical discussion of "investments in whiteness," see George Lipsitz, *The Possessive Investment in Whiteness: How White People Profit from Identity Politics* (Philadelphia: Temple University Press, 1998).

4. On the "politics of identity and recognition," see Charles Taylor, *Multiculturalism: Examining the Politics of Recognition*, edited and introduced by Amy Gutmann (Princeton: Princeton University Press, 1994).

5. Participating in the Wingspread gathering were William R. Jones, Robert C. Williams, Leonard Harris, Joyce Mitchell Cook, Howard McGary, and this writer.

6. First Pan-African Congress: Paris, 1912; the Second Pan-African Congress, held in 1921, met in three sessions (London, Brussels, Paris); the Third Pan-African Congress was held in London (and Lisbon) in 1923; the Fourth Pan-African Congress was held in New York in 1927; the Fifth Congress was held in Manchester (England) during 1945. See Kwame Anthony Appiah, "Pan-Africanism," in *Africana: The Encyclopedia of the African and African American Experience*, ed, Kwame Anthony Appiah and Henry Louis Gates Jr. (New York: Basic *Civitas* Books, 1999), 1484–86.; and British Broadcasting Corporation, "The Story of Africa: Between World Wars (1914–1945)." www.bbc.co.uk/worldservice/africa/features/storyofafrica/13chapter5.shtml.

7. I was an invited observer in the delegation from the Unites States and certainly shared the sense of, the hope for, transcontinental (and transhistorical) identification and solidarity to be gained and/or reinforced by the agenda and engagements of the congress.

8. See, for example, Nick Nesbitt, "Négritude," in *Africana: The Encyclopedia of the African and African American Experience*, ed. Kwame Anthony Appiah and Henry Louis Gates Jr. (New York: Basic *Civitas* Books, 1999), 1404–8.

9. For works presented during this conference see H. Odera Oruka and Dismas Masolo, eds., *Philosophy and Cultures: Proceedings of the Second Afro-Asian Philosophy Conference, Nairobi* [Kenya], *October/November 1981* (Nairobi: Bookwise, 1983).

10. See H. Odera Oruka, *Sage Philosophy: Indigenous Thinkers and Modern Debate on African Philosophy* (Leiden: Brill Academic Publishers, 1990).

11. Kwame Gyekye and Kwasi Wiredu, eds., *Person and Community: Ghanaian Philosophical Studies* (Washington, DC: Council for Research in Values and Philosophy, 1992).

12. On the poignant matter of "social death," see Orlando Patterson, *Slavery and Social Death: A Comparative Study* (Cambridge: Harvard University Press, 1982).

13. *Black Fire: An Anthology of Afro-American Wrting* (New York: William Morrow, 1968), edited by LeRoi Jones [Amiri Baraka] and Larry Neal, is a seminal collection of writings by makers of the Black Arts and Black Consciousness/Black Power Movements.

14. Routledge and Roman & Littlefield are the publishers of my two books, the former of *On Race and Philosophy* (1996), the latter of *Critical Social Theory in the Interests of Black Folks* (2005), and Maureen MacGrogan was my Routledge editor.

15. Significant examples of major resource collections are Blackwell Publisher's additions to its Companions to Philosophy series: *A Companion to African Philosophy*, edited by Kwasi Wiredu (2004), and *A Companion to African-American Philos-*

ophy, edited by Tommy L. Lott and John P. Pittman (2003). Also significant here is Blackwell Publisher's additions to its Critical Reader series: *Cornel West: A Critical Reader*, edited by George Yancy (2001), and *Fanon: A Critical Reader*, edited by Lewis R. Gordon, T. Denean Sharlpey-Whiting, and Renée T. White (1996).

16. Works published in the Routledge series include Paget Henry's *Caliban's Reason: Introducing Afro-Caribbean Philosophy* (2000); Lewis R. Gordon's *Existentia Africana: Understanding Africana Existential Thought* (2000); Clarence Sholé Johnson's *Cornel West and Philosophy* (2002); and Anthony Bogues's *Black Heretics, Black Prophets: Radical Political Intellectuals* (2003).

17. See Kwame Gyekye, *An Essay on African Philosophical Thought: The Akan Conceptual Scheme* (Philadelphia: Temple University Press, 1995).

18. For a wealth of information and resources regarding Caribbean philosophy, see the section of the Web site "PHILWEB: Philosophy Resources On- and Off-line" at www.phillwebb.net/Regions/Caribbean/Caribbean.htm.

19. An exception in this regard is George Yancy's edited collection *African-American Philosophers: 17 Conversations* (Routledge, 1998) in which Yancy, through interviews, dialogued with seven women philosophers of African descent: Angela Y. Davis, Adrian M. S. Piper, Michele M. Moody-Adams, Anita L. Allen, Naomi Zack, Joy James, and Joyce Mitchell Cook. Yancy was able to focus on the personal histories, needs, and concerns of women philosophers of African descent as articulated in their own words.

20. For other writings by Davis, see *The Angela Y. Davis Reader*, ed. Joy James (Malden, MA: Blackwell, 1998).

21. See, for example, among many writings on the subject by Molefi K. Asante, his *Afrocentricity: The Theory of Social Change* (Buffalo, NY: Amulefi Publishing, 1980); *The Afrocentric Idea* (Philadelphia: Temple University Press, 1987); and *Kemet, Afrocentricity, and Knowledge* (Trenton, NJ: Africa World Press, 1990).

Bibliography

Allen, Anita. *Uneasy Access: Privacy for Women in a Free Society*. Totowa, NJ: Rowman & Littlefield, 1988.

Appiah, Kwame Anthony. *Assertion and Conditionals*. Cambridge: Cambridge University Press, 1985.

———. *For Truth in Semantics*. Oxford, UK: Basil Blackwell, 1986.

———. *In My Father's House: Africa in the Philosophy of Character*. New York: Oxford University Press, 1992.

———. "Racisms." In *Anatomy of Racism*, ed. David Theo Goldberg. Minneapolis: University of Minnesota Press, 1990.

Birt, Robert. "Alienation in the Later Philosophy of Jean-Paul Sartre." *Man and World* 19 (1986): 293–309.

Birt, Robert, ed. *Blackness and the Quest for Authenticity*. Lanham, MD: Roman & Littlefield, 2005.

Blyden, Edward Wilmot. *Africa and Africans: Proceedings on the Occasion of a Banquet, Given at the Holborn Restaurant, August 15, 1903, to Edward W. Blyden*. London: C. M. Phillips, 1903.

———. *Liberia: Past, Present, and Future*. Washington, DC: M'Gill & Witherow, 1869.

———. *The Negro in Ancient History*. Washington, DC: M'Gill & Witherow, 1869.

Bogues, Anthony. *Black Heretics, Black Prophets: Radical Political Intellectuals*. New York: Routledge, 2003.

Boxill, Bernard. *Blacks and Social Justice*. Rev. ed. Lanham, MD: Rowman & Littlefield, 1992.

———. "A Lockean Argument for Black Reparations," *Journal of Ethics* 7, no. 1 (2003): 63–91.

———. "The Morality of Reparations II." In *A Companion to African-American Philosophy: Blackwell Companions to Philosophy*, ed. John P. Pittman and Tommy L. Lott. Malden, MA: Blackwell Publishing, 2003.

———. "Power and Persuasion." *Journal of Social Philosophy* 32, no. 3 (2001): 382–85.

———. "Two Traditions in African American Political Philosophy." *Philosophical Forum* 24 (1992–1993): 119–35.

———. "Washington, Du Bois, and *Plessy V. Ferguson*." *Law and Philosophy* 16, no. 3 (1997): 299–330.

Boxill, Bernard, ed. *Race and Racism*, New York: Oxford University Press, 2001.

Butler, Broadus N. and Kolaja, Jiri. "Dimensions of Identification." *Personalist* 41 (July 1960): 318–23.

Cook, Joyce Mitchell. "On the Nature and Nurture of Intelligence." *Philosophical Forum* 9 (1978): 289–302.

Carruthers, Jacob H. *Essays in Ancient Egyptian Studies*. Los Angeles: University of Sankore Press, 1984.

Carruthers, Jacob H., ed. *Kemet and the African Worldview: Research, Rescue and Restoration*. Los Angeles: University of Sankore Press, 1986.

Darby, Derrick. "Are Worlds without Natural Rights Morally Impoverished?" *Southern Journal of Philosophy* 37, no. 3 (1999): 397–417.

———. "Feinberg and Martin on Human Rights." *Journal of Social Philosophy* 34, no. 2 (2003): 199–214.

———. "Rights Externalism." *Philosophy and Phenomenological Research* 68, no. 4 (2004): 620–34.

———. "Two Conceptions of Rights Possession." *Social Theory and Practice* 27, no. 3 (2001): 387–417.

———. "Unnatural Rights." *Canadian Journal of Philosophy* 33, no. 1 (2003): 49–82.

Davis, Angela Y. "Afro Images: Politics, Fashion, and Nostalgia." *Critical Inquiry* 21, no. 1 (1994): 37–45.

———. *Blues Legacies and Black Feminism: Gertrude "Ma" Rainey, Bessie Smith, and Billie Holiday*. New York: Random House, 1998.

———. "Marcuse's Legacies." In *Herbert Marcuse: A Critical Reader*, ed. John Abromeit. New York: Routledge, 2004.

———. "Racialized Punishment and Prison Abolition." In *A Companion to African-American Philosophy: Blackwell Companions to Philosophy*, ed. Tommy L. Lott and John P. Pittman. Malden, MA: Blackwell Publishing, 2003.

———. *Women, Culture, and Politics*. New York: Vintage Books, 1990.

———. *Women, Race, and Class*. New York: Random House, 1981.

Delany, Martin. *The Condition, Elevation, Emigration and Destiny of the Colored People of the United States*. Philadelphia: Author, 1852.

Du Bois, W. E. B. "The Conservation of Races" (1897). Reprinted in *African-American Social and Political Thought, 1850–1920*, ed. Howard Brotz. New Jersey: Transaction, 1992.

———, ed. *The Souls of Black Folk*. Chicago: A. C. McClurg, 1903.

Eddins, Berkeley. "Speculative Philosophy of History, A Critical Analysis." *Southern Journal of Philosophy* 6 (1968): 52–58.

Equiano, Olaudah. *The Interesting Narrative of the Life of Olaudah Equiano, or Gustavus Vassa, the African, Written by Himself*, ed. Shelly Eversley. London: Printed for and sold by T. Wilkins et al.; New York: Modern Library, 2004.

Eze, Emmanuel Chukwudi. *Achieving Our Humanity: The Idea of a Postracial Future*. New York: Routledge, 2001.

———, ed. *Postcolonial African Philosophy: A Critical Reader*. Malden, MA: Blackwell, 1997.

———, ed. *African Philosophy: An Anthology*. Malden, MA: Blackwell, 1988.

———, ed. *Race and the Enlightenment*. Malden, MA: Blackwell, 1997.

Frey, Charles A. *From Egypt to Don Juan: The Anatomy of Black Studies*. Lanham, MD: University Press of America, 1988.

———. *Level Three: A Black Philosophy Reader*. Lanham, MD: University Press of America, 1980.

Garcia, J. L. A. "The Heart of Racism." *Journal of Social Philosophy* 27 (1996): 5–47.

Garnet, Henry Highland. "An Address to the Slaves of the United States of America" (1848). In *Walker's Appeal and Garnet's Address: To the Slaves of the United States of America*. Nashville: James C. Winston, 1994.

Gates, Henry Louis, Jr., and Nellie Y. McKay, eds. *The Norton Anthology of African American Literature*. New York: Norton, 2004.

Gordon, Lewis R. "African-American Philosophy: Theory, Politics, and Pedagogy." *Philosophy of Education* (1998): 39–46.

———. *Bad Faith and Antiblack Racism*. Atlantic Highlands, NJ: Humanities Press, 1995.

———. "Critical Reflections on Three Popular Tropes in the Study of Whiteness." In *What White Looks Like: African-American Philosophers on the Whiteness Question*, ed. George Yancy. New York: Routledge, 2004.

———. *Existence in Black: An Anthology of Black Existential Philosophy*. New York: Routledge, 1997.

———. *Existentia Africana: Understanding Africana Existential Thought*. New York: Routledge, 2000.

———. *Fanon and the Crisis of European Man: An Essay on Philosophy and the Human Sciences*. New York: Routledge, 1995.

———. *Her Majesty's Other Children: Sketches of Racism from a Neocolonial Age*. Lanham, MD: Roman & Littlefield, 1997.

———. "Identity and Liberation: An Existential Phenomenological Approach." In *Phenomenology of the Political*, ed. Kevin Thompson. Dordrecht: Kluwer, 2000.

———. "Meta-Ethical and Liberatory Dimensions of Tragedy: A Schutzean Portrait." In *Alfred Schutz's Sociological Aspect of Literature*, ed. Lester Embree. Dordrecht: Kluwer, 1998.

———. *Not Only the Master's Tools: African-American Studies in Theory and Practice*. Boulder, CO: Paradigm, 2006.

Glaude, Eddie. *Exodus: Religion, Race, and Nation in Early Nineteenth-Century Black America*. Chicago: University of Chicago Press, 2000.

Glaude, Eddie, ed. *Is It Nation Time?: Contemporary Essays on Black Power and Black Nationalism*. Chicago: University of Chicago Press, 2002.

Glaude, Eddie, and Cornel West, eds. *African American Religious Thought: An Anthology*. Louisville, KY: Presbyterian Publishing, 2004.

Gooding-Williams, Robert. "Black Neoconservatism: A Critical Introduction." *Praxis International* 7 (1987): 133–42.

———. "Comments on Bernd Magnus's *A Bridge Too Far*: Asceticism and Eternal Recurrence." *Southern Journal of Philosophy* 37 (1999): 113–18.

———. "Egos, Monsters, and Bodies: Response to Shapiro and Conway." *International Studies in Philosophy* 36, no. 3 (2004): 117–25.

———. "Literary Fiction as Philosophy: The Case of Nietzsche's Zarathustra." *Journal of Philosophy* 83 (1986): 667–75.

———. "Politics, Racial Solidarity, Exodus!" *Journal of Speculative Philosophy* 18, no. 2 (2004): 118–28.

———. "Race, Multiculturalism and Democracy." *Constellations* 5, no. 1 (1998): 18–41.

———. "Zarathustra contra Zarathustra." *International Studies in Philosophy* 35, no. 4 (1998).

———. "Zarathustra's Dionysian Modernism." *International Studies in Philosophy* 36, no. 4 (2001).

Harris, Joseph, ed. *Africa and Africans as Seen by Classical Writers: African History Notebook*. Vol. 2. Washington, DC: Howard University Press, 1981.

Harris, Leonard. "Alain L. Locke, 1885–1954," in *The Blackwell Guide to American Philosophy*, ed. Armen T. Marsoobian. Malden, MA: Blackwell Publishing, 2000.

———. "The Great Debate: W. E. B. DuBois vs. Alain Locke on the Aesthetic." *Philosophia Africana: Analysis of Philosophy and Issues in Africa and the Black Diaspora* 7, no. 1 (2004): 15–39.

———. "The Harlem Renaissance and Philosophy." In *A Companion to African-American Philosophy: Blackwell Companions to Philosophy*, ed. Tommy L. Lott and John P. Pittman. Malden, MA: Blackwell Publishing, 2003.

———. "The Philosophy of Alain Locke." *Ethics* 101, no. 1 (1990).

———. "Pragmatism and the Problem of Race." *Transactions of the Charles S. Peirce Society* 41, no. 2 (2005).

———. "Racism: Key Concepts in Critical Theory." *Continental Philosophy Review* 35, no. 1 (2002).

Harris, Leonard, ed. *American Philosophies: An Anthology*. Malden, MA: Blackwell Publishing, 2001.

———. *The Critical Pragmatism of Alain Locke*. Lanham, MD: Roman & Littlefield, 1999.

———. *Philosophy Born of Struggle: Anthology of Afro-American Philosophy from 1917*. Dubuque, IA: Kendall/Hunt, 1983.

Hegel, Georg Wilhelm Friedrich. *The Philosophy of History*. New York: Dover, 1956.

Henry, Paget. "African-American Philosophy: A Caribbean Perspective." In *A Companion to African-American Philosophy: Blackwell Companions to Philosophy*, ed. Tommy L. Lott and John P. Pittman. Malden, MA: Blackwell Publishing, 2003.

———. "Between Hume and Cugoano: Race, Ethnicity and Philosophical Entrapment." *Journal of Speculative Philosophy* 18, no. 2 (2004): 129–44.

———. *Caliban's Reason: Introducing Afro-Caribbean Philosophy*. New York: Routledge, 2000.

———. "Myth, Language, and Habermasian Rationality: Another Africana Contribution." In *Perspectives on Habermas*, ed. Lewis Edwin Hahn. New York: Open Court, 2000.

———. "Rastafarianism and the Reality of Dread." In *Existence in Black: An Anthology of Black Existential Philosophy*, ed. Lewis R. Gordon. New York: Routledge, 1997.

———. "Whiteness and Africana Phenomenology." In *What White Looks Like: African-American Philosophers on the Whiteness Question*, ed. George Yancy. New York: Routledge, 2004.

Hord, Fred Lee, et al., eds. *I Am Because We Are: Readings in Black Philosophy*, Amherst: University of Massachusetts Press, 1995.

Hume, David. "Of National Characters." In *The Philosophical Works of David Hume*, vol. 3. Boston: Little, Brown, 1854.

James, Joy. "The Academic Addict: Mainlining (& Kicking) White Supremacy (WS)." In *What White Looks Like: African-American Philosophers on the Whiteness Question*, ed. George Yancy. New York: Routledge, 2004.

———. "Black Feminism: Liberation Limbos and Existence in Gray." In *Existence in Black: An Anthology of Black Existential Philosophy*, ed. Lewis R. Gordon. New York: Routledge, 1997.

————. *The New Abolitionists: (Neo)slave Narratives and Contemporary Prison Writings.* Albany: State University of New York Press, 2005.

————. "Radicalizing Feminism from 'The Movement Era.'" In *A Companion to African-American Philosophy: Blackwell Companions to Philosophy,* ed. Tommy L. Lott and John P. Pittman. Malden, MA: Blackwell Publishing, 2003.

————. *Shadowboxing: Representations of Black Feminist Politics.* New York: St. Martin's Press, 1999.

————. *Transcending the Talented Tenth.* New York: Routledge, 1997.

Johnson, Charles. *Being and Race: Black Writing Since 1970.* Bloomington: Indiana University Press, 1988.

Johnson, Clarence Sholé. "An Analysis of John Mbiti's Treatment of the Concept of Event in African Ontologies." *Quest: Philosophical Discussions* 9, no. 2 (1996): 139–57.

————. *Cornel West and Philosophy: The Quest for Social Justice.* New York: Routledge, 2003.

————. "Hume on Character, Action, and Causal Necessity." *Auslegung: A Journal of Philosophy* 16, no. 2 (1990): 149–64.

————. "Paulin Hountondji, African Philosophy, and Philosophical Methodology." *Southern Journal of Philosophy* 36, no. 2 (1998): 179–95.

————. "(Re)Conceptualizing Blackness and Making Race Obsolescent." In *White on White/Black on Black,* ed. George Yancy. Lanham, MD: Rowman and Littlefield, 2005.

————. "Teaching the Canons of Western Philosophy in Historically Black Colleges and Universities: The Spelman College Experience." *Metaphilosophy* 26, no. 4 (1995): 413–23.

————. "Yet Another Look at Cognitive Reason and Moral Action in Hume's Ethical System." *Journal of Philosophical Research* 17 (1992): 225–38.

Johnston, Percy E., ed. *Afro-American Philosophies: Selected Readings from Jupiter Hammon to Eugene C. Holmes.* Upper Montclair, NJ: Montclair State College Press, 1970.

Jones, William R. "Functional Ultimacy as Authority in Religious Humanism." *Religious Humanism* 12 (1978): 28–32.

————. *Is God a White Racist?* Rev. ed. Boston: Beacon Press, 1997.

————. "The Legitimacy and Necessity of Black Philosophy: Some Preliminary Considerations." *Philosophical Forum* 9 (1978): 149–60.

Kant, Immanuel. *Observations on the Feeling of the Beautiful and Sublime* (1764). Trans. John T. Goldthwait. Berkeley: University of California Press, 1960.

Keita, Lancinay. "Rationality and Social Choice: The Fallacy of the Arrow Paradox." *Second Order* 6 (1977): 75–89.

Kirkland, Frank M. "Gadamer and Ricoeur: The Paradigm of the Text." *Graduate Faculty Philosophy Journal* 6 (1977): 131–44.

————. "Hegel's Critique of Psychologism." In *Phenomenology: East and West: Essays in Honor of J. N. Mohanty,* ed. Frank M. Kirkland. Dordrecht: Kluwer, 1993.

———. "Husserl and Hegel: A Historical and Religious Encounter." *Journal of the British Society for Phenomenology* 16 (1985): 70–87.

———. "Modernisms in Black." In *A Companion to African-American Philosophy: Blackwell Companions to Philosophy*, ed. Tommy L. Lott and John P. Pittman. Malden, MA: Blackwell Publishing, 2003.

———. "The Problem of the Color Line: Normative or Empirical, Evolving or Non-Evolving." *Philosophia Africana: Analysis of Philosophy and Issues in Africa and the Black Diaspora* 7, no. 1 (2004): 57–82.

Lawson, Bill E. "Booker T. Washington: A Pragmatist at Work." In *Pragmatism and the Problem of Race*, ed. Bill E. Lawson and Donald F. Koch. Bloomington: Indiana University Press, 2004.

———. "Locke and the Legal Obligations of Black Americans." *Public Affairs Quarterly* 3 (1989): 49–63.

———. "Microphone Commandos: Rap Music and Political Ideology." In *A Companion to African-American Philosophy: Blackwell Companions to Philosophy*, ed. Tommy L. Lott and John P. Pittman. Malden, MA: Blackwell Publishing, 2003.

———. "Property of Persons: On a Plain Reading of the United States Constitution." *Journal of Ethics* 1, no. 3 (1997): 291–303.

Lawson, Bill E., ed. *The Underclass Question*, Philadelphia: Temple University Press, 1992.

Lawson, Bill E., and Kirkland, Frank, eds. *Frederick Douglass: A Critical Reader*. Malden, MA: Blackwell Publishing, 1999.

Lawson, Bill E., and McGary, Howard, eds. *Between Slavery and Freedom: Philosophy and American Slavery*. Bloomington: Indiana University Press, 1992.

Lott, Tommy Lee. "Aesthetics and Politics in Contemporary Black Film Theory." In *Film Theory and Philosophy*, ed. Richard C. Allen. New York: Clarendon Press, 1997.

———. "African Retentions." In *A Companion to African-American Philosophy: Blackwell Companions to Philosophy*, ed. Tommy L. Lott and John P. Pittman. Malden, MA: Blackwell Publishing, 2003.

———. "Ascombe on Justifying Claims to Know One's Bodily Position." *Philosophical Investigations* 12 (1989): 293–307.

———. *The Invention of Race: Black Culture and the Politics of Representation*. Malden, MA: Blackwell Publishing, 1999.

———. "Motivation and Egoism in Hobbes." *Kinesis: Graduate Journal in Philosophy* 6 (1974): 112–25.

———. "Nationalism and Pluralism in Alain Locke's Social Philosophy." In *Defending Diversity*, ed. Lawrence Foster. Amherst: University of Massachusetts Press, 1994.

———. "Subjugation and Bondage: Critical Essays on Slavery and Social Philosophy." *Teaching Philosophy* 22, no. 4 (1999).

Lott, Tommy L., and Bernasconi, Robert, eds. *The Idea of Race*. Indianapolis, IN: Hackett, 2000.

Lott, Tommy Lee, and Pittman, John P., eds. *A Companion to African-American Philosophy: Blackwell Companions to Philosophy*. Malden, MA: Blackwell Publishing, 2003.

McGary, Howard, and Bill E. Lawson, eds. *Between Slavery and Freedom: Philosophy and American Slavery*. Bloomington: Indiana University Press, 1992.

McGary, Howard. "Achieving Democratic Equality: Forgiveness, Reconciliation, and Reparations." *Journal of Ethics* 7, no. 1 (2003): 93–113.

———. "Forgiveness." *American Philosophical Quarterly* 26 (1989): 343–51.

———. "Morality and Collective Liability." *Journal of Value Inquiry* 20 (1986): 157–65.

———. "The New Conservatism and the Critique of Equity Planning." *Philosophy and Geography* 7, no. 1 (2004): 79–93.

———. "On Violence in the Struggle for Liberation." In *Existence in Black: An Anthology of Black Existential Philosophy*, ed. Lewis R. Gordon. New York: Routledge, 1997.

———. *Race and Social Justice*. Oxford: Blackwell Publishing, 1999.

———. "South Africa: The Morality of Divestment." *Philosophical Forum* 18 (1987): 203–12.

Meier, August. *Negro Thought in America, 1880–1915*. Ann Arbor: University of Michigan Press, 196

Menkiti, Ifeanyi. "On the Normative Conception of a Person." In *A Companion to African Philosophy: Blackwell Companions to Philosophy*, ed. Kwasi Wiredu. Malden, MA: Blackwell Publishing, 2004.

———. "Person and Community in African Traditional Thought." In *African Philosophy: An Introduction*, ed. Richard A. Wright. Washington, DC: University Press of America, 1979.

Mills, Charles W. *Blackness Visible: Essays on Philosophy and Race*. Ithaca, NY: Cornell University Press, 1998.

———. "Do Black Men Have a Moral Duty to Marry Black Women?" *Journal of Social Philosophy* 25 (June 1994): 131–53.

———. *From Class to Race: Essays in White Marxism and Black Radicalism*. Lanham, MD: Roman & Littlefield, 2003.

———. "Ideal Theory as Ideology." *Hypatia: A Journal of Feminist Philosophy* 20, no. 3 (2005): 165–84.

———. "Non-Cartesian Sums: Philosophy and the African-American Experience." *Teaching Philosophy* 17 (September 1994): 223–43.

———. *The Racial Contract*. Ithaca, NY: Cornell University Press, 1999.

———. "Under Class Under Standings." *Ethics* 104 (July 1994): 855–81.

Moody-Adams, Michelle M. *Fieldwork in Familiar Places: Morality, Culture, and Philosophy*. Cambridge: Harvard University Press, 1997.

———. "Gender and the Complexity of Moral Voices." In *Feminist Social Thought*, ed. Diana Meyers. New York: Routledge, 1997.

———. "Race, Class, and the Social Construction of Self-Respect." In *African-American Perspectives and Philosophical Traditions*, ed. John P. Pittman. New York: Routledge, 1997.

Mosley, Albert. "A Defense of Affirmative Action." In *Contemporary Debates in Applied Ethics*, ed. Andrew Cohen. Malden, MA: Blackwell Publishing, 2005.

———. "Music in the Black Atlantic." *Philosophia Africana: Analysis of Philosophy and Issues in Africa and the Black Diaspora* 6, no. 1 (2003): 23–30.

———. "Negritude, Nationalism, and Nativism: Racists or Racialists?" In *African Philosophy: Selected Readings*, ed. Kwame Anthony Appiah. Englewood Cliffs, NJ: Prentice Hall, 1995.

———. "On the Aesthetics of Black Music." *Journal of Aesthetic Education* 35, no. 3 (2001): 94–98.

———. "Preferential Treatment and Social Justice." In *Terrorism, Justice and Social Values. Social Philosophy Today*, vol. 4. Lewiston, ME: Mellen Press, 1990.

———. "Witchcraft, Science, and the Paranormal in Contemporary African Philosophy." In *African Philosophy: New and Traditional Perspectives*, ed. Lee Brown. Oxford: Oxford University Press, 2004.

———. "Witchcraft, Science, and the Skeptical Inquirer: Conversations with the Late Prof. Peter Bodunrin." *Philosophical Papers* 30, no. 3 (2001): 289–306.

Mudimbe, V. Y. *The Surreptitious Speech: Préseance Africaine and the Politics of Otherness, 1947–1987*. Chicago: University of Chicago Press, 1992.

Mudimbe, V. Y. "African Philosophy as an Ideological Practice: The Case of French-Speaking Africa." *African Studies Review* 26 (September-December 1983): 133–54.

———. *The Idea of Africa*. Bloomington: Indiana University Press, 1994.

———. *The Invention of Africa: Gnosis, Philosophy and the Order of Knowledge*. Bloomington: Indiana University Press, 1988.

Mudimbe, V. Y., ed. *Nations, Identities, Cultures*. Durham, NC: Duke University Press, 1997.

Mutiso, Gideon-Cyrus M., and S. W. Rohio, eds. *Readings in African Political Thought*. London: Heinemann, 1975.

Outlaw, Lucius T., Jr. *Critical Social Theory in the Interests of Black Folks*. Lanham, MD: Rowman & Littlefield, 2005.

———. *On Race and Philosophy*. New York: Routledge, 1996.

Patterson, Orlando. *Slavery and Social Death: A Comparative Study*. Cambridge: Harvard University Press, 1982.

"Philosophy and Black Experience." *Philosophical Forum* 9 (Winter-Spring 1977–1978). Special issue.

Pinkney, Alphonso. *Red, Black, and Green: Black Nationalism in the United States*. Cambridge: Cambridge University Press, 1976.

Piper, Adrian. "Critical Hegemony and Aesthetic Acculturation." *Nous* 19 (1985): 29–40.

———. "Hume on Rational Final Ends," *Philosophy Research Archives* 14 (1989): 193–228.

———. "Making Sense of Value." *Ethics* 106, no. 3 (1996): 525–37.

———. "Moral Theory and Moral Alienation." *Journal of Philosophy* 84 (1986): 102–18.

———. "Passing for White, Passing for Black." *Transition* 58 (1992): 4–32.

———. "Personal Continuity and Instrumental Ratinality in Rawls' Theory of Justice." *Social Theory and Practice* 13 (1987): 49–76.

———. "Seeing Things." *Southern Journal of Philosophy* 29 (1990): 29–60.

———. "The Triple Negation of Colored Women Artists." In *Feminism-Art-Theory: An Anthology*, ed. Hilary Robinson. Malden, MA: Blackwell Publishing, 2001.

Pittman, John P. "Punishment and Race." *Utilitas: A Journal of Utilitarian Studies* 9, no. 1 (1997): 115–30.

———. "'Radical Historicism,' Antiphilosophy, and Marxism." In *Cornel West: A Critical Reader*, ed. George Yancy. Oxford: Blackwell, 2001.

———. "Response: Rortyan Policing?" In *Handled with Discretion: Ethical Issues in Police Decision Making*, ed. John Kleinig. Lanham, MD: Rowman & Littlefield, 1996.

Pittman, John, ed. *African-American Perspectives and Philosophical Traditions*. New York: Routledge, 1997.

Pittman, John P., and Tommy L. Lott. *A Companion to African-American Philosophy*. Malden, MA: Blackwell, 2003.

Radford-Curry, Blanche. "On the Social Construction of a Women's and Gender Studies Major." In *Gender and Academe: Feminist Pedagogy and Politics*, ed. Sara Munson Deats and Lagretta Tallent Lenker. Lanham, MD: Rowman & Littlefield, 1994.

Radford-Curry, Blanche, Helen Bannan, Nancy Greeman, and Ellen Kimmel. "Institutional Inertia to Achieving Diversity: Transforming Resistance into Celebration." *Educational Foundations* vol. 6 no. 2, pp 89–111, (Spring 1992).

Radford-Curry, Blanche, Nancy Greenman, and Ellen Kimmel. "Choosing Change." *American Philosophical Association's Newsletter on the Black Experience*, Spring 1992.

Scott, Jacqueline. "Nietzsche and Decadence: The Revaluation of Morality." *Continential Philosophy Review* 31, no. 1 (1998): 59–78.

———. "Nietzsche and the Problem of Women's Bodies." *International Studies in Philosophy* 31, no. 3 (1999): 65–75.

———. "On the Use and Abuse of Race in Philosophy: Nietzsche, Jews, and Race." In *Race and Racism in Continental Philosophy*, ed. Robert Bernasconi. Bloomington: Indiana University Press, 2003.

Senghor, Léopold Sédar. *Nationhood and the African Road to Socialism*. Trans. Mercer Cook. Paris: Présence Africaine, 1962.

Serequeberhan, Tsenay. *The Hermeneutics of African Philosophy: Horizon and Discourse*. New York: Routledge, 1994.

———. *Our Heritage: The Past and the Present of African-American and African Existence*. Lanham, MD: Roman & Littlefield, 2000.

Serequeberhan, Tsenay, ed. *African Philosophy: The Essential Readings*. New York: Paragon House, 2000.

Shelton, La Verne. "A Diachronic Semantics for Inexact Reference." *Notre Dame Journal of Formal Logic* 24 (1983): 67–88.

———. "On the Ramification of Inexactness." *Philosophy Research Archives* 9 (1983): 347–68.

Snowden, Frank M., Jr. *Blacks in Antiquity*. Cambridge, MA: Belknap Press, 1970.

Stewart, Maria. "Religion and the Pure Principles of Morality, the Sure Foundation on which We Must Build." Boston: Garrison & Knapp, 1831.

Sundstrom, Ronald R. "Being and Being Mixed-Race." *Social Theory and Practice* 27 (2001): 285–307.

———. "Race as a Human Kind." *Philosophy and Social Criticism* 28 (2002): 91–115.

Taylor, Paul C. "Appiah's Uncompleted Argument: W. E. B. Du Bois and the Reality of Race." *Social Theory and Practice* 26, no. 1 (2001): 103–28.

———. "Intuitionistic Sets and Ordinals." *Journal of Symbolic Logic* 61, no. 3 (1996): 705–44.

———. "Malcolm's Conk and Danto's Colors; or, Four Logical Petitions Concerning Race, Beauty, and Aesthetics." *Journal of Aesthetics and Art Criticism* 57, no. 1 (1999): 16–20.

———. "Pragmatism and Race." In *Pragmatism and the Problem of Race*, ed. Bill E. Lawson. Bloomington: Indiana University Press, 2004.

———. *Race: A Philosophical Introduction*. Cambridge: Polity Press, 2003.

———. "Silence and Sympathy." In *What White Looks Like: African-American Philosophers on the Whiteness Question*, ed. George Yancy. New York: Routledge, 2004.

———. "Three Questions about Race, Racism, and Reparations." *Journal of Social Philosophy* 36, no. 4 (2005): 559–67.

———. "What's the Use of Calling Du Bois a Pragmatist?" *Metaphilosophy* 35, nos. 1–2 (2004): 99–114.

Truth, Sojourner. *Ar'n't I a Woman*, speech given at the National Women's Convention, Akron, Ohio, 1851. Reprinted in *The Norton Anthology of African American Literature*, ed. Henry Louis Gates Jr. and Nellie Y. McKay. New York: Norton, 2004.

Thomas, Laurence. "Becoming an Evil Society: The Self and Strangers," *Political Theory* 24, no. 2 (1996): 271–94.

———. *The Family and the Political Self*. Cambridge/New York: Cambridge University Press, 2006.

———. "Forgiving the Unforgivable?" In *Moral Philosophy and the Holocaust*, ed. Eve Garrard. Aldershot: Ashgate Publishing, 2003.

———. "Moral Equality and Natural Inferiority." *Social Theory and Practice* 31, no. 3 (2005): 379–404.

———. "Moral Flourishing in an Unjust World." *Journal of Moral Education* 22, no. 2 (1993): 83–96.

―――. "Moral Psychology." In *The Blackwell Guide to Ethical Theory*, ed. Hugh LaFollette. Cambridge: Blackwell, 2000.

―――. "The Moral Self in the Face of Injustice." In *Social and Political Philosophy: Contemporary Perspectives*, ed. James P. Sterba. New York: Routledge, 2001.

―――. "Morality and a Meaningful Life." *Philosophical Papers* 34, no. 3 (2005): 405–27.

―――. "Morality and Human Diversity." *Ethics* 103, no. 1 (1992): 117–34.

―――. "Self-Respect, Fairness, and Living Morally." In *A Companion to African-American Philosophy: Blackwell Companions to Philosophy*, ed. Tommy L. Lott and John P. Pittman. Malden, MA: Blackwell Publishing, 2003.

―――. "Sexism and Racism: Some Conceptual Differences." *Ethics* 90 (1980): 239–50.

―――. "Sexual Desire, Moral Choice, and Human Ends." *Journal of Social Philosophy* 33, no. 2 (2002): 178–92.

Wells-Barnett, Ida B. *A Red Record: Tabulated Statistics and Alleged Causes of Lynchings in the United States, 1892–1893–1894*. Chicago: Donohue & Henneberry, 1894.

West, Cornel. "Afterward: Philosophy and the Funk of Life." In *Cornel West: A Critical Reader*, ed. George Yancy. Oxford: Blackwell Publishers, 2001.

―――. *The American Evasion of Philosophy: A Genealogy of Pragmatism*. Madison: University of Wisconsin Press, 1989.

―――. *Democracy Matters*. London: Penguin Books, 2004.

―――. "Keeping Faith." *Ethics* 105, no. 4 (1995).

―――. *Keeping Faith: Philosophy and Race in America*. New York: Routledge, 1993.

―――. *Marxist Theory and the Specificity of Afro-American Oppression*. Urbana: University of Illinois Press, 1988.

―――. "Philosophy and the Afro-American Experience," in *A Companion to African-American Philosophy: Blackwell Companions to Philosophy*, ed. John P. Pittman and Tommy L. Lott. Malden, MA: Blackwell Publishing, 2003.

―――. *Prophesy Deliverance: An Afro-American Revolutionary Christianity*. Louisville, KY: Westminster John Knox Press, 1982.

―――. *Prophetic Fragments: Illuminations of the Crisis in American Religion and Culture*, Grand Rapids, MI: William B. Eerdmans, 1988.

―――. *Race Matters*. Boston: Beacon Press, 1993.

West, Cornel and Sealy, Kevin Shawn, ed. *Restoring Hope: Conversations on the Future of Black America*. Boston: Beacon Press, 1997.

Wheatley, Phillis. "To the University of Cambridge, in England" and "On Imagination," in her *Poems on Various Subjects, Religious and Moral*. London: Printed for A. Bell, bookseller, Aldgate; and sold by Messrs. Cox and Berry, King-street, Boston, 1773.

Wiredu, Kwasi. *Philosophy and an African Culture*. Cambridge: Cambridge University Press, 1980.

Wright, Richard A., ed. *African Philosophy: An Introduction*. Lanham, MD: University Press of America, 1984.

Yancy, George. "Black Women's Experiences, Philosophy of Religion and Womanist Theology: An Introduction through Jacquelyn Grant's Hermeneutics of Location." *American Philosophical Association Newsletter on Philosophy and the Black Experience* 2, no. 1 (Fall 2002): 56–65.

———. "In the Spirit of the A.M.E. Church: Gilbert Haven Jones as an Early Black Philosopher and Educator." *A.M.E. Church Review* 118, no. 388 (2002): 43–57. Reprinted in *American Philosophical Association Newsletter on Philosophy and the Black Experience* 2, no. 2 (Spring 2003): 42–48.

———. "Thomas Nelson Baker: The First African-American to Receive the Ph.D. in Philosophy." *Western Journal of Black Studies* 21, no. 4 (1997): 253–60.

———. "Whiteness and the Return of the Black Body." *Journal of Speculative Philosophy* 19, no. 4 (2005): 215–41.

Yancy, George, ed. *African-American Philosophy: 17 Conversations.* New York: Routledge, 1999.

———. *Cornel West: A Critical Reader.* Malden, MA: Blackwell Publishers, 2001.

———. *The Philosophical I: Personal Reflections on Life in Philosophy.* Lanham, MD: Rowman & Littlefield, 2002.

———. *What White Looks Like: African-American Philosophers on the Whiteness Question.* New York: Taylor & Francis/Routledge, 2004.

———. *White on White/Black on Black.* Lanham, MD: Rowman & Littlefield, 2005.

Zack, Naomi. *Bachelors of Science: Seventeenth Century Identity, Then and Now.* Philadelphia: Temple University Press, 1996.

———. "Philosophy and Racial Paradigms." In *A Companion to African-American Philosophy: Blackwell Companions to Philosophy,* ed. John P. Pittman and Tommy L. Lott. Malden, MA: Blackwell Publishing, 2003.

———. *Philosophy of Science and Race.* New York: Taylor & Francis, 2002.

———. *Race and Mixed Race.* Philadelphia: Temple University Press, 1994.

———. "Reparations and the Rectification of Race." *Journal of Ethics* 7, no. 1 (2003): 139–51.

———. *Thinking about Race,* 2nd ed. Belmont, CA: Thomson Wadsworth, 2006.

———. "Women of Color and Philosophy." *Hypatia: A Journal of Feminist Philosophy* 20, no. 1 (2005).

What Is Afro-Caribbean Philosophy?* 5

LEWIS R. GORDON
Temple University

AFRO-CARIBBEAN philosophy is a subset of Africana philosophy and Caribbean philosophy. By Africana philosophy, I mean the set of philosophical reflections that emerged by and through engagement with the African diaspora, and by Caribbean philosophy, I mean both philosophy from the region and philosophies about the unique problems of theorizing Caribbean reality. The latter could also be characterized as the discourse on the convergence of reason and the New World.

The etymology of the word "Caribbean" points to the Caribs, a group of Native peoples, in addition to the earlier-arrived Taínos or Arawaks, among others, living in the region at the time of Columbus's landing. The term "cannibal," by the way, also has its roots in Carib, and the name "Caliban," which refers to the villain in Shakespeare's *Tempest*, is also a variation of the word Carib. "Taínos" and "Arawaks" were not the names of the earlier people; those names were ascribed to them by European archaeologists in the first half of the twentieth century. As we will see, the etymology of cannibal betrays the colonial logic that rationalizes much that happened in the region, and that logic contextualizes the philosophy there as well.

Afro-Caribbean philosophy is a form of philosophy rooted in the modern world and that takes the question of modernity as one of its central concerns. It is modern because the Caribbean itself is a modern creation. Although the indigenous people preceded that creation, its convergence

---

*Special thanks to Jane Anna Gordon and Paget Henry for comments on an early draft of this chapter.

with the African diaspora, marked by the consequences both of exploration and slavery, is indigenous to the modern world.

Afro-Caribbean philosophy, then, consists of the philosophical meditations on the question of African presence in the Caribbean and the modern questions of blackness raised by that presence. The latter, however, raise additional questions since "blackness" is, as Frantz Fanon points out near the end of his introduction in *Black Skin, White Masks*, "a white construction" (p. 14). By this, he means that the people who have become known as black people are descendants of people who had no reason to regard themselves as such. As a consequence, the history of black people has the constant motif of such people *encountering* their blackness from the "outside," as it were, and then developing, in dialectical fashion, a form of blackness that transcends the initial, negative series of events. Again, paraphrasing Fanon, this time from *A Dying Colonialism*, it may have been whites who created the concept of the Negro, but it was the Negro who created the concept of negritude.

Although other groups have been yoked to the categories of Negro and blackness in the modern world in such places as Australia and the Polynesian islands, it is the descendants of the people kidnapped and enslaved from the coasts of the Atlantic and along the Arabic and East Indian trade routes who are most commonly linked to those terms. Thus, when Las Casas, the famed priest who sought salvation for the indigenous peoples of the Americas and to ward off their impending genocide through recommending the enslavement of West Africans, began his reflections on the New World predicament, the categories were already being formed as those inherited by generations into the present. It should be borne in mind, however, that these early formulations did not necessarily refer to the crystallized, reductive notions of blackness that dominated racial consciousness into the nineteenth and twentieth centuries. After all, the early, founding moments were also those of a complex war of hybrid populations. In January 1492, for instance, Ferdinand II of Aragon and Isabella I of Castile had managed to drive the Moors, who had ruled the region for nearly eight hundred years, out of the Iberian Peninsula, but that achievement was not regarded as the end of that war of several hundred years, and the expectation of its continuation meant that the Age of Exploration was also the continuation of, in the minds of the Spaniards and the Portuguese, their war against *their* former colonizers. Ironically, then, modern colonialism was founded on a particular kind of *anticolonialism*—namely, against the colonization of Christians, which was later qualified as against Europeans, who were presumed to be only Christians. This fact is no doubt a lesson that many efforts at decolonization in the twentieth century did not learn from the past. Crucial, then, is for us to understand that there is a history of the formation of modern blackness that is missing in contemporary discussions. The Muslim, Jewish, as well as Berber, Arabic, and other North African dimensions of the societies that became known as Portugal, Spain, and even Italy should be understood in the collisions they had with the indigenous peoples of the Americas. That hybrid population in the midst of war in the Mediterranean came to the New World expecting to meet a mediating Arab community that stood between them and India, and that misunderstanding forged a philosophical anthropology marked as much by orthodoxy and infidels as by expectations of meeting friends and foe in the dynamics of war. Such expectations and fears guided as well the Age of Exploration from the Mediterranean along the costs of Africa, a continent about which, given the demographics of the Mediterranean communities, they knew a bit more than is presented in historical narratives that lay claim to ignorant travelers. That so much of central Africa was located along trade routes that extended to the eastern coasts of the continent meant that at least various forms of Arabic—in addition to the creolized languages they used for trade, such as, eventually Swahili—stood as the lingua franca between groups of indigenous peoples.

Caribbean philosophy, then, was already being formed by the reflections of these early encounters of so many divergent communities, and in its core it was as it had to have been: a reflection on humanity through a robust realization of human difference and similarity—in short, philosophical anthropology. The profound divisions that occurred over time between the various groups, however, led to a phenomenon of denied interiority to the subjugated populations, to the point of there being a single narrative of reality as the perspective of domination. In effect, indigenous and black perspectives suffered the loss of their ability to appear.

The "reappearance" of black reality in the New World, in the form of resistance in the face of near-overwhelming white encirclement, was the Haitian Revolution of the late eighteenth into the early nineteenth century, through which perhaps the greatest intellectual effort to articulate the humanity and dignity of black people in the nineteenth century emerged in 1885 in Anténor Firmin's *The Equality of the Human Races*. Firmin was born in Haiti during the forty-sixth year of its independence. His life in many ways brings to the fore the side of the Haitian Revolution that is not often written about in the constant stream of denunciations of its history: There was much innovation as the former slaves experimented and attempted to build what they knew was a beacon of hope for enslaved people worldwide.

Firmin's entire education was in Haiti. He studied at the Lycée National du Cap-Haitien and the Lycée Pétion in Port-au-Prince. He chose law as his profession and became a successful politician, which took him to Paris in 1883 as a diplomat. He was invited to join the Anthropology Society in Paris in 1884, where he was appalled at the racist anthropological theories espoused by his colleagues in the face of his presence as their clear contradiction. Although more serious in their methodological approaches than the extremely popular Count Arthur de Gobineau's *Essai sur L'Inégalité des Races Humaines* (*Essay on the Inequality of Human Races*, 1853–1855), their conclusions revealed clear convergence with that racist diatribe—the supposed superiority of the Aryan race; the innate inferiority of the Negro; the search for a polygenic account of the emergence of different races, in effect, a collapse of race into species differentiation; and more. De Gobineau's text was translated into several other European languages, which included five editions in German, and it is included in the Oxford Library of French Classics. The influence of de Gobineau's work brings home one of the features of modern civilization that is the brunt of much criticism in Afro-Caribbean and the wider Africana philosophy: Influence in the white world is not a function of being correct, truthful, or excellent; it is a world, unfortunately, that asserts its superiority through the luxury of rewarded mediocrity.

The logic of the situation begged as many questions as it was supposed to answer. The presence of Firmin as a member of the Anthropology Society should have contradicted the thesis of black inferiority, but he was rationalized into the logic of exceptionalism, where he achieved as an exception to the rule but would fail as an instance of it. Firmin's response was to write his own account of race in direct response to de Gobineau. The result was *The Equality of the Human Races*. The scale of Firmin's achievement in that work, and its near absence of notoriety save for specialists in the Afro-Francophone world, is perhaps one of the great travesties of the impact of racism on the history of ideas. Nearly every contemporary debate in race theory and Africana philosophy is touched upon in an insightful way in that great work of more than a century past. Firmin returned to Haiti in 1888, where he eventually became foreign minister in 1891, during which he successfully prevented the United States from acquiring the Môle of St. Nicolas, the deep-sea harbor in which Columbus first entered the island. The incident led to the American ambassador, Frederick Douglass, who had not trusted his white American colleagues because of the humiliations he suffered from their ignoring the significance of his position, to be relieved from his post, and Firmin was held in ill repute for agreeing to negotiate with the United States in the first place. He was made minister of Paris in 1900, the year in which he attended the First Pan-African Congress in London as ex-*président légitime* of Haiti, but was drawn into conflict with Haiti in what became known as the Firmin Insurgency of 1902, which led to his seeking exile in the island of St. Thomas. He continued writing on social and political matters, especially Pan-Africanism and Pan-Caribbean politics, before dying shortly after attempting to secure his presidential leadership of Haiti in a 1911 insurrection.

This synopsis of Firmin's life reveals much irony, for his political thought located him in the tradition of black republicanism, exemplified by commitment to a domination-free society governed by nonarbitrary laws, as this quotation attests:

> The wish I formulate for the people of my race, wherever they may live and govern themselves in the world, is that they turn away from any thing that smacks of arbitrary practices, of systematic contempt for the law and for freedom, and of disdain of legal procedures and distributive justice. Law, justice, and freedom are eminently respectable values, for they form the crowning structure of the moral edifice which modern civilization has been laboriously and gloriously building on the accumulated ruins of the ideas of the Middle Ages.[1]

Although Firmin wrote *The Equality of the Human Races* as a scientist and defended what he called a "positivist" conception of science, which he claimed was in the spirit of August Comte (1798–1857), his achievement in the text is also a magnificent example of philosophical anthropology and philosophy of human science. There is not enough space here to provide a detailed account of his thought, but an illustration by way of his critique of Kant should provide an indication of his importance to philosophy. He begins with a reflection on method. One cannot study the human being as one would ordinary natural objects, he argues, because the human being is a contradictory subject. "Man can lower himself to the lowest depths of ignorance and complacently wallow in the muddy swamps of vice, yet he can also rise to the resplendent heights of truth, goodness, and beauty."[2] Philosophers and scientists have attempted to resolve these contradictions by splitting the human subject into either an overly formalized idealism or a reductive naturalism. To illustrate his point, Firmin argues that Kant's moral philosophy illuminates his anthropology more than his *Pragmatica Anthropology*. In the former, Kant separates morality from what he calls moral anthropology, where the former is rational and the latter is simply empirical. This division leads to Kant using the term "anthropology" in a way that is very different from the scientists of his day, who regarded it as the natural study of the human being. Kant regarded their work as properly "physical geography," and his theory of human difference is, in many ways, a geographical theory of intelligence. Hegel, Firmin argues, is an heir to Kant in this regard, since he, too, sees race ultimately as geographical. In effect, Kant and Hegel were engaged in a form of geographical idealism.

Yet as the scientists criticized the philosophers for their idealism, they failed to see the errors of their naturalistic reductionism. The scientists of the eighteenth century simply presupposed that the human being could be studied in the same manner as plants, other animals, and other natural phenomena. What is missing in their analysis, Firmin argues, is an understanding of the implications of social life. Natural history must give way, then, to a form of unnatural history since the human being makes his or her own history. The human being, as Firmin proposes, emerges in a human world, which leads to anthropology as "the study of Man in his physical, intellectual, and moral dimensions, as he is found among the different races which constitute the human species."[3] Although Firmin refers to the "different races," it is important to notice that he added "which constitute the human species." His criticism of his colleagues is that they sought, in their effort to articulate a great distance between the Caucasian and Negro, to advance a theory of species differentiation instead of racial differentiation. Racial differentiation could only make sense for members of the same species. To advance his case, Firmin took on many of the racist claims propagated by mainstream naturalists of his day, such as those against race mixing. The fertility of mixed-race offspring dispels the notion of species difference. As well, the claims of polygenesis—that whites and blacks evolved from completely different animal ancestors—is a variation of the species difference argument, which is not only proven wrong by racial mixture but also by the fact that contemporary versions of each group are manifestations of even older mixtures. Here, Firmin's argument precedes much of what was found in critical race theory by the last quarter of the twentieth century.

What should also be noticed is that although Firmin allied himself with the positivist science of his day, his thought clearly transcends positivist reductionism. For instance, he focused on the historical question of classification not in terms of individuals, although he offers analyses of their thought, but in terms of *systems of knowledge*. He understood, and was in fact explicit, about the limits involved in constructing an anthropology and of how the orders of knowledge of the nineteenth century were in fact constructing the very subject they had set out to study. Readers familiar with the thought of Michel Foucault (1926–1984) could easily recognize Firmin's reflection as in stream with an archaeology of knowledge and its role in the constitution of subjects of inquiry: That he recognized the role of racial impositions on the subject matter and the underlying investments involved in geography and natural history meant that he was aware of the genealogical organization of thought on human subjects. More, his understanding of social life and the question of moral imposition or the impact of rules on the organization of human subjects means, as well, that he was a precursor in the area of philosophy of social science that examines problems of the constitution of social reality. Firmin understood, in other words, as Alfred Schutz (1899–1959) later pointed out in his *Phänomenologie des inneren Zeitbewusstsein* (*Phenomenology of the Social World*, 1928), that social life is an achievement, not a determined reality. This made him a precursor, as well, of social constructivism, but his version is rooted in a very thick conception of history.

Firmin also introduced a concept in Africana thought that was later taken up by the Guyanese revolutionary Walter Rodney (1942–1980)— namely, the concept of *underdevelopment*. Firmin writes throughout the text of what he calls the "regeneration of the black race." By this, he means that it was not the natural condition of blacks to be in an inferior position to whites and that the actual history of blacks in Africa is much different from what has been perpetrated by eighteenth- and nineteenth-century Eurocentric writings on Africa and Haiti. He offers a history of ancient Africa that predates the writings of the Senegalese Cheikh Anton Diop (1923–1986). The Europeanizing and Asianizing of Ancient Egypt is one instance of the exceptionalist rule, whereby an ancient African nation is literally taken out of Africa because of an analytical reduction of civilization into things European and Asian. That the history of Africa is one of a rapid change and spiraling degeneration during the slave trade suggests that a process of underdevelopment led to the question-begging situation of black inferiority. This is what Rodney ultimately argued in his classic work *How Europe Underdeveloped Africa* (1972).

The concept of regeneration brings to the fore a problem of modern historiography, namely, the notion that the European qua European lacks a primitive past. It is an analytical notion in which, for example, when Neanderthals are discovered by recent archaeological and anthropological evidence to have been white skinned, the discussion of their intelligence shifts and a greater effort to articulate their humanity unfolds in the research. In short, a white primitive becomes an oxymoron, and, in effect, the ascription of intelligence functions retroactively from the present to the past and returns to the present. Whites thus function as the telos, as the aim, of the human species. It is, in effect, the reassertion of an old logic, namely, Aristotelianism, where there is a search for the telos or aim of living phenomena. Darwinism, properly speaking, should not make any teleological claims. But social Darwinism falls into this trap, and the logic from race to racism follows. The concept of regeneration suggests that the past was not one of any human race being inferior to another but that historical forces come into play to subordinate, by force, some groups of human beings over others. Regeneration suggests that every individual member of each group of human beings, as living beings, is in a generative process of achieving his or her potential, but that potential is not a metaphysical external Prime Mover. It is in what individuals in each group may strive for in the absence of domination. We see here the basis of Firmin's republicanism.

Firmin's ideas, however, fell upon deaf ears. This was so primarily because of the strategic isolation of Haiti by the United States and its allies in the region. For Firmin's thought to have "appeared" beyond the borders of Haiti required the Haitian people themselves to have appeared beyond the stereotypes and disavowals of their humanity, poignantly analyzed by Sibylle Fischer recently in *Modernity Disavowed* (2005). How could such thought have its day in a world that could only see such people as violent usurpers in ragged clothing with pitchforks and torches held high?

Firmin was not the only nineteenth-century Caribbean thinker to see the importance of bringing nuance to the understanding of Africa in the modern world. A scholar of great repute from the Caribbean island of St. Thomas, Virgin Islands, George Wilmot Blyden (1832–1912) migrated to Liberia where he launched a stellar career as a teacher, researcher, and statesman. Blyden's work was more social scientifically focused in the areas of linguistics, history, and sociology than Firmin's work, which focused on philosophical and empirical anthropology. Blyden's insights along the way offered much for the philosophy of culture. For instance, he was critical of Alexander Crummell's project of Christianizing Africa, arguing, in *African Life and Customs* (1908), that it is much easier to change a people's theology than their religion. Blyden saw the effort to change the normative basis of how people lived as having a damaging effect, although one could engage them at the level of rational reflection on the implications of their customs and thoughts. Central in this regard is his study of the Muslim populations of Western Africa, where he observed the difference between the impact of Christianity and Islam on blacks. The former, he concluded, had a negative effect of demanding subservience in the psychic and social life of blacks, which he considered demoralizing, whereas the latter afforded more dignity since it was more aligned with traditional African conceptions of self-assertiveness. With regard to modernization, he was a pioneer of the view that modernization need not only be European and that it was possible to develop a distinctively African form of modernity.

The question of formulating a *black* form of modernity was taken up in the next great effort at Afro-Caribbean appearance through the political genius and the grand effort of Jamaican-born Marcus Mosiah Garvey (1887–1940). After traveling through the islands in his adolescent years, he was struck by the seeming universal status of blacks at the lowest level of each society. After spending time in London, he was invited to the United States by Booker T. Washington in 1916, but Washington had died by the time of Garvey's arrival. He stayed in the United States and was so successful in organizing the black masses that he was for a time the undisputed most influential individual among the people of the black world. He founded the Universal Negro Improvement Association and African Community League under a program of race pride and economic self-reliance. An extraordinarily gifted speaker with an understanding of the organizing force of spectacles, Garvey understood that black populations needed symbols that represented possibility in their lives in addition to the material infrastructures he was arguing for. Since there are many studies of Garvey's life that chronicle his conflict with W. E. B. Du Bois, his eventual arrest in 1925 for tax evasion, and his deportation from the United States in 1927, I will not explore the details of those matters here. What is crucial is that along the way Garvey set the framework for a form of black nationalism of a prophetic and philosophical character. The prophetic side emerged from his political argument that black liberation rested upon the liberation of the African continent from colonialism. Prophesying the emergence of a royal liberator in Ethiopia, Garvey became the major prophetic figure for what became Rastafari in Jamaica. That movement came into being at the crowning of Emperor Tafari Makonnen in 1930, the avowed 111th emperor in the succession of King Solomon. Ras (King) Tafari adopted the name Haile Selassie ("Might of the Trinity") on that occasion, and some of the followers of Garvey in Jamaica regarded those series of events to be the fulfillment of Hebrew messianic prophecy. The name they adopted, Rastafari, exemplify his name, and their subsequent philosophical and religious thought has had an enormous impact on the representation of black pride to this day.

Garvey's philosophical thought focused on the affirmation of the black self. For Garvey, it was crucial for black people to value themselves, but this thought was linked to his political philosophy, where such value was not simply at an individual level but required, as well, a nation through which such value could emerge as historical. In short, black pride required black nationhood. The imperative of liberating the African continent and the many ethnic groups there returned, but the concept of nation advanced here undergirds the many ethnicities through the concept of race. In other words, the African states had to be founded on the black nation, which, given Garvey's argument, was diasporic.

The next significant moment of black appearance in the Caribbean was the return of Aimé Césaire (1913–) to the island of Martinique in 1939 and the publication of his classic *Cahier d'un retour au pays natal* (*Return to My Native Land*), published in 1947. Although there were other Caribbean writers exploring similar themes, what was unique about Césaire was that he inaugurated this stage *in* the Caribbean itself. Trinidadian-born C. L. R. James (1904–1989), for instance, had published *The Black Jacobins*, his classic 1938 study of the Haitian Revolution, in the United States, and it took time for the text to be understood as a contribution to Caribbean historicism instead of only Caribbean history. James's writings were, as well, regarded more as work in Marxism and what could later be called Afro-Caribbean Marxism. Césaire and his wife Suzanne Césaire had returned to Martinique after playing their role, along with Léopold Senghor and Léon Gontian Damas, in the development of what Aimé Césaire coined as "negritude," whose basic tenet was to affirm being black and being proud of it. In his essay, "West Indians and Africans," in *Toward the African Revolution*, Fanon testified to the "scandal" created by Césaire, a dark-skinned Martinican, expressing pride instead of shame in his appearance. Césaire's thought, most exemplifed in his poetry, argued for positive black identification with Africa and for an aesthetic that subverted the notion of Eurocentric/white superiority over the African/black.

Césaire's thought had an extraordinary impact on perhaps the greatest Afro-Caribbean thinker—Frantz Fanon (1925–1961). I will not focus in detail on Fanon's biography since he is unquestionably the Afro-Caribbean thinker who is best known and on whom the most biographies have been written. The short version is that he fought in the French Resistance in World War II, returned to Martinique briefly after the war, and then went to France to study psychiatry (with FrançoisTosquelles) and philosophy (with Maurice Merleau-Ponty). As the head of psychiatry at Blida-Joinville hospital in Algeria, he developed a series of revolutionary innovations in humanistic psychiatry and challenged the "primivitist" school of psychiatry that was influential in the study of colonized subjects at the time. He eventually joined the Algerian National Liberation Front in the Algerian War but died from pneumonia while seeking treatment for leukemia in Bethesda, Maryland.

The impact of Fanon's thought on Afro-Caribbean philosophy cannot be overestimated. Nearly all of the central issues in this area of thought for the next half of the twentieth century emerged from his ideas. Although for a time he was more known for his ideas on decolonization and post-colonization in *Les Damnés de la terre* (*The Damned of the Earth*, but available as *The Wretched of the Earth*), published in 1961, it is *Peau noire, masques blancs* (*Black Skin, White Masks*), published in 1952, that outlines most of the problematics of contemporary African philosophy. In that work, Fanon takes on the theme of Prospero and Caliban through raising the question of epistemological colonization. He argues that race and racism are functions of the social world, but the social world often hides its own dependence on human agency. He also challenges the ethical system that dominates modern thought—namely, liberalism and its promise of assimilation of all human subjects. Fanon points out that many black people attempt to enter that sphere of recognition in good faith only to find a distorted image thrown back at them in the form of an alien and alienated subject. Whether through the resources of language, sexual relationships, or the constitution of dream life, the black subject always finds himself or herself struggling with the dialectics of recognition, in which the white world always serves as the standard for the truly human mode of being. The dialectics of recognition mean that blacks stand in a strange relation to theoretical work such as philosophy, whose idol is Reason itself. They faced the phenomenon of Reason taking flight whenever blacks attempted to enter the equation. Fanon also challenged several influential tropes in the study of race and racism. The first was the self–other dialectic. For Fanon, colonialism and racism placed whole groups of people below that dialectic, which meant that they could only live it between each other. At the interracial level of black and white, there was no such dialectic. There was, simply, such a relation between whites, but beyond whites there was neither self nor others. In short, the human minimum was denied by the systems of colonization and racism. The result of Fanon's analysis was that one could not simply apply the Western human sciences to the study of racialized colonial subjects. Their logic often broke down. Lacanian psychoanalysis, for instance, did not work for the Martinican subject because both the Martinican female and the Martinican male sought recognition from white males, which, in effect, meant that Martinican males did not exist as Lacanian men. How could this be so if sex were ontologically

basic, as presupposed by psychoanalysis? Fanon showed that colonialism—
a social phenomenon—intervened and disrupted the patriarchal order of
Lacanian categories. He showed the same for Hegelian categories, in
which recognition is also sought *by the master* in the ordinary Hegelian
schema, but it is not so in the racialized schema faced by Afro-Caribbean
subjects. And Fanon showed that the resources of language faced similar
limitations. The semiotic limits occurred in the regional transcendence of
"blacks." In short, the Afro-Caribbean often attempted to master the colonizing language in order to transcend racial difference, but he or she often found the contradictions emerging from such mastery itself: (1) There
seemed no way to be black *and* a master of the colonial language, yet (2)
there being blacks who mastered it meant that there was something wrong
with those blacks. They had, in other words, illicit use of licit grammar and
words. The structure was, in other words, deeply neurotic, but it was so on
the level of a lived reality of constant failure. Thus, Fanon raised the question of an Afro-Caribbean philosophy as one that posed a philosophical
anthropology premised upon the need to formulate an alternative social
world.

Ironically, although Fanon wrote those reflections in 1952, *Black Skin,
White Masks* was not immediately recognized in the Caribbean. In France,
it was somewhat of a scandal since the official French view was that there
was no racial discrimination in France and that French colonialism, in effect, offered colonial subjects access to the (French) universal. But in the
islands, the process of decolonization began to reach through the Anglophone, Francophone, and Hispanophone worlds in ways that brought the
question of black emancipation to the table of international affairs as many
African nations gained independence. Crucial in this regard was the Cuban
Revolution in 1959. For Fidel Castro placed, among his objectives, the
question of racial justice since the overwhelming number of poor Cubans,
especially those that worked the sugarcane fields, were black. Eric Williams
had earlier argued, in *Capitalism and Slavery* (1944), that the causes of such
historical circumstances were primarily economic, and such a case offered
much for efforts at social emancipation premised upon Marxist-centered
thought.

Added to these developments in the 1960s was the growing discourse
of underdevelopment as a new stage of colonial assertion or "neocolonialism," which meant that black emancipation gained a new formulation
through more historical-minded scholars and activists. Central among
them was the Guyanese historian Walter Rodney (1942–1980), whose *How
Europe Underdeveloped Africa* (1972) and earlier pamphlet *Grounding with My*

Brothers (1969) brought a fusion of historical themes under a new stage of Afro-Caribbean historical consciousness in the notions of underdevelopment and lumpen-proletariat politics of social transformation through Rastafari. Although Firmin was the first to raise the problem of underdevelopment, the concept has been mostly associated with Rodney because of the influence of Marxism on twentieth-century African and Afro-Caribbean political economic thought. Orthodox Marxism argued that the proletariat—the working-class consequences of industrialism—held the universal dimensions of the next stage in the ineluctable movement of history. A problem that emerged for Third World peoples is what to do in places where there was no infrastructural development, where there was no industrial working class. In effect, the response from orthodox Marxism amounted to telling colonized and racialized subjects to wait for their turn. In effect, the response of James in *Black Jacobins*, that of Fanon in *Les Damnés de la terre*, and that of Rodney was to offer alternative models of revolution with shared premises but different conclusions. Revolution in the Third World, in other words, required a different logic because of the fact of racial oppression. In other words, the struggle that was being waged from the Afro-Caribbean was not simply a matter of class membership but *human existence*. Thus, the place of philosophical anthropology and the logic of recognizing "lumpen" populations took a more central role. The Rastafari movement, in its symbols of recognizing "natural" blackness such as dreadlocks and its cultural links with music and rituals around marijuana that led to direct conflicts with the Jamaican (and other Caribbean) governments, brought these questions to the fore.

Afro-Caribbean thought for most of the 1980s was heavily locked in discussions of political economy and history. A change emerged in the 1990s, however, when African American academic philosophy began to gain influence on African American studies in North American universities. African American academic philosophy began to formulate a set of problematics that conjoined the world of black public intellectuals with those of academic professionals. A group of Afro-Caribbean intellectuals surfaced who were a mixture of the developments in the United States and those in the Caribbean. Some of them were predominantly Caribbean in their orientation, and others were predominantly U.S. black in their upbringing. The effect was similar to rap and hip-hop culture, where Caribbean musicians, vinyl aficionados, dancers, and poets fused with the Hispanophone and Anglophone Caribbean with U.S. black Anglophone culture. The Committee on Blacks in the American Philosophical Association at first consisted of such a matrix: Blacks from the United

States and those from Puerto Rico, Jamaica, and Barbados met under one, racial rubric ("Black") to discuss philosophical issues most relevant to them. The early meetings of that group were primarily focused on the intellectual identities of Anglo-analytical philosophy and American pragmatism. It is perhaps safe to say that the two exemplars of those models by the early 1990s were Bernard Boxill (Barbadian) in terms of the former and Cornel West (U.S. black) in terms of the latter. Ironically, the committee itself was originally organized by William R. Jones (U.S. black), who inaugurated his career with a dissertation on Jean-Paul Sartre's philosophical anthropology and who developed his own brand of humanism that served as a foundation of that stage of black existential and phenomenological philosophy. Others in that group included Lucius Outlaw (critical theory and phenomenology), Howard McGary (analytical philosophy), and Leonard Harris (pragmatism). By the mid-1990s, that group included Charles Mills (Jamaican analytical philosopher), Robert Gooding-Williams (U.S. black and specialist in European continental philosophy), and Naomi Zack (U.S. proponent of "mixed race" and analytical philosophy but with existential sympathies). That was the context in which my own work came on the scene in 1993, at first through a series of presentations and articles, and then in 1995 through the publication of my books *Bad Faith and Antiblack Racism* and *Fanon and the Crisis of European Man*. Crucial here, however, was also the work of organizing the U.S. history of African-American philosophy through the interviews and anthologies put together by George Yancy (U.S. black who concentrates in African American philosophy and critical race theory). Also, in terms of organizing the U.S. history of African American philosophy, Yancy's *Cornel West: A Critical Reader* is significant as it brought together for the first time in American history a critical cadre of philosophers to reflect upon the work of a living black philosopher. All of this posed the question of whether such a correlate could emerge in the Caribbean context.

Much was happening at the same time in Caribbean literature through such writers as the Barbadian George Lamming, whose contribution to Anglo-Caribbean existentialism was contemporaneous with Fanon's in the Francophone Caribbean; the Guyanese Wilson Harris, whose concerns of consciousness place him in the phenomenological wing; the Cuban-born but Jamaican Sylvia Wynter, who represents the poststructural development; and the Antiguan Jamaica Kincaid, whose novels and essays raise the question of the political geography of the "island" dimension of Afro-Caribbean consciousness. As well, there was a sociological wing of writers thinking through questions of freedom and consciousness, although they were not working in concert. The work of the Jamaican Orlando Patterson raised the historical-Hegelian formulations, but no writer exemplified commitment to the philosophical dimension of the sociological wing more than the Montserrat-born Antiguan sociologist and philosopher Paget Henry, who took on the editorship of the *C. L. R. James Journal* in the late 1980s. Henry had already made a name for himself as the father of Antiguan political economy in his classic work *Peripheral Capitalism and Development in Antigua* (1985), and his coedited work, *C. L. R. James's Caribbean* (1992), had served as an exemplary fusion of black British cultural studies and Caribbean historicism. Under his editorship of the *C. L. R. James Journal*, the historicist dimension of that journal began to explore developments in African and African American philosophy. It was, however, the publication of *Bad Faith and Antiblack Racism* that signaled a decision for Henry to delve more deeply into philosophy at the level of embedded work in the sociology of philosophy, which, in this case, meant *doing philosophy* instead of simply studying it.

Bad Faith and Antiblack Racism announced the existential phenomenological wing of African American and Afro-Caribbean philosophy. The text argued that a renewed reflection on the role of the theorist in the study of race and racism was necessary, and this reflective movement raised the question of bad faith. The reality of bad faith meant that any philosophical anthropology faced its own metastability, by which is meant that thought as an object of consciousness placed itself outside of an identity relationship with itself. This meant, further, that any reflective human endeavor always encounters its own incompleteness. For Henry, this meant that the question of the modern black consciousness was being posed and, with that, the question of the black self. Moreover, *Bad Faith and Antiblack Racism* argued that the historicist turn was limited in that it reflected only part of the problem. Colonialism and racism were not only matters of historical events, they were also questions about the constitution of new *kinds of beings*. In other words, they raised new, ontological problems and problematics. Henry's historicism up to this point took the form of a fusion of the archaeological poststructuralism of Michel Foucault and the Marxist historicism of C. L. R. James. In both, however, he found it difficult to find an Afro-Caribbean self. The existential phenomenological posing of the creation of new kinds of beings and of how they live the consciousness of who or "what" they are offered the possibility of analyzing such subjects. *Bad Faith and Antiblack Racism* and *Fanon and the Crisis of European Man* put forward the thought of Fanon as foundational for this stage of

African American and Afro-Caribbean thought, and, combined, the two books played their part in the case for the now-canonical place of Fanon in postcolonial and Caribbean studies, which in turn led to Henry thinking through the categories of his organization of Afro-Caribbean thought.

The results of Paget Henry's research came to the fore in the benchmark year of 2000. There, Afro-Caribbean philosophy was marked by the publication of *Caliban's Reason: Introducing Afro-Caribbean Philosophy* and my *Existentia Africana: Understanding Africana Existential Thought*, which, although not explicitly on Afro-Caribbean philosophy, is a contribution to that area by virtue of its being heavily informed by the thought of Fanon. I will here focus on *Caliban's Reason*, however, since it is the text that placed this stage of Afro-Caribbean philosophy into its current schema.

The title *Caliban's Reason* points to the ongoing theme of Shakespeare's *Tempest* as the primary metaphor of modern colonization and racialization. Here, however, we see the theme of double consciousness come to the fore. First, there is the form of double consciousness in which one sees oneself only through the eyes of others. For Caliban, reality emerges through Prospero's eyes. In Eurocentric scholarship, reality is solely a function of what emerges through European perspectives. So, an Afro-Caribbean that subscribes to that view will only see himself or herself through Eurocentric eyes that regard the Caribbean as marginal at best and, at worst, primitive or inferior. That, argues Henry, was the way the Caribbean regarded itself. There is, however, another stage of double consciousness, where Caliban realizes the contradictions of the world as presented by Prospero. That stage is able to issue a critique of Eurocentrism and pose the possibility of seeing the self beyond the negative versions constructed by European modernity. This form of double consciousness involves recognizing how the Caribbean self (Caliban) was misrepresented. But this representation does not mean reinscribing Prospero's normativity; it does not, that is, require showing that Caliban is "as good as" Prospero. It requires understanding the problems of a Prospero-centered logic in the first place. Henry's response, then, is not to deny the achievements of European thought. His response is to demand an examination of the contributions from Africa.

Raising the question of the *intellectual* contributions of the Afro-Caribbean to Caribbean life brought Henry to a tradition that goes back to Césaire. By raising this question, he brought to the table of ideas a different understanding of Africa in the Caribbean. There, Henry argues that what Africans brought to the New World were their unique visions of time and the distribution of values. Concerns of predestination governed (and still govern) the lives of many traditional African societies. The existential problematic thus focuses on problems of agency and human-centered action. How were these concerns affected by colonialism, slavery, and racialization?

Henry argues that a repression of the African self emerged in the historical process of its dehumanization. Afro-Caribbean philosophy therefore faces an important mission: the liberation of the Afro-Caribbean self from the yoke of its dehumanization. Such a task was twofold. First, it takes the form of the constructive arguments toward such self-recognition. Second, it involves the historical reconstruction of the *intellectual history* of such efforts. *Caliban's Reason* takes on both tasks, although most of the text does so through presenting a careful discussion of the variety of thinkers and ideas that constitute the body of Afro-Caribbean thought. The presentation is done through a taxonomy of what Henry considers to be the major groups of Afro-Caribbean philosophy: (1) the historicists and (2) the poeticists. The former are primarily concerned with problems of social change and political economy. The latter are primarily concerned with the imagination, the conceptions of the self as represented by literature and poetry. Prime examples of historicists for Henry include C. L. R. James and his followers, which include the Antiguan Leonard Tim Hector (1942–2002) and the later Fanon. The poeticist wing includes Wilson Harris and Sylvia Wynter. The categories are not meant to be exclusive, however, so there are historicist contributions by poeticists and vice versa. Fanon and Wynter, as well as the Martinican Edouard Glissant, for instance, made both historical and poetic contributions. Wilson Harris's call for the primacy of the imagination in the Caribbean is also linked to his Hegelian-like notion of a supraconsciousness over and through all living things, which, although poetic, is also historical. Henry then examined how different movements in the Afro-Caribbean were affected by these categories.

One movement that seemed to defy these categories was African American philosophy and its impact on the development of Afro-Caribbean philosophy. Many of the problematics formulated by African American philosophy are faced in Afro-Caribbean philosophy. For instance, in his discussion of prophetic pragmatism, whose chief proponent is U.S.-born Cornel West, Henry points out that a major shortcoming is the failure to recognize the African dimensions of the hybrid "African American." It is as if the African American were born in North American modernity without an African continued presence and an African past. Henry points out the importance of the phenomenological turn in African

American philosophy, which raises the question of the unique forms of consciousness posed by African America. To that, he adds the value of a *historicist* dimension to phenomenological treatments of the constitution of African America, one that historicizes the African *and* other dimensions, and the importance of such an approach to the study of the constitution of the Caribbean self. Another category is Afro-Caribbean analytical philosophy, or what he sometimes calls Afro-Caribbean "logicism." There, through the work of Bernard Boxill and Charles Mills, he sees the Afro-Caribbean proponents of logical analysis of language. In relation to the analytical group, he also examines what he calls "the linguistic turn" in Afro-Caribbean thought, whose chief proponents are U.K.-born Paul Gilroy's Birmingham School form of cultural studies and Jamaican-born David Scott's Foucauldianism, wherein there is the poststructural appeal to the basis of the self in the linguistic formations of modern societies. Henry offers a critique of this turn, pointing out that it leads to a form of linguistic structuralism that evades the inner life or lived reality of the peoples of the region. The problem of language, after all, is central for the philosophical enterprise. The body of literature he explores, for instance, constitutes the discourse through which Afro-Caribbean life and problems can be understood. At the close of the text, Henry points out that there are unresolved historical questions in the Caribbean and that they could benefit from a dialogue with the poeticists, who demand a role for political imagination. But more, Henry raises—there, later in a series of articles in the *C. L. R. James Journal,* and for the volume (*After Man—the Human*) in honor of Sylvia Wynter edited by B. Anthony Bogues—the crucial role of transcendental reflection in Caribbean philosophy. By transcendental, he means the move from poetic interpretation and historicist examinations of temporality to the self-reflective analysis of preconditions and conditions of possibility. In short, Afro-Caribbean phenomenology, in addition to its historical and poetic dimensions, raises the question of Afro-Caribbean transcendentalism. For Henry, this means taking seriously the question of creolization in the Caribbean, wherein sources of transcendentalism are offered not only in the phenomenological writings from the 1990s and since 2000, but also in the past, through the elements offered by the Indo-Caribbean tradition and its creolization with Africa and Europe. In addition, the clear role of double consciousness in Caribbean thought requires an explicit engagement with the work of W. E. B. DuBois and its relevance to the Caribbean in the form of what Henry calls "potentiated double consciousness," the form of double consciousness that transcends the first stage mired in the dialectics of recognition.

There has been an array of works from a new generation of Afro-Caribbean philosophers since 2000. These writers have expanded the meaning of the Caribbean philosopher to take on the historic legacy of the Caribbean writer, whose goal is a set of issues that includes philosophy but is not limited to it. Such writers include the Barbadian Clevis Headley, the Jamaican B. Anthony Bogues, the Puerto Rican and U.S. Virgin Islander Gertrude James Gonzalez de Allen, Jamaican-descended political theorist Neil Roberts, Puerto Rican–born Nelson Maldonado-Torres, Jamaican-born classicist and philosopher Patrick Goodin, as well as a group of African philosophers who have joined the discussion such as Nigerian-born Nkiru Nzegwu, Ayotunde Bewaji, and Lawrence Bamikole, as well as the great Ghanaian philosopher Kwazi Wiredu, whose pragmatist writings are also now being read in the Caribbean context, and the Kenyan cofounding father of sage philosophy, Frederick O'Chieng Odhiambo. Nelson Maldonado-Torres, Gertrude James Gonzalez de Allen, Jorge Garcia (Puerto Rican), Jorge Gracia (Cuban), Ofelia Shutte (Cuban), and Linda Martín Alcoff (Panamanian), among others, have been producing work that could be labeled "Latin Caribbean philosophy." Maldonado-Torres has, however, been the most active in developing the *Afro*-Caribbean aspects of this philosophy and in taking the Fanonian side to a new dimension into what he calls a "postcontinental" philosophy. Here, Maldanado-Torres raises the question of the differences between the kinds of consciousness developed for continental formulations versus those governed by the logic of islands. Maldonado-Torres raises questions of going beyond such logics at the linguistic levels as well as the regional levels—especially in terms of how one formulates the notion of "America" and the "Americas"—in the constitution of liberated selves. Maldonado-Torres, through the work of the Lithuanian Jew Emmanuel Levinas and the Argentinian philosopher, historian, and theologian Enrique Dussel, also raises the question of ethics in Caribbean struggles for liberation. Unlike Fanon's work and my own, which question the role of ethics after colonialism, Maldonado-Torres has attempted to reconcile ethics with postcolonial liberation.

Henry's reflections on phenomenology have also been joined by groups of North American scholars in dialogue with Afro-Caribbean philosophy. These include the philosopher and therapist Marilyn Nissm-Sabat, who had already began exploring the postcolonial phenomenological dimensions of Afro-Caribbean philosophy on developmental questions of maturation from *Fanon and the Crisis of European Man* onward, and the philosopher and poet Janet Borgerson, who has extended the treatment of embodied bad faith from *Bad Faith and Antiblack Racism* to feminist critical discussions in philosophical treatments of marketing, power, and gender performance. Stephen Haymes, the award-winning philosopher of education and cultural critic, has also taken the existential phenomenological route in his recent writings, which explore problems of memory and trauma and how New World black slaves developed unique forms of pedagogies through which to assert their humanity. Kenneth Knies has also taken on these questions of the constitution of the self in phenomenology, but he raises the question of the disciplinary underpinning of such questions in what he calls "post-European science." My own work is also in dialogue with this development in the field as efforts at what I call "shifting the geography of reason." In effect, this research asks the question of what happens when reason no longer runs out the door when the black walks in the room. The argument here takes several turns. First, it addresses the metatheoretical question of theory itself. Critics of Afro-Caribbean philosophy take the position that building new theory is an imperial project and that properly postcolonial thought, as Afro-Caribbean thought should be, should focus on criticism, on tearing down the master's house, so to speak. The response to this approach argues that being locked in negative critique collapses into reactionary thought and politics. The aim should not be about what to tear down but what to build up. The role of theory is to use all of its resources—from its many genealogical trends (creolization)— to build livable homes. This means, second, understanding what disciplinary formations could offer such a domicile. The error in most disciplinary formations is that they treat themselves as "closed," "absolute," or "deontological." The result is disciplinary decadence, which involves the closing off of epistemological possibilities of disciplinary work. This form of decadence is particularly acute at the level of method, where a methodology does not emerge since such questions are closed. In effect, the discipline and its method become "complete." Life returns to disciplinary practices, however, through being willing to transcend the discipline itself. I call this "a teleological suspension of disciplinarity." What this means is that the thinker concludes that there are issues so important to pursue that method and disciplinary commitment must fall to the wayside if they inhibit exploration of those issues. In the case of philosophy, disciplinary suspensions—that is, the decision to go beyond philosophy—enable the emergence of new philosophy. Afro-Caribbean philosophy, from this point of view, is the construction of new philosophy through Afro-Caribbean philosophers' willingness to go beyond philosophy, paradoxically, for the sake of philosophy.

At the institutional level, what has resulted since 2000 is that there are now philosophy departments at the universities in the Anglo-Caribbean, and there are now institutes and centers for Caribbean thought, as well as a Caribbean Philosophical Association. Richard Clarke and his colleagues at the University of the West Indies at Cave Hill in Barbados held a conference on philosophy and Caribbean cultural studies in 2001, which stimulated discussions of ideas on that island in the form of continued, annual symposia, and the University of the West Indies at Mona, Jamaica, held a series of large, public seminars honoring such people of letters as Sylvia Wynter (2002), George Lamming (2003), and Stuart Hall (2004). Discussions initiated at the onset of these seminars led to the founding of the Caribbean Philosophical Association in 2003. Taking on the motto of "shifting the geography of reason," the Caribbean Philosophical Association meets annually at countries and provinces that vary linguistically—that is, Anglophonic (Barbados, 2004), Hispanophonic (Puerto Rico, 2005), Francophonic (Montreal, Quebec, 2006)—and has begun production of a series of volumes, through the editorship of Clevis Headley and Marina Banchetti, in which problems in the philosophy of science, language, religion, gender, and aesthetics are explored in the Caribbean context. There are now also students pursuing master's degrees and doctoral degrees in the Caribbean with a focus on Afro-Caribbean philosophy. Within those ranks, there is much interest in the thought of Caribbean women writers, and there is growing engagement between Afro-Caribbean feminists and U.S. feminist philosophers for the emerging area of Afro-Caribbean feminist philosophy. Recent developments include work on historical figures, such as T. Denean Sharpley-Whiting's work on the role of the Nardal sisters and Suzanne Césaire in the development of negritude and Kristin Waters's work on the Jamaican Mary Seacole, as well as the growing scholarship on such women as Jamaica Kincaid and the Haitian writer Edgwin Danticat, and there is feminist constructivist work by philosopher Jeanette (Jan) Boxill on contemporary problems ranging from social justice to philosophies of sport.

To conclude, then, Afro-Caribbean philosophy has placed the question of the Afro-Caribbean self as a primary concern of the identity dimension of its philosophical anthropology, and it has placed explorations of how such conceptions of the self relate to historical questions of social change as its teleology. Afro-Caribbean philosophy is also concerned with a variety of questions in other areas of philosophy, such as the relationship of European philosophical categories to the creolized ones of the Caribbean, as well as the historical task of constructing Caribbean intellectual history. It is not, however, a philosophy that is obsessed with similitude or the pressures to be philosophy as understood in the northern hemisphere. In seeking its own path, Afro-Caribbean philosophy exemplifies the paradox of becoming more philosophical through the effort of going beyond philosophy itself.

Notes

1. Anténor Firmin, *Equality of Human Races: A Nineteenth Century Haitian Scholar's Response to European Racialism,* trans. Asselin Charles with intro. by Carolyn Fleuhr-Lobban (New York: Taylor & Francis, 1999), lvii.
2. Firmin, *Equality of the Human Races,* 3.
3. Firmin, *Equality of the Human Races,* 10.

Bibliography

Banchetti-Robino, Marina, and Cleavis Headley, eds. *Shifting the Geography of Reason,* vol. 1. London: Cambridge Scholars Press, 2006.

Bernal, Martin. *Black Athena: The Afroasiatic Roots of Classical Civilization.* New Brunswick, NJ: Rutgers University Press, 1987.

———. *Black Athena Writes Back: Martin Bernal Responds to His Critics,* ed. David Chioni Moore. Durham, NC: Duke University Press, 2001.

Bewaji, John Ayotunde (Tunde) Isola. "Philosophy in History and History of Philosophy as Academic Politics." *International Readings on Theory, History and Philosophy of Culture* (UNESCO Moscow) 18 (2004), *Differentiation and Integration of Worldviews: Philosophical and Religious Experience*: 194–232.

Bogues, B. Anthony. *Black Heretics, Black Prophets: Radical Political Intellectuals.* New York: Routledge, 2003.

Boxill, Bernard. *Blacks and Social Justice.* Lanham, MD: Rowman & Littlefield, 1992.

Boxill, Jan, ed. *The Moral Significance of Sports.* Forthcoming.

———. *Sports Ethics: An Anthology.* Malden, MA: Blackwell Publishers, 2003.

Blyden, Edward W. *African Life and Customs.* Baltimore, MD: Black Classics, 1994.

———. *A Paper on "Christianity, Islam, and the Negro Race."* London: Whittingham & Co., 1887.

Césaire, Aimé. *Cahier d'un retour au pays natal.* 2nd ed. Ed. Abiole Irele. Columbus: Ohio State University Press, 2000.

Chrisman, Laura. "Journeying to Death: Gilroy's *The Black Atlantic*." In *Black British Culture and Society: A Text Reader,* ed. Kwesi Owusu Comedia, 453–64. London: Routledge, 2000.

———. "Rethinking Black Atlanticism." *Black Scholar* 30, nos. 3–4 (Fall–Winter 2000): 12–17.

Collins, Randall. *Sociology of Philosophies: A Global Theory of Intellectual Change.* Cambridge, MA: Harvard/Belknap Press, 1998.

Cugoano, Quobna Ottobah. *"Thoughts and Sentiments on the Evil of Slavery" and Other Writings*. Ed. with intro. and notes by Vincent Carretta. New York: Penguin Books, 1999.

DuBois, W. E. B. *The Conservation of Races*. Washington, DC: American Negro Academy Occasional Papers, No. 2, 1897.

———. *The Souls of Black Folk* (1903). With intros. by Nathan Hare and Alvin F. Poussaint, revised and updated bibliographies. New York: Signet Classic/New American Library, 1969.

Dussel, Enrique. *Beyond Philosophy: Ethics, History, Marxism, and Liberation Theology*. Trans. and ed. Eduardo Mendieta. Lanham, MD: Rowman & Littlefield, 2003.

———. *The Underside of Modernity*. Ithaca, NY: Humanity Books, 1996.

Eze, Emmanuel, ed. *African Philosophy*. Oxford: Blackwell, 1998.

———. *Race and the Enlightenment: A Reader*. Oxford: Blackwell, 1997.

Fanon, Frantz. *Black Skin, White Masks*. Trans. Charles Lamm Markman. New York: Grove Press, 1967.

———. *A Dying Colonialism*. Trans. Haakon Chevalier with intro. by Adolfo Gilly. New York: Grove Weidenfeld, 1967.

———. *Les Damnés de la terre*. Preface by Jean-Paul Sartre. Paris: François Maspero éditeur S.A.R.L., 1961; Paris: Éditions Gallimard, 1991.

———. *Peau noire, masques blancs*. Paris: Éditions du Seuil, 1952.

———. *Sociologie d'une révolution: l'an V de la révolution algérienne*. 2nd ed. Paris: François Maspero, 1975/1968 [1959].

———. *Toward the African Revolution*. Trans. Haakon Chevalier. New York: Grove Press, 1967.

———. *The Wretched of the Earth*. Trans. Constance Farrington with intro. by Jean-Paul Sartre. New York: Grove Press, 1963.

Finch, Charles, III. *Echoes from the Old Darkland: Themes from the African Eden*. Decatur, GA: Khenti, 1996.

———. "From the Nile to the Niger: The Evolution of African Spiritual Concepts." In *A Companion to African-American Studies*, ed. Lewis Gordon and Jane Anna Gordon, 453–75. Malden, MA: Blackwell, 2006.

Firmin, Anténor. *Equality of Human Races: A Nineteenth Century Haitian Scholar's Response to European Racialism*. Trans. Asselin Charles with intro. by Carolyn Fleuhr-Lobban. New York: Taylor & Francis, 1999.

Fischer, Sibylle. *Modernity Disavowed: Haiti and the Cultures of Slavery in the Age of Revolution*. Durham, NC: Duke University Press, 2004.

———. "Unthinkable History? Some Reflections on the Haitian Revolution, Historiography, and Modernity on the Periphery." In *A Companion to African-American Studies*, ed. Lewis R. Gordon and Jane Anna Gordon. Malden, MA: Blackwell, 2006.

Foucault, Michel. *Discipline and Punish: The Birth of the Prison*. Trans. Alan Sheridan. New York: Vintage, 1979.

——. *The Order of Things: An Archaeology of the Human Sciences*. Trans. Alan Sheridan. New York: Vintage, 1973.

Garvey, Marcus. *Marcus Garvey: Life and Lesson*. Ed. Robert A. Hill and Barbara Bair. Berkeley: University of California Press, 1988.

——. *The Philosophy and Opinions of Marcus Garvey, Or, Africa for the Africans*. New York: Majority Press, 1986.

——. *Selected Writings and Speeches of Marcus Garvey*. Ed. Bob Blaisdell. New York: Dover, 2005.

Gilroy, Paul. *Against Race*. Cambridge: Harvard University Press, 2001.

——. *The Black Atlantic: Modernity and Double Consciousness*. Cambridge: Harvard University Press, 1993.

Gobineau, Comte Arthur de. *Essai sur l'inegalité des races humaines*. Présentation de Hubert Juin. Paris: P. Belfond, 1967.

Gordon, Jane Anna. *Why They Couldn't Wait: A Critique of the Black–Jewish Conflict over Community Control in Ocean Hill–Brownsville (1967–1971)*. New York: Routledge Farmer, 2001.

Gordon, Lewis R. *Bad Faith and Antiblack Racism*. Ithaca, NY: Humanity Books, 1995/1999.

——. *Disciplinary Decadence: Living Thought in Trying Times*. Boulder, CO: Paradigm Publishers.

——. *Fanon and the Crisis of European Man: An Essay on Philosophy and the Human Sciences*. New York: Routledge, 1995.

——. *Existentia Africana: Understanding Africana Existential Thought*. New York: Routledge, 2000.

——. *Her Majesty's Other Children: Sketches of Racism from a Neocolonial Age*. Lanham, MD: Rowman & Littlefield, 1997.

——. "Through the Zone of Nonbeing: A Reading of *Black Skin, White Masks* in Celebration of Fanon's Eightieth Birthday." *C.L.R. James Journal* 11, no. 1 (Summer 2005): 1–43.

——. "The Unacknowledged Fourth Tradition: An Essay on Nihilism, Decadence, and the Black Intellectual Tradition in the Existential Pragmatic Thought of Cornel West." In *Cornel West: A Critical Reader*, ed. George Yancy, 38–58. Malden, MA: Blackwell Publishers, 2001.

Gordon, Lewis R., ed. *Existence in Black: An Anthology of Black Existential Philosophy*. New York: Routledge, 1997.

Gordon, Lewis R., with Jane Anna Gordon, eds. *A Companion to African-American Studies*. Malden, MA: Blackwell Publishers, 2006.

——. *Not Only the Master's Tools: African-American Studies in Theory and Practice*. Boulder, CO: Paradigm Publishers, 2006.

Gordon, Lewis R., with T. Denean Sharlpey-Whiting, and Renée T. White, eds. *Fanon: A Critical Reader*. Oxford: Blackwell Publishers, 1996.

Gramsci, Antonio. *Selections from the Prison Notebooks*. New York: International Publishers, 1971.

Gyekye, Kwame. *An Essay on African Philosophy: The Akan Conceptual Scheme*. Philadelphia, PA: Temple University Press, 1995.

———. *Tradition and Modernity: Philosophical Reflections on the African Experience*. New York: Oxford University Press, 1997.

Hallen, Barry. *A Short History of African Philosophy*. Bloomington: Indiana University Press, 2002.

Headley, Clevis. "Race, African American Philosophy, and Africana Philosophy: A Critical Reading of Lewis Gordon's *Her Majesty's Other Children*." *Philosophia Africana* 4, no. 1 (March 2001): 56–57.

Hegel, G. W. F. *Phenomenology of Spirit*. Trans. A. V. Miller, with analysis by J. N. Findlay. Oxford: Oxford University Press, 1979.

———. *The Philosophy of History*. With prefaces by Charles Hegel and the translator, J. Sibree, and a new intro. by C. J. Friedrich. New York: Dover Publications, 1956.

———. *Philosophy of Right*. Trans. with notes by T. M. Knox. Oxford: Clarendon, 1967.

Henry, Paget. "African and Afro-Caribbean Existential Philosophies." In *Existence in Black: An Anthology of Black Existential Philosophy*, ed. Lewis R. Gordon, 11–36. New York: Routledge, 1997.

———. "African Philosophy in the Mirror of Logicisms: A Review/Essay." *C.L.R. James Journal* 4, no. 1 (Winter 1993): 70–80.

———. "Afro-American Studies and the Rise of African American Philosophy." In *A Companion to African-American Studies*, ed. Lewis R. Gordon with Jane Anna Gordon, 223–45. Malden, MA: Blackwell, 2006.

———. "Between Hume and Cugoano: Race, Ethnicity, and the Philosophical Entrapment." *Journal Speculative Philosophy* 18, no. 2 (2004): 120–48.

———. *Caliban's Reason: Introducing Afro-Caribbean Philosophy*. New York: Routledge, 2000.

———. "Cultural Dependence in the Age of Informatic Capitalism." *Radical Philosophy Review* 5, nos. 1–2 (2002–2003): 28–53.

———. "Myth, Language, and Habermasian Rationality: Another Africana Contribution." In *The Library of Living Philosophers: Habermas*, ed. by Lewis Hahn. Chicago, IL: Open Court, 2001.

———. "Rastafarianism and the Reality of Dread." In *Existence in Black: An Anthology of Black Existential Philosophy*, ed. Lewis R. Gordon, 157–64. New York: Routledge, 1997.

———. "Self-Formation and the Call: An Africana Perspective." *Listening: A Journal of Religion and Culture* 36, no. 1 (Winter 2001): 27–45.

Henry, Paget, with José Itzigsohn, eds. "Introduction: Special Symposium on Development," *Radical Philosophy Review* 5, nos. 1–2 (2002–2003): 26–27.

Hord (Mzee Lasana Okpara), Ford, and Jonathan Scott Lee. *I Am Because We Are: Readings in Black Philosophy*. Amherst: University of Massachusetts Press, 1995.

Hume, David. *Dialogues Concerning Natural Religion and the Posthumous Essays, "Of the Immortality of the Soul" and "Of Suicide."* Ed. with an intro. by Richard H. Popkin. Indianapolis, IN: Hackett, 1980.

———. *A Treatise of Human Nature.* Ed. David Fate Norton and Mary J. Norton, intro. by David Fate Norton. Oxford: Oxford University Press, 2000.

Husserl, Edmund. "Philosophy as Rigorous Science." In *Phenomenology and the Crisis of Philosophy*, trans. and ed. by Quentin Lauer, 71–147. New York: Harper & Row, 1965.

Hymans, Jacques Louis. *Léopold Sédar Senghor: An Intellectual Biography.* Edinburgh: Edinburgh University Press, 1971.

James, C. L. R. *American Civilization.* Ed. Anna Grimshaw and Keith Hart. Oxford: Blackwell, 1993.

———. *The Black Jacobins: Toussaint L'Ouverture and the San Domingo Revolution.* New York: Vintage, 1989.

Jaspers, Karl. *Philosophy of Existence.* Trans. and intro. by Richard F. Grabay Philadelphia: University of Pennsylvania Press, 1971.

———. *Truth and Symbol.* Trans. with an intro. by Jean T. Wilde, William Kluback, and William Kimmel. Albany, NY: New College and University Press, 1959.

Jones, Leroi (Amiri Baraka). *Blues People: The Negro Experience in White America and the Music That Developed from It.* New York: William Morrow and Company, 1963.

Jones, William R. *Is God a White Racist?: A Preamble to Black Theology.* Boston: Beacon, 1998.

Kant, Immanuel. *Critique of Pure Reason.* Trans. and ed. by Paul Guyer and Allen W. Wood. New York: Cambridge University Press, 1998.

Kierkegaard, Søren. *Fear and Trembling*, and *Repetition.* Ed. and trans. with intro. and notes by Howard V. Hong and Edna H Hong. Princeton: Princeton University Press, 1983.

Knies, Kenneth Danziger. "The Idea of Post-European Science: An Essay on Phenomenology and Africana Studies." In *Not Only the Master's Tools: African-American Studies in Theory and Practice*, ed. Lewis R. Gordon with Jane Anna Gordon, 85–106. Boulder, CO: Paradigm Publishers, 2006.

Kwame, Safro. "Feminism and African Philosophy." In *Readings in African Philosophy: An Akan Collection*, ed. by Safro Kwame, 251–71. Lanham, MD: University Press of America, 1995.

Lamming, George. *In the Castle of My Skin.* Intro. by Richard Wright. New York: Collier, 1970.

Levtzion, Nehemia, and Jay Spaulding, eds. *Medieval West Africa: Views from Arab Scholars and Merchants.* Princeton: Marcus Weiner Publishers, 2003.

MacIntyre, Alisdair. *After Virtue: A Study in Moral Theory.* South Bend, IN: Notre Dame University Press, 1984.

Maldonado-Torres, Nelson. "The Cry of the Self as a Call from the Other: The Paradoxical Loving Subjectivity of Frantz Fanon." *Listening: A Journal of Religion and Culture* 36, no. 1 (Winter 2001): 46–60.

————. "Toward a Critique of Continental Reason: Africana Studies and the Decolonization of Imperial Cartographies in the Americas." In *Not Only the Master's Tools: African-American Studies in Theory and Practice*, ed. Lewis R. Gordon with Jane Anna Gordon, 51–84. Boulder, CO: Paradigm Publishers, 2006.

Masolo, D. A. *African Philosophy in Search of Identity.* Bloomington: Indiana University Press, 1994.

————. "Sartre Fifty Years Later: A Review of Lewis Gordon's *Fanon and the Crisis of European Man.*" *American Philosophical Association Newsletter on Philosophy and the Black Experience* 97, no. 2 (Spring 1998): 24–29.

Mbembe, Achille. *On the Postcolony.* Berkeley: University of California Press, 2001.

McClendon, John. *C. L. R. James's* Notes on Dialectics: *Left Hegeliamism or Marxian-Leninism?* Lanham, MD: Lexington Books, 2005.

Mills, Charles. *The Racial Contract.* Ithaca, NY: Cornell University Press, 1991.

Mudimbe, V. Y. *The Idea of Africa.* Bloomington: Indiana University Press, 1994.

————. *The Invention of Africa: Gnosis, Philosophy, and the Order of Knowledge.* Bloomington: Indiana University Press, 1990.

Nietzsche, Friedrich. *On the Genealogy of Morals.* Trans. W. Kaufmann and R. J. Hollingdale, intro. by W. Kaufmann. New York: Vintage, 1989.

Nissim-Sabat, Marilyn. *For Love of Humanity.* Forthcoming.

Nzegwu, Nkiru. "Colonial Racism: Sweeping out Africa with Mother Europe's Broom." In *Racism and Philosophy*, ed. Susan E. Babbitt and Sue Campbell, 124–56. Ithaca, NY: Cornell University Press, 1999.

————. *Family Matters: Feminist Concepts in African Philosophy of Culture.* Albany: State University of New York Press, forthcoming.

————. *Issues in Contemporary African Art.* Binghamton: International Society for the Study of Africa, 1998.

————. "Philosophers' Intellectual Responsibility to African Females." *American Philosophical Association (APA) Newsletter* 96, no. 1 (November 1996): 130–35.

————. "Questions of Identity and Inheritance: A Critical Review Anthony Appiah's *In My Father's House.*" *HYPATIA: A Journal of Feminist Philosophy* 2, no. 1 (Winter 1996): 176–99.

Oyewùmí, Oyèrónké. *The Invention of Women: Making an African Sense of Western Gender Discourses.* Minneapolis: University of Minnesota Press, 1997.

Patterson, Orlando. *Freedom.* Vol. 1, *Freedom in the Making of Western Culture.* New York: Basic Books, 1992.

————. *Slavery and Social Death.* Rev. ed. Cambridge: Harvard University Press, 2005.

Redding, Robert, Jr., ed. *Two Early African American Philosophers.* Foreword by Lewis R. Gordon. Forthcoming.

Ricoeur, Paul. *From Text to Action: Essays in Hermeneutics, II.* Trans. Kathleen Blamey and John B. Thompson. Evanston, IL: Northwestern University Press, 1991.

Schmitt, Carl. *The Concept of the Political.* Trans. George Schwab. Chicago: University of Chicago Press, 1996.

Schopenhauer, Arthur. *The World as Will and Idea.* Trans. R. By Haldane and J. Kemp London: Kegan Paul, Trench, Trubner, 1883.

Schrag, Calvin. "Note on Kierkegaard's Teleological Suspension of the Ethical." In *Collected Papers: Betwixt and Between,* by Søren Kierkegaard, 27–32. Albany: State University of New York Press, 1994.

Schutz, Alfred. *Collected Papers.* Vol. 1, *The Problem of Social Reality,* ed. with intro. by Maurice Natanson and preface by H. L. Van Breda. The Hague: Martinus Nijhoff, 1962.

———. *The Phenomenology of the Social World.* Trans. by George Walsh and Frederick Lehnhert, with intro. by George Walsh. Evanston, IL: Northwestern University Press, 1970.

Senghor, Léopold Senghor. *Liberté: I.* Paris: Seuil, 1964.

Sharpley-Whiting, T. Denean. *Negritude Women.* Minneapolis: University of Minnesota Press, 2002.

Spinoza, Benedicto. *Ethics.* Ed. and trans. G. H. R. Parkinson. Oxford: Oxford University Press, 2000.

———. *Theological-political Treatise.* Trans. Samuel Shirley, intro. and annotation by Seymour Feldman. Indianapolis, IN: Hackett, 2001.

Taiwo, Olufemi. "On the Misadventures of National Consciousness: A Retrospect on Frantz Fanon's Gift of Prophecy." In *Fanon: A Critical Reader,* ed. Gordon et al., 255–71. Oxford: Blackwell Publishers, 1996.

Taylor, Charles. *Multiculturalism and the Politics of Recognition: An Essay.* Ed. with commentary by Amy Gutmann. Princeton: Princeton University Press, 1992.

West, Cornel. *Prophesy, Deliverance!: An Afro-American Revolutionary Christianity.* Philadelphia: Westminster Press, 1982.

———. *Keeping Faith: Philosophy and Race in America.* New York: Routledge, 1994.

Williams, Eric. *Capitalism and Slavery.* Chapel Hill: University of North Carolina Press, 1944.

Williams, Patrick, and Laura Chrisman, eds. *Colonial Discourse and Post-colonial Theory: A Reader.* New York: Columbia University Press, 1994.

Wilson, William Julius. *The Declining Significance of Race: Blacks and Changing American Institutions.* Chicago: University of Chicago Press, 1980.

———. *The Truly Disadvantaged: The Inner City, the Underclass, and Public Policy.* Chicago: University of Chicago Press, 1990.

Wiredu, Kwasi. *Cultural Universals and Particulars: An African Perspective.* Bloomington: Indiana University Press, 1996.

Wiredu, Kwasi, ed. *A Companion to African Philosophy.* Malden, MA: Blackwell, 2004.

Wynter, Sylvia. "Columbus, the Ocean Blue, and Fables That Stir the Mind: To Reinvent the Study of Letters." In *Poetics of the Americas: Race, Founding, and Textuality,* ed. Bainard Cowan and Jefferson Humphries, 141–64. Baton Rouge: Louisiana State University Press, 1997.

————. "Is 'Development' a Purely Empirical Concept or also Teleological?: A Perspective from 'We the Underdeveloped.'" In *Prospects for Recovery and Sustainable Development in Africa*, ed. Aguibou Y. Yansané, 299–316. Westport, CT: Greenwood Press, 1996.

————. "On How We Mistook the Map for the Territory, and Re-Imprisoned Ourselves in Our Unbearable Wrongness of Being, of *Désêtre*: Black Studies Toward the Human Project." In *Not Only the Master's Tools: African-American Studies in Theory and Practice*, ed. Lewis R. Gordon and Jane Anna Gordon, 107–72. Boulder, CO: Paradigm, 2006.

Yancy, George, "Political and Magical Realist Semiotics in Kamau Brathwaite's Reading of *The Tempest.*" *CLR James Journal* 12, no. 1 (2006): 85–108.

Yancy, George, ed. *African-American Philosophy: 17 Conversations*. New York: Routledge, 1999.

————. *Cornel West: A Critical Reader*. Malden, MA: Blackwell Publishers, 2001.

————. *The Philosophical I: Personal Reflections on Life in Philosophy*. Lanham, MD: Rowman & Littlefield, 2002.

————. *What White Looks Like: African-American Philosophers on the Whiteness Question*. New York: Taylor & Francis/Routledge, 2004.

What Is Latin American Philosophy?   6

JORGE J. E. GRACIA
State University of New York at Buffalo

WHY ASK "WHAT is Latin American philosophy"? The reasons we ask questions vary considerably. Questions have many purposes, and their purposes often reveal something about the kind of answers that those who ask them seek to provide. It makes sense, then, to ask for the purposes behind the question presented in the title of this chapter.

I see at least four that are interesting for us to consider in this context. First, a pedagogical purpose: When I teach a course on Latin American philosophy, I need to decide which thinkers to discuss and which texts to assign to students. This entails that I know what Latin American philosophy is, that is, what qualifies as Latin American philosophy and what does not.

A second purpose is historiographical. Some of us are interested in the history of Latin American philosophy, and this again requires that we determine the object of investigation. Questions about authors and materials to be studied surface again.

A third purpose has to do with issues of validation and authenticity. It is quite clear that some of those who teach and study Latin American philosophy are concerned with establishing its legitimacy, perhaps because they are philosophers who consider themselves to be Latin American or because they are Latin Americans and think that it is a good thing for us to have a philosophy of our own. This goes along with the fact that "philosophy" is an honorific term, perhaps not as honorific as "novelist" or "artist," but nonetheless appreciated enough so that every culture and ethnic and national group would like to have one.

Finally, there is an ideological purpose. Some of those who ask and answer the question of what Latin American philosophy is have as their primary aim to grind a certain ideological ax. They are concerned with it not for a love of knowledge in general, or even of knowledge about Latin American philosophy in particular, but rather because the study of Latin American philosophy will help them reach some other aim, be that political, religious, or what have you.

Aristotle noted long ago that the purpose, that is, what he called "telos," determines both what something is and its function. The telos of a human being for him, for example, is the acquisition of a certain kind of knowledge. And this telos determines what is both distinctive of humans (rationality) among other similar beings (animals) and the human function (to reason). If we take this idea seriously in the case we are considering—and it is particularly pertinent because the study of Latin American philosophy is a purposeful human activity—then we should expect that there might be differences in what is considered Latin American philosophy among those who study it, depending on the purposes they have in mind. Teachers will primarily have a pedagogical aim and consider their object of study differently perhaps than historiographers. And something similar could be said about those who have an ideological aim or those who search for validation and authenticity.

In the case of some other subjects, perhaps there might not be significant differences because the object of study has fairly well-established boundaries and its aim is also agreed upon. When we are concerned with cancer, for example, matters appear easier, at least in principle, insofar as the overall aim of the study of cancer is to cure and eradicate the decease. Anything that contributes to this aim is fair game to the investigator.

But Latin American philosophy poses difficulties because the purpose in studying it is not so clear or uniform and what qualifies as Latin American is not well-established. True, some authors and texts are clearly part of Latin American philosophy and regarded as such by everyone. No one disputes that Antonio Caso, Risieri Frondizi, Leopoldo Zea, and Francisco Miró Quesada are Latin American philosophers. Although there are disagreements as to the value and originality of their work, this work is uniformly accepted as philosophical and belonging in the canon of Latin American philosophy. Hence, any course on Latin American philosophy can, and perhaps should, include the study of these figures without apology, and the same goes for anyone interestd in the historiography of Latin American philosophy. Even those motivated by ideology or validation consider them part of the canon and either use them to support the case they

want to make or consider them exceptions of one kind or another to
whatever principles they wish to peddle. In short, the authors mentioned,
and their work, are part of what we call Latin American philosophy,
whether anybody likes it or not.

It is equally clear that many philosophers do not qualify as Latin American and their work is not part of the corpus of Latin American philosophical texts. Aristotle, Thomas Aquinas, Descartes, and Habermas, for
example, do not qualify, and no one working on Latin American philosophy would be taken seriously if he or she said that they were part of Latin
American philosophy, even though some Latin American philosophers have
been heavily influenced by their ideas. References to these authors in works
or courses on Latin American philosophy are acceptable, but their work is
not studied as Latin American. To understand Frondizi's views on the self,
for example, references to von Erhenfeld are essential, for Frondizi used this
philosopher's ideas about value and Gestalt to develop his own views. But it
is obvious that whereas Frondizi is clearly a Latin American philosopher,
and part of the Latin American philosophical canon, von Erhenfeld is not.

The authors I have mentioned pose no problems for the pedagogue or
historiographer of Latin American philosophy. But problems surface when
we consider texts and authors such as the *Popol Vuh* (the text that narrates
the Mayan creation myth), Bartolomé de Las Casas, Sor Juana Inés de la
Cruz, Simón Bolívar, Francisco Romero, Frantz Fanon, José Gaos, Héctor
Neri-Castañeda, Jorge Luis Borges, and Renzo Llorente.

The problem with the *Popol Vuh*, for example, is twofold. First, this is
not a clearly philosophical text in the most widespread Western understanding of the term. After all, there are many texts like this in the Western tradition and they are never included in the philosophical canon.
Consider, for example, the Egyptian *Book of the Dead* and the biblical books
of Genesis and Job. Even the *Iliad* and the *Odyssey* are not generally included in courses on the history of philosophy except to illustrate the
change historians of philosophy see between religious and literary texts and
the work of the pre-Socratics. If this is so, then why should we include the
Popol Vuh in the study of Latin American philosophy? Perhaps for the sake
of validation, to render philosophical legitimacy to the peoples of Latin
America before the Iberians arrived? Or perhaps the issue is ideological,
namely, that one wishes to change the way we generally think of philosophy in the West because one has some other idea in mind about the nature
of philosophy and its role in the social context.

Bartolomé de Las Casas poses a different problem. He is a Spaniard who
lived part of his life in Latin America and applied the scholastic philosophy

developed in the Middle Ages and practiced during his time in the Iberian peninsula to the Latin American context, particularly to the question of the humanity and rights of conquered peoples. His place of origin and the philosophical framework that he used count against him being part of the Latin American philosophical canon, but his concern with issues arising from the Latin American context, his advocacy for the well-being of pre-Columbian peoples, and the influence he exerted in the way both Latin Americans and non–Latin Americans think about these issues suggest that he should be included in the canon. Besides, no one can doubt that Las Casas's scholastic mode of argumentation fits what is considered philosophical in the West, and the philosophical issues raised by the conquest cannot be raised without mentioning Las Casas or his work. His work is clearly philosophical and inspired by the Latin American situation. Should we include him for ideological reasons, because he said the right things and defended the oppressed pre-Columbian populations or because otherwise there would be no Latin American philosophy at the time? So what do we do with him and why?

The case of Sor Juana is difficult in a different way. Because she was a woman, she was prevented from writing philosophy in the way that was common at the time. So in a sense we do not have any work from her that can be classified as philosophical strictly speaking. Yet, this prohibition did not prevent her from precisely making a case against philosophy in rational and rhetorical terms. She wrote poems that have ethical or moral relevance, although her style, as a humanist, was not what counts as strictly philosophical in the West. Keep in mind that Renaissance humanists have a hard time being included in the Western philosophical curriculum or the philosophical research canon. When was the last time you saw a course in philosophy that discussed the work of Lorenzo Valla, or a history of philosophy that does more than mention his name as a humanist? So on what basis should we include Sor Juana in a course on Latin American philosophy or include her as a figure to be studied in the historiography of Latin American philosophy when similar authors in Europe are generally excluded from consideration in courses and studies of European philosophy? Because she is a woman and we want to validate women's philosophical capacity? Because there is a certain ideological ax that we want to grind? Because the history of Latin American philosophy makes no sense without reference to her?

Francisco Romero fits well the criteria of Western philosopher: His writing is in line with standard philosophical texts, he was influenced by well-accepted Western philosophers, and the topics he discusses are common in the history of European philosophy. Yet, he was born in Spain, not Argentina. He was an immigrant to Argentina, just like I am in this country. Is he part of Latin American philosophy, then? In my case, my name appears on some lists of American philosophers, so there is no reason why he should be treated differently. But before we decide to include him we need to discuss the criteria of inclusion.

The case of Frantz Fanon is more complicated. He wrote in French and was born in Haiti. Does Latin America include this part of the world? Since the French created the term "Latin America," I am sure they would answer affirmatively, but few authors take this French part of the Americas into consideration when studying Latin American philosophy, and no anthologies of Latin American philosophy include the work of authors from this part of the Americas. There is, of course, a very serious bias against anything not Spanish speaking. Even Brazilian authors have problems of inclusion. But anything outside of the Iberian sphere of influence is almost automatically excluded. So on what basis do we include Fanon: ideology, validation, an expanded version of Latin America?

José Gaos is also a difficult case. He came to Latin America as an older person, fleeing from the political instability in Spain, but his impact on Mexico in particular was enormous. No history of Mexican philosophy makes sense without examining this impact, and perhaps no history of Latin American philosophy does either. Moreover, he also appropriated much that could be considered as arising from the Mexican situation; one could argue that he philosophizes from a Mexican context. But should we include reference to him as we do with José Ortega y Gasset (who also had an enormous influence on Latin American philosophy) and Ginés de Sepúlveda (who had no influence but engaged Las Casas in a philosophical controversy arising in Latin America), or do we include him as we would include Caso or Frondizi? I believe one can easily find cases outside Latin America, say in the United States, that pose similar questions.

Héctor Neri-Castañeda was born in Guatemala and emigrated to the United States when he was already trained in philosophy. But his entire career took place in this country and his thought has no discernible relation to anything Latin American. Indeed, like Mario Bunge, he seems to have shunned anything dealing with Latin America and Latin American thought, although he was very much in favor of promoting the interests of Latinos in the United States. Can we include him in a course on Latin American philosophy as part of that philosophy? And if we do, do we do it merely because of ideology, legitimation, or pride?

Everyone agrees that Jorge Luis Borges had a fantastic intellect, that his work was highly suggestive philosophically, and that he is a great writer. But is his work part of Latin American philosophy? The issue here is the nature of the work, not the Latin American credentials of the author. Some have argued that Borges's work is part of Latin American philosophy, and in order to include it they erase the distinction between philosophy and literature.[1] This proposal has a clear ideological and validation aim in the Latin American context, although similar proposals about the inclusion of literary figures in philosophy have been made in other contexts as well.[2] Those who argue for this position accept that "academic philosophy" in Latin America has not been particularly original, interesting, or of high quality, whereas Latin American literature is at the top of the charts. Moreover, no one questions that much of this literature is very philosophical (as with Borges, for example). So, why not change the definition of philosophy to include literature and then have great philosophy and philosophers in Latin America, the likes of Borges?

Finally we come to Renzo Llorente. Here is a son of Cuban immigrants, trained in the United States, living in Spain, speaking with a Castilian accent, and interested in Latin American philosophy. Is he a Latin American philosopher? Is his work to be included in the canon of Latin American philosophy? He tells me that he has never thought of including it.

Clearly we have no problem including the likes of Caso and Frondizi, or excluding the likes of von Erhenfeld and Descartes, but when we get to Las Casas, Sor Juana, Borges, and the others mentioned, we do. So, what should we do? Who is to be included in Latin American philosophy and what criteria are we going to use to determine inclusion? And how are we going to conceive Latin American philosophy in order to do this? These are the pertinent questions that we need to answer. Some of these belong to the philosophical historiography of Latin America, but some also include larger questions about the nature of philosophy and how to conceive it.

Before I turn to the philosophical dimension of these questions, it should be useful to look at how Latin Americans themselves have posed the question of Latin American philosophy and what general positions they have adopted with respect to it.

I. Latin Americans' View of Latin American Philosophy

Latin Americans themselves have been very concerned with Latin American philosophy.[3] Two topics have dominated the discussions. One is framed in terms of a question: Is there a Latin American philosophy? Another concerns itself with distinguishing what is frequently called academic and nonacademic philosophy, although other terms are also used such as Western and non-Western, European and autochthonous, genuine and imported, authentic and inauthentic, and so on. Both topics involve an understanding of philosophy in general and of Latin American philosophy in particular. Elsewhere I have discussed in some detail the three most common approaches to the first topic and their understanding of philosophy: the universalist, culturalist, and critical. Here I present an abbreviated version of that discussion.[4]

The universalist views philosophy as a universal discipline and no different from science, for example. Philosophy, like mathematics or physics, has an object that it studies and a method it employs in doing so. But neither the effectiveness of the method nor the truth value of the conclusions it reaches depend on particular circumstances or perspectives. Either material objects are composed of matter and form or they are not, and so Aristotelian hylomorphism is either true or false. The question of whether there is Latin American philosophy, then, depends on whether Latin Americans have been able to produce the kind of universal discipline that one expects when one has science as a model. Its problems are common to all humans, its method is also common, and its conclusions are supposed to be true, regardless of particular circumstances. Just as water is composed of a certain proportion of hydrogen and oxygen, so there are certain conditions that determine the sameness of an artifact over time. Most universalists see Latin American philosophy as largely a failure in this respect.

The culturalist thinks on the contrary that truth is always perspectival, dependent on a point of view and that the method to acquire it is always dependent on a cultural context. Philosophy, then, is a historical, nonscientific enterprise concerned with the elaboration of a general point of view from a certain personal or cultural perspective. But is there a Latin American philosophy? Why not, they ask? If Latin Americans have engaged in developing views from their perspective as individuals or as Latin Americans, and using whatever means they have found appropriate to do so, there cannot but be a Latin American philosophy.

Finally, the critical approach considers philosophy a result of a social condition and closely related to those conditions. Some conditions are conducive to the production of philosophy, or what is sometimes called "authentic philosophy," whereas others are not. So, is there a Latin American philosophy? For most critics the conditions operative in Latin

America preclude the development of philosophy, because all the philosophy developed in Latin America is inauthentic and therefore not true philosophy. The dependance of Latin America on ideas imported from elsewhere, or its situation as dominated, prevents its philosophy from being authentic; it is a borrowed, subservient philosophy.

The second topic that has dominated discussions of Latin American philosophy by Latin Americans is concerned with the kind of philosophy that is practiced in Latin America. One type is the philosophy developed in the academy, similar to what the scholastics developed in schools. It is a result of school activities and developed for academic purposes, the solution of puzzles of interest primarily to academics. The other type is the philosophy developed outside the academy, and this responds to the needs and conditions under which it is developed. Its mode of expression is not academic, even sometimes antiacademic, frequently becoming literary or polemical, and concerned with real problems and issues confronted by Latin Americans rather than with scholarly issues.

Often culturalists and critical philosophers accuse universalists of being academic philosophers and therefore of not being authentic or responsive to the needs of Latin America. Universalists respond by accusing culturalists and critical philosophers of not doing philosophy at all but rather of developing the kind of personal or cultural narrative that has no scientific or universal value.

It should be obvious that both positions beg the question insofar as both begin with a preestablished conception of philosophy that delegitimizes the other. The issue, then, does not have to do with Latin American philosophy as such, but with the nature of philosophy.

It should also be clear that the answer that is given to the questions we have asked is not descriptive but rather prescriptive. We are normatively told what is or is not Latin American philosophy and therefore how we should think about and deal with it in the classroom and as historiographers.

So far little headway has been made when it comes to answering the question we have raised in a way that does not beg the question or even is useful for understanding the issues involved. In this chapter, I propose a model to answer the question. The model is the conception of Latin American philosophy as an ethnic philosophy. This should serve us both to see how it is different from and similar to other philosophies, and it should help us decide what to include in courses on Latin American philosophy and in its study. But what is an ethnic philosophy?

II. Latin American Philosophy as Ethnic Philosophy

An ethnic philosophy is the philosophy of an ethnos. So we must begin by adopting a conception of ethnos.

A. Ethnos

For purpose of this analysis, I shall adopt the notion of an ethnos that I have defended elsewhere: An ethnos is a subgroup of individual humans who satisfy the following conditions: (1) they belong to many generations; (2) they are organized as a family and break down into extended families; and (3) they are united through historical relations that produce features which, in context, serve (i) to identify the members of the group and (ii) to distinguish them from members of other groups.[5]

The main feature of an ethnic group is that it is like a large family in which no members necessarily have to share a common feature in order to belong to it. The basic principle of this view, which I like to call the "familial-historical view of ethnicity," is that there is no necessarily identifiable feature, or set of features, that is common to all members of an ethnic group throughout the history of the group. This accounts for the lack of agreement among members of ethnic groups, and among those who study them, concerning any particular conditions, or even kinds of conditions, that are necessary and sufficient for ethnicity. Even the most superficial research indicates that different groups and individuals do not agree on any conditions; ethnic groups are not homogeneous. We must, then, abandon the project of trying to conceive ethnic groups in terms of any constant and empirically discernible features. This means, in turn, that in order to belong to an ethnic group it is not necessary that one share a feature or set of features with other members of the group, which explains why, in his attempt to characterize ethnicity, Weber concluded that it is not feasible to go beyond vague generalizations.[6] Indeed, contrary to what many think, it is not even necessary that the members of the group name themselves in any particular way or have a conscious sense of belonging to the group. Some of them may in fact consider themselves so and even have an awareness, or sense, of themselves as a group, but it is not necessary that all of them do.

Members of an ethnos are tied by the same kind of thing that ties the members of a family, as Wittgenstein would say.[7] They belong to the same group because they are historically related, as a father is to a daughter, an aunt to a nephew, and grandparents to grandchildren. Wittgenstein's metaphor of family resemblance is particularly appropriate in this case, but the metaphor of the family must be interpreted correctly to avoid any misunderstanding of it as requiring genetic ties. One does not need to be tied genetically to other members of a family to be a member of the family. Indeed, perhaps the most important foundation of a family, namely marriage, takes place between people who are added to a family through contract, not a genetic link. And in-laws become members of families indirectly, again not through genesis. This means that the very notion of resemblance used by Wittgenstein is misleading if it is taken as requiring a genetic connection. It also means that any requirements of coherence and homogeneity do not apply. Families are not coherent wholes composed of homogeneous elements; they include members that differ substantially from each other and may clash in various ways. Physical features vary widely within the same family, and views of the world, politics, and religion, for example, can be quite opposed.

This does not entail that other factors do not play roles in particular contexts in the constitution of ethnic groups, contributing both to their creation and preservation. To deny that they do would be to be blind to reality. According to the familial-historical view, history generates relations that in turn generate properties among members of groups and serve to unite them among themselves and to distinguish them from others in particular contexts. But what would these features have to do with, but political organization, territorial boundaries, language, religion, culture, race, genetic lineage, experience, self-awareness, and other-group identification? Indeed, this is the reason why ethnicity is frequently confused both with nationality and race, and why it is often also understood in purely cultural terms. It is easy to think of an ethnic group in terms of national origin (e.g., Cuban), race (e.g., "black"), language (e.g., Catalan), religion (e.g., Jewish), or culture (e.g., Arab) precisely because these are factors that play a role in ethnic unity.

Another important consequence of this understanding of ethnicity is that there are seldom strict boundaries between ethne. There are some people who clearly belong, and some that clearly do not belong, but there are others whose membership is not clear. This is not a consequence of the familial-historical view but rather something quite evident in our experience of ethne. My view merely accommodates it. Consider the case of Latinos in the United States. I clearly belong because I was born in Cuba, have unique historical relations to other Cubans and some other Latin Americans, share in a composite Hispanic culture some of whose features are common to some other Latinos, and so on. Clearly, my sons-in-law are not Latinos. One has English ancestry and his contact with Latin cultures is only second hand, through marriage. And something similar can be said about the other. But what are we to say about the children they have with my daughters? Are they Latinos? The case is not clear, is it? In short, ethnic boundaries are not always strict, and I say "not always" because there are some ethne in which they seem to be, while in others they are not.

B. Ethnic Philosophy

When we apply this notion of ethnicity to philosophy, we get the view that an ethnic philosophy is the philosophy of an ethnos, and insofar as it is so, and members of ethne do not necessarily share features in common, then what the philosophy of a particular ethnos is exactly will not require any features in common with other philosophies outside the ethnos or even within the ethnos throughout its history. This, I claim, is the best way of understanding the unity of Latin American philosophy.

Historians of philosophy have worked very hard trying to find something common to all philosophy in Latin America, but they have failed miserably. I count myself among those who have tried, but reality has defeated us. It is indisputable that there are common elements between various philosophers, or even some philosophical movements, in Latin America. There is much that is common among scholastic authors in Latin America, or among positivists, for example. But it is not possible to find anything common throughout the history of Latin American philosophy even if we consider only those authors that everyone agrees are part of it. But we can explain the unity of Latin American philosophy if we understand it as an ethnic philosophy. Latin American philosophy is one insofar as all its parts are related in various ways that have helped develop particular properties in context and that separate Latin American philosophy from the philosophy of France or from American philosophy. The unity of the philosophy, just like that of an ethnos, has to do with contextual historical relations, and these also help to distinguish it from other philosophies in context.

Note that what determines membership in an ethnos consists of both the internal and external factors that shape it in a unique way in context. And so it is with its philosophy: Latin American philosophy is the philosophy the Latin American ethnos has developed in the circumstances in which the members of the ethnos have found themselves throughout history. It makes no sense to impose on an ethnic philosophy criteria that are not ethnic. We cannot apply to Latin American philosophy criteria that were developed in

Indian, or French, or British philosophy, and then say that because it does not fit those criteria, it is not philosophy or not good philosophy. What Latin American philosophy is, when it is understood ethnically, can be asked only in the context of the Latin American ethnos.

Note that, as with an ethnos, membership qualifications are negotiated and depend on a variety of factors, some external and some internal. Membership has to do with what actually happens historically. One of the factors is what the members of the ethnos itself think, but this is neither a necessary nor a sufficient condition of inclusion or exclusion.

So what is the advantage of this view? It explains the continuity of Latin American philosophy throughout its history. It also explains that such philosophy may include texts that are not included in the history of philosophy in other ethne, or in scientific, universal philosophy. And it also explains how Latin America philosophy is different and why it is different from other philosophies. Moreover, it also serves to solve some of the problems concerning inclusion and exclusion raised at the beginning of this chapter, or at least to raise questions regarding it that are interesting. What do we do with the *Popol Vuh*, Las Casas, Sor Juana, Bolívar, Romero, Fanon, Gaos, Neri-Castañeda, Borges, and Llorente? Are they part of Latin American philosophy?

What do we do with the *Popol Vuh* and similar pre-Columbian texts? Susana Nuccetelli and Gary Seay include these texts in their recent anthology, but they speak of them as "thought" rather than philosophy.[8] And Elizabeth Millán-Zaibert and I come right out and say that they are not philosophy strictly speaking; indeed, we do not include them in our anthology cited earlier. On the other hand, Miguel León-Portilla and others have argued that they are to be considered part of Latin American philosophy. Who is right?

If we were to adopt a strict understanding of philosophy as we have it (as exemplified in college curricula, journals, and other similar venues) in the West, they could not qualify. We do not include Genesis or the Egyptian *Book of the Dead* among the sources that are discussed in courses on Western philosophy, so why should we include the *Popol Vuh*? On what bases can we justify their inclusion in a course on or in an investigation into Latin American philosophy? Legitimacy? Ideology? Authenticity? Pedagogy? Historiography?

However, if we adopt an ethnic conception of Latin American philosophy, then the issue becomes something different and more complex, for then it turns on how these texts are related to the ethnos and what counts as philosophy for the ethnos. If there is such an ethnos as Latin American—

and this is a question that needs to be addressed, of course—then we can ask whether these texts are part of what counts as philosophy in the context of this ethnos. This means that whether they are to be accepted or not as Latin American philosophy is not measured by some exclusively external standard of rationality, topical relevance, or methodology. For membership in an ethnos is contextual and historical, and what counts as something belonging to the ethnos, such as its philosophy, is not determined exclusively from the outside. It is negotiated between the outside and the inside, and it is determined for particular times and places, just as the ethnic identity is.

So, is the *Popol Vuh* to be included in Latin American philosophy? The issue now shifts to whether pre-Columbians can be considered part of the Latin American ethnos and why. Moreover, the question for us here has also to do with how the Latin American ethnos functions, is regarded by others, and regards itself. Tomorrow is another day, of course, and things might change. But this is just as it should be, for ethne are fluid historical phenomena.

Still, you probably want me to tell you what I think about the *Popol Vuh*: Does it belong or not to Latin American philosophy? I do not want to answer the question because I do not find it philosophically interesting. The interesting issue has to do rather with the kind of question we should ask in order to determine whether the *Popol Vuh* is part of Latin American philosophy or not. Once the right kind of question is asked, I contend, we can proceed to examine possible answers, most of which will have to be dealt with in disciplines other than philosophy, such as history and sociology. But the issues that the question I propose raises are very different from what Latin Americans and historiographers of Latin American philosophy have been asking thus far.

Let me add three more comments before I move to the next section, where I compare Latin American philosophy with other philosophies. First, an ethnic philosophy, just like an ethnos, has no strict boundaries for all times and places. What counts as Latin American philosophy considered ethnically may vary a great deal throughout the history of the ethnos. Second, an ethnic philosophy depends on the existence of the ethnos. If Latin Americans do not constitute an ethnos, then the whole notion of an ethnic Latin American philosophy falls apart. Third, what is included in Latin American philosophy, considered ethnically, can be much more, or much less, than if it is conceived differently.

So, now we see that what I have said about the *Popol Vuh* applies, mutatis mutandis, to the other cases I raised. We need to answer the question of whether these authors and their work can be considered part of the philosophy of a Latin American ethnos.

Now, when we adopt an ethnic understanding of Latin American philosophy, we also encounter questions about its relationship to other philosophies. How is it related to "scientific, universal" philosophy? How is it related to British, European, French, Iberian, Roman, Greek, and Western philosophies?

III. Latin American Philosophy and Other Philosophies

The first issue that we need to settle is whether these other philosophies are themselves ethnic or whether they are not. We all know that science is heavily influenced by its context and the culture and environment in which it occurs. But we also know that science attempts to divest itself from those trappings and achieve a status that goes beyond such contexts. And I think it is clear that it often succeeds. The claim "Taking an aspirin pill everyday generally helps prevent heart attacks in males" has been shown to be true.

Of course, the issue concerned with the independence of science from culture is not undisputed.[9] Some philosophers think that science can never entirely divest itself from its context, whereas others believe it can. We cannot settle this issue here, but we should be able to agree that most scientists regard science as striving to make claims that are not bound by context or perspective (the terminology varies from author to author), and science succeeds in doing so. This means that science can never be considered ethnic, as least in its purpose, and that what counts as science cannot be tied necessarily to an ethnos. In this, science is very different from ethnic philosophy, such as I have presented in the case of Latin American philosophy.

So, we may ask, are British, European, French, Iberian, Roman, Greek, and Western philosophies ethnic? Clearly, most philosophers in these groups have considered themselves to be nonethnic. Indeed, many of them have considered themselves to be scientists of a sort. But there has always been a group of philosophers, some even considered to be antiphilosophers by others, who have argued that some, or all, of these philosophies are the sort of thing I have claimed to be ethnic. Others think that, although these philosophies might have included ethnic elements at some point, their aim has always been scientific and universal, and this aim sufficiently justifies their universal status. Why? Because the standards for inclusion as good philosophy have to do with methods and standards of truth that are not ethnically bound.

Obviously, we are not going to settle this issue here, nor do we need to in order to make the point I want to make. The point is that we can conceive Latin American philosophy in two ways. We can think of it in ethnic terms, as the expression of a particular group of people who have been related in various ways in a historical context and who have developed a view about the world, including philosophy, that is informed by the circumstances in which they have found themselves. If we do this, we can then proceed to ask about which texts and figures fit that model, and the standards of inclusion are probably going to be different from those adopted in a nonethnic model of Latin American philosophy. In the nonethnic model, what counts are the standards that philosophers all over the world have been trying to develop independently of ethnic contexts. So only what meets those standards that is produced by Latin Americans or in Latin America qualifies as philosophy. And the label "Latin American" merely refers to provenance.

Now, depending on whether one considers philosophy ethnically or universally, the same Latin American author or text may or may not count as part of philosophy. We probably would want to say that the *Popul Vuh* counts as part of Latin American philosophy considered ethnically, but it is clear that it does not count as part of universal philosophy. The cases of Romero and Frondizi are different, for they count as part of both. And could there be someone who counts as part of universal philosophy in Latin America and not as part of Latin American philosophy considered ethnically? There is no reason why not, although it would depend on the criteria of inclusion in Latin American philosophy. At present there would not be anyone, for the criteria of inclusion in Latin American philosophy conceived ethnically includes those who work in universal philosophy.

One corollary of this position is the need to keep a broad conception of philosophy within which there are many varieties of the discipline. In the sixties and seventies, it was a common thing for practitioners of British ordinary language philosophy to go around departments of philosophy saying that other people in the departments who did not practice their kind of philosophy were not philosophers and that their work did not count as philosophy. This dismissive attitude has never been absent in the United States, and it is frequently found in Latin America, both among analytic and Continental philosophers, to name just two widespread philosophical traditions.

What can one gain from this attitude, except a sense of power in disenfranchising others? Would it not be more fruitful for everyone to try to understand what the other is doing that he or she calls philosophy? This is what I have tried to do here. My aim has been to show that there is a way of understanding philosophy in ethnic terms, apart from its understanding as, say, a science. Moreover, understanding philosophy ethnically explains why in certain parts of the world philosophy is more broadly conceived than in other parts and includes religious treatises and literature. Indeed, what counts as philosophy, understood ethnically, is very much a matter of context. To open the door to the understanding of philosophy in this way does not in any way undermine doing philosophy in some other way, for example, as a science, if that is indeed possible, which brings me to a last point.

We should be aware that many of the philosophies that have been peddled as scientific are anything but that. Recall that the very notion of science has changed much in the history of the West, let alone in the history of the world. What the medievals conceived as science is quite different from what the moderns conceived as science. For the medievals science consisted in the development of a deductive system in which conclusions followed necessarily from premises that were self-evident or based on self-evident premises, whereas for authors such as Bacon and Mill, science was a primarily inductive enterprise. So here again, talk about a scientific philosophy must be qualified and contextualized, for what that may mean can be very different, depending on what one understands by science.

If scientific philosophy is philosophy that imitates science as this is practiced in the West today, I do not know that there are any current scientific philosophers. Just read the most "scientific" of them and you will find many holes, unsupported statements, unwarranted speculation, unempirical claims, and unquestioned assumptions, let alone undefined terms and shoddy methodology. Not too long ago, one of my daughters, who teaches medicine at a fancy university, told me that she was doing some research on the relation between race and medicine. I suggested that she look at some philosophical literature on the subject, and she did. But she found it completely useless, full of hot air, unsupported claims, and ideological assumptions. I was not surprised. Philosophy is not science and it has never been science, when science is conceived in the terms in which it is carried out in science departments of universities today. Those philosophers who claim that what they are doing is scientific, as the members of the Vienna Circle did, are generally ignorant of science and blind to the enterprise in which they are engaged.

Of course, one can be in favor of clarity and rigor. One can be concerned with the same kinds of problems that Plato and Aristotle were concerned with. One can even understand that to do certain conceptual analyses logic is necessary, a point that Abelard made several centuries ago, repeating, without knowing it, a claim implied in much of what Aristotle and some other ancient philosophers did. And one can strive, as scientists do, to make claims whose truth does not depend on particular perspectives or cultures. But none of this entails that only philosophy that does so is philosophy, for even the greatest practitioners of clarity and rigor often fall short of the standard they would like to meet. Indeed, many of them are not even trying to be clear and rigorous in practice. And something similar can be said about their method and aims. It makes better sense to say that some of them practice philosophy with certain standards in mind or that they belong to a philosophical tradition in which clarity and rigor are part of the modus operandi, although most philosophers who engage in self-criticism know that the validity of such standards is a matter of debate among philosophers and no general agreement about what they are has been achieved, even among those who claim to have and follow them. There are philosophers that follow other standards, and there are philosophers whose standards are set by their ethnic context, and this should not disqualify them from being labeled philosophers, even if they cannot be labeled "scientific" philosophers.

IV. Universalism, Culturalism, and Critical Philosophy Revisited

So how is the proposal I have presented concerning Latin American philosophy different from the universalist, culturalist, and critical views? In several ways. It accepts the view, contrary to what many hard culturalists argue, that there is a legitimate conception of philosophy that is not bound by context or perspective in aim or method, but this has to be qualified in two ways: First, the aim does not necessarily translate into a reality; indeed, it becomes very difficult to find philosophy that is completely neutral to context and perspective, even if its method is codified in noncontextual or nonperspectival terms. Second, this does not entail that philosophy is scientific in any sense of science that is current today, although it may still be a rigorous enterprise that aims for universal validity.

The view presented, then, differs from the culturalist view in that it makes room for a universalist philosophy, and it differs from the universalist view in that it locates the universalist aspect of philosophy in its aim and method, rather than on a certain achievement of that aim even when the method is implemented. It also differs from the culturalist view in that the culturalist view is not an ethnic view. For the culturalist, what is important is the cultural perspective from which the philosophy is developed and the originality that is supposed to result from that. But in ethnic philosophy what is important is the identity of an ethnos and what is considered philosophy for that ethnos. This means that ethnic philosophy is not bound by any particular criteria, for ethne are changing realities whose parameters are historically contingent. (And a similar criticism can be made of the critical position.) Questions of authenticity, domination, and so on do not enter into the picture at all unless they are relevant for a particular ethnic philosophy.

Having said this, it should be clear that the overall aim of my answer to the question—What is Latin American philosophy?—has been to open a window to a dimension of reality that we otherwise would miss. And, of course, the reason for this window is that we need to decide what to study and what to teach when we teach Latin American philosophy. We also need to answer the question Latin Americans have posed about the existence of their philosophy. Finally, there is also a deeper philosophical aim, namely, the opening of a window to a different set of questions and ways of posing the problems of the nature of Latin American philosophy in particular and of philosophy in general. Rather than sitting in judgment about what philosophy is or is not from a particular conception of the discipline, I have suggested a way of initiating a discussion that is more profitable insofar as it engages a set of issues that otherwise would be ignored. If, as Aristotle said, curiosity is characteristic of humans, then we should welcome openings of this sort rather than positions that preclude further discussion.

Is the distinction between ethnic and nonethnic philosophy useful when thinking about Latin American philosophy? I think so. If we adopt the ethnic model, we are able to see things that we would not see otherwise, and vice versa with the nonethnic model. As historians of philosophy and as philosophers interested in Latin American philosophy and the philosophically interesting historiographical issues raised by it, we can profit from both models, and it is fruitless to insist that we adopt one to the exclusion of the other.[10]

Notes

1. See José Luis Gómez Martínez, "Posmodernidad, discurso antrópico y ensayística latinoamericana," *Dissens, Revista Internacional de Pensamiento Latinoameri-*

cano 2 (1996): 45; and Pedro Lange Churrión and Eduardo Mendieta, "Philosophy and Literature: The Latin American Case," *Dissens* 2 (1996): 37-40.

2. See Gómez Martínez, "Posmodernidad," 45 and 46. Ermanno Bencivenga, William Irwin, Jorge Gracia, and Deborah Knight explore this question in Jorge Gracia, Carolyn Korsmeyer, and Rodolphe Gasché, eds., *Literary Philosophers: Borges, Calvino, Eco* (New York: Routledge, 2002).

3. The literature on this topic is quite extensive. Jorge Gracia and Iván Jaksić have collected the main texts in *Filosofía e identidad cultural en América Latina* (Caracas: Monte Avila, 1988). For sources in English, see the third part of Jorge Gracia and Elizabeth Millán-Zaibert, eds., *Latin American Philosophy for the Twenty-First Century* (Buffalo, NY: Prometheus Books, 2004).

4. See chapter 5 of Jorge Gracia, *Hispanic/Latino Identity* (Oxford: Blackwell, 2000).

5. This view is developed in Jorge Gracia, *Surviving Race, Ethnicity, and Nationality: A Challenge for the Twenty-First Century* (Lanham, MD: Rowman & Littlefield, 2005).

6. Max Weber, "What is an Ethnic Group?" in *The Ethnicity Reader: Nationalism, Multiculturalism and Migration,* ed. M. Guibernau and J. Rex (Cambridge: Polity Press, 1997), 22 and 24. See also Everett C. Hughes, *Our Work, Race, and the Sociological Imagination,* ed. L. A. Coser (Chicago: University of Chicago Press, 1994), 91.

7. Ludwig Wittgenstein, *Philosophical Investigations,* trans. by G. E. M. Anscombe (New York: Macmillan, 1981), § 67.

8. Susana Nuccetelli and Gary Seay, eds., *Latin American Philosophy: An Introduction with Readings* (Upper Saddle River, NJ: Prentice Hall, 2004).

9. See, for example, the discussion in Martin Kusch, ed., *The Sociology of Philosophical Knowledge* (Dordrecht: Kluwer, 2000).

10. I am grateful to William Cooper, Renzo Llorente, Michael Monahan, Gregory Pappas, and Arleen Salles for various suggestions and criticisms based on an earlier draft of this paper.

Bibliography

Ardao, Arturo. "Assimilation and Transformation of Positivism in Latin America." *Journal of the History of Ideas* 24 (1963): 515–22.

Beuchot, Mauricio. *The History of Philosophy in Colonial Mexico.* Trans. Elizabeth Millán. Foreword by Jorge J. E. Gracia. Washington, DC: Catholic University of America Press, 1998.

Crawford, William Rex. *A Century of Latin American Thought,* 3rd ed. New York: Praeger, 1966.

Cruz Costa, João. *A History of Ideas in Brazil: The Development of Philosophy in Brazil and the Evolution of National History.* Berkeley: University of California Press, 1965.

Dascal, Marcelo, ed. *Cultural Relativism and Philosophy: North and Latin American Perspectives.* Leiden, Netherlands: E. J. Brill, 1991.

Davis, Harold Eugene. *Latin American Social Thought: The History of Its Development since Independence, with Selected Readings.* Washington, DC: University Press of Washington, 1963.

———. *Latin American Thought: A Historical Introduction.* New York: Free Press, 1972.

Fernández Retamar, Roberto. *Calibán and Other Essays.* Trans. Edward Baker. Minneapolis: University of Minnesota Press, 1980.

Ferrater Mora, José. *La filosofía en América. Vol. 1, Actas del IX Congreso Interamericano de Filosofía.* Caracas: Sociedad Venezolana de Filosofía, 1979.

Frondizi, Risieri. "Is There an Ibero-American Philosophy?" *Philosophy and Phenomenological Research* 9 (1948–1949): 345–55.

———. "On the Unity of the Philosophies of the Two Americas." *Review of Metaphysics* 4 (1951): 617–22.

Gaos, José. *En torno a la filosofía mexicana.* Intro. by Leopoldo Zea. Mexico City: Alianza, 1980.

Gaos, José, ed. *Antología del pensamiento de lengua española en la edad contemporánea.* Mexico City: Séneca, 1945.

Gómez Martínez, José, ed. Proyecto Ensayo Hispánico. Available from www .ensayistas.org.

Gómez Robledo, Antonio. *La filosofía en el Brasil.* Mexico City: Imprenta Universitaria, 1946.

Gracia, Jorge J. E. "Ethnic Labels and Philosophy," in *Latin American Philosophy: Currents, Issues, Debates,* ed. Eduardo Mendieta. Bloomington: Indiana University Press, 2003.

———. *Filosofía hispánica: Concepto, origen y foco historiográfico.* Pamplona, Spain: Universidad de Navarra, 1998.

———. *Hispanic/Latino Identity: A Philosophical Perspective.* Oxford: Blackwell, 2000.

Gracia, Jorge J. E., ed. *Latin American Philosophy Today.* Double issue of *The Philosophical Forum* 20, nos. 1–2 (1988–1989).

Gracia, Jorge J. E., and Mireya Camurati, eds. *Philosophy and Literature in Latin America: A Critical Assessment of the Current Situation.* Albany: State University of New York Press, 1989.

Gracia, Jorge J. E., and Iván Jaksić, eds. *Filosofía e identidad cultural en América Latina.* Caracas, Venezuela: Monte Avila, 1988.

Gracia, Jorge J. E., and Elizabeth Millán-Zaibert, eds. *Latin American Philosophy for the 21st Century: The Human Condition, Values, and the Search for Identity.* New York: Prometheus, 2004.

Gracia, Jorge J. E., Eduardo Rabossi, Enrique Villanueva, and Marcelo Dascal, eds. *Philosophical Analysis in Latin America.* Dordrecht, Netherlands: Kluwer, 1984.

More extensive Spanish edition: *El análisis filosófico en América Latina.* Mexico City: Fondo de Cultura Económica, 1985.

Jaksić, Iván. *Academic Rebels in Chile: The Role of Philosophy in Higher Education and Politics.* Albany: State University of New York Press, 1989.

León-Portilla, Miguel. *Time and Reality in the Thought of the Maya.* 2nd ed. Norman: University of Oklahoma Press, 1988.

Liss, S. B. *Marxist Thought in Latin America.* Berkeley: University of California Press, 1984.

Löwy, M., ed. *Marxism in Latin America from 1909 to the Present: An Anthology.* Trans. M. Pearlman. Atlantic Highlands, NJ: Humanities Press, 1990.

Martí, Oscar R. "Is There a Latin American Philosophy?" *Metaphilosophy* 1 (1983): 46–52.

Mayz Vallenilla, Ernesto. *El problema de América.* Caracas, Venezuela: Ediciones de la Universidad Simón Bolívar, 1992.

Mendieta, Eduardo, ed. *Latin American Philosophy: Currents, Issues, Debates.* Bloomington: Indiana University Press, 2003.

Miró Quesada, Francisco. "The Impact of Metaphysics on Latin American Ideology." *Journal of the History of Ideas* 29 (1963): 539–52.

Nuccetelli, Susana. *Latin American Thought: Philosophical Problems and Arguments.* Boulder, CO: Westview Press, 2002.

Nuccetelli, Susana, and Gary Seay, eds. *Latin American Philosophy: An Introduction with Readings.* Upper Saddle River, NJ: Prentice Hall, 2004.

Redmond, W. *Bibliography of the Philosophy in the Iberian Colonies of America.* The Hague: Nijhoff, 1972.

Roig, Arturo Andrés. "Nuestra América frente al panamericanismo y el hispanismo: la lectura de Leopoldo Zea." In *América Latina. Historia y destino. Homenaje a Leopodo Zea,* ed. Horacio Cerutti-Guldberg, 279–84. Mexico City: Universidad Nacional Autónoma de México, 1992.

———. *Teoría y crítica del pensamiento latinoamericano.* Mexico City: Fondo de Cultura Económica, 1981.

Romero, Francisco. *Sobre la filosofía en America.* Buenos Aires: Raigal, 1952.

Sáenz, Mario, ed. *Latin American Perspectives on Globalization: Ethics, Politics, and Alternative Visions.* Lanham, MD: Rowman & Littlefield, 2002.

Salles, Arleen, and Elizabeth Millán-Zaibert, eds. *The Role of History in Latin American Philosophy.* Albany: State University of New York Press, 2005.

Sánchez Reulet, A., ed. *Contemporary Latin American Philosophy: A Selection with an Introduction and Notes.* Trans. W. R. Trask. Albuquerque: University of New Mexico Press, 1954.

Sasso, Javier. *La filosofía latinoamericana y las construcciones de su historia.* Caracas, Venezuela: Monte Ávila, 1998.

Schutte, Ofelia. *Cultural Identity and Social Liberation in Latin American Thought.* New York: State University of New York Press, 1993.

Stabb, Martin S. *The Dissenting Voice: The New Essay of Spanish America, 1960–1985*. Austin: University of Texas Press, 1995.

———. *In Quest of Identity: Patterns in the Spanish American Essay of Ideas, 1890–1960*. Chapel Hill: University of North Carolina Press, 1967.

Woodward, R. L., ed. *Positivism in Latin America: 1850–1900: Are Order and Progress Reconcilable?* Lexington, MA: Heath, 1971.

Zea, Leopoldo. *El pensamiento latinoamericano*. Barcelona: Ariel, 1976.

———. *The Latin-American Mind*. Trans. James H. Abbott and Lowell Dunham. Norman: University of Oklahoma Press, 1963.

———. *Positivism in Mexico*. Austin: University of Texas Press, 1974.

———. *The Role of the Americas in History*. Savage, MD: Rowman & Littlefield, 1992.

What Is American Indian Philosophy?   **7**
Toward a Critical Indigenous Philosophy

DALE TURNER
Dartmouth College

> *"So you are saying that human agreement decides what is true
> and what is false?"—It is what humans say that is true and
> false; and they agree in the language they use. That is not
> agreement in opinions but in form of life.*

> —LUDWIG WITTGENSTEIN, PHILOSOPHICAL INVESTIGATIONS (§ 241)

> *I sell the shadow to support the substance.*

> —SOJOURNER TRUTH

MARILYN NOTAH VERNEY has a straightforward definition of American Indian philosophy: "I refer to the beliefs and teachings of my people as American Indian philosophy."[1] The invocation of the Eurocentric term "philosophy" does not pose a problem for Verney, nor should it. American Indian philosophy constitutes, more or less, one of many "ways of knowing" the world. Professional philosophers, however, are less inclined to view philosophy in the same spirit. Most contemporary professional philosophers would not seriously consider the claim that philosophy is simply *a way* of thinking about the world. But, as I will try to show in this chapter, the claim raises some serious concerns for an indigenous intellectual culture. What exactly are American Indian "ways of knowing the world"? More importantly, do these ways of knowing constitute philosophy in the Western European sense—and does it matter? These are important questions, especially for the next generation of indigenous intellectuals.

I claim that understanding an indigenous way of knowing the world (however we label it) embraces a different kind of intellectual activity than does engaging what I call a "critical indigenous philosophy." The addition of the word "critical" means that we must engage the discourses, practices, and institutions that are used to characterize indigenous rights, sovereignty, and nationhood within a constitutional democracy. The purpose of this chapter is to reflect upon what it means to make a distinction between, and to understand better, the relationship between indigenous ways of knowing the world and a critical indigenous philosophy.[2]

In order to make the distinction between indigenous ways of knowing the world and a critical indigenous philosophy I must begin with the following caveat: However I use the term "philosophy" I do not use it to mean the same thing as "spirituality."[3] Indigenous spirituality embraces what Wittgenstein calls a "form of life."[4] It is this distinctive way of living one's life that makes indigenous cultures distinctive. A critical indigenous philosophy, on the other hand, engages different sets of practices; it arises out of a particular kind of cross-cultural dialogue between American Indian ways of knowing the world, of which American Indian spirituality plays an important part, and the legal and political practices of the dominant culture. These practices guide the politicized "discourses" of American Indian rights, sovereignty, and nationhood that define the contemporary legal and political relationship tribes have with the American state.[5]

The discourses of rights, sovereignty, and nationhood have been and continue to be used to marginalize, distort, and delegitimate American Indian understandings of their political identity. But colonialism is woven deep into the fabric of American Indian intellectual life. For better or worse, American Indians use these discourses to defend and assert their rights, sovereignty, and nationhood within the legal and political practices of the state. Over the course of the relationship American Indians have come to understand only too well how tribal sovereignty is understood in American law and implemented in federal Indian policies.

But there is an uneasy tension between American Indian spirituality and a critical indigenous philosophy. The tension is highlighted when we consider an important third kind of intellectual activity. This third activity, what I call "indigenous philosophy," has evolved out of the long ongoing dialogue between Western European and indigenous cultures. What distinguishes indigenous philosophy from indigenous spirituality, as I intend it, is that indigenous philosophy represents an attempt to *explain* to the dominant culture—usually in English—the meaning and content of indigenous ways of thinking about the world. What distinguishes indigenous philosophy from a *critical* indigenous philosophy is the explicit political nature that I attach to a critical indigenous philosophy.

In Canada, the United States, New Zealand, and Australia indigenous peoples de facto possess "special" forms of political recognition that the state has incorporated into its legal and political practices. These forms of political recognition distinguish indigenous peoples from other minority groups within these four constitutional democracies. Indigenous peoples take their "special" status within the state very seriously. It matters, though, how we go about asserting and defending this special status; more importantly, it matters who participates in the legal and political practices of the state.

In this chapter, I defend two claims. First, I argue that American Indian spirituality ought to remain embedded in our communities and that our survival as distinctive indigenous nations is rooted in the need to maintain our distinctive relationships to our homelands. Second, I argue that a critical indigenous philosophy offers *a way* for American Indians to assert and defend the integrity of our indigeneity and that we can be empowered to do so by engaging the discourses of rights, sovereignty, and nationhood of the state.[6] Taken together, these two claims raise a deep colonial tension: The source of our indigeneity lies in our relationships to our homelands; yet, in order to defend the political integrity of these relationships we must engage the legal and political discourses of the state. In other words, indigenous peoples can only empower themselves politically by using the legal and political discourses of the state.

My discussion follows in two sections. In the first section, I explain why we must begin our investigation of a critical indigenous philosophy by distinguishing it from indigenous spirituality. There must be a clear distinction between the two because they embrace radically different attitudes about the world. American Indian spirituality embraces a way of living that is in accordance with so-called traditional ways of knowing. (It is not my task to articulate the meaning and content of American Indian spirituality. Understanding the distinctive cultural practices that characterize indigenous spiritual traditions involves a kind of learning process that goes well beyond the written text.) My task, rather, is to keep indigenous spirituality out of contemporary critical discussions of indigenous rights, sovereignty, and nationhood.[7]

A critical indigenous philosophy, on the other hand, has a much more clearly defined purpose in the dominant culture—at least as I understand it. Contact with Europeans and the reality of colonialism has created the need for a critical indigenous philosophy. A critical indigenous philosophy asserts and defends the integrity of indigenous rights, sovereignty, and nationhood by explicitly engaging the legal and political discourses of the state. The difficult task facing contemporary indigenous intellectuals is that they must engage these discourses guided by indigenous ways of knowing the world. How to do so effectively (and justly) is a major problem for contemporary indigenous leadership.

In the second section, I examine more closely what I mean by a critical indigenous philosophy. With the signing of treaties we began the slow insidious process of negotiating away our humanity. We have resisted whitewashed interpretations of history and have come to bear the consequences of its uses in law and politics. At the same time, survival has dictated that we gradually become skilled at using concepts like "rights," "sovereignty," and "nation." Although we have had to resist consistently the unilateral imposition of American policies, it has taken a devastating toll on the well-being of American Indian communities. A critical indigenous philosophy continues to evolve *because* of the ongoing colonial relationship. Once one has a better understanding of the history of the legal and political relationship between American Indians and the American state, one appreciates the need to assert and protect the rights, sovereignty, and nationhood that we believe we still possess.

Ultimately, I argue that a critical indigenous philosophy necessitates a peculiar kind of division of intellectual labor in Indian Country. In other words, not only do we need to separate indigenous spirituality from a critical indigenous philosophy, but also we have to be acutely aware of *who* participates in the legal and political discourses of the state. The relationship between traditional "wisdom keepers," or "sage philosophers," and what I will call "word warriors" is complex.[8] But the relationship hinges on an important conditional: *If* indigenous peoples assert that they possess distinctive ways of understanding the world and that these differences matter politically, then they need to be able, and empowered, to engage the legal and political discourses of the state. Our cultural survival, then, is dependent on how well we can assert and defend our rights, sovereignty, and nationhood within the contemporary legal and political practices of the dominant culture.

Indigenous Spirituality:
Political and Metaphysical

American Indian spirituality is rooted in the special relationships that many American Indians have with their homelands. These relationships embrace complex, culturally specific sets of practices that form a background from which American Indians make sense of the world. Perhaps this background can be explained; that is, the rules that govern American Indian behavior can be articulated using the English language. For example, there is no reason why a medicine person couldn't explain, in English, what he or she *means* by American Indian spirituality. But it does not follow that from that explanation we have gained a rich understanding of American Indian beliefs and teachings. The kinds of explanations of indigenous spirituality that are generated in English constitute what I call "indigenous philosophy."

It is important to distinguish between these two kinds of intellectual endeavors. Indigenous spirituality has a very long cultural tradition that is rooted in precontact indigenous communities and, as I understand it, is practiced using indigenous languages. Colonialism, on the other hand, has created indigenous philosophy. As I mentioned above, indigenous philosophy is an attempt to articulate the meaning and content of indigenous spirituality using Western European philosophical categories. The question of whether indigenous spirituality is *more* authentic than indigenous philosophy raises complex problems of translatability and commensurability. Indigenous peoples themselves have become divided over what counts as an authentic explanation of indigenous thought—and for good reasons.

I do not know how to solve the problems of commensurability and translatability. My point is not that indigenous spirituality can be subsumed into indigenous philosophy, but rather that indigenous spirituality ought to be left alone and indigenous philosophy ought to be woven into a critical indigenous philosophy. Western European–educated indigenous intellectuals need to understand that it is not our place to explain the meaning and content of our ways of knowing. We are best situated to engage the legal and political practices of the state in order to assert and defend our homelands. For example, in the United States the concept of tribal sovereignty has normative weight in American law—without its legitimacy tribes would not be empowered at all.

In describing what a critical indigenous philosophy means, I have to cordon off indigenous spirituality from indigenous philosophy. This is for two reasons. First, the concept of "spirituality" is a deeply contested concept in the English language and certainly within Western European intellectual cultures. Most professional philosophers are hostile to claims that a term like spirituality can be the foundational concept for an entire philosophical system of thought. Its "metaphysics," at least by Western European philosophical standards, is messy to say the least. Second, I do not believe that we need to engage in a "messy" metaphysics, because our primary purpose in explaining a *critical* indigenous philosophy is political, not metaphysical. Indigenous spirituality belongs to indigenous peoples and, for the most part, is rooted in indigenous communities. Indigenous peoples may choose to explain their world in a certain language, but this language is not the language required to assert and defend their rights, sovereignty, and nationhood.

African philosophers have been vigorously debating the relationship between their so-called traditional forms of knowledge (rooted in African communities), Western-educated African philosophers who discuss these forms of knowledge in an academic context, and African philosophers who simply participate in Western professional philosophy. On one end of the debate, there are those who argue that legitimate African philosophers are those who possess local forms of "traditional" knowledge, expressed in their own languages. These special philosophers, called "sage philosophers," are the sole source of African philosophical authenticity.[9] Then there are those who do a kind of "ethnophilosophy," which means they explain and legitimate African ways of thinking about the world by engaging and/or embracing Western European philosophical frameworks.[10] Paulin Hountondji has criticized these two approaches by attempting to reconcile Western philosophical thought with the fact that he remains deeply committed to defending the integrity of a distinctive African philosophy.[11]

These debates around the issue of what constitutes an "authentic" African philosophy are integral to a critical indigenous philosophy. What we need to determine first is what makes the North American context unique. What makes it unique is the fact that the Canadian and American states continue to recognize that indigenous peoples possess special forms of legal and political recognition. In Canada, since 1982, Aboriginal rights have been explicitly protected in the Canadian Constitution.[12] In the United States, federally recognized tribes possess a form of sovereignty, called "tribal sovereignty," that recognizes that tribes possess limited powers of self-governance. Both of these forms of political recognition are definitively embedded in the legal and political practices of the state.[13]

So, why is this a problem for Aboriginal peoples of Canada and American Indians of the United States? The main problem with these forms of political recognition is that the discourses of rights and sovereignty legitimate the power structures of the state. The question to ask is whether the forms of political empowerment that tribes exercise represents a tacit consent to the colonial practices of the state. More to the point, does the ongoing participation in the legal and political relationship constrain future tribal efforts to renew more tribal-centric forms of governance? The tension between indigenous spirituality and a critical indigenous philosophy resurfaces because indigenous peoples must defend their political integrity by engaging the legal and political practices of the state and they must do so by claiming that a source of their political distinctiveness lies outside the discourses of the state.

In an American context, tribes possess a limited form of political empowerment legitimated by the discourse of tribal sovereignty. In addition, tribes possess rights that have been characterized as "extra" and "pre" constitutional in nature.[14] What this means is that tribes possess a form of political empowerment that lies outside the legitimacy of the state. From an American Indian perspective, the source of this form of political empowerment lies in American Indians' distinctive relationships with their homelands. The normative justification for these "explanations" is embedded within indigenous ways of understanding the world—ways that are guided by indigenous understandings of spirituality.

It is not my place to provide these explanations. I am not a medicine person, so I have to be very careful about what I can and cannot say about indigenous knowledge. These kinds of explanations are not legitimized within the contemporary legal and political practices of the state; rather, their rightful place is found within the languages of indigenous communities themselves. Given the American state's miserable record of accommodating American Indian normative explanations of ownership of their homelands, we should be much more conscientious about bringing those explanations out of our communities and into places like courts of law.

This is no mere reality check for indigenous peoples. When one begins to understand the Indian/white historical relationship better, one begins to see that for over two hundred years American Indians have been explaining themselves to the dominant culture. Their very survival demanded that they assert and defend what they believed belonged to them. The shift in political power, which culminated in the formation of the American state, has had devastating effects in Indian Country. Indeed, to think of the arrival and subsequent empowerment of Europeans over Indian lands as anything other than an invasion is to misunderstand Indian history.[15] Although, it must be mentioned that the historical relationship has not always been a relationship of *complete* domination: American Indians have both resisted and participated in the ongoing relationship and have come to understand the importance of being able to assert and defend their rights, sovereignty, and nationhood within the legal and political practices of the state.

The generally accepted view in American Indian law is that tribes have been politically recognized as "nations" since the Worcester case of 1832. In this case, Justice Marshall stated:

> [The] settled doctrine of the law of nations is, that a weaker power does not surrender its independence—its right to self-government, by associating with a stronger, and taking its protection. A weak state, in order to provide for its safety, may place itself under the protection of one more powerful, without stripping itself of the right of government, and ceasing to be a state.[16]

This form of legal and political recognition situated American Indians in an empowering place in the American political landscape. At least in principle. The concept of tribal sovereignty remains *the* normative concept that drives the contemporary political relationship between tribes (also a normative term) and the state. The meaning of tribal sovereignty, if it is to empower tribes, must be interpreted in ways that are actually put to use in contemporary legal and political rights discourse. A critical indigenous intellectual culture is charged with securing these empowering interpretations.

The point of this brief diversion into policy is to show that American Indians must be strategic about the meaning and content of their legal and political rights because these forms of political recognition gain their legitimacy within the existing normative political practices of the state. From an American Indian perspective, though, these discourses represent only one dimension of the dialogue. There are other kinds of understandings of political legitimacy that indigenous peoples situate within a distinctively spiritual context. A richer understanding of indigenous rights, sovereignty, and nationhood weaves together the three kinds of intellectual activities I cited earlier. The first centers on traditional indigenous ways of knowing the world—ways that are guided by complex spiritual relations of power. These systematic forms of knowledge, in a less colonized world, would be recognized as "indigenous philosophy" proper. In other words, "philosophy" would be understood in Verney's unproblematic way of using the term. These praxis-oriented philosophies would embrace very specialized and privileged forms of knowledge and practices that would be articulated in indigenous languages and expressed in indigenous cultural practices.[17] The second activity uses the normative categories of contemporary Western European philosophy to explain the meaning and content of indigenous ways of knowing the world. The language used, at least in the United States, would mostly be English, which carries with it its own intrinsic set of epistemological and political problems. In the third activity, indigenous intellectuals must explicitly assert and defend the integrity of indigenous philosophies within a global community. Western European philosophical frameworks can play a central role in explaining the meaning and content of indigenous rights, sovereignty, and nationhood, but they must do so in a way that does not undermine the legitimacy of indigenous ways of knowing the world.

Although a critical indigenous philosophy requires all three kinds of intellectual activities, it functions within the dominant intellectual culture by cordoning off the spiritual dimension of indigenous philosophical thought from the Western European discourses of rights, sovereignty, and nationhood. To answer the question of why this cordoning off of indigenous spirituality is necessary, we turn to explicating the importance of developing a critical indigenous philosophy.

Toward a Critical Indigenous Philosophy

The importance of cordoning off indigenous "spirituality" is to give primacy to the political claim about the nature of the legal and political relationship. Indigenous views of spirituality are rooted in our communities and ought to remain there (although this claim is not without its problems). The fact remains that the legal and political relationship demands that American Indians find empowering ways of explaining their political distinctiveness—their indigeneity. It is this persistent *demand* for explanation that creates a critical indigenous philosophy. But a serious problem arises: How should we understand the relationship between so-called traditional forms of knowledge and the legal and political discourses that are used to determine the meaning and content of tribal sovereignty? Further, why is this a problem in the first place? Why bother with "traditional" forms of knowledge at all, especially since the reality of contemporary tribal life clearly demands that, if American Indians want to have any rights *at all*, they must by necessity engage the legal and political practices of the state?

The conditions of a critical indigenous philosophy flow from the demand for explanation. But indigenous peoples do more than simply engage the dominant culture's "practices of governance." The relations of power created out of the ongoing legal and political relationship are interwoven into indigenous practices of freedom.[18] No matter how oppressive the dominant culture's policies have been, indigenous peoples have always met these policies with resistance guided by the belief that they remain self-determining peoples. But this discourse of "self-determination" is itself

part of the ongoing historical relations of power. In other words, indigenous peoples cannot "escape" the discourse of rights, sovereignty, and nationhood. How a particular indigenous community chooses to engage (or
embrace) these discourses is as diverse as Indian Country itself. An effective critical indigenous philosophy is driven by a conditional: If indigenous
peoples claim that they possess different ways of understanding the world
and that these differences matter legally and politically, then they must engage the dominant culture's practices of governance. How we ought to
"engage" these practices remains the central problem for a contemporary
indigenous intellectual culture.

This conditional creates the necessary division of intellectual labor in
indigenous communities. In order to maintain the distinctive nature of indigenous ways of thinking about the world, indigenous peoples need to be
empowered to actually be able to protect them. This form of empowerment has both cultural and political dimensions. The complex relationship
between indigenous ways of knowing the world and Western European
worldviews has shaped indigenous identity for centuries now. In order for
indigenous communities to have important internal dialogues over how
they want to assert and protect their ways of thinking about the world, they
need to be able to actually have a meaningful dialogue. By meaningful I
mean nothing more than this: The kinds of dialogues they have must end
up being useful for indigenous communities.

But this dialogue requires not only the participation of all indigenous
citizens; in many instances it requires that their communities be protected
from the destructive influences of the dominant culture. Indigenous communities need people who engage the dominant culture's practices of governance and are empowered to affect public policies that are actually
implemented in their communities. I have argued elsewhere that, from an
indigenous perspective, it matters greatly who participates in these largely
Western European legal and political practices.[19] A critical indigenous philosophy, then, evolves out of a complex dialogue between indigenous ways
of knowing the world and the practices of governance that are used to situate indigenous peoples within the larger legal and political practices of the
state.

So, why does it matter "who" participates in the legal and political practices of the state? We must remember the conditional I mentioned earlier:
If indigenous peoples assert that they possess distinctive ways of understanding the world and that these differences matter politically, then they
need to be able, and empowered, to engage the legal and political discourses of the state. We need American Indians who not only speak the

discourses of rights, sovereignty, and nationhood, but know how to use these languages effectively in contemporary American Indian politics. The problem is that these people do not do so in a cultural vacuum. The critical dimension of a critical indigenous philosophy integrates indigenous spirituality into the ways that indigenous intellectuals engage the discourses of rights, sovereignty, and nationhood.

The problem of integration, or reconciliation, of indigenous knowledge with the discourses of the state reinforces the need for a division of intellectual labor. Indigenous peoples have to take the position that the survival of their knowledge will always be threatened by the dominant culture. It follows that indigenous peoples themselves must take control of keeping indigenous knowledge alive and protecting this privileged knowledge from disappearing. Indigenous wisdom keepers are charged with keeping their traditional knowledge alive—but they cannot do so alone. The threats of cultural annihilation from the outside are real and, as has been demonstrated too many times, can be overwhelmingly destructive.

Indigenous wisdom keepers are charged with educating and maintaining the spiritual life of the community. This is an activity that looks inward to the well-being of the community. It is important to point out that the spirituality I am referring to embraces indigenous people's understandings of who they are as human beings. Some European-educated indigenous peoples—what I call "word warriors"—are charged with asserting and defending the rights, sovereignty, and nationhood of indigenous communities within the legal and political practices of the dominant culture. The difficult part of making this distinction is that both types of intellectuals belong to indigenous communities, yet they spend a large part of their lives in different cultures. It is a colonial irony that in order for tribes to continue to survive as distinctive self-determining peoples they must invoke a kind of self-imposed cultural schizophrenia!

Unfortunately, we are no closer to understanding the meaning of indigenous philosophy. Indigenous philosophy occupies a strange intellectual space between the discourses of indigenous spirituality and nonindigenous intellectual culture. What it does mean is that indigenous philosophy is not a privileged form of knowledge embedded solely in indigenous cultures.

I am claiming that if one is chosen to be taught, then the path is an arduous one that involves many years of study. One has to live in a fundamentally different way in order to understand indigenous spirituality. Our spiritual ways have been threatened since the earliest times of the relationship, yet they are still alive. Once we lose our spiritual knowledge, we may continue to be indigenous peoples, especially in a legal and political sense,

but we will have lost something deeply intrinsic to our well-being as indigenous peoples. This is why I defend a more protectionist approach. At
this point in the historical relationship, indigenous peoples cannot afford to
put their spiritual traditions up for negotiation in the intellectual culture of
the dominant culture.

It follows that philosophy, as it is understood in the Western European
intellectual tradition, can be of use to indigenous peoples, but mainly as a
kind of political activity. Indigenous rights, sovereignty, and nationhood
have been interpreted and put to use in law and politics by nonindigenous
peoples for far too long. Indigenous leaders have become adept at using the
law, but the legal and political practices of the state cannot accommodate
indigenous understandings of spirituality. If indigenous rights, sovereignty,
and nationhood are the only discourses available to indigenous leaders,
then they must find more creative and empowering ways of participating
in the legal and political practices of the dominant culture. Further, as I
have been trying to show, they must do so while defending the integrity of
indigenous ways of understanding who they are as indigenous peoples. I
refer to this philosophical activity as a "critical indigenous philosophy."

Of course, a critical indigenous philosophy is not without its problems.
One problem is the issue of commensurability. If all we have is the language of the dominant culture, then why do we need "indigenous" philosophy at all—shouldn't everyone be doing Western European
philosophy? In a sense this is true: The dialogue over the meaning of indigenous rights, sovereignty, and nationhood is framed in the language of
the dominant culture. But we must appreciate that if word warriors are
empowered in the legal and political practices of the state, then the discourses themselves should evolve in ways that accommodate indigenous
ways of understanding the world. The real difficulty lies in the kind of dialogue word warriors ought to engage that can reconcile both the discourses of the dominant culture and indigenous ways of knowing the
world. Indigenous peoples need to have a dialogue among themselves
about the meaning of indigeneity and what role it ought to play in a modern, evolving cosmopolitan world. It is this spiritual and intellectual activity that the next generation of indigenous intellectuals must see as central
to the future well-being of their communities.

Summary

In my discussion, I've characterized three related kinds of intellectual practices: indigenous spirituality, indigenous philosophy, and a critical indige-

nous philosophy. Indigenous spirituality predates the arrival of Europeans and finds its roots in the ceremonies and ways of knowing the world that are articulated in indigenous languages. Colonialism essentially created indigenous philosophy. It is a way for indigenous (and nonindigenous) peoples to explain indigenous ways of understanding the world using the philosophical categories of the dominant culture. The relationship between the two highlights issues of commensurability, translatability, and authenticity. The reality is that indigenous understandings of who they are have little, if any, currency in contemporary American Indian politics. I have called for the explicit creation of a critical indigenous philosophy that asserts and defends the rights, sovereignty, and nationhood of indigenous peoples within existing contemporary indigenous politics. Indigenous intellectuals need to become much more effective at engaging the discourses of rights, sovereignty, and nationhood, but must do so guided by the wisdom of their indigenous ways of knowing. An indigenous intellectual community (consisting of medicine people, indigenous philosophers, and other indigenous intellectuals), then, must work out the spiritual and philosophical dilemmas associated with asserting a form of political distinctiveness in a global world while retaining strong cultural ties to its communities. How to do so effectively remains the most serious and pressing issue for an indigenous intellectual community.

Notes

1. Marilyn Notah Verney, "On Authenticity," in *American Indian Thought*, ed. Anne Waters (Malden, MA: Blackwell Publishing, 2004), 133. Also, a word about terminology. I prefer the term "American Indian" when I am referring to the indigenous people of the United States. Otherwise, in this chapter I will use the term "indigenous," which carries with it a broader, more international connotation.

2. By examining a constitutional democracy I intentionally limit myself to discussion of indigenous issues in Canada, the United States, New Zealand, and Australia. The fact that indigenous politics is part of the broader political practices associated with constitutional democracies is significant.

3. Although the term "spirituality" is problematic, I believe most indigenous people prefer it to the term "religion."

4. The idea of a form of life comes from Wittgenstein's later philosophy. Crudely speaking, a form of life embraces a particular way of seeing and understanding the world. For Wittgenstein, a form of life is understood not as an exegetical system of thought; rather, it exists in our everydayness.

5. See David E. Wilkins, *American Indian Politics and the American Political System* (New York: Rowman & Littlefield, 2002); Charles F. Wilkinson, *American Indians, Time, and the Law: Native Societies in a Modern Constitutional Democracy* (New

Haven: Yale University Press, 1987); and Colin Calloway, *First Peoples: A Documentary Survey of American Indian History* (Boston: Bedford/St.Martin's, 1999).

6. Broadly speaking, indigeneity characterizes the source of what makes indigenous peoples unique in the legal and political relationship.

7. This point highlights the difference between indigenous spirituality and indigenous philosophy. Whether indigenous philosophy is able to justly "translate" or "capture" the meaning and content of indigenous spirituality raises thorny issues of commensurability, translatability, and authenticity. It is my intention, at least in this discussion, to emphasize the importance of separating indigenous spirituality from the discourses of indigenous rights, sovereignty, and nationhood.

8. The term "sage philosophers" comes from the African philosopher Odera Oruka. See his *Sage Philosophy: Indigenous Thinkers and Modern Debate on African Philosophy* (Leiden: Brill, 1990). A "word warrior" is "an indigenous person who has been educated in the legal and political discourses of the dominant culture. The primary responsibility of word warriors is to be intimately familiar with the legal and political discourses of the state *while remaining citizens of indigenous nations*." Dale Turner, *This Is Not a Peace Pipe: Towards a Critical Indigenous Philosophy* (Toronto: University of Toronto Press, 2006), 119.

9. See Oruka, *Sage Philosophy*.

10. I have been using "indigenous philosophy" to mean "ethnophilosophy." For an account of African ethnophilosophy see Placide Tempels, *Bantu Philosophy*, trans. Colin King (Paris: Presence Africaine, 1969). For an interesting discussion of ethnophilosophy see Anthony Kwame Appiah, *In My Father's House: Africa in the Philosophy of Culture* (New York: Oxford University Press, 1992), 92–94.

11. See Paulin J. Hountondji, *African Philosophy: Myth and Reality*, trans. Henri Evans (Bloomington: Indiana University Press, 1996); and *The Struggle for Meaning: Reflections on Philosophy, Culture, and Democracy in Africa* (Athens: Ohio University Center for International Studies, 2002).

12. Section 35(1) reads, "The existing Aboriginal and treaty rights of the Aboriginal peoples of Canada are hereby recognized and affirmed."

13. Cf. note 5.

14. This fact of American constitutional law goes back to *Talton v Mayes*, 163 U.S. 376 (1896).

15. See Calloway, *First Peoples*; and David Stannard, *American Holocaust: The Conquest of the New World* (New York: Oxford University Press, 1993).

16. From Jill Norgren, *The Cherokee Cases: Two Landmark Federal Decisions in the Fight for Sovereignty* (Norman: University of Oklahoma Press, 1996), 119.

17. The question of whether indigenous philosophies can be articulated in English is a thorny issue. As I lay out the intellectual projects, indigenous philosophy proper would have to be articulated in an indigenous language. Articulating indigenous philosophies in English raises important epistemological and political problems that need to become central to a *critical* indigenous philosophy.

18. The relationship between "practices of governance" and "practices of freedom" comes from Michel Foucault. See James Tully, "Political Philosophy as a Critical Activity," *Political Theory* 30, no. 4 (August 2002): 533–55.

19. See Turner, *This Is Not a Peace Pipe.*

Bibliography

Alexie, Sherman. *The Lone Ranger and Tonto Fistfight in Heaven.* New York: Harper Perennial, 1994.

Alfred, Gerald. *Heeding the Voices of Our Ancestors: Kahnawake Mohawk Politics and the Rise of Native Nationalism.* Toronto: Oxford University Press, 1995.

Alfred, Taiaiake. *Peace, Power, Righteousness: An Indian Manifesto.* Toronto: Oxford University Press, 1999.

Allen, Paula Gunn. *The Sacred Hoop: Recovering the Feminine in American Indian Traditions.* Boston: Beacon Press, 1986.

Asch, Michael. *Home and Native Land: Aboriginal Rights and the Canadian Constitution.* Toronto: Methuen, 1984.

Basso, Keith. *Wisdom Sits in Places: Landscape and Language among the Western Apache.* Albuquerque: University of New Mexico Press, 1987.

Bataille, Gretchen. *American Indian Women, Telling Their Lives.* Lincoln: University of Nebraska Press, 1984.

Berkhofer, Robert F., Jr. *The White Man's Indian: Images of the American Indian from Columbus to the Present.* New York: Vintage Press, 1978.

Bonnin, Gertrude (Zitkala Sa). *American Indian Stories.* Lincoln: University of Nebraska Press, 1921.

———. *Old Indian Legends.* Lincoln: University of Nebraska Press, 1985.

Bordewich, Fergus M. *Killing the White Man's Indian: Reinventing Native Americans at the End of the Twentieth Century.* New York: Anchor Books, 1996.

Borrows, John. *Recovering Canada: The Resurgence of Indigenous Law.* Toronto: University of Toronto Press, 2002.

Boudinot, Elias. *Cherokee Editor: The Writings of Elias Boudinot,* ed. Theda Perdue. Athens: University of Georgia Press, 1996.

Brown, Dee. *Bury My Heart at Wounded Knee: An Indian History of the American West.* New York: Holt, Rinehart and Winston, 1970.

Burt, Larry W. *Tribalism in Crisis: Federal Indian Policy, 1953–1961.* Albuquerque: University of New Mexico Press, 1982.

Cairns, Alan C. *Citizens Plus: Aboriginal Peoples and the Canadian State.* Vancouver, BC: University of British Columbia Press, 2000.

Cajete, Gregory. *Native Science: Native Laws of Interdependence.* Santa Fe, NM: Clearlight, 2000.

Champagne, Duane. *Distinguished Native American Political and Tribal Leaders.* Salt Lake City, UT: Onyx Press, 2002.

Champagne, Duane, and Jay Strauss, eds. *Native American Studies in Higher Education: Models for Collaboration between Universities and Indigenous Nations.* Detroit, MI: Visible Ink Press, 1994.

Churchill, Ward. *Fantasies of the Master Race: Literature, Cinema and the Colonization of American Indians,* ed. M. Annette Jaimes. Monroe, ME: Common Courage Press, 1992.

———. *From a Native Son: Selected Essays in Indigenism, 1985–1995.* Boston: South End Press, 1996.

———. *Struggle for the Land: Indigenous Resistance to Genocide, Ecocide, and Expropriation in Contemporary North America.* Monroe, ME: Common Courage Press, 1993.

Cohen, Felix. *Handbook of Federal Indian Law.* Washington, DC: Government Printing Office, 1942.

Cook, Noble David. *Born to Die: Disease and the New World Conquest, 1492–1650.* Cambridge, UK: Cambridge University Press, 1998.

Cook-Lynn, Elizabeth. *Why I Can't Read Wallace Stegner and Other Essays: A Tribal Voice.* Madison: University of Wisconsin Press, 1996.

Cook-Lynn, Elizabeth, and Mario Gonzalez. *The Politics of Hallowed Ground: Wounded Knee and the Struggle for Indian Sovereignty.* Urbana: University of Illinois Press, 1998.

Copway, George. *The Life, History, and Travels of Kah-ge-ga-gah-bowh: A Young Indian Chief of the Ojibway Nation.* Albany, NY: Weed and Parsons, 1847.

Cronon, William. *Changes in the Land: Indians, Colonists, and the Ecology of New England.* New York: Hill and Wang, 1983.

Crosby, Alfred. *The Columbian Exchange: Biological and Cultural Consequences of 1492.* Westport, CT: Greenwood Press, 1972.

Crow Dog, Mary. *Lakota Woman.* New York: Grove Weidenfeld, 1990.

Cruikshank, Julie. *Life Lived Like a Story: Life Stories of Three Yukon Native Elders.* Lincoln: University of Nebraska Press, 1990.

Debo, Angie. *A History of the Indians of the United States.* Norman: University of Oklahoma Press, 1970.

Deloria, Ella. *Waterlily.* Lincoln: University of Nebraska Press, 1988.

Deloria, Philip. *Playing Indian.* New Haven: Yale University Press, 1998.

Deloria, Philip, and Neal Salisbury, eds. *The Blackwell Companion to American History.* Malden, MA: Blackwell Publishing, 2001.

Deloria, Vine, Jr. *American Indian Policy in the Twentieth Century.* Norman: University of Oklahoma Press, 1985.

———. *Behind the Trail of Broken Treaties: An Indian Declaration of Independence.* New York: Dell, 1974.

———. *Custer Died for Your Sins: An Indian Manifesto.* New York: Macmillan, 1970.

———. *God Is Red: A Native View of Religion.* Golden, CO: North American Press, 1994.

———. *The Metaphysics of Modern Existence*. San Francisco: Harper and Row, 1979.

———. *Red Earth, White Lies: Native Americans and the Myth of Scientific Fact*. New York: Scribner, 1995.

Deloria, Vine, Jr., and Clifford Lytle. *American Indians, American Justice*. Austin: University of Texas Press, 1983.

———. *The Nations Within: The Past and Future of American Indian Sovereignty*. New York: Pantheon Books, 1984.

Deloria, Vine, Jr., and David Wilkins. *Tribes, Treaties, and Constitutional Tribulations*. Austin, TX: University of Texas Press, 1999.

Dickason, Olive Patricia. *Canada's First Nations: A History of Founding Peoples from Earliest Times*. Toronto: McClelland and Stewart, 1992.

Drinnon, Richard. *Facing West: The Metaphysics of Indian-Hating and Empire-Building*. Norman: University of Nebraska Press, 1977.

Eastman, Charles. *From the Deep Woods to Civilization: Chapters in the Autobiography of an Indian*. Lincoln: University of Nebraska Press, 1977.

———. *Old Indian Days*. New York: McClure, 1907.

———. *The Soul of an Indian and Other Writings from Ohiyesa*. San Rafael, CA: New World Library, 1993.

Erdrich, Louise. *Love Medicine: A Novel*. New York: Holt, Rinehart and Winston, 1984.

Erdrich, Louise. *Tracks: A Novel*. New York: Holt, Rinehart and Winston, 1988.

Fire, John (Lame Deer), and Richard Erdoes. *Lame Deer, Seeker of Visions: The Life of a Sioux Medicine Man*. New York: Simon and Schuster, 1972.

Fixico, Donald. *The Invasion of Indian Country in the Twentieth Century: American Capitalism and Tribal Natural Resources*. Boulder: University of Colorado Press, 1998.

———. *Termination and Relocation: Federal Indian Policy, 1945–1960*. Albuquerque: University of New Mexico Press, 1986.

Forbes, Jack D. *Columbus and Other Cannibals*. New York: Autonomedia, 1992.

———. *Native American Philosophy: Social and Political Implications*. Medelingen van het Juridisch Instituut mo. 22, Jurisdiche faculteit, Erasmus Universiteit, Rotterdam, 1983.

———. *Racism, Scholarship, and Cultural Pluralism in Higher Education*. Davis: University of California, Davis, 1977.

———. *Tribes and Masses: Explorations in Red, White, and Black*. Davis, CA: D-Q University Press, 1978.

Forbes, Jack D., ed. *The Indian in America's Past*. Englewood Cliffs, NJ: Prentice Hall, 1964.

Francis, Lee. *Native Time: A Historical Time Line of Native America*. New York: St. Martin's Press, 1996.

Geiogamah, Hanay, and Jaye T. Darby. *Stories of Our Way: An Anthology of American Indian Plays*. Los Angeles: UCLA American Indian Studies, 2000.

Getches, David H., Daniel M. Rosenfelt, and Charles F. Wilkinson. *Case and Materials on Federal Indian Law.* St. Paul, MN: West Publishing, 1979.

Green, Rayna Diane. *Women in American Indian Society.* New York: Chelsea House, 1992.

Grinde, Donald A., Jr. *The Iroquois and the Founding of the American Nation.* San Francisco: Indian Historian Press, 1977.

Grinde, Donald A., Jr., and Bruce E. Johansen. *Exemplar of Liberty: Native American and the Evolution of Democracy.* Los Angeles: University of California Press, 1991.

Hanke, Lewis. *Aristotle and the American Indians.* Bloomington: Indiana University Press, 1959.

Harjo, Joy (1994). *The Women Who Fell Through the Sky: Poems.* New York: W. W. Norton, 1994.

Harjo, Joy, and Gloria Bird, eds. *Reinventing the Enemy's Language: Contemporary Native Women's Writing of North America.* New York: W. W. Norton, 1997.

Harris, Leonard, Scott Pratt, and Anne Waters. *American Philosophies: An Anthology.* Oxford, UK: Blackwell, 2001.

Horn, Gabriel. *Contemplations of a Primal Mind.* Novato, CA: New World Library, 1996.

Hotinonsionne (The Longhouse People). *Kaianerekowa—The Great Law of Peace.* Rooseveltown, NY: Akwesasne Notes, 1975.

Hoxie, Frederick, ed. *The Encyclopedia of North American Indians.* Boston: Houghton Mifflin, 1996.

Jaimes-Guerrero, M. A., ed. *The State of Native America: Genocide, Colonization, and Resistance.* Boston: South End Press, 1992.

Jennings, Francis. *The Invasion of America.* New York: W. W. Norton, 1976.

Johansen, Bruce E. *Debating Democracy: Native American Legacy of Freedom.* Santa Fe, NM: Clearlight, 1998.

Johnson, Troy. *The Indian Occupation of Alcatraz and the Rise of Indian Activism.* Champaign: University of Illinois Press, 1996.

Josephy, Alvin M., Jr. *500 Nations: An Illustrated History of North American Indians.* New York: Knopf, 1994.

———. *Red Power: The American Indian's Fight for Freedom.* New York, NY: McGraw-Hill, 1971.

Kappler, Charles J. *Indian Treaties, 1778–1883.* New York: Interland, 1973.

Krupat, Arnold. *For Those Who Came After: A Study of Native American Autobiography.* Berkeley: University of California Press, 1985.

Krupat, Arnold. *Red Matters: Native American Studies (Rethinking the Americas).* Philadelphia: University of Pennsylvania Press, 2002.

Kymlicka, Will. *Multicultural Citizenship: A Liberal Theory of Minority Rights.* Oxford: Oxford University Press, 1995.

Las Casas, Bartolomé de. *History of the Indies.* Trans. and ed. Andree Collard. New York: Harper and Row, 1971.

Lyons, Oren, John Mohawk, Vine Deloria Jr., et al. *Exiled in the Land of the Free: Democracy, Indian Nations, and the U.S. Constitution*. Santa Fe, NM: Clearlight, 1992.

Mankiller, Wilma Pearl. *Mankiller: A Chief and Her People*. New York: St. Martin's Press, 1993.

Mathews, John Joseph. *Sundown*. Norman: University of Oklahoma Press, 1988.

Mathiessen, Peter. *In the Spirit of Crazy Horse: The Story of Leonard Peltier*. New York: Viking, 1991.

————. *Indian Country*. New York: Penguin, 1984.

McNeil, Kent. *Emerging Justice: Essays on Indigenous Rights in Canada and Australia*. Saskatoon: Native Law Centre, University of Saskatchewan, 2001.

Means, Russell, and Marvin J. Wolf. *Where White Men Fear to Tread: The Autobiography of Russell Means*. New York: St. Martin's Press, 1995.

Meriam, Lewis, et al. *The Problem of Indian Administration*. Baltimore, MD: Johns Hopkins Press, 1928.

Mihesuah, Devon A. *American Indians: Stereotypes and Realities*. Atlanta, GA: Clarity, 1996.

Mihesuah, Devon A., and Angela Cavender Wilson, eds. *Indigenizing the Academy: Native Scholars and Scholarship on Natives*. Lincoln: University of Nebraska Press, 2004.

Momaday, N. Scott. *House Made of Dawn*. New York: Harper and Row, 1968.

————. *The Man Made of Words*. New York: St. Martin's Press, 1997.

Monture-Angus, Patricia. *Journeying Forward: Dreaming First Nations' Independence*. Halifax, NS: Fernwood Publishing, 1999.

Moses, L. G., and Raymond Wilson. *Wild West Shows and the Images of American Indians, 1883–1933*. Albuquerque: University of New Mexico Press, 1996.

Nabokov, Peter. *A Forest of Time: American Indian Ways of History*. Cambridge, UK: Cambridge University Press.

Nagel, JoAnne. *American Indian Ethnic Renewal: Red Power and the Resurgence of Identity and Culture*. New York: Oxford University Press, 1996.

Nannum, Hurst. *Autonomy, Sovereignty and Self-Determination*. Philadelphia: University of Pennsylvania Press, 1990.

Neihart, John C. *Black Elk Speaks*. Lincoln: University of Nebraska Press, 1998.

Norgren, Jill. *The Cherokee Cases: The Confrontation of Law and Politics*. New York: McGraw-Hill, 1996.

Ortiz, Alfonso, ed. (1979, 1983). *Handbook of American Indians*, vol. 9 and vol. 10. Washington, DC: Smithsonian Press.

Ortiz, Alfonso, and Richard Erdoes. *American Indian Trickster Tales*. Rear Collingdale, PA: Diane, 2002.

Ortiz, Roxanne Dunbar. *Indians of the Americas: Human Rights and Self-Determination*. Westport, CT: Praeger, 1984.

Ortiz, Simon. *From Sand Creek: Rising in This Heart Which Is Our America*. New York: Thunder's Mouth Press, 1981.

Ortiz, Simon. *Speaking for a Generation: Native Writers on Writing.* Tucson: University of Arizona Press, 1998.

Owens, Louis. *I Hear the Train: Reflections, Inventions, Refractions.* Norman: University of Oklahoma Press, 2001.

———. *Mixedblood Messages: Literature, Film, Family, Place.* Norman: University of Oklahoma Press, 1998.

Penn, W. S. *As We Are Now: Mixblood Essays on Race and Identity.* Berkeley: University of California Press, 2000.

Pokagon, Simon. *Red Man's Greeting.* Hartford, MI: C. H. Engle, 1893.

Reid, Bill, and Robert Bringhurst. *The Raven Steals the Light.* Vancouver: Douglas and McIntyre, 1984.

Ridington, William Robin. *Trail to Heaven: Knowledge and Narrative in a Northern Native Community.* Iowa City: University of Iowa Press, 1988.

Royal Commission on Aboriginal Peoples. *Report of the Royal Commission on Aboriginal Peoples.* 5 vols. Ottawa: Minister of Supply and Services, 1996.

Shattuck, Petra, and Jill Norgren. *Partial Justice: Federal Indian Law in a Lineal Constitutional System.* Oxford: Berg, 1991.

Smith, Linda Tuhiwai. *Decolonizing Methodologies: Research and Indigenous Peoples.* New York: St. Martin's Press, 1999.

Smith, Paul Chaat, and Robert Alan Warrior. *Like a Hurricane: The American Indian Movement from Alcatraz to Wounded Knee.* New York: New Press, 1996.

Standing Bear, Luther. *Land of the Spotted Eagle.* Boston: Houghton Mifflin, 1933.

Stannard, David E. *American Holocaust: Columbus and the Conquest of the New World.* New York: Oxford University Press, 1992.

Steiner, Stan. *The New Indians.* New York: Harper and Row, 1967.

Thorton, Russell. *American Indian Holocaust and Survival: A Population History since 1492.* Norman: University of Oklahoma Press, 1987.

Todorov, Tzvetan. *The Conquest of America.* New York: Harper and Row, 1987.

Trask, Haunani-Kay. *From a Native Daughter: Colonialism and Sovereignty in Hawai'i.* Monroe, ME: Common Courage Press, 1993.

Tully, James. *Strange Multiplicity: Constitutionalism in an Age of Diversity.* Cambridge: Cambridge University Press, 1995.

Vizenor, Gerald. *Manifest Manners: Postindian Warriors of Survivance.* Hanover, NH: University of New England Press, 1994.

———. *The People Named the Chippewa: Narrative Histories.* Minneapolis: University of Minnesota Press, 1984.

Wa, Gisday, and Delgam Uukw. *The Spirit in the Land: Statements of the Gitksan and Wet'suwet'en Hereditary Chiefs in the Supreme Court of British Columbia 1987–1990.* Gabriola, BC: Reflections, 1992.

Wallace, Paul A. *The White Roots of Peace.* Santa Fe: Clearlight Publishing, 1997.

Warrior, Robert Alan. *Tribal Secrets: Recovering American Indian Intellectual Traditions.* Minneapolis: University of Minnesota Press, 1995.

Weatherford, Jack. *Indian Givers: How Indians Transformed the World.* New York: Crown Books, 1989.

Weaver, Jace. *Defending Mother Earth: Native American Perspectives on Environmental Justice.* New York: Orbis Books, 1997.

Wilkins, David. *American Indian Politics and the American Political System.* Lanham, MD: Rowman & Littlefield, 2002.

————. *American Indian Sovereignty and the U.S. Supreme Court: The Making of Justice.* Austin: University of Texas Press, 1997.

Wilkinson, Charles F. *American Indians, Time, and the Law: Native Societies in a Modern Constitutional Democracy.* New Haven: Yale University Press, 1987.

Williams, Robert A., Jr. *The American Indian in Western Legal Thought: The Discourses of Conquest.* New York: Oxford University Press, 1990.

Wilshire, Bruce. *The Primal Roots of American Philosophy: Pragmatism, Phenomenology, and Native American Thought.* University Park: Pennsylvania State University Press, 2000.

Womack, Craig. *Red on Red: Native American Literary Separatism.* Minneapolis: University of Minnesota Press, 1999.

Wub E Ke Niew. *We Have a Right to Exist: A Translation of Aboriginal Indigenous Thought. The First Book Ever Published from an Ahnishinahbaeotjibway Perspective.* New York: Black Thistle Press, 1995.

Young Bear, Ray. *Black Eagle Child.* Iowa City: University of Iowa Press, 1992.

What Is Asian American Philosophy? 8

DAVID HAEKWON KIM
University of San Fransisco

ASIA, THE PACIFIC ISLANDS, and the Americas have long been joined by migration, trade, and the imaginations of the people who have occupied these areas. But, since roughly the late nineteenth century, the movement toward global capitalism and the spread of imperialism began to consolidate this loose network of relations into a large connective region. The transformation was not unlike what had been transpiring across the Atlantic, perhaps the "Black Atlantic." And the coalescing processes involved here, as with the Atlantic, raise myriad questions about political economy, ethical relations, and historical self-understanding. By the late twentieth century, one conception of this regional formation came to be expressed in a popular celebratory language centered around the idea of a "Pacific Rim." And it has been criticized sharply by a host of scholars and activists.[1] For the discourse highlights commerce, tourism, cross-cultural experience, migration, and the like without giving sufficient attention to, often even masking or mystifying, the wars, atrocities, poverty, colonialism, dehumanizing labor, political suppression, and environmental devastation that fill the history of this region as conditions or effects of global capitalism and imperialism.

For better or worse, then, Asia, the Pacific Islands, and the Americas have inter-suffused each other with increasing intensity for more than a century. And so, not unlike the idea of European philosophy, Asian philosophy, or some other philosophy organized around human, and often ethnoracial, geographic categories, there seems to be a basis for a "Pacific regional philosophy," "Amerasian philosophy," or some such philosophical orientation. This chapter, however, focuses on a subset of such an approach, namely the

part that concerns U.S.-Asia-Pacific relations and more particularly, though
not exclusively, the social worlds of Asians in America. For convenience,
"Asian American philosophy" will be used to designate the philosophy born
of that context. As will become clearer, I join many who regard the United
States to be an empire and to have been so long before its current Eurasian
or Middle Eastern incursions. Consequently, I take the political geography
of this nation to stretch *far* beyond the confines of its formal fifty states.
Since roughly the late nineteenth century, the United States has asserted various kinds of dominion across Latin America, many of the Pacific Islands,
and much of East Asia. So we will need to broaden our conception of
"Asians in America" and, hence, "Asian America" and "Asian American
philosophy" as we enlarge our geopolitical gaze from a fifty-states republic
to a multicontinental empire.

In giving an account of Asian American philosophy, a good deal of
backdrop has to be provided, like the history of Asian Americans and of
America in Asia. In fact, some important aspects of the backdrop will
themselves need elaboration. For example, we will need some discussion of
modern Asia as such and some related political epistemology. I think it goes
without saying that the wider American public knows little about these
histories, let alone their implications. For the civic narratives of the United
States often rewrite in "Grand Republic" style the history of America in
the Asia-Pacific and of Asians and Pacific Islanders in America. And the
U.S. educational system largely follows suit or ignores the "difficult" historical facts altogether. And with the philosophical focus of this chapter,
the problem is compounded by a peculiar situation in which classical Asian
philosophy has come to represent virtually all of Asian philosophy in the
Western academy. Since what might be called "modern Asian philosophy,"
of which Asian American philosophy is partly an instance, receives almost
no hearing in Western philosophy, there is no preexisting niche into which
Asian American philosophy can be readily inserted. A good bit of ground
clearing, then, is in order. So this chapter slowly builds up to a discussion
of Asian American philosophy.

In the first section, I consider the peculiar reception of classical Asian
philosophy by Western philosophy and how this points to larger concerns
about Orientalism and colonial modernity in Asia. The second section
characterizes both the sociohistorical condition that configures modern
Asian philosophy and modern Asian philosophy itself. In the third and final section, I present an account of Asian America and Asian American
philosophy that is continuous with the earlier discussion of modern Asia
and modern Asian philosophy. And given the fairly wide unfamiliarity with

Asian America, my discussion of it is a fairly concrete, historically informed, political philosophical description.

Asian Philosophy and Modernity's Orient

At the outset, some clarification of the expression "classical Asian philosophy" is in order. Largely following convention, I mean to include under this label the originary texts primarily of Hinduism, Daoism, Buddhism, and Confucianism. Included as well are the many centuries of critical, sometimes divergent, reflection upon them (e.g., Theravada as opposed to Mahayana Buddhism, Mozi's critique and Mencius's reinvigoration of Confucianism, etc.) and recent discussions and advances on that general body of thought. So, for example, comparative studies of the nature of consciousness from the standpoints of Buddhism and of analytic philosophy would be included under this heading (though not exclusively so). In addition, some positions on Confucianism and human rights could be cited as instances of such philosophy (and other kinds as well). I include both examples under the rubric of classical Asian philosophy (without confining them there) because both have the explicit aim of bringing to the comparative dialogue a classical Asian system conceived as such even if interpreted by means of the best contemporary analyses available. In a similar vein, though twentieth-century neo-Confucianist work might be called "contemporary Asian philosophy," that title would be shorthand for the more ponderous "contemporary classical Asian philosophy." Thus, the guiding concern here is system retention, not recency of analysis.[2] I leave open the question of how much retention is needed for establishing conceptual continuity. And, of course, significant conceptual modifications can result in a position sufficiently hybrid as to call into question whether the work remains solely or even minimally a classical Asian system. For instance, somebody might develop a position that deeply integrates political liberalism and Confucianism, maybe a kind of Rawlsian Confucianism or a Confucianist Rawlsianism. The work, then, (if coherent) would potentially be a case of both classical Asian philosophy and Western philosophy. Consequently, the phenomenon of theoretical hybridity is acknowledged, and the borders around the concept of classical Asian philosophy are recognized to be permeable.

Recently, ethnoracial philosophy, especially in its critical modes, has begun to amass some interest in the North American scene. The last few decades have witnessed a surge of creative activity in philosophical work from Africana and African American, Latin American and Latino, and

Native American approaches.[3] At the first-order level, these areas have been productive for many decades, in some cases centuries, despite their near banishment from Western philosophy. And, in recent years, such institutional erasure has been an important theme in the metaphilosophy of each of these fields, generating new moral epistemic perspectives for reconstructing philosophy.

Significantly, Asian philosophy does not follow suit. Like the other ethnoracial philosophies, this one faces the communicative difficulties arising from racism, imperialism, Eurocentrism, and the like. Yet, quite unlike its cousins, Asian philosophy has had a long history of Western defenders. Importantly, this history of advocacy has identified Asian philosophy almost exclusively with one of its main species, namely *classical* Asian philosophy. I shall return to this point later. In any case, the Western advocacy has sometimes been dialogical and nuanced. At other times, it has involved stiff binary thinking or exoticizing romanticism. All the same, enough positive interest by enough philosophers of the West has enabled classical Asian philosophy to occupy some sort of position within the domain of philosophy proper as conceived by Western philosophy. This makes classical Asian philosophy unique among ethnoracial philosophies. For, in contrast, all the other non-Western, non-Asian philosophies have struggled for even basic philosophical recognition from Western audiences. It is hardly surprising, then, that East–West philosophy has been and continues to be both the paradigm and statistical norm for cross-cultural or global philosophy in the West. But, in spite of being granted philosophical status, it seems quite clear that classical Asian philosophy has been relegated to an inferior position within the Western framework. This problematic inclusion and the more thoroughgoing exclusion of other ethnoracial philosophies, together, indicate complexity in the racial politics of metaphilosophy. As it turns out, this politics is deeply linked to the larger modern scene in which the confrontation of Asia and the West transformed Asia and to an extent the West as well. And we get a natural entry into this sociohistorical situation through a consideration of classical Asian philosophy's special position in Western philosophy.

Whatever may be the full story of classical Asian philosophy's unique reception, I think it cannot have as its center the apparently innocent idea that early Western proponents of classical Asian philosophy simply understood and appreciated the special philosophical character and potential contributions of this foreign system of thought. For, first of all, why didn't other non-Western systems receive similar, even if not equal, appreciation? One might contend that only classical Asian philosophy involves a recognizable form of philosophical argumentation and admits of the classic distinctions between metaphysics, epistemology, and ethics. The basic problem with this view, however, is that it is simply false: Latin American philosophy, to take just one example, reveals these same features, at the very least because of its hybridity, yet receives nothing even remotely close to the treatment Asian philosophy has received. As noted in Latin Americanist metaphilosophy, such evidently philosophical movements as positivism, analytic philosophy, and existentialism have all made their way through the continent and exerted real influence in the philosophy there.[4] Even if one rejects all of these movements, nobody, so far as I know, denies that they involve philosophical argumentation, address the classic subdivisions of philosophy, and, therefore, can lay claim to the title of philosophy. Yet Latin American philosophy remains almost entirely outside of Western philosophical discussion.

Moreover, even if those features of Western philosophy were largely absent from most or all non-Western systems, there is no reason why Western philosophy could not in any case learn from these other systems of thought, either in and of themselves or through the partial reconstruction of their terms. Consider that in philosophy of art, few deny that aesthetic discourse, art itself, and their entwined histories are basic required areas of knowledge and even sources of insight in spite of their not being philosophy. And in philosophy of science, a solid grasp of evolution, Newtonian mechanics, relativity, quantum mechanics, and the history of science is largely considered fundamental to doing good work in this field. So to do metaphilosophy well, and especially to venture making universalist or globalist claims, shouldn't it be imperative that one study the great systems of thought the world over? As it turned out, little of this was done in any comprehensive way, often not even in a partial way. And yet the universalisms or globalisms have endured, whether Western or Western-Asian systems have formed the heart.

Once we observe the larger scene, then, we find we cannot look simply at the intrinsic merits of classical Asian philosophy and the intellectual integrity of its Western advocates. Something further or something else is involved. Attention must also be paid, it seems, to the way such Western advocacy institutionally tracked the merits of classical Asian philosophy. Again, the general *type* of reason that would motivate engagement with Asian philosophy—that is, appreciation of a culturally distinctive philosophical system's internal merits or wider philosophical contributions—applies also to other non-Western, non-Asian philosophies. As well, the scope of the Western universalisms or globalisms common to East-West philosophy would seem to necessitate not simply an examination of Asian philosophy but a far more ranging assessment of ethnoracial systems of thought. So philosophical cross-cultural appreciation by itself fails to explain interest in classical Asian philosophy, and insistence on it skirts an issue with which it is enmeshed, namely the peculiar singularity of classical Asian philosophy's legitimated status. Whatever the full story might be, it seems difficult to plausibly deny here the long-standing reign of the Hegelian world-historical hierarchy in which it is believed that only the expressions of Asian civilizations begin to approach those of Europe.[5] The turn toward Asia, it seems, was also a turn away from Africa and the indigenous Americas, among other places. Incidentally, the entrenchment of this Hegelian structure might help to explain why, once admitted into philosophy proper, classical Asian philosophy, presumably stagnant or immature, was so often relegated to the margins and only the stalwart would defend a place for it at the center.

A full account of how and why this Hegelian configuration emerged is beyond this chapter, but *that* it did seems clear. As well, that its legacy continues should also be evident. This presses upon us the question of what accounts for the distinctive institutional turn toward Asia in the first place? Here we can find help in the literature on Orientalism and imperialism in Asia. And we come upon a second reason why the hierarchical legitimation of classical Asian philosophy is not merely a matter of Western advocates of classical Asian philosophy moving against the grain and appreciating the world of ideas aright.

Upon a nineteenth- or early twentieth-century imperial map of the world, one will find planted on *nearly every territory on the planet* the flag of England, France, Spain, Portugal, Holland, Belgium, Russia, Italy, Germany, the United States, or Japan. As we should know, though it is often conveniently forgotten, domination was the global order of the day. The mechanisms of control took many forms. Whichever was employed in a given territory, the exercise of infiltrative powers had to be massive and sustained to suitably reorganize the colony or semi-colony. And it would be a serious historical error to suppose that the Euro-American and Japanese imperial networks were only economic, political, and military in nature. The wars that changed the face of the planet and maintained essentially a global white supremacy (and a white-Japanese one in East Asia) were fought across the mental landscape as across the literal towns and countrysides of the world. Occupying forces sought to divest the populace not only of the more overt means of insurgency but also, through various administrative and ideological structures, the ability to control information, education, and cultural production.

Focusing on Europe's East (and to an extent America's West), Edward Said has famously argued that the West's self-conception was profoundly shaped by its material domination and correlated discursive containment of the Orient so-called. And he explained this in terms of the stronger thesis that Europe discursively created the Orient and, through the Orient's intensive relation to Europe, the West itself. Moreover, he contended that even apparently innocuous or positive conceptions of the Orient could be in the grips of a latent dominative structure.[6] On such an account, therefore, it is no surprise that a West obsessed so with the East would have a number of its scholars hit upon the major philosophical developments of Asia and many end up actually appreciating them. And, on a more contentious note, a Saidian analysis might yield the judgment that even the Western advocacy of classical Asian philosophy could not but play a hegemonic role and was thereby accommodated in the so-called marketplace of ideas. Now, whether or not one accepts this notion of inevitable complicity, the larger dominative context indicates that Western appreciation of Asian philosophy, even when genuine and nuanced, must be understood within broader *patterns* or *tendencies*. We must shift the context from mere cross-cultural encounter to *interpolity domination*.

As mentioned, this relation of subjection was not only political and economic, but cultural and conceptual. And the discourse of the Orient did not always outright derogate the peoples and cultures of Asia. It also depicted Asians in other distorting ways, ways that made them appear, for example, safe, manageable, or in need of Western aid. For instance, and maybe most obviously, Asians were often depicted as lacking the ability to govern themselves in a rational manner due allegedly to certain of their cultural traits or more inherently bodily dispositions. Correlatively, Westerners regarded themselves as having the ability to play a positive role in the aid or governance of Asians. This role may have been meaningful on a number of different fronts, from the pleasures of racial contempt to the "moral satisfaction" of uplifting "inferior indegenes" to the more obvious benefits of regional control and economic advantage. And there are many other kinds of cases of conceptual distortions that facilitated polity domination. Consider, as a further example, that Asian cultures might have been regarded as a complementing counterpart, but ultimately an inferior one, to Western culture. Specifically, certain Western theorists who were not hyperrationalists might have mapped onto the East-West polarity the emotion-reason, religion-science, and femi-nine-masculine dichotomies, respectively. This seems to have been rather common. But, unlike many others, these theorists might have val-ued both terms of the dichotomies and, hence, both East and West so conceived, even as they valued more highly the West-reason-science-masculine cluster. In such cases, Asians would be safely, perhaps even deftly, circumscribed or contained within the psyche and could be ad-mitted under qualified conditions into some domains of the imperial polity. A variant of this last example might involve the commodification of Asian culture, food, religion, and even people as some sort of exotic, perhaps even cognitively sophisticated, product for Western cultural consumption. In these latter kinds of cases, there can be dominative Orientalism without overtly arrogant or destructive intentions.

With some modifications, Said can be understood as putting forward two projects. First, in politics, history, and arguably philosophy, he makes the imperial domination and discursive containment of the Orient a *tena-cious datum*, one that should be salient across a *range* of theoretical frame-works. Second, he offers a Foucauldian-Gramscian analysis of this datum. This distinction is easily overlooked or underappreciated. The separation of the two claims means that even if one rejects the latter effort out of an aversion to Foucault or Gramsci, one must still contend with the first. Per-haps Said can be imagined here as saying that even the middle-road polit-ical liberal must acknowledge the Eurocentric linguistic and inferential patterns of the common discourse on the Orient and the West; that this was deeply shaped by the epistemic authorities and culture-makers whose polity economically and militarily dominated the peoples of Asia; and that such domination was in turn facilitated by the misshapen discourse. Noth-ing in the prior sentence necessarily invokes Foucault or Gramsci, but the datum of discursive containment and more generally of colonial moder-nity are preserved. Consequently, as we shift our focus from mere cross-cultural encounter to interpolity domination, we can see that the imperialist scene, with its project of discursive derogation or management, is comprehensible from a number of theoretical standpoints.

The foregoing clarifies the significant conceptual pull or undertow to-ward the so-called Orient experienced by the West. This should hardly sur-prise given the profound enmeshment of "Orient" and "West." Consequently, the focus on Asian philosophical systems in the Western project of global or universalist philosophy seems deeply, even if not reduc-tively, linked to the specific kind of Western preoccupation with Asia that characterized colonial modernity. Another implication is that we must bring some measure of critical scrutiny to Western advocacy of Asian philosophy, even if we do not regard it as inevitably complicitous with imperialism in Asia. Western characterizations of both the nature of classical Asian philosophy and the need for its inclusion within the wider philosophical forum must be examined for blatant or subtle Orientalism. And there is nothing rude or mean about this. The need for such scrutiny is an unfortunate result of the complex political and epistemic situation described. There is no claim made here that every discussion of Asia and classical Asian philosophy is Orientalist or Orientalist in the same way or degree. The focus has been directed upon patterns and tendencies. Something stronger, more totalistic, like that delivered in a Saidian analysis, will be preferred by some, but general structures are all that are needed for the case at hand.[7]

A final consideration is that anticolonialism and anti-Orientalism too must take care lest they inadvertently employ subtle Orientalist forms of thought. This is an important and controversial area of analysis. For some might contend that the use of binary thinking, which is common to Orientalism, in the project of anticolonialism ends up reinscribing Orientalism. Others seem to maintain that the intended or actual use of the ideas, binary or not, is more important for determining the status of the ideas. However we decide on this and related issues, it is clear that there are serious and far-ranging epistemological implications of discursive containment and colonial domination.[8] And, for the purposes of this chapter, that is the main point I wish to emphasize.

I have discussed how the consolidation of a Hegelian structure and the condition of Orientalism, together, complicate any simple claim to the effect that Western defenders of classical Asian philosophy were simply following their philosophical conscience during cross-cultural encounters. One aspect of the situation not yet discussed is the transformation of Asian philosophy and the development of new forms of Asian thought. In various ways, these new forms would come to bear the marks of the Orientalist modernity to which they were in part replies. And, subsequently, these modern Asian philosophies would go unrecognized by Western philosophy in ways that partly separate them from classical Asian philosophy and partly link them to non-Western, non-Asian philosophies. I turn now to these new developments and the bifurcation within Asian philosophy.

Modern Asian Philosophy

As noted earlier, "classical Asian philosophy" includes the originary teachings primarily of Hinduism, Buddhism, Daoism, and Confucianism, and the critical scrutiny and creative elaboration and revision they have received across the centuries up to the present moment. And there is nothing absolute here: evolution, hybridity, and multiple instantiation of disparate philosophical systems are all acknowledged possibilities. What I have called "modern Asian philosophy" makes essential reference to elements of the earlier discussion, such as imperialism, Orientalism, and modernity. It gathers reflections, mostly since the nineteenth century (and possibly in some cases since the sixteenth century), on the experience of Asians and diasporic Asians in their colonial and postcolonial lifeworlds and world-systems.[9] There is incredible diversity across the lives and situations of modern Asians. But the broader colonial context and its legacies have been powerfully unifying *at an overarching level* and serve thereby to give some cohering force to the rubric of modern Asian philosophy. I cannot offer a full account of Orientalist modernity and its legacies. But in what follows I quickly note three relevant aspects of Asian modernity. They concern certain dialectics that emerged within the sociopolitical contexts faced by Asians and the subsequent transnationalization of many features of those contexts. Afterward, I briefly elaborate on one of these aspects, the colonial dialectic of Asian modernity, to flesh out some lines of thought that get taken up later. I then turn to modern Asian philosophy.

By the mid- to late nineteenth century, virtually all Asian peoples had to contend with existing or impending Western and Japanese domination. As noted earlier, the social worlds of Asians have been permeated by an Orientalist modernity consisting of racial, economic, cultural, and military subjection. Importantly, the formative moments within this tragic modern context have not always been one-sided. The social worlds of Asians have also been shaped by their own resistance against precisely this vast subordinating condition. The confrontation and creation took many forms, and I will discuss some of them shortly. But suffice it to say for now that this responsiveness on the part of Asians generated a kind of dialectic within colonial modernity. And many instances of it were politically radical and some very concretely threatening to Western hegemony. Among the most spectacular manifestations of the formative colonial dialectic have been the many mass-based anticolonial movements, violent and nonviolent, that emerged in many areas and forms since the late nineteenth century. Perhaps the Gandhian and Maoist variants were the most globally influential.

After WWII, a wave of formal decolonization began spreading across Asia, the Middle East, and Africa. Importantly, however, most and possibly all decolonized nations faced an enormous difficulty, namely that formal political liberty did not guarantee true autonomy. For stronger nations

could avail themselves of various international structures, especially economic ones, to subtly or overtly encroach upon or control weaker or fledg-
ling nations. Thus, as many have noted, postcolonial nations of Asia could
be, and very often were, subjected to an indirect, economic, or "neo" colonialism. And this often occurred with the aid or through the agency of a
dictator or set of socioeconomic elites drawn from the ranks of the people
themselves. But within this postcolonial neocolonial context, as in the previous explicitly colonial condition, Asians continued to shape some part of
their situation through their various replies to their altered world. And so
a kind of postcolonial dialectic emerged as Asians both challenged and
were influenced by their sociopolitical surroundings. Interestingly, colonial
and postcolonial dialectics of the kinds mentioned here could be simultaneously present in Asia since not all nations were decolonized at the same
time. Consequently, perhaps it should not be surprising that postcolonial
Philippines and especially postcolonial South Korea (and colonial Puerto
Rico) were in their respective ways gathered in a neocolonial fashion by
the United States and made to be participants in the explicitly imperial war
against Vietnam.

Finally, consider that since the last few decades a number of transpacific
transnational processes have emerged and coalesced in modern Asian and
American experience. The most obvious case is the massive migration of
Asians to the United States after the immigration reforms of 1965. The
population of Asians in America has more than tripled since the anti-Asian
immigration blockades were lifted. As a result, currently more than half of
Asian Americans are foreign born.[10] Moreover, some Asians are now shut-
tling back and forth so often across the Pacific that their identities seem no
longer to have classic attachments to nation-states. And, apart from populations and migration, the matrices of business, trade, and investment that
straddle the Pacific have become so pronounced a phenomenon that we
now have a new lingo by which to discuss the matter, like "Pacific Rim,"
"the Four Dragons," and so on. We also have a growing awareness of the
problem of outsourcing to Asia and the ubiquitous presence of sweatshops.
The effects of economic transnationalism can even be seen in the institutional structure of Asian studies. At the scholarly level, much funding is
now being made available by organizations with close ties to national or international commerce agencies.[11] And, at the student level, it seems that
undergraduates frequently adopt an Asian studies major or minor to supplement their business major.

As I have noted earlier, I do not offer here a full account of these three
aspects of the modern Asian experience. Many books could be written on

each and still other features. Nevertheless, before turning to an account of modern Asian philosophy, I think it would be helpful to consider briefly at least some of the details of the colonial dialectic that emerged within Orientalist modernity since it offers a natural narrative starting point and since many of its aspects remain relevant.

In the colonial dialectic, Asian thought was often arrayed against Western dominion and tended to gravitate around a sociopolitical conception configured by two sets of distinctions. One distinction separated culture and thought from science and technology in the examination of a society.[12] The other consisted of a wide-ranging comparative relation—actually many of them—between "Orient" and "West." Sometimes, East and West were conceptualized as normatively contrastive antipodes (e.g., the bad materialistic West versus the good spiritual East), as complements to each other (e.g., the scientific West and the spiritual East), as being only superficially different (e.g., the basic unity of all religious strivings, East and West), and perhaps in still other ways. Also, importantly, some sort of world-historical self-consciousness distinctive to modernity typically undergirded and integrated, not always coherently, both sets of distinctions. Nobody could deny that the world had radically changed with the dominative presence of the West and the modernization processes brought in its wake. The urgent task at hand, at every level of consciousness, culture, and the polity, was to reconceptualize and sustain a viable way of life in the face of these changes. But whether Asians sought a hermetic retreat from or a full, even self-effacing, insertion into the modernizing world-trajectory, the presence of a colonizing West and a transformed world were *constant* and *essential* reference points.[13] Unsurprisingly, we find here many of the ideas that concerned Said about colonial discourse in the service of imperialism and even anti-imperialism. A brief tour of some of the replies to Orientalist modernity should be considered. And there are conceivably many ways to proceed. For expository ease, I offer a mostly standard story.

On the one end of the spectrum, an Asian theorist might have rejected every form of classical Asian outlook and thoroughly embraced some version of modern Western thought as well as modern Western science. This would have been modernization-as-Westernization of a total kind. I am uncertain if there were any prominent thinkers who adhered completely to this program.[14] For it would be difficult to completely extirpate earlier cultural influences and, hence, totally Westernize in taking up this sort of project. But surely the agendas of some at least approximated this extreme. On the other end, an Asian theorist might have stayed the course, as it were, and maintained more or less the same classical philosophic system and scientific or technological outlook as premodern thinkers. I do not know how many pursued this route to its extreme. It seems not uncommon for new and powerful globalizing influences to be met by the entrenchment of local cultural forms. But few, it seems, could totally reject the efficacy or benefits of Western science and technology, whether perceived in the form of medicine, railroads, or machine guns.[15] Here, too, there may have been some who approached this pole asymptotically. Most, however, followed some sort of intermediate path, and a variety of such paths emerged. Significantly, none of these conceptual options (nor the related new questions and issues taken up by extant classical Asian philosophy) would have been intelligible or felt to be urgently important were it not for the variegated structures of Orientalist modernity. Considered this way, we get a clearer sense of how there can be such a thing as "modern Asian philosophy" in spite of the diversity of Asian experience and thought. I think we can usefully differentiate at least three kinds of conceptual replies lying between total rejection of and total continuity with premodern Asian life-forms.

First, many endorsed the idea of maintaining fundamentally classical Asian culture and thought, even if partly nourished by Western streams, and adopting Western science and technology. The late nineteenth-century Japanese traveler and writer Fukuzawa Yukichi has often been identified with marrying the concepts of "Eastern Spirit" and "Western Science."[16] Later, some members of the Kyoto School of philosophy, who have subsequently been accused of complicity with Japanese imperialism, contended that Europe had reached a spiritual crisis that could only be resolved through enlightenment derived from a generally Asian but distinctively Japanese cultural form inspired largely by Buddhist tenets.[17] But setting aside this grand salvific trajectory, the basic idea of Asian culture combined with Western science, and their union placed on a modernization path, has been prevalent across modern Asia. And some version of this idea, with or without the modernization impetus, has been, if not the primary, at least one of the main ways in which an "alternative modernity" was theorized by many Asian intellectuals and pursued by a host of Asian political leaders.

Second, some espoused a less purist conception of alternative modernity and developed more consciously syncretic East–West hybrid social forms to accompany the adoption of Western science and technology. Sun-Yat Sen (founder of the Chinese Republic), for example, appealed to a broadly Confucianist sense of rightness in moral and political dealings and advocated a partly sinicized version of Western civic nationalism.[18]

Third, some sought to raise within Asia what they conceived to be a Western variant of alternative modernity in the form of anarchist revolution and community or, later, Marxist revolution and communism. On this conception, the political economy of capitalism was the central explanatory structure (or at least a very significant one, in the case of anarchism). So modernity was conceived to be fundamentally marked by an intensification of class inequality, state suppression, and imperialism. Marxists in particular, especially after the work of Lenin, regarded global imperialism to be the highest stage of capitalism. With the order of the day conceived this way, anarchism and Marxism, though generated in the West, were understood as fundamentally opposed to the West as it had in fact historically developed and opposed as well to the feudal inequities and governmental corruption of their own Asian societies.[19] Many who advocated this agenda shaped radical Western thought to fit their local contexts, which in turn sometimes influenced Western radicalism itself. The "Sinified Marxism" of Mao Zedong and its global influence, especially in the 1960s, is an obvious instance.[20] An earlier and interesting example is the "Third World" influence of the Indian Marxist Manabendranath Roy on Lenin regarding conceptions of national liberation generated at the Third Communist International in the interwar years.[21] Now, it might be argued that this third type of alternative modernity, insofar as it has a partly hybridized theoretical outlook, was a species of the second type. This might be so. But the reconception of modernity in anarchism and particularly Marxism, combined with the subsequent historical importance of Marxism's expansion and revolutionary impetus in Asia during the Cold War, seem to justify this third type of Asian alternative modernity having its own conceptual niche. Moreover, this would accommodate the fact that many who espoused this sort of agenda regarded alternative modernity of the first and much of the second kind to be alternatives in name only and to be in actuality Asian ideologies that facilitated the spread of global capitalism and imperialism, which lay at the heart of colonial modernity.

In sum, I have very briefly noted a spectrum of responses to Western dominion.[22] And let me emphasize that I do not regard the three intermediary positions discussed above, all variants of a claim to Asian alternative modernity, to be exhaustive of the replies lying between complete continuity with and complete denunciation of the precolonial era. Let me also add that some cases may not easily conform to these rubrics, though they will likely be linked to them.[23] But, even if limited in some ways, this characterization of the modern Asian spectrum covers a wide array of cases, reveals the operations of a complex colonial dialectic, and clarifies at some level of generality the social world inhabited and partly shaped by Asians.[24]

Clearly, this brief portrait of the modern Asian condition plays an important role in characterizing modern Asian philosophy. But we also need a general way of describing the formation of a philosophy and applying it to the case at hand. And in light of the first section of this chapter, this general account combined with the general portrait would clarify further why modern Asian philosophy is not merely contemporary classical Asian philosophy. Here, we encounter the problem of what unifies the philosophy in question. Some may seek an essence, a set of necessary and sufficient conditions for all the cases that fall under a particular philosophical label. Like many, I think this has dim prospects. Others, and I follow them, focus on family resemblances or on the collection of cases in accord with a coherent metatheoretical project. We can borrow insight from the work of Lucius Outlaw on how Africana philosophy is formed.

> How, then, to speak of "commonalities" or "unity" sufficient to underwrite Africana philosophy as a disciplinary field of studies with distinct boundaries and intellectual and praxiological coherence? The only appropriate way of doing so is by first recognizing that the unifying commonalities sought for are provided through the third-order organizational, classificatory, or archaeological strategies involved in "gathering" people and discursive practices under "Africana" and "philosophy," respectively. I say "third order" because the gathered discursive practices are themselves "second order" in that they are reflections on "first order"—that is to say *lived*—experiences of the various African and African-descended persons and peoples.[25]

If we apply Outlaw's metaphilosophical conception, modern Asian philosophy can be understood in terms of the following three general levels.

First and obviously, it recognizes that there are lived experiences of Asians and diasporic Asians. As I have told the story, these experiences will often bear the marks of their transformed world, and specifically the colonial and postcolonial dialectics and the transnational circuits discussed above. I think this forms the *nucleus* of the starting point for modern Asian philosophy. But there are other relevant kinds of experience at this first-order level, and their relevance derives from the deeply relational and relationally expansive nature of colonial modernity, Orientalism, and anticolonialism. For example, many kinds of Western or white experiences are linked to Orientalist modernity, whether they involve contempt, exoticization, calculating indifference, outrage, or solidarity. Significantly, some non-Asian non-Western experiences are also relevant and interestingly manifold. For example, Marcus Garvey and W. E. B. Du Bois, whatever differences they had, often paired Africa and Asia, and Pan-Africanism and Pan-Asianism, in their critical perspectives upon global colonial modernity.[26] And one of the hallmarks at the start of the postcolonial era is the 1955 Bandung Conference focused upon Afro-Asian cooperation and shared resistance against neocolonialism.[27]

Second, modern Asian philosophy is concerned with reflections, philosophical and philosophically related, upon these lived experiences or the wider context informing them. There are many—too many—such examples, and a good number of them overlap in interesting ways: Filipino anticolonial thought in the work of José Rizal,[28] Carlos Bulosan,[29] José Sisson,[30] and others; May 4th "Chinese Occidentalism,"[31] as in the writings of Kang Youwei[32] and Liang Qichao;[33] Gandhism and the debate over its viability,[34] as seen in the work of Sri Aurobindo,[35] Rabindranath Tagore,[36] Ashis Nandy,[37] and others; Maoism,[38] as seen not only in the work of Mao himself, of course, but in revolutionary movements across the world since the 1960s; the Kyoto School,[39] as exemplified by the work of Nishida Kitaro, Nishitani Keiji, Miki Kiyoshi, and others; Asian Marxisms, like the work of Tran Duc Thao,[40] Manabendranath Roy,[41] and others; Asian existentialism, as seen in the work of Lu Xun[42] and Kenzaburo Oe;[43] Korean anticolonial and liberatory thought in the Tonghak movement[44] and later in Minjung thought,[45] as in the work of Kim Chi-Ha;[46] subaltern studies, as seen in the work of Gayatri Spivak[47] and Dipesh Chakrabarty;[48] Asian feminism, as in the writings of Trinh Minh Ha,[49] Uma Narayan,[50] Neferti Tadiar,[51] and others; a host of work that might be grouped under critical Asian studies and Asian American studies, as in the work of Edward Said,[52] Arif Dirlik,[53] Lisa Lowe,[54] Gary Okihiro,[55] E. San Juan Jr.,[56] David Palumbo-Liu,[57] Colleen Lye,[58] and so on; and still other rubrics, to be sure. Importantly, there are other kinds of reflections on Asian experience (and related non-Asian experiences). The ones listed just now are mostly Asian reflections on Asian experience. Beyond historical reclamation, like the sort just given, it is unclear whether Asian reflections necessarily form the nucleus of this second-order level as Asian experience does at the first-order level. Perhaps it may not be necessary to weigh in on this issue. In any case, it is important to recognize that non-Asian reflections on Asian and related experiences can certainly form a part of modern Asian philosophy. The sort of Afro-Asian outlook of W. E. B. Du Bois, for example, can and arguably should play an important role at this second-order level.[59]

Third, modern Asian philosophy "gathers" these second-order practices, these philosophical or philosophically related reflections upon the lived experience and world-system of Orientalist modernity and its legacies, through a coherent metadiscursive project. The project here is critical, ethical, and liberatory.[60] And I leave open the question of how radical the project must be. Such a question will itself be an important issue in modern Asian philosophy. Still, some concrete considerations are in order, and in what follows I do not think that any of the normative claims are beyond the conceptual reach of middle-road liberalism.[61] I think the driving idea at this third-order level is that we should not be mere observers of the tragedy of Orientalist modernity and its enduring legacies, nor mere bystanders in relation to those who struggle against it. Rather, we should be participants in the ongoing struggle, heeding the ethical call and seeking justice and social transformation. In this postcolonial era, neocolonial subjection continues to sully the rights, diminish the powers, and increase the vulnerabilities of vast numbers of Asians in subordinated polities. More urgently, this subjection, even if not solely responsible, continues to conduce to the poverty of literally millions of people, the deterioration of their environments, and the suppression of indigenous democratic movements. Relatedly, we have yet to see any serious reparation efforts for the countless injuries inflicted or goods stolen during at least the explicitly colonial era of Asia. Nor have we seen any civic culture in the United States that seriously grapples with these matters and resists thereby the political epistemology that hides or distorts the cruel facts that make the U.S.-Asia-Pacific region, among other things, a troubling ethical set of relations. In light of these considerations, we must find ways of understanding and transforming the lives and social worlds of modern Asians and the Asian diaspora. In doing so, we should strive to prevent not only Asian replications of Western colonialism, as with Japan earlier, but Asian variants of neocolonialism or complicity with it.[62] And with the global age upon us, modern Asian philosophy, though it may have Asia as a focal point, must have a global scope. In a way that classical Asian philosophy and so much of Western philosophy could barely imagine, modern Asian philosophy must be a philosophy of solidarity.

With the foregoing conception of modern Asian philosophy before us, it is interesting to consider where some of the more philosophical figures noted above appear in explicitly philosophical texts. Many that have been mentioned—like Liang Qichao, the Kyoto School, Mao, Gandhi, and so on—appear, unsurprisingly, in Asian philosophy texts with a contemporary focus, but exactly how is worth noting. They rarely make an appearance in contemporary studies of Confucianism, Daoism, Hinduism, and Buddhism. And they never show up in books on *modern Asian* philosophy as such since there have been no such texts in the first place as far as I know. They do, however, appear in studies under *nation-based* headings. There are anthologies and histories of Indian, Chinese, Japanese, and Korean philosophy that fit this model.[63] They indicate that not all Asian philosophy is classical Asian philosophy, even if the conception of Asian thought in Western philosophy and East-West philosophy in particular is largely dominated by a focus on Hinduism, Confucianism, Daoism, and Buddhism. More interestingly, these nation-configured texts highlight conceptual continuity across good portions of the relevant histories covered but rely mostly on national continuity when they provide space for famous texts and figures that represent rupture in the conceptual lineages. Unsurprisingly, all of them, in some fashion or other—and most of them in a very clear way—present their respective modern philosophies as deeply connected to various of the elements of Orientalist modernity that I have discussed throughout this chapter.[64] Modern Asian philosophy as I conceive it, then, gathers and unifies a cross-section of each of these and other national philosophical lineages (as well as non-national ones) under the international, intercontinental, ethical rubric of Orientalist modernity, its legacies, and the ongoing struggle against these. Having offered a general account of modern Asian philosophy, I think some loose ends can be tied, even if only loosely.

First, I do not think that modern Asian philosophy can only be produced by Asians. Unless imagination and reflection do nothing more than record experience, there is no reason why such philosophy could not be produced by non-Asians interested in various aspects of Orientalist modernity and various kinds of Asian experiences of it. Perhaps another way of putting it is that modern Asian philosophy does not require any special modern Asian cultural sensibility, either in the sense of a Pan-Asian cultural outlook, whatever that might be, or one based on a specific Asian nation or ethnicity. Only the right sort of thematic focus and ethical concern about the relevant issues seems required.

Moreover, consider that modern Asian philosophy and classical Asian philosophy may be co-instantiated, and of course this admits of degrees. Some of what falls under the first and second types of claims to alternative modernity would offer examples. So the liberatory emphasis of modern Asian philosophy, though historically focused on Orientalist modernity, is by no means opposed in principle to consideration of Buddhism, Confucianism, Hinduism, and Daoism for their liberatory potential. This consideration underscores that, in the first place, modern Asian philosophy will likely involve some sort of East-West hybridity, but that the Asian element involved may not be sufficient or may not be of the right kind for the philosophy in question to count as both modern and classical Asian philosophy. There is no space for adequate discussion of this here. But let me note that this hybridity need not involve explicitly Asian philosophical elements mixed with Western philosophy. It can involve general Asian cultural elements or reflections about Asian concerns or realities with which Asian and Western philosophy proper can be brought into dialogue.[65] Moreover, cases of Asian or Western theory that may not be regarded as philosophy proper, like postcolonial theory, can be brought into the mix.[66] In a related vein, I should also note that the framework provided here can potentially accommodate the idea of postmodern realities or of postmodernist thought. Indeed, some of the globalized and decentered economic realties of the "Pacific Rim" seem to demand attention to what might be involved in the "next phase" of the trajectories and frameworks considered here. And, as it turns out, Western postmodernism—for instance, the influence of Derrida and Foucault—has already played a part in some of the reflections that could be gathered by modern Asian philosophy.

Finally, I should note that a variety of correlates to modern Asian philosophy exist or could in principle. There can be regional, subregional, supraregional, and more purely conceptual differences between philosophies linked to modern Asian philosophy. For example, a related regional correlate could be Australasian philosophy, which might be concerned philosophically with the thought and experiences of the lower region of Asia, the Pacific Islands, Australia, and New Zealand. Another, a subregional one, might be Asian English philosophy, which might cover the reflections and experiences of Asians in England and in the British empire. Presumably, the experience of the South Asian diaspora would loom large in such an orientation. Asian American philosophy would also be of this type since it would concern at least in part the Asian diaspora in the United States. But since the United States is a transpacific empire, Asian American philosophy would be very nearly a regional philosophy. A supraregional case might be called Asiana philosophy, which could be a philosophy of the reflections and experiences of Asians in the world generally. Perhaps its structure, like its syntactical schema, would parallel that of Africana philosophy. Finally, a more conceptually based approach would include Asian existentialism, Asian critical theory, and the like.

Ironically, I think it is arguable that modern Asian philosophy is the first robust form of Asian philosophy. Classical Asian philosophy is undergirded by an Asian concept primarily in terms of the general location of the origin and development of Hinduism, Buddhism, Daoism, and Confucianism. We need to ask, here, why such a wide geographic entity, Asia, should be thought to track and link these systems of thought usefully? Why not use subregional or national categories, or even no such categories at all? The idea of Asia seems not to do much work as a way of picking out the four main constituents of classical Asian philosophy. What really makes them, severally and collectively, Asian philosophy is their relation to the West, particularly the way the West has dyadically, contrastively, and hierarchically positioned Western thought over Asian thought. The deeper commonality, then, is not so much geography of origins but a certain negativity, that is non-Westernness of a certain kind as dictated largely by the West. In contrast, in modern Asian philosophy, Asia is important less as descriptive geography and far more as a site of historical and ongoing ethical struggle, and this includes the struggle against the very dyadic hierarchical relation that undergirds the collation of Hinduism, Buddhism, Daoism, and Confucianism.

Asian American Philosophy

A general account of Asian America is needed to serve as context and offer some content for an articulation of Asian American philosophy. It is also necessary because relatively few have even a basic familiarity with Asian America, even though no conception of America would be complete without it. As it turns out, there is a great deal of complexity and ambiguity here, and thus many ways to characterize Asian America. In what follows, I offer a mostly standard account of two very general directionally based conditions that form Asian America. One concerns the Eastward diasporic movement of Asians to America and the various kinds of racial exclusion they faced. The other focuses on the westward racial imperial movement of the United States into and across the Pacific to large tracts of East Asia. Interestingly, these two sorts of accounts are not always combined analytically, even when aspects of each are noted in a single discussion. The resulting blend may perhaps be deemed unusual. But there is no denying both kinds of movement as constitutive of Asian America.[67]

In the previous section, I suggested that we conceive of mid–nineteenth-century Asia onward in terms of an Orientalist modernity with deep and wide-ranging consequences for virtually all Asian peoples. Much of the focus was on the dominative presence of Western empires and the Japanese empire, and the complicated responses that emerged. One of the significant effects of this general condition, and it is interesting to consider to what extent it was anticipated, was the migration of so many of the affected peoples to various of these empires. Latent in the discussion thus far has been the pervasive role of race as a hierarchical organizing principle of interpolity and intrapolity relations of an imperial system. Even if economic exploitation and correlated regional control were the engines of imperialism, race played a significant role. The rhetoric that justified imperial incursions in Asia typically adverted to white supremacist (or Japanese supremacist) ideologies at various levels of the imperial populace. So when racialized Asians wanted to migrate to Europe, America, or Australia, a serious problem for white supremacist nations emerged. For the very people who on racial grounds were deemed incapable of self-government, and probably even of being governed, were about to pass, perhaps "swarm," across the borders.

In the case of the United States, formally racialized immigration blockades were constructed early on when Asia–America contact intensified in the nineteenth century. The first major piece of legislation was the Chinese Exclusion Act of 1882. The rhetoric that won its passage appealed to inassimilability, more strictly biological inferiority, civilizational threat, and white labor displacement. But, since this exclusion act hardly plugged the legal hole through which other Asians could enter, Congress passed in 1917 a widening of the blockade to prohibit entry from the "barred Asiatic zone," which covered roughly the Middle East all the way to the Pacific Islands.[68] All the while, Irish, Eastern Europeans, and Southern Europeans were being admitted in massive numbers. As these particular kinds of Europeans were being "whitened" and many even joining in the reviling of Asians, the civic structure of the United States was becoming powerfully formally arrayed against the alien-seeming and apparently inassimilable Asiatic or Oriental. As it turned out, these formal measures would not be fully lifted until as late as 1965.[69] Consequently, the fact that people of Asian descent comprise a relatively small proportion of Americans, roughly 5 percent, was a legally engineered feat. And so Asians did not *merely* increase their numbers through post-1965 immigration; their numbers increased because the state *promoted* them from the lower strata of a human hierarchy.

Relatedly, those Asians who did gain entry before 1965 faced a barrage of serious racially discriminatory laws. They ranged from, most fundamentally, prohibitions against naturalization (except U.S.-born Asians) to denials of land ownership to various kinds of anti-Asian "Jim Crow" exclusions, including antimiscegenation laws. An overall structure of legalized disenfranchisement, then, was a basic life situation with which most Asians in America had to contend. And, of course, all this pertains to formal subordination. Demeaning social norms, segregation, cruel labor conditions, outbreaks of violence, stints of racial terrorism, and other such conditions were further outrages of their American experience. I think the significance of these events and the overall situation can hardly be overstated, for they indicate that the concept and reality of the Asian as legal pariah or citizen antithesis inform some of the deepest ideas of what it meant to be an *American* and what it meant for America to be *America*. Such meanings must be decoded to make plain their white normativity and, from the late nineteenth century onward, the specifically, though not uniquely, Orientalist character of that normativity. Whatever else may have been true, then, racism in a variety of forms was not an aberration but a central part of the social world that formed Asian America. Even in this twenty-first century, it is not uncommon to witness one of the more benign but revealing legacies of the earlier period, as when an Asian American, perhaps even a fourth-generation Chinese American, is asked "Where are you from?" and disallowed any answer with an American location.

Obviously, a crucial feature of this troubling history is the role of race. Earlier, I discussed Orientalism as a discursive structure that served Western imperialism in various ways. But its field of saturation includes the ideological terrain of domestic race relations. American Orientalism has a long and complicated history. And it is a telling fact that this history exists in spite of the relatively low number of Asians in the United States for such a long period of time. Clearly, then, Americans have been deeply fixated on the Oriental. As it turns out, American Orientalism has put forward many figurations of the Asian in popular culture from the nineteenth century onward. Cultural theorist Robert Lee tracks them and characterizes how Asians have been regarded variously as pollutant, coolie, deviant, "yellow peril," model minority, and "gook."[70] Perhaps one of the most peculiar aspects of Asian racialization is the simultaneous presence of positive-sounding and negative depictions, like "model minority" and "yellow peril," respectively. According to historian Gary Okihiro, these depictions must be understood not as an evolution of tropes but as a unified phenomenon in which Asians are variously discursively contained to suit the needs of the hegemonic political context. This is why negative and positive stereotypes can morph into each other "when the situation requires," as when Asian values, previously a civilizational threat, could, through an emphasis on family and industry, make Asians an assimilation exemplar, or when too much of the model minority turns into a kind of Asiatic peril that would deny whites their share to some social goods.[71] Recently, literary theorist Colleen Lye has contended that such recurring racial praise-and-blame is best understood as two aspects of a "racial form" whose underlying idea is economic efficiency and whose basic function is to help preserve the economic order of the United States at various crisis points in its profoundly Asia-enmeshed modernity, from the early problem of cheap immigrant labor to the Great Depression to interimperial rivalry with Japan.[72] The work of these and other Asian Americanists offers cogent and compelling (and sometimes conflicting) ways of thinking about how and why Asians have been Orientalized.[73]

Clearly, we still reside in a period in which Asians are racialized as a kind of model minority and as a kind of potential threat, and perhaps in still other ways. It is troubling that such racialization persists many years after formal civic equality has been achieved and so-called colorblindness has become ascendant in the public discourse. In terms of negative racial regard, anti-Asian hate crimes and potentially consequential racial stereotyping remain serious problems.[74] In the last couple of decades, we have witnessed recurring versions of yellow perilism in the Democratic National Committee's campaign finance scandal in the 1990s; the unfounded incarceration of the alleged Chinese spy Wen Ho Lee; the eruption of anti-Asian sentiment in the wake of the U.S. spy plane incident on Hainan Island; and the continual demonization of North Korea. And, since 9-11, anti-Arab and anti-Muslim sentiment have escalated the number of hate crimes and intensified the general prejudice against South Asians and Asian Muslims. But, as noted, racial "praise" in the form of the model minority myth also endures. It will be a long time before the image of math whiz kids, SAT fanatics, violin virtuosos, and the like are delinked from the idea of the Asian American. What makes the model minority myth a serious problem is that it continues to racialize Asians and, as Okihiro has pointed out, does so in a way that strategically keeps in play a host of negative perceptions. It also implies criticism of blacks, Latinos, and Native Americans for failing to "pull themselves up by the bootstraps" and thereby erases the racio-economic struggles they (and some subgroups of Asian Americans) continue to face. And insofar as people of any color buy into any aspect of the model minority myth, the solidarity so needed for eliminating racism and injustice is obstructed. In addition, such domestic racial "praise" conceptually unites with and reinforces an internationalist model minority rendering of economically "successful" nations (i.e., the "dragons" or "tigers" of East Asia) and thereby masks the history of imperialism and Orientalism discussed at length already and the continuing legacies of economic and political subordination.

As the foregoing reveals, one of the most conspicuous features of current and historical racism against Asians is the centrality of Asia-America relations. Although virtually all acknowledge this, many restrict the referents and delimit the significance of this internationalism to human migration and commerce across the Pacific. But Asian America must be understood in terms of a westward movement of America itself to Asia, not just the eastward movement of the Asian diaspora to America. For there is no way to deny the historical fact that the nation-state that excluded diasporic Asians from or within its formal boundaries is the very same that infiltrated, invaded, dominated, or codominated various nations in the Pacific and in Eastern Asia. This marks an important asymmetry between the Asia-Pacific and the Africa-Atlantic, and it indicates a rough structural similarity between the Asia-Pacific and Latin America.[75] On strictly classic political grounds that any political liberal can in principle recognize, it is clear that America participated as an imperial power in the Orientalist modernity discussed throughout this chapter. Indeed, American late modernity overlaps significantly with the Orientalist modernity of modern Asia.

Interestingly, those who write out empire from the internationalism of Asian racialization do not deny, and of course cannot, the recurring presence of wars. Although most of the small wars of the American twentieth century were fought in Latin America, most of the large-scale wars had an Asian or Pacific theater, and only one of these was initiated because of an outright attack on U.S. territory.[76] This is more alarming when we consider how racialized and vicious the wars have been, from the Philippines, to Japan, to North Korea, to Vietnam.[77] And of course, it is only in Asia that a nuclear weapon has ever been used, and directly upon a civilian populace at that. And Asia is also the only place where a second such weapon has ever been used, again directly upon a civilian populace. For many, the atomic bombing of Hiroshima and Nagasaki, and the genocide perpetrated in the Vietnam War, count as paradigm instances of atrocity and of evil.[78] Arguably, however, other U.S. wars in Asia offer further paradigms. As recent studies of the U.S. wars in the Philippines and in Korea reveal, all kinds of barbarity were perpetrated directly upon civilian populaces in ways that would remind many of the subsequent war in Vietnam.[79] And if it is claimed that the U.S. war with Japan did not involve any atrocities, it is still noteworthy that the mutual and racialized savagery made the Pacific front of WWII markedly different than the European front.[80] These brief considerations already give an indication that all has not been well in the history of the so-called Pacific Rim.

Although wars may render empires naked, peace is the context in which they flourish since it is in conditions of stability and normalcy that the conditions of economic control and exploitation can ripen. The larger and longer context of the wars indicates that the United States has maintained an empire in Asia and the Pacific for more than a century. And this condition of dominance has been codified in America's foreign policy and Supreme Court rulings. In getting a general sense of this history, a natural starting point would be the series of annexations, or colony formations, at the end of the nineteenth century. In that period, America had entered a new phase of its modernity. It had traversed and claimed all the contiguous territory to the Pacific, consolidated Jim Crow after the freeing of slaves, developed a sense of racio-national mission in Manifest Destiny, contended with a troubled economy, and imagined the economic prospects of crossing a new Asia-Pacific frontier. Its short successful war against Spain in 1898 offered the occasion for the United States to absorb the former Caribbean and Pacific colonies of Spain—Puerto Rico, the Philippines, Guam, and Cuba in part. By other means, the United States also annexed Hawai'i and half of Samoa. Although each of these nations or kingdoms is relatively small, they offered strategic positions within the center of the Atlantic and the center and base of the Pacific. These tactical positions, combined with an informal control of Latin America and in particular Panama (an Atlantic-Pacific gateway), enabled the United States to have an imperial reach that encompassed enormous tracts of waterways so crucial for transport and trade.

Preserving this hegemony is what made it so crucial for the Supreme Court to pass a series of decrees known as the Insular Cases from 1901 across the next couple decades. Basically, these rulings rendered the Caribbean and Pacific acquisitions colonies without an obvious route to statehood or national independence. Though both states (e.g., New York) and territories (e.g., Puerto Rico and Guam) must act in accord with the U.S. Constitution, they play by different rules and receive uneven powers and benefits. This is why only states can send representatives to Congress with voting power and other kinds of real influence, whereas insular territories can send only representatives with limited voice and no vote. I think most would see this arrangement, at least in the abstract, as clearly antidemocratic. It reveals one aspect of the formal and codified nature of U.S. imperialism. Yet the Insular cases went unchallenged in the jurisprudence of the U.S. Constitution, and this remains true even to this very day.[81] As the twentieth century progressed, America would consolidate various kinds of formal and informal dominion over nearly the entirety of Latin America and large portions of East Asia, granting it a multicontinental and multihemispheric empire—in a word, an *Amerasian* empire.[82]

We now have a way of understanding more fully the wars mentioned previously. After purchasing the Philippines from a defeated Spain, the United States faced a Philippines that declared its independence, and thus began the Philippine-American War (1899–1902), the first major antiimperial war against the United States in the twentieth century. As the Philippine-American War continued, and the waterways and land bases were being secured, the United States began to strengthen its position in Asia. Through the Open Door Policy (1899–1900), the United States was able to join various European empires and Japan in dissecting the commercial ports of China as sites of economic or early neocolonial domination, helping thereby to render China a semicolonial country. The significance of China's colonial dissection is that unlike the dissection of Africa, there was a minimum of formal political governance so that full economic exploitation could be conducted without the fetters of colonial bureaucracy. And once the United States had pacified the Philippine resistance, important opportunities for imperial consolidation emerged. Japan was emerging as an important imperial rival in the Asia-Pacific. So when Japan defeated Russia in 1905 in what amounted to an interimperial war, the United States used the peace negotiations to establish some rules for its geopolitical chess game. In the Taft-Katsura Memorandum (1905), Japan and the United States secretly negotiated a deal in which Japan would steer clear of the U.S.-possessed Philippines, and the United States would leave alone Korea as Japan moved to annex it as a part of its own empire-building project. Later, further agreements, like the Root-Takahira Agreement (1908), would be added to consolidate a peaceable imperialist status quo in the Asia-Pacific that was structurally similar to what the United States had been developing in Latin America. In hindsight, however, we know that no diplomacy would prevent that "Day of Infamy," December 7, 1941, when the attack on Pearl Harbor propelled America's entry into WWII and into violent struggle with its longtime Pacific imperial rival.

Both the event and remembrance of Pearl Harbor offer a revealing context for thinking about U.S. imperialism. Pearl Harbor has a mythic presence in our civic culture. Every December 7, an air of patriotic solemnity enters the national consciousness and the "cost of liberty" is collectively remembered. What never gets discussed, however, is why there was any U.S.

military base in Hawai'i in the first place, why Japan roughly simultaneously attacked a U.S. military base in the Philippines, and why Japan claimed to be doing all this in the name of liberating Asia. The questions have their answer in the fact that Japan was extending its empire by attacking two of the most important Pacific military outposts of a rival empire. What never gets discussed on December 7 is the fault of *both* the United States and Japan, and the fraudulence of both of their claims as liberators. A military base was set up at Pearl Harbor only because, first, U.S. businessmen led a coup d'etat against Queen Liliuokalani of the Kingdom of Hawai'i and, second, the United States later annexed Hawai'i as a colony. And it was not until as late as 1959—eighteen years after Pearl Harbor—that Hawai'i was granted statehood.[83] Infamy, therefore, preceded December 7, 1941.

After World War II, America continued its imperial enterprise, and it took on a seething character as the Cold War escalated. Although missing from the U.S. education system for obvious reasons, an established scholarly record reveals that in the name of defeating communism, the United States supported dictators and the suppression of indigenous democracy movements in various parts of Asia (and elsewhere in the Third World), like the Philippines, Indonesia, South Korea, South Vietnam, Cambodia, Thailand, and Okinawa.[84] And, of course, the hot wars of the Cold War, the large ones in any case, were fought in Asia. Although not obvious, the Korean War admits of an imperialistic reading.[85] And with less controversy, the Vietnam War can be viewed as an imperialist war. One aspect of that war that reveals empire at work is the fact that various U.S. colonial and neocolonial satellites were pushed into a war that surely none of them would otherwise have been involved in: The neocolonial Philippines offered logistical support, and neocolonial South Korea and colonial Puerto Rico offered extensive military support with tragic consequences for all sides. Much has been said about the Vietnam War, and much continues to be said about it in America's twenty-first-century wars. So I leave the matter. But one of the obvious legacies of America's hegemonic, and often catastrophically violent, presence in modern Asia is the proliferation of military bases in Japan, South Korea, Okinawa, Guam, various Pacific Islands, and, for a long period of time, the Philippines. In this context, it is interesting to consider what the world and America would have been like if an enlarged China rimmed the California-Oregon-Washington coast with a similarly monolithic military presence, with spy planes hovering over the coast of San Francisco and Los Angeles, and tens of thousands of white women "servicing" Chinese soldiers on Chinese military bases in Hawai'i and the small islands nearby San Diego and San

Francisco. Clearly, world history would have to have been radically different. The inversion of this imagined scenario, America enlarged, however, is radically normalized to the point of being very nearly a nonissue for the civic culture of the United States.

The foregoing only touches upon American imperialism. But perhaps even this much conveys in a concrete fashion how Asian America is constituted in part by the westward movement of the U.S. nation-state.[86] And by considering how this enlarged America has overlapped geopolitically with East Asia for more than a century, we can also see in a general way how the U.S. participated in Asia's colonial modernity and, therefore, how Asian America is deeply linked to modern Asia.[87] Earlier, I noted that modern Asia should be conceived in terms of an Orientalist modernity and that this in turn be understood in terms of a colonial dialectic, a postcolonial dialectic, and a more recent complex set of transnational processes. Many imperial nations could be mentioned in accounts of these aspects of modern Asia. But, in light of the foregoing, no full account can leave out the United States in a consideration of any of these three respects.

One of the most important developments in the history of Asian America is a consciousness that tied together various elements of both the racial exclusions and the racial imperialism that constitute Asian America. More specifically, in the 1960s and 1970s, people of various Asian ethnic groups faced a horrendous war in Vietnam and contended with a system of racial oppression in the United States. And with the model afforded by the black liberation movement and the readings of various progressive or revolutionary leaders, particularly from the Third World, a unifying political consciousness arose among people of various Asian ethnic groups in America, generating the antiracist, anti–imperialist Asian American movement and the very title, "Asian American."[88] One participant, Glenn Omatsu, characterizes the efforts of the Asian American movement within the larger context in the following way:

> They were struggles that confronted historical forces of racism, poverty, war, and exploitation. They were struggles that generated new ideologies, based mainly on the teachings and actions of Third World leaders. And they were struggles that redefined human values—the values that shape how people live their daily lives and interact with each other. Above all, they were struggles that transformed the lives of "ordinary people." . . . For Asian Americans, these struggles profoundly changed our communities. They spawned numerous grassroots organizations. They created an extensive network of student organizations and Asian American Studies classes. They recovered buried cultural traditions as well as produced a new gen-

eration of writers, poets, and artists. But most importantly, the struggles deeply affected Asian American consciousness. They redefined racial and ethnic identity, promoted new ways of thinking about communities, and challenged prevailing notions of power and authority.[89]

Omatsu goes on to say that members of the movement read from Marx, Lenin, Mao, Fanon, Malcolm X, Che Guevara, Kim Il-Sung, W. E. B. Du Bois, Paulo Freire, the Black Panther Party, the Young Lords, and other resistance struggles, and that they engaged with such ideas as "Third World consciousness, participatory democracy, community building, historical rooting, liberation, and transformation."[90]

Clearly, the experiences and reflections of activists of the Asian American movement, like Omatsu, offer an important kind of paradigm for Asian American philosophy. As I have noted earlier, Asian American philosophy can be understood in part as an instance or species of modern Asian philosophy. As such, Asian American philosophy gathers thought, which may not always be explicitly philosophical, on the lived experiences of the relevant agents. The Asian American movement activists are one type of such agent. But, as I have discussed in this third section of the chapter, America has been an empire whose geopolitical dimensions far exceed the fifty states. So, though Asians in fifty-states America, like the activists, are obviously salient for Asian American philosophy's raw materials, as it were, so are those Asians who have been deeply affected by U.S. imperialism outside of the formal fifty states. In other words, on account of geopolitical expansion, Asian American philosophy is significantly different from, say, a hypothetical Asian Canadian or Asian Brazilian philosophy.

Imperialism changes the geographic scope and the moral status of an imperial nation's sovereignty without negating the empire's nationhood. So if one wishes to build a philosophy in part or whole around the idea of a nation, there is no reason in principle why this project could not continue with an imperial nation and adopt a correspondingly widened scope and a critical moral stance. Therefore, those Asians who reside in America enlarged are the subjects salient to Asian American philosophy. For ease, let us call Asians in America proper or in fifty-states America "Asian Americans" and Asians in America enlarged "Asian/Americans," where the slash or solidus symbol signifies inclusiveness and perhaps some indeterminacy with respect to the ideas that straddle it.[91]

Now, one might contend that Asian Americans are the *main* subjects of Asian American philosophy or, more plausibly, have *more* of a claim to this. After all, if both the existence of Asians in America proper and of America in Asia constitute Asian America, then wouldn't Asians in America proper, which is a part of America enlarged, have double the claim on being subjects of Asian American philosophy? I think this is a plausible line of thought. And, importantly, notice that it concedes the point I have been making and simply adds gradations of salience to the broadened conception of Asian America and Asian American philosophy. However, I think this "double claim" cannot be absolute. Ultimately, Asian American philosophy, in virtue of its links to modern Asian philosophy, has a liberatory stance: The geography matters primarily because the ethical relations do. So the "double claim" derives what force it has primarily, though not exclusively, from its ethical demand. And there is no reason in principle why the of the experiences or thought of Asian/Americans, say in the Philippines, Korea, or Okinawa, could not in certain cases or kinds of cases have a more compelling ethical salience than certain of the experiences or thought of Asian Americans, say in San Francisco or New York City. Therefore, Asian American experience and thought may have prima facie more salience for Asian American philosophy, but even then it is unclear just how strong that prima facie status is. In fact, certain kinds of Asian/American experience and thought, like those strongly pertaining to U.S. imperialism and other ethically charged conditions, may have an equal if not greater claim on Asian American philosophy. In any case, Asian/American experience and thought cannot be excluded simply on account of the absence of U.S. citizenship or absence from a physical location in America's fifty states. In fact, too much insistence on the special claim of Asian Americans on Asian American philosophy runs the risk of trivializing or obscuring the facts and moral import of America's dominative history in Asia. And this potentially represents a serious ethical problem, namely, Asian Americans obscuring and thereby aiding in the domination of Asians in Asia. The lure of a narrow Asian American nationalism that facilitates continued U.S. hegemony in Asia represents another and little discussed kind of model minority dynamic, where it is the Asian American empire-assimilationist, probably of the middle class, who stands over the Asian/American anti-imperialist.

As discussed in this third section, the lived experience of Asian Americans involves being racialized as Asian in the dominant, as opposed to subordinated, polity of an Amerasian empire. Some of the most explicitly self-conscious Asian Americans were, like Omatsu, involved in or impacted directly by the Asian American movement. And, as seen in Omatsu's compelling remarks, they reveal a striking sense of the moral unities of being an Asian in an imperialized Asia and being an Asian in an imperial America. Specifically, this was filtered through the prism of the Vietnam War: Through moral bonds of identification, these Asian Americans saw themselves mirrored in some fashion in the lives of Vietnamese peasants waging war against the United States. And the corresponding sense of identity and action was modeled to an extent by the moral protest and antiracist racial identity offered in the black liberation movement. And, as for Asian/Americans outside of fifty-states America, their lived experience has involved the colonial and postcolonial dialectics and the transnational conditions touched upon in the previous section of this chapter and partly elaborated in this third section.

Asian American philosophy, therefore, gathers all the kinds of experiences mentioned and many kinds of philosophically relevant reflection upon them.[92] At the ground level, Asian American philosophy can be expressed in treatments of a variety of issues that are shared with and have received a good deal of illumination from the interdisciplinary field of Asian American studies. But, to highlight some more explicitly philosophical work, consider the following possible themes and, where available, citations of directly relevant research: immigration, assimilation, citizenship,[93] imperialism,[94] war, democracy, neocolonialism, exploitation, labor, transnationalism, racism,[95] racial identity,[96] East-West comparison, the prospects of Asian American culture, exoticization,[97] intracolored and Third World solidarity or conflict, the complex heterogeneity of the Asian American community, global capitalism, modernity, indigeneity, gendered aspects of virtually every topic just listed, sex workers at U.S. military bases and mail order brides,[98] and surely still other themes. At a more metaphilosophical level, it could investigate such issues as how Asian American and Asian/American realities should be linked; how modern Asian philosophical thought, not just Euro-American philosophy, can illuminate Asian American philosophical issues; whether and how classical Asian philosophy might play a role in Asian American philosophical treatments; how Western thought has been influenced by classical or modern Asian philosophical work;[99] how Western thought has neglected or aided in the suppression of Asian American or modern Asian realities or reflections;[100] how Euro-American philosophy can contribute or be reconstructed to contribute to Asian American philosophy;[101] how modern Asian and Asian American thought intersects with other forms of non-Western or hybrid theoretical traditions;[102] how modern Asian and Asian American philosophy might be linked substantively with other forms of liberation thought;[103] the experience or disciplinary practice of Asians and Asian Americans in the philosophical profession;[104] the pedagogy of Asian American philosophy;[105] and surely still other issues.

As its name suggests, Asian American philosophy can also be seen as a kind of American philosophy. I have placed greater emphasis on modern Asian philosophy in situating Asian American philosophy because it highlights, against the obscuring tendencies of our civic culture, the ethical, geopolitical, and ideational intersuffusion of Asia and America in a more compelling way than does an approach that merely focuses on Asian American philosophy as a kind of American philosophy. Moreover, *at this juncture,* explaining Asian American philosophy by means of modern Asian philosophy seems to offer more clarity and robustness so far as I can tell. American philosophy has a general nation–geographic structure and is typically identified with transcendentalism and pragmatism, and sometimes partly with Anglo-American analytic philosophy. Due to the primarily descriptive nature of this structure, as opposed to the normative and liberatory one that characterizes modern Asian philosophy, I am unclear as to whether there is an especially compelling reason, which is not to say there is no reason, to think of Asian American philosophy mainly in terms of American philosophy. Of course, the critical normative impulse in modern Asian philosophy can be extended to the context at hand to fashion a kind of critical American philosophy. And this seems to have already been done in the case of, for example, African American philosophy. As I understand it, this philosophy is not simply a complex meditation on the African American condition, but this with the aim of contributing to the transformation of that very condition. Asian American philosophy, then, can be conceived along these lines as well. Although I have opted to explain Asian American philosophy through modern Asian philosophy, the critical Americanist strategy of explication is clearly an important project. Indeed, some elements of such an approach, reconfigured in certain ways, should be evident in the foregoing account. In any case, given the transpacific conditions that bridge Asia, the Pacific Islands, and America, modern Asia constitutes Asian America profoundly and concretely, even if not totally. And given the imperialist realities of Asian America, the same holds for Asian America constituting modern Asia. And so, even on a critical American characterization, modern Asian philosophy will still offer an important referent and much of Asian American philosophy will still offer a way of philosophizing in the mode of modern Asian philosophy.[106]

Conclusion

In the U.S. wars of the twenty-first century, it is a striking fact about our civic culture that the past wars in Asia have come to serve as hermeneutic devices. The attacks of 9-11 have been likened to Pearl Harbor. The wars in, and occupations of, Afghanistan and especially Iraq have been linked to the military and moral quagmire of Vietnam. The domestic and worldwide protest against these wars and occupations has been similarly analogized to the domestic and global dissent against the U.S. war in Vietnam. And finally the suppression of and backlash against Arabs, South Asians, and Muslims in the United States have been likened to the internment of Japanese Americans after Pearl Harbor.[107] Perhaps the specters of imperialisms past are haunting the United States in its more recent Eurasian/Middle Eastern incursions. If the foregoing account holds, however, such past dominion never fully ceased. It is not just ghosts but the living that demand our attention. And now the ethical call is being issued not only from Asia (and the Americas and Africa) but also from the Middle East.

It is illuminating to pair this set of retrospective hermeneutics with a premonition that issued from the era of the Vietnam War and the Asian American movement. Consider, here, the haunting words of Jean-Paul Sartre after he condemned U.S. genocide in Vietnam:

> [T]he links of the *One World*, this universe upon which the United States wishes to impose its hegemony, are ever closer. For this reason, of which the American government is well aware, the present act of genocide—as a reply to a people's war—is conceived and perpetuated in Vietnam not only against the Vietnamese but against humanity. When a peasant falls in his ricefield, mown down by a machine gun, we are all struck. In this way, the Vietnamese are fighting for all men, and the Americans against all men. Not in the figurative sense or the abstract. And not only because genocide in Vietnam would be a crime universally condemned by the law of nations. But because, gradually, the threat of genocide is extended to the whole human race, backed up by the threat of atomic warfare, i.e. the absolute point of total war, and because this crime, perpetrated every day before the eyes of all, makes all those who do not denounce it the accomplices of those who commit it. . . . In this sense, imperialist genocide can only become more radical—because the group aimed at, to be terrorized, *through the Vietnamese nation*, is the human group in its entirety. (italics his)[108]

I do not know how concretely Sartre may have anticipated U.S. expansion into the Middle East. And, arguably, he overstates his case when he says that the United States aims to specifically "terrorize," as opposed to control or dominate, all of humanity "through the Vietnamese nation." But it seems clear that from the moral lens of modern Asia and Asian America, he discerned at least the outlines of a global trajectory of American hegemony. Our civic culture, as it asks whether Iraq is another Vietnam, seems to barely apprehend what Sartre began to envision decades ago from Vietnam itself. In such a time as this, Asian American philosophy (and modern Asian philosophy) may have not simply an interest in but an ethical mandate to stand with threatened humanity.

Notes

1. See the excellent compilation of essays in Arif Dirlik, ed., *What Is in a Rim? Critical Perspectives on the Pacific Region Idea* (Boulder, CO: Westview Press, 1993), and in Rob Wilson and Arif Dirlik, eds., *Asia/Pacific as Space of Cultural Production* (Durham, NC: Duke University Press, 1995).

2. Perhaps one further example might be helpful. In the current publication scene, we regularly see updated works on Plato, Aristotle, Aquinas, Descartes, Locke, Hume, Kant, and others. We also see their positions applied to contemporary issues, like abortion (e.g., virtue ethics and abortion), liberal democracy (e.g., social contract theory and modern constitutions), feminism (e.g., Hume as an early semi-feminist), and so on. Given the way I am using the expression "classical Asian philosophy," I would here use the expression, "classical Greek philosophy," "classical European philosophy," or "classical Western philosophy" in a parallel fashion, and the qualifier "contemporary" to signify the recency of the work in question. Again, sufficient system retention is what concerns me.

3. Here is a sampling of this and related work. Enrique Dussel, *The Underside of Modernity: Apel, Ricoeur, Rorty, and Taylor and the Philosophy of Liberation*, trans. Eduardo Mendieta (Atlantic Highlands, NJ: Humanities Press, 1996); Anthony Appiah, *In My Father's House: Africa in the Philosophy of Culture* (New York: Oxford University Press, 1992); Ofelia Schutte, *Cultural Identity and Social Liberation in Latin American Thought* (Albany: State University of New York Press, 1993); Lucius Outlaw Jr., *On Race and Philosophy* (New York: Routledge, 1996); Lewis Gordon, *Existentia Africana: Understanding Africana Existential Thought* (New York: Routledge, 2000), and Lewis Gordon, ed., *Existence in Black: An Anthology of Black Existential Philosophy* (New York: Routledge, 1997); George Yancy, *African-American Philosophers, 17 Conversations* (New York: Routledge, 1998), and George Yancy, *What White Looks Like: African-American Philosophers on the Whiteness Question* (New York: Routledge, 2004); Charles Mills, *Blackness Visible: Essays on Philosophy and Race* (Ithaca, NY: Cornell University Press, 1997); P. H. Coetzee and A. P. J. Roux, eds., *The African Philosophy Reader* (New York: Routledge, 1998); Eduardo Mendieta, ed., *Latin American Philosophy* (Bloomington: University of Indiana Press, 1999), and "Is There a Latin American Philosophy," *Philosophy Today*, SPEP Supplement, vol. 43 (1999): 50–61; Jorge Gracia, *Hispanic/Latino Identity: A Philo-*

sophical Perspective (Oxford: Blackwell, 2000); Walter Mignolo, *Local Histories/ Global Designs: Coloniality, Subaltern Knowledges, and Border Thinking* (Princeton: Princeton University Press, 2000); Scott Pratt, *Native Pragmatism: Rethinking the Roots of American Philosophy* (Bloomington: University of Indiana Press, 2002); Anne Waters, ed., *American Indian Thought: Philosophical Essays* (Malden, MA: Blackwell, 2004); Yoko Arisaka, "Asian Women: Invisibility, Locations, and Claims to Philosophy," In *Women of Color and Philosophy*, ed. Naomi Zack (New York: Blackwell, 2000); Gary Mar, "Re-Orienting Philosophy," *American Philosophical Association Newsletter on Asian and Asian American Philosophers and Philosophies* 2, no. 2 (Spring 2003): 27–30; Nelson Maldonado-Torres, "The Topology of Being and the Geopolitics of Knowledge," *City: Analysis of Urban Trends, Culture, Theory, Policy, Action* 8, no.1 (April 2004): 29–56; Elizabeth Kassab, "Integrating Modern Arab Thought in Postcolonial Philosophies of Culture," *American Philosophical Association Newsletter* 4, no.1 (Fall 2005): 2–7.

4. See Mendieta, "Is There Latin American Philosophy?" and Enrique Dussel, "Philosophy in 20th-century Latin America," in Mendieta, ed., *Latin American Philosophy*.

5. This does not necessarily mean that all East-West scholars endorsed this Hegelian outlook. Again, the critical evaluation concerns overall institutional structure. Though, let me add that all such scholars may still have some responsibility for helping to rectify the situation.

6. Edward Said, *Orientalism* (New York: Vintage, 1978). And for some important emendations, applications, or criticisms of his account, see James Clifford, *The Predicament of Culture: Twentieth-Century Ethnography, Literature, and Art* (Cambridge: Harvard University Press, 1988); Lisa Lowe, *Critical Terrains: French and British Orientalisms* (Ithaca, NY: Cornell University Press, 1991); Aijaz Ahmad, *In Theory: Classes, Nations, Literatures* (New York: Verso, 1992); J. J. Clarke, *Oriental Enlightenment: The Encounter between Asian and Western Thought* (New York: Routledge, 1997); and Richard King, *Orientalism and Religion: Post-Colonial Theory, India, and the Mystic "East"* (London: Routledge, 1999).

7. There is an important implication of moving to a focus on patterns and tendencies without holding a stronger Saidian thesis. Many contend that while Said correctly points to a tradition of anti-Asian Orientalism, he goes too far and fails to acknowledge unproblematic exceptions to his claim. I think these kinds of accounts sometimes misconceive the Foucauldian-Gramscian structure of Said's account. But, more fundamentally, they forget that, by its very nature, the highlighting of exceptions does not unseat a claim to patterns and tendencies, since exceptions are *compatible* with them. Incidentally, I think such accounts often do not delve very deeply into how pro-Asian theorists from the West can nevertheless present accounts that are discursively managerial. There is no contradiction in positively cast discursive containment.

8. See, for example, Xiaomei Chen, *Occidentalism: A Theory of Counter-Discourse in Post-Mao China* (New York: Oxford University Press, 1995); Arif Dirlik, *The*

Postcolonial Aura: Third World Criticism in an Age of Global Capitalism (Boulder, CO: Westview Press, 1997); and Shu-Mei Shih, *The Lure of the Modern: Writing Modernism in Semicolonial China, 1917–1937* (Berkeley: University of California Press, 2001).

9. The history of Western imperialism in Asia has a wider temporal stretch than the present focus. For example, following Magellan's sixteenth-century "discovery" of the Philippines, the Spanish empire colonized the Philippines and Guam. And in the eighteenth century, the British colonized South Asia. Moreover, various Pacific islands were colonized before the late nineteenth century. Bearing this in mind, much of the emphasis here will be on the mid-to-late nineteenth century onward.

10. See Yen Le Espiritu, *Asian American Women and Men* (Thousand Oaks, CA: Sage Press, 1996).

11. See the introduction and some of the essays in Masao Miyoshi and Harry Harootunian, eds., *Learning Places: The Afterlives of Area Studies* (Durham, NC: Duke University Press, 2002).

12. Of course, many now doubt whether that distinction is clear or defensible.

13. For a sampling of readings on various Asian responses to Western imperialism and modernity, see Wm. Theodore de Bary, Wing-Tsit Chan, and Burton Watson, eds., *Sourcebook of Chinese Tradition*, vol. 2 (New York: Columbia University Press, 1964); Wm. Theodore de Bary, ed., *Sourcebook of Indian Tradition*, vol. 2 (New York: Columbia University Press, 1958); Ryusaku Tsunoda, Wm. Theodore de Bary, and Donald Keene, eds., *Sourcebook of Japanese Tradition*, vol. 2 (New York: Columbia University Press, 1961); and Yongho Ch'oe, Peter Lee, and Wm. Theodore de Bary, eds., *Sourcebook of Korean Tradition*, vol. 2 (New York: Columbia University Press, 2000).

14. Perhaps the May 4th intellectual, Hu Shih, comes close. Incidentally, he was influenced by Dewey's pragmatism. See de Bary et al., *Sourcebook of Chinese Tradition*, vol. 2, ch. 24.

15. See, for example, the debate by Korean neo-Confucianists over "Western implements," in Ch'oe et al., *Sources of Korean Tradition*, vol. 2, ch. 29.

16. See his *Autobiography of Fukuzawa Yukichi*, trans. Eiichi Kiyooka (Tokyo: Hokuseido Press, 1960).

17. Interestingly, in this case, Western modernity and Asia's alternative modernity were conceived to be integrally unified in a single world trajectory. For a sampling of the writings of the Kyoto School, see David A. Dilworth and Valdo H. Viglielmo with Agustin J. Zavala, eds. and trans., *Sourcebook for Modern Japanese Philosophy: Selected Documents* (Westport, CT: Greenwood Press, 1998). And for commentary or context, see James W. Heisig, *Philosophers of Nothingness: An Essay on the Kyoto School* (Honolulu: University of Hawai'i Press, 2001); James Heisig and John C. Maraldo, eds., *Rude Awakenings: Zen, the Kyoto School, and the Question of Nationalism* (Honolulu: University of Hawai'i Press, 1995); Stephan Tanaka, *Japan's Orient: Rendering Pasts into History* (Berkeley: University of California Press, 1993);

Harry Harootunian, *Overcome by Modernity: History, Culture, and Community in Interwar Japan* (Princeton: Princeton University Press, 2000); and Yoko Arisaka, "The Nishida Enigma: 'The Principle of the New World Order' (1943)," *Monumenta Nipponica* 51, no. 1 (1996), and "Beyond 'East and West': Nishida's Universalism and Postcolonial Critique," *Review of Politics* 59, no. 3 (Summer 1997): 541–60.

18. See Sun Yat-Sen, *San Min Chu I: The Three Principles of the People*, 2nd ed. (Taipei, Taiwan: China Publishing, 1990), and *China and Japan: Natural Friends— Unnatural Enemies: A Guide for China's Foreign Policy* (Shanghai: China United Press, 1941).

19. Marxism in Asia is a much discussed topic. See, for example, Hélène Carrère d'Encausse and Stuart Schram, *Marxism in Asia* (London: Penguin, 1969); and Tani Barlow, ed., *New Asian Marxisms* (Durham, NC: Duke University Press, 2002). For more on anarchism in Asia, see Arif Dirlik, *Anarchism in the Chinese Revolution* (Berkeley: University of California Press, 1993); and Benedict Anderson, *Under Three Flags: Anarchism and the Anti-Colonial Imagination* (New York: Verso, 2006).

20. See Mao Tse-Tung, *Mao Tse-Tung: Selected Works*, vols. 1–5 (New York: International Publishers, 1954, 1956); and Arif Dirlik, Paul Healy, and Nick Knight, eds., *Critical Perspectives on Mao Zedong's Thought* (Atlantic Highlands, NJ: Humanity Press, 1997). And I am indebted here to some illuminating discussions with Chris Connery on Maoism and what he calls the "World '60s."

21. For a sampling of his work, see Sibnarayan Ray, ed., *Selected Works of M. N. Roy*, vols. 1–4 (Oxford: Oxford University Press, 1987–2000).

22. For some sophisticated treatments of this theme in the early twentieth-century Chinese context, see Rebecca Karl, *Staging the World: Chinese Nationalism at the Turn of the Twentieth Century* (Durham, NC: Duke University Press, 2002); Shu-Mei Shih, *The Lure of the Modern*; and Chow Tse-Tsung, *The May 4th Movement: Intellectual Revolution in Modern China* (Cambridge: Harvard University Press, 1960).

23. For example, in the first couple decades of the twentieth century, Liang Qichao, a central political thinker in pre-Republic China, both shifted the focus from a cultural to a nation-based conception of China and the West, and endorsed a modernization historical trajectory of the world that deflated the pretensions of the West's historical self-understanding. Arguably, some of his views resonated with and may have partly paved the way for the more radical views of Li Dazhao, one of the founders of Chinese Marxism, and later Mao Zedong, both proponents of the third alternative modernity project. For more on Liang Qichao's important views, see Joseph R. Levenson, *Liang Ch'i-Ch'ao and the Mind of Modern China* (Berkeley: University of California Press, 1953); and Yang Xiao, "Liang Qichao's Political and Social Philosophy," in *Contemporary Chinese Philosophy*, ed. Chung-Ying Cheng and Nicholas Bunnin (Malden, MA: Blackwell, 2002).

24. For simplicity, I have left aside a complicating factor, namely that colonial modernity in much of Asia was sometimes layered with Japanese imperialism set

atop Western imperialism. This is pertinent here because many East Asians received Western training from Japan, read Western works through Japanese translations, or sought refuge in Japan when their viewpoints were formally denounced by their homeland governments. Stephan Tanaka's *Japan's Orient* offers a historical account of much of this complexity. And an account of early twentieth-century Chinese intellectuals facing this situation can be found in Shu-Mei Shi, *The Lure of the Modern*.

25. Lucius Outlaw Jr., *On Race and Philosophy* (New York: Routledge, 1996), 86.

26. See Bill Mullen and Cathryn Watson, eds., *W. E. B. DuBois on Asia: Crossing the Color Line* (Jackson: University of Mississippi, 2005).

27. Richard Wright, *The Color Curtain: A Report on the Bandung Conference* (Jackson: University of Mississippi Press, 1994); and Christopher J. Lee, ed., *Bandung and Beyond* (Athens: Ohio University Press, forthcoming).

28. José Rizal, *Noli Me Tangere,* trans. Ma. Soledad Lacson-Locsin (Honolulu: University of Hawai'i Press, 1997); Ambeth Ocampo, *Rizal without the Overcoat* (Pasig City, Philippines: Anvil, 2000); and Anderson, *Under Three Flags.*

29. Carlos Bulosan, *America Is in the Heart* (Seattle: University of Washington Press, 1974); and Susan Evangelista, ed., *Carlos Bulosan and His Poetry: A Biography and Anthology* (Seattle: University of Washington Press, 1985).

30. José Sisson, *The Philippine Revolution: The Leader's View* (New York: Taylor and Francis, 1989).

31. See Chow Tse-Tsung, *The May 4th Movement*; Shu-Mei Shih, *The Lure of the Modern*; and Karl, *Staging the World.*

32. "Kang Youwei and the Reform Movement," in de Bary et al., *Sources of Chinese Tradition*, vol. 2, 60–73; Hsiao Kung-Ch'uan, *A Modern China and a New World: K'ang Yu-wei, Reformer and Utopian, 1858–1927* (Seattle: University of Washington Press: 1975).

33. Liang Qichao, *History of Chinese Political Thought during the Early Tsin Period,* trans. L. T. Chen (New York: Harcourt, Brace & Co., 1930), and "A People Made Anew," in Wm. Theodore de Bary et al., *Sources of Chinese Tradition,* vol. 2, 93–97; Joseph Levenson, *Liang Ch'i-Ch'ao and the Mind of Modern China*; and Yang Xiao, "Liang Qichao's Political and Social Philosophy," in Chung-Ying Cheng, ed., *Contemporary Chinese Philosophy.*

34. Homer A. Jack, ed., *The Gandhi Reader: A Sourcebook of his Life and Writings* (New York: Grove Press, 1956); J. N. Mohanty, *Essays on Indian Philosophy Traditional and Modern,* ed. Purushottama Bilimoria (Delhi, India: Oxford University Press, 1993); and Harold Coward, ed., *Indian Critiques of Gandhi* (Albany: State University of New York Press, 2003).

35. Peter Heehs, ed., *The Essential Writings of Sri Aurobindo* (New York: Oxford University Press, 1998).

36. Krishna Dutta and Andrew Robinson, eds., *Rabindranath Tagore: An Anthology* (New York: St. Martin's Press, 1999).

37. Ashis Nandy, *The Intimate Enemy: Loss and Recovery of Self under Colonialism* (New York: Oxford University Press, 1988).

38. Mao Tse-Tung, *Mao Tse-Tung: Selected Works,* vol. 1–5; Dirlik, et al., eds., *Critical Perspectives on Mao Zedong's Thought*; and Bill Martin, "Still Maoist after All These Years," in Bill Martin, *Politics in the Impasse: Explorations in Postsecular Social Theory* (Albany: State University of New York Press, 1996).

39. Many have regarded important members of the Kyoto School as complicit in some fashion or other with Japanese imperialism. Since, very shortly, I will emphasize the liberatory aspect of modern Asian philosophy, it may seem odd that I mention the Kyoto School here. I do so simply because ascertaining their complicity or innocence is an interestingly relevant issue and an important debate in the field. And even if they were in whole or part imperialist, we can still ask whether their accounts retain elements of philosophical and liberatory value. For a wide sampling of the work of the Kyoto School, see Dilworth, et al., eds. and trans., *Sourcebook for Modern Japanese Philosophy*.

40. Tran Duc Thao, *Phenomenology and Dialectical Materialism*, trans. Daniel J. Herman and Donald V. Morano (Boston: D. Reidel, 1986); and Shawn McHale, "Vietnamese Marxism, Dissent, and the Politics of Postcolonial Memory: Tran Duc Thao, 1946–1993," *Journal of Asian Studies* 61, no. 1 (February 2002): 7–31.

41. Ray, ed., *Selected Works of M. N. Roy*, vols. 1–4.

42. Lu Xun, *Silent China: Selected Writings of Lu Xun*, ed. and trans. Gladys Yang (New York: Oxford University Press, 1973); and Leo Ou-Fan Lee, *Voices from the Iron House: A Study of Lu Xun* (Bloomington: Indiana University Press, 1987).

43. Kenzaburo Oe, *Hiroshima Notes* (Tokyo, Japan: YMCA Press, 1981).

44. Ch'oe et al., eds., *Sources of Korean Tradition,* vol. 2, ch. 30; Jong-Sun Noh, *Religion and Just Revolution: Third World Perspective* (Seoul, Korea: Voice Publishing House, 1987); and Hee-Sung Keel, "Haewol's Ethics of Threefold Reverence and Its Significance for Environmental Ethics Today," unpublished ms. I am grateful to Hee-Sung Keel for illuminating discussions about the sources and possibilities of twentieth century Korean thought, and for that matter, East-West thought more generally.

45. Yong-Bok Kim, "Messiah and Minjung: Discerning Messianic Politics over against Political Messianism," in *Third World Liberation Theologies: A Reader*, ed. Deane W. Ferm (Maryknoll, NY: Orbis Books, 1986), ch. 33.

46. Kim Chi Ha, *The Gold-Crowned Jesus and Other Writings,* ed. Chong Sun Kim and Shelly Killen (Maryknoll, NY: Orbis Books, 1978).

47. Gayatri Spivak, *The Post-Colonial Critic: Interviews, Strategies, Dialogues*, ed. Sarah Harasym (New York: Routledge, 1990).

48. Dipesh Chakrabarty, *Provincializing Europe: Postcolonial Thought and Historical Difference* (Princeton: Princeton University Press, 2000).

49. Trinh Minh Ha, *Woman, Native, Other: Writing Postcoloniality and Feminism* (Bloomington: Indiana University Press, 1989).

50. Uma Narayan, *Dislocating Cultures: Identities, Traditions, and Third World Feminism* (New York: Routledge, 1997).

51. Neferti X. M. Tadiar, *Fantasy-Production: Sexual Economies and Other Philippine Consequences for the New World Order* (Hong Kong: Hong Kong University Press, 2004).

52. Said, *Orientalism*.

53. Dirlik, *The Postcolonial Aura*.

54. Lisa Lowe, *Immigrant Acts: On Asian American Cultural Politics* (Durham, NC: Duke University Press, 1996).

55. Gary Okihiro, *Margins and Mainstreams: Asians in American History and Culture* (Seattle: University of Washington Press, 1994).

56. E. San Juan Jr., *Racism and Cultural Studies: Critiques of Multicultural Ideology and the Politics of Difference* (Durham, NC: Duke University Press, 2002).

57. David Palumbo-Lui, *Asian/American: Historical Crossings of a Racial Frontier* (Stanford: Stanford University Press, 1999).

58. Colleen Lye, *America's Asia: Racial Form and American Literature, 1893–1945* (Princeton: Princeton University Press, 2005).

59. Bill Mullen, *Afro-Orientalism* (Minneapolis: University of Minnesota Press, 2004).

60. I think a case could be made for modern Asian philosophy that is more descriptively based. However, the critical and liberatory orientation here seems to make the case more plausibly since it gets at the normative relations that ultimately undergird our ostensibly geographic categories in this context.

61. Much of this immediate discussion concerns political economy, neocolonialism, political epistemology, and reparations for imperialism. I think all of these topics can in some form be accommodated by the conceptual architecture of liberalism. For some examples, see practically any of the political texts of Noam Chomsky, like *Reasons of State* (New York: New Press, 2003); Charles Mills, *The Racial Contract* (Ithaca, NY: Cornell University Press, 1997), and *Blackness Visible*; and my "Empire's Entrails and the Geography of 'Amerasia,'" *City: Analysis of Urban Trends, Culture, Theory, Policy, Action* 8, no. 1 (April 2004): 57–88. Consider also the references to world-systems theory and underdevelopment theory in the political liberalism of Allen Buchanan's "Rawls's Law of Peoples: Rules for a Vanished Westphalian World," *Ethics* 110 (July 2000): 697–721.

62. I think this overall characterization resonates with much of the spirit of the formative discipline-cohering agendas posited by Outlaw for Africana philosophy: "the effort to forge and articulate new identities and life agendas by which to survive and to flourish in the limiting situations of racialized oppression and New World relocations" and "the effort to recover or reconstruct life-defining, identity-confirming meaning-connections to lands and cultures of the African continent, its peoples, and their histories." See Outlaw, *On Race and Philosophy*, 89.

63. Wing-Tsit Chan, ed. and trans., *A Sourcebook in Chinese Philosophy* (Princeton: Princeton University Press, 1963); Chung-Ying Cheng and Bunnin, eds., *Contemporary Chinese Philosophy*; Mohanty, *Essays on Indian Philosophy Traditional and Modern*; Dilworth, et al., eds., *Sourcebook for Modern Japanese Philosophy*; and

Korean National Commission for UNESCO, ed., *Korean Philosophy: Its Tradition and Modern Transformation* (Elizabeth, NJ: Holly Int'l, 2004).

64. Quite possibly, some of the authors or editors might balk at the overall characterization I have offered. Still, as I have noted, some elements of the characterization seem to recur throughout these works. I think a general concern that some may have—if not these authors and editors, then others, surely—is the extent to which I have politicized (though not reductively, I think) the history of philosophy. As it turns out, my view may be still more extreme for some. Though I have focused on the modern period, I am open in principle to accounts of *classical* Asian philosophies, like Hinduism, Buddhism, Confucianism, and Daoism, requiring reference to political elements. For example, as Thomas Wilson argues, the creation of Confucianist canons in twelfth-century China by their very nature excluded as they included material from the history of Confucianist thought. And this complicated process was both formal and linked to the interests of the sociopolitical elite. See his *Genealogy of the Way: The Construction and Uses of the Confucian Tradition in Late Imperial China* (Stanford: Stanford University Press, 1995).

65. Martha Nussbaum has extended a generally Western liberalism to the case of India, gender, and poverty. At the very least, her deeply considered views are strongly relevant to modern Asian philosophy. And, as I have described modern Asian philosophy just now, her account might be an instance of it. See Martha Nussbaum, *Women and Human Development: The Capabilities Approach* (New York: Cambridge University Press, 2000), and Martha Nussbaum and Jonathan Glover, eds., *Women, Culture, and Development: A Study of Human Capabilities* (New York: Oxford University Press, 1995).

66. See, for example, Robert Young, *Postcolonialism: A Historical Introduction* (Malden, MA: Blackwell, 2001).

67. There are other relevant movements—for instance, transatlantic Asian migration to the United States and northward migration from Latin America—following upon earlier transpacific and transatlantic movement from Asia. So the emphasis on transpacific movement to the United States is heuristic, and its value lies in its greater coverage of cases and its more familiar links to American modernity.

68. The two exceptions, which would later be denied that status, were Japan and the Philippines. A limited number of Japanese were allowed entry due to the U.S. government's efforts to relieve tension with a rival Asian imperial nation. And a limited number of Filipinos were allowed to immigrate due to their status as colonial subjects of the American empire.

69. For more on these formal measures, see Mae Ngai, *Impossible Subjects: Illegal Aliens and the Making of Modern America* (Princeton: Princeton University Press, 2004).

70. Robert Lee, *Orientals: Asian Americans in Popular Culture* (Philadelphia: Temple University Press, 1999).

71. Okihiro, *Margins and Mainstreams*, ch. 5.

72. Lye, *America's Asia*.

73. In this vein, I have also benefited from the work of Lowe, *Immigrant Acts*; and Palumbo-Lui, *Asian/American*.

74. A 2001 survey, conducted *prior* to the Hainan spy plane incident, on American views of Chinese Americans and to an extent Asian Americans reveals some rather serious lingering racist perceptions. In this survey, 68 percent of respondents stated some measure of dislike toward Chinese Americans, and within that group, 25 percent indicated having "very negative" attitudes toward them. Also, 24 percent of respondents disapproved of marriage with an Asian American, a percentage surpassed only by marriage with an African American (at 34%). Furthermore, respondents who oppose minority leadership were the most "uncomfortable" with the idea of an Asian American, over any other minority group representative, as president of the United States, CEO of a Fortune 500 company, or supervisor at work. These statistics are taken from *American Attitudes toward Chinese Americans and Asian Americans: A Committee of 100 Survey*, available at www.committee100.org.

75. It also suggests the need for an emendation in the concept of Americaneity proffered by Aníbal Quijano and Immanuel Wallerstein in "Americaneity as a Concept, or the Americas in the Modern World-System," *International Social Science Journal* 44, no. 134 (1992): 549–54.

76. For the small wars in Latin America, see Greg Grandin, *Empire's Workshop: Latin America, the United States, and the Rise of the New Imperialism* (New York: Metropolitan Books, 2006).

77. See Angelo Velasco Shaw and Luis Francia, eds., *Vestiges of War: The Philippine-American War and the Aftermath of an Imperial Dream, 1899–1999* (New York: New York University Press, 2002); John Dower, *War without Mercy: Race and Power in the Pacific War* (New York: Pantheon, 1986); Bruce Cumings, *North Korea: Another Country* (New York: New Press, 2004); Marilyn Young, *The Vietnam Wars, 1945–1990* (New York: Harper Perennial, 1991); Noam Chomsky, *At War with Asia: Essays on Indochina* (New York: Vintage Books, 1970); and Takashi Fujitani, Geoffrey White, and Lisa Yoneyama, eds., *Perilous Memories: The Asia-Pacific War(s)* (Durham, NC: Duke University Press, 2001).

78. See, for example, Claudia Card, *The Atrocity Paradigm: A Theory of Evil* (New York: Oxford University Press, 2002).

79. Shaw and Francia, eds., *Vestiges of War*; and Cumings, *North Korea*.

80. Dower, *War without Mercy*.

81. See Christine Barnett and Burke Marshall, eds., *Foreign in a Domestic Sense: Puerto Rico, American Expansion, and the Constitution* (Durham, NC: Duke University Press, 2001).

82. I discuss this at length in "Empire's Entrails."

83. Importantly, many indigenous Hawaiians would have preferred independence. And this is expressed in the current indigenous sovereignty movement in Hawai'i. See, for example, Haunani-Kay Trask, *Native Daughter: Colonialism and Sovereignty in Hawaii* (Honolulu: University of Hawai'i, 1999).

84. See, for example, Mark Selden, ed., *Remaking Asia: Essays on the Uses of American Power* (New York: Pantheon Books, 1974); Bruce Cumings, *Parallax Visions: Making Sense of American-East Asian Relations at the End of the Century* (Durham, NC: Duke University Press, 1999); and Chalmers Johnson, *Blowback: The Costs and Consequences of American Empire* (New York: Owl Books, 2004).

85. Some of the makings of such a case can be found in Cumings, *North Korea*. This is not the place to make this sort of argument. But let me note that the dividing line between North and South Korea was decided without any Korean involvement. This already should raise some suspicions. Let me also note that as with Pearl Harbor and the U.S. entry into World War II, both sides can be blameworthy. And this seems to hold for the Korean War as well, with both North Korea and the United States deserving blame, of different kinds of course.

86. A more complete discussion here would connect these thoughts with the sort of account offered by Aníbal Quijano in "Coloniality of Power, Eurocentrism, and Latin America," *Nepantla: Views from the South* 1, no. 3 (2000): 533–80. In a related vein, a fuller discussion would consider Asia-Latin American issues, like the nineteenth-century coolie bondage of Chinese, Indians, and others in various parts of Latin America. The topic of Asian coolies in Latin America, especially the Chinese in Cuba, is illuminatingly discussed by Lisa Yun, *The Coolie Speaks: Chinese Indentured Laborers and African Slaves in Cuba* (Philadelphia: Temple University Press, 2007).

87. In thinking this way, I am indebted to the work of David Palumbo-Liu and Colleen Lye, who make extended cases for this, with different sorts of emphases, in *Asian/American* and *America's Asia*, respectively. I am also indebted to the work of Walter Mignolo, whose account of border thinking offers a rough parallel in the case of Latino/Latin America. See his "The Larger Picture: Hispanics/Latinos (and Latino Studies) in the Colonial Horizon of Modernity," in *Hispanics/Latinos in the United States: Ethnicity, Race, and Rights*, ed. Jorge Gracia and Pablo De Greif (New York: Routledge, 2000). Finally, a special note of thanks to Linda Martín Alcoff and Eduardo Mendieta from whom I have benefited tremendously from the many conversations we have had on this and related issues of Latin America.

88. For more on this, see Yen Le Espiritu, *Asian American Panethnicity: Bridging Institutions and Identities* (Philadelphia: Temple University Press, 1992); and Helen Zia, *Asian American Dreams: The Emergence of an American People* (New York: Farrar, Straus, and Giroux, 2000). And for vignettes from the activists themselves, see Steve Louie and Glenn Omatsu, eds., *Asian Americans: The Movement and the Moment* (Los Angeles: UCLA Asian American Studies Center Press, 2001); and Fred Ho, with Carolyn Antonio, Diane Fujino, and Steve Yip, *Legacy to Liberation: Politics and Culture of Revolutionary Asian Pacific America* (San Francisco: Big Red Media, 2000).

89. Glenn Omatsu, "The 'Four Prisons' and the Movements of Liberation: Asian American Activism from the 1960s to the 1990s," in *The State of Asian*

America: Activism and Resistance in the 1990s, ed. Karin Aguilar-San Juan (Boston: South End Press, 1994), ch. 1, 20.

90. Omatsu, "The 'Four Prisons,'" 30.

91. The idea for using the solidus or slash comes from David Palumbo-Liu's *Asian/American*. See his book for a much fuller discussion of the possibilities of this linguistic convention.

92. For some related and interesting work on Asian American intellectual history, see Henry Yu, *Thinking Orientals: Migration, Contact, and Exoticism in Modern America* (New York: Oxford University Press, 2001); Augusto Espiritu, *Five Faces of Exile: The Nation and Filipino American Intellectuals* (Stanford: Stanford University Press, 2005); and Peter Chua, "U.S. Empire and Social Thought: Dewey, Mead, and the Philippine Problem," in a special edition of *Philosophy Today*, "Asian American and American Philosophy," ed. David H. Kim and Ronald Sundstrom, forthcoming.

93. Ronald Sundstrom, *The Browning of America and the Evasion of Social Justice* (Albany: State University of New York Press, forthcoming); and Falguni Sheth, "The Eclipse of Early Twentieth Century Asian Indian Immigration in American Racial and Postcolonial Discourses," in Kim and Sundstrom, eds., "Asian America and American Philosophy."

94. See my "Empire's Entrails."

95. Falguni Sheth, "The Technology of Race: Enframing, Violence, and Taming the Unruly," *Radical Philosophy Review* 7, no. 1 (2004).

96. See Ronald Sundstrom, "Falling into the Olongapo River," *American Philosophical Association Newsletter on Asian and Asian-American Philosophers and Philosophies* 2, no. 2 (Spring 2003): 25–27; Emily Lee, "The Meaning of the Visible Differences of the Body," *American Philosophical Association Newsletter on Asian and Asian-American Philosophers and Philosophies* 2, no. 2 (Spring 2003): 34–37, and "Ambivalence and Ambiguity," in Kim and Sundstrom, eds., "Asian America and American Philosophy"; Tommy Lott, "The Role of the Body in Asian-Pacific-American Panethnic Identity," *American Philosophical Association Newsletter on Asian and Asian-American Philosophers and Philosophies* 2, no. 2 (Spring 2003): 37–40; Janet Farrell Smith, "Multiplicity within Identity: Asian American Cultural Experience in the Plural," *American Philosophical Association Newsletter on Asian and Asian-American Philosophers and Philosophies* 4, no. 1 (Fall 2004); Linda Martín Alcoff, *Visible Identities: Race, Gender, and the Self* (New York: Oxford University Press, 2006).

97. Yoko Arisaka, "Exoticism and the Phenomenology of Racialized Desire," in David H. Kim, ed., *Passions of the Color Line* (Albany, NY: SUNY Press, forthcoming).

98. Lauri Shrage, *The Moral Dilemmas of Feminism* (New York: Routledge, 1994), ch. 5 and 6.

99. Clarke, *Oriental Enlightenment*; and Arthur Christy, *The Orient in American Transcendentalism: A Study of Emerson, Thoreau, and Alcott* (New York: Columbia University Press, 1932).

100. David H. Kim, "The Unexamined Frontier: Dewey, Pragmatism, and America Enlarged," in *Pragmatism, Nation, and Race: Community in the Age of Empire*, ed. Eduardo Mendieta and Chad Kautzer (Bloomington: Indiana University Press, forthcoming); and Chua, "U.S. Empire and Social Thought."

101. Mariana Ortega, "Homogeneity, Heterogeneity, and Self: William James and New Asian and Latina Voices in the 'U.S. American' Intellectual Landscape," in Kim and Sundstrom, eds., "Asian America and American Philosophy"; Kyoo Lee, "Buttery Flies: Marking Asian American Irony and Its Interstitial Edges with Derrida, Rorty, and West," in Kim and Sundstrom, eds., "Asian America and American Philosophy"; and Gary Mar, "Democratizing the Disciplines: Noam Chomsky and Asian American Studies," in Kim and Sundstrom, eds., "Asian America and American Philosophy."

102. Grace Lee Boggs, *Living for Change: An Autobiography* (Minneapolis: University of Minnesota Press, 1998); Ortega, "Homogeneity, Heterogeneity, and Self"; Lee, "Ambivalence and Ambiguity"; Kim, "Empire's Entrails."

103. Gary Mar, "What Does Asian American Studies Have to Do with Philosophy," *American Philosophical Association Newsletter on Asian and Asian-American Philosophers and Philosophies* 2, no. 2 (Spring 2003): 27–30.

104. Yoko Arisaka, "Asian Women: Invisibility, Locations, and Claims to Philosophy," in *Women of Color and Philosophy*, ed. Naomi Zack (New York: Blackwell, 2000); David H. Kim, "Asian American Philosophers: Absence, Politics, and Identity," *American Philosophical Association Newsletter on Asian and Asian-American Philosophers and Philosophies* 1, no. 2 (Spring 2002): 25–28; and Darrell Moore, "Edward Said and Asian American Philosophical Practice," unpublished ms.

105. Gary Mar, "New Media and New Pedagogy in Asian American Studies: Strategies for Transforming Knowledge into a Pedagogy of Empowerment," *American Philosophical Association Newsletter on Asian and Asian-American Philosophers and Philosophies* 3, no. 1 (Fall 2003): 19–32.

106. In writing this chapter, I have been indebted to the vision and generosity of the volume's editor, George Yancy.

107. For an interesting and important angle on this connection, see Gary Okihiro, "Safeguarding Democracy: Asian Americans and War," *American Philosophical Association Newsletter on Asian and Asian-American Philosophers and Philosophies* 2, no. 2 (Spring 2003): 24–25.

108. Jean Paul Sartre, "Vietnam: Imperialism and Genocide," in *Between Existentialism and Marxism* (New York: William Morrow, 1976), 83.

Bibliography

Ahmad, Aijaz. *In Theory: Classes, Nations, Literatures.* New York: Verso, 1992.

Anderson, Benedict. *Under Three Flags: Anarchism and the Anti-Colonial Imagination.* New York: Verso, 2006.

Arisaka, Yoko. "Asian Women: Invisibility, Locations, and Claims to Philosophy." In *Women of Color and Philosophy*, ed. Naomi Zack, ch. 9. New York: Blackwell, 2000.

———. "Beyond 'East and West': Nishida's Universalism and Postcolonial Critique." *Review of Politics* 59, no. 3 (Summer 1997): 541–60.

———. "Exoticism and the Phenomenology of Racialized Desire." In *Passions of the Color Line*, ed. David H. Kim. Albany: State University of New York Press, forthcoming.

———. "The Nishida Enigma: 'The Principle of the New World Order (1943).'" *Monumenta Nipponica* 51, no. 1 (1996).

Barlow, Tani, ed. *New Asian Marxisms*. Durham, NC: Duke University Press, 2002.

Barnett, Christine, and Burke Marshall, eds. *Foreign in a Domestic Sense: Puerto Rico, American Expansion, and the Constitution*. Durham, NC: Duke University Press, 2001.

Boggs, Grace Lee. *Living for Change: An Autobiography*. Minneapolis: University of Minnesota Press, 1998.

Bulosan, Carlos. *America Is in the Heart*. Seattle: University of Washington Press, 1974.

Card, Claudia. *The Atrocity Paradigm: A Theory of Evil*. New York: Oxford University Press, 2002.

Carrère d'Encausse, Hélène, and Stuart Schram. *Marxism in Asia*. London: Penguin, 1969.

Chakrabarty, Dipesh. *Provincializing Europe: Postcolonial Thought and Historical Difference*. Princeton: Princeton University Press, 2000.

Chan, Wing-Tsit, ed. and trans. *A Sourcebook in Chinese Philosophy*. Princeton: Princeton University Press, 1963.

Chen, Xiaomei. *Occidentalism: A Theory of Counter-Discourse in Post-Mao China*. New York: Oxford University Press, 1995.

Cheng, Chung-Ying, and Nicholas Bunnin, eds. *Contemporary Chinese Philosophy*. Malden, MA: Blackwell, 2002.

Ch'oe, Yongho, Peter Lee, and Wm. Theodore de Bary, eds. *Sourcebook of Korean Tradition*. Vol. 2. New York: Columbia University Press, 2000.

Chomsky, Noam. *At War with Asia: Essays on Indochina*. New York: Vintage Books, 1970.

———. *Reasons of State*. New York: New Press, 2003.

Chow Tse-Tsung. *The May 4th Movement: Intellectual Revolution in Modern China*. Cambridge: Harvard University Press, 1960.

Christy, Arthur. *The Orient in American Transcendentalism: A Study of Emerson, Thoreau, and Alcott*. New York: Columbia University Press, 1932.

Chua, Peter. "U.S. Empire and Social Thought: Dewey, Mead, and the Philippine Problem." *Philosophy Today*, special issue, "Asian America and American Philosophy," ed. David H. Kim and Ronald Sundstrom, forthcoming.

Clarke, J. J. *Oriental Enlightenment: The Encounter between Asian and Western Thought.* New York: Routledge, 1997.

Clifford, James. *The Predicament of Culture: Twentieth-Century Ethnography, Literature, and Art.* Cambridge: Harvard University Press, 1988.

Committee of 100. *American Attitudes toward Chinese Americans and Asian Americans: A Committee of 100 Survey.* www.committee100.org.

Coward, Harold, ed. *Indian Critiques of Gandhi.* Albany: State University of New York Press, 2003.

Cumings, Bruce. *North Korea: Another Country.* New York: New Press, 2004.

———. *Parallax Visions: Making Sense of American-East Asian Relations at the End of the Century.* Durham, NC: Duke University Press, 1999.

de Bary, Wm. Theodore, ed. *Sourcebook of Indian Tradition.* Vol. 2. New York: Columbia University Press, 1958.

de Bary, Wm. Theodore, Wing-Tsit Chan, and Burton Watson, eds. *Sourcebook of Chinese Tradition.* Vol. 2. New York: Columbia University Press, 1964.

Dilworth, David A., and Valdo H. Viglielmo with Agustin J. Zavala, eds. and trans. *Sourcebook for Modern Japanese Philosophy: Selected Documents.* Westport, CT: Greenwood Press, 1998.

Dirlik, Arif. *Anarchism in the Chinese Revolution.* Berkeley: University of California Press, 1993.

———. *The Postcolonial Aura: Third World Criticism in an Age of Global Capitalism.* Boulder, CO: Westview Press, 1997.

Dirlik, Arif, ed. *What Is in a Rim? Critical Perspectives on the Pacific Region Idea.* Boulder, CO: Westview Press, 1993.

Dirlik, Arif, Paul Healy, and Nick Knight, eds. *Critical Perspectives on Mao Zedong's Thought.* Atlantic Highlands, NJ: Humanity Press, 1997.

Dower, John. *War without Mercy: Race and Power in the Pacific War.* New York: Pantheon, 1986.

Dussel, Enrique. "Philosophy in 20th-Century Latin America." In *Latin American Philosophy,* ed. Eduardo Mendieta. Bloomington: University of Indiana Press, 1999.

———. *The Underside of Modernity: Apel, Ricoeur, Rorty, and Taylor and the Philosophy of Liberation.* Trans. Eduardo Mendieta. Atlantic Highlands, NJ: Humanities Press, 1996.

Dutta, Krishna, and Andrew Robinson, eds. *Rabindranath Tagore: An Anthology.* New York: St. Martin's Press, 1999.

Espiritu, Augusto. *Five Faces of Exile: The Nation and Filipino American Intellectuals.* Stanford: Stanford University Press, 2005.

Evangelista, Susan, ed. *Carlos Bulosan and His Poetry: A Biography and Anthology.* Seattle: University of Washington Press, 1985.

Fujitani, Takashi, Geoffrey White, and Lisa Yoneyama, eds. *Perilous Memories: The Asia-Pacific War(s).* Durham, NC: Duke University Press, 2001.

Fukuzawa Yukichi. *Autobiography of Fukuzawa Yukichi.* Trans. Eiichi Kiyooka. Tokyo: Hokuseido Press, 1960.

Gordon, Lewis. *Existentia Africana: Understanding Africana Existential Thought.* New York: Routledge, 2000.

Grandin, Greg. *Empire's Workshop: Latin America, the United States, and the Rise of the New Imperialism.* New York: Metropolitan Books, 2006.

Harootunian, Harry. *Overcome by Modernity: History, Culture, and Community in Interwar Japan.* Princeton: Princeton University Press, 2000.

Heehs, Peter, ed. *The Essential Writings of Sri Aurobindo.* New York: Oxford University Press, 1998.

Heisig, James. *Philosophers of Nothingness: An Essay on the Kyoto School.* Honolulu: University of Hawai'i Press, 2001.

Heisig, James, and John C. Maraldo, eds. *Rude Awakenings: Zen, the Kyoto School, and the Question of Nationalism.* Honolulu: University of Hawai'i Press, 1995.

Ho, Fred, with Carolyn Antonio, Diane Fujino, and Steve Yip. *Legacy to Liberation: Politics and Culture of Revolutionary Asian Pacific America.* San Francisco: Big Red Media, 2000.

Hsiao Kung-Ch'uan. *A Modern China and a New World: K'ang Yu-wei, Reformer and Utopian, 1858–1927.* Seattle: University of Washington Press, 1975.

Jack, Homer A., ed. *The Gandhi Reader: A Sourcebook of His Life and Writings.* New York: Grove Press, 1956.

Johnson, Chalmers. *Blowback: The Costs and Consequences of American Empire.* New York: Owl Books, 2004.

Kang Youwei. "Kang Youwei and the Reform Movement." In *Sourcebook of Chinese Tradition,* ed. Wm. Theodore de Bary, Wing-Tsit Chan, and Burton Watson, vol. 2, 60–73. New York: Columbia University Press, 1964.

Karl, Rebecca. *Staging the World: Chinese Nationalism at the Turn of the Twentieth Century.* Durham, NC: Duke University Press, 2002.

Kassab, Elizabeth. "Integrating Modern Arab Thought in Postcolonial Philosophies of Culture." *American Philosophical Association Newsletter* 4, no. 1 (Fall 2005): 2–7.

Keel, Hee-Sung. "Haewol's Ethics of Threefold Reverence and Its Significance for Environmental Ethics Today." Unpublished ms.

Kenzaburo, Oe. *Hiroshima Notes.* Trans. Toshio Yonezawa. Tokyo: YMCA Press, 1981.

Kim Chi Ha. *The Gold-Crowned Jesus and Other Writings.* Eds. Chong Sun Kim and Shelly Killen. Maryknoll, NY: Orbis Books, 1978.

Kim, David H. "Asian American Philosophers: Absence, Politics, and Identity." *APA Newsletter on Asian and Asian American Philosophers and Philosophies* 1, no. 2 (Spring 2002): 25–28.

———. "Empire's Entrails and the Geography of 'Amerasia,'" *City: Analysis of Urban Trends, Culture, Theory, Policy, Action* 8, no. 1 (April 2004): 57–88.

———. "The Unexamined Frontier: Dewey, Pragmatism, and America Enlarged." In *Pragmatism, Nation, and Race: Community in the Age of Empire,* ed. Eduardo

Mendieta and Chad Kautzer. Bloomington: Indiana University Press, forthcoming.

Kim, David H., and Ronald Sundstrom, eds. "Asian America and American Philosophy." Special edition of *Philosophy Today* (forthcoming).

Kim, Yong-Bok. "Messiah and Minjung: Discerning Messianic Politics over against Political Messianism." In *Third World Liberation Theologies: A Reader*, ed. Deane W. Ferm, ch. 33. Maryknoll, NY: Orbis Books, 1986.

King, Richard. *Orientalism and Religion: Post-Colonial Theory, India, and the Mystic "East."* London: Routledge, 1999.

Korean National Commission for UNESCO, ed. *Korean Philosophy: Its Tradition and Modern Transformation*. Elizabeth, NJ: Holly Int'l, 2004.

Le Espiritu, Yen. *Asian American Panethnicity: Bridging Institutions and Identities.* Philadelphia: Temple University Press, 1992.

———. *Asian American Women and Men*. Thousand Oaks, CA: Sage Press, 1996.

Lee, Christopher J., ed. *Bandung and Beyond*. Athens: Ohio University Press, forthcoming.

Lee, Emily. "Ambivalence and Ambiguity." *Philosophy Today*, special issue, "Asian America and American Philosophy," ed. David H. Kim and Ronald Sundstrom, forthcoming.

———. "The Meaning of the Visible Differences of the Body." *American Philosophical Association Newsletter on Asian and Asian-American Philosophers and Philosophies* 2, no. 2 (Spring 2003): 34–37.

Lee, Kyoo. "Buttery Flies: Marking Asian American Irony and Its Interstitial Edges with Derrida, Rorty, and West." *Philosophy Today*, special issue, "Asian America and American Philosophy," ed. David H. Kim and Ronald Sundstrom, forthcoming.

Lee, Leo Ou-Fan. *Voices from the Iron House: A Study of Lu Xun*. Bloomington: Indiana University Press, 1987.

Lee, Robert. *Orientals: Asian Americans in Popular Culture*. Philadelphia: Temple University Press, 1999.

Levenson, Joseph R. *Liang Ch'i-Ch'ao and the Mind of Modern China*. Berkeley: University of California Press, 1953.

Liang Qichao. *History of Chinese Political Thought during the Early Tsin Period*. Trans. L. T. Chen. New York: Harcourt, Brace & Co., 1930.

———. "A People Made Anew." In *Sourcebook of Chinese Tradition*, ed. Wm. Theodore de Bary, Wing-Tsit Chan, and Burton Watson, vol. 2, 93–97. New York: Columbia University Press, 1964.

Lott, Tommy. "The Role of the Body in Asian-Pacific-American Panethnic Identity." *American Philosophical Association Newsletter on Asian and Asian-American Philosophers and Philosophies* 2, no. 2 (Spring 2003): 37–40.

Louie, Steve, and Glenn Omatsu, eds. *Asian Americans: The Movement and the Moment*. Los Angeles: UCLA Asian American Studies Center Press, 2001.

Lowe, Lisa. *Critical Terrains: French and British Orientalisms*. Ithaca, NY: Cornell University Press, 1991.

———. *Immigrant Acts: On Asian American Cultural Politics.* Durham, NC: Duke University Press, 1996.

Lu Xun. *Silent China: Selected Writings of Lu Xun.* Ed. and trans. Gladys Yang. New York: Oxford University Press, 1973.

Lye, Colleen. *America's Asia: Racial Form and American Literature, 1893–1945.* Princeton: Princeton University Press, 2005.

Maldonado-Torres, Nelson. "The Topology of Being and the Geopolitics of Knowledge." *City: Analysis of Urban Trends, Culture, Theory, Policy, Action* 8, no. 1 (April 2004): 29–56.

Mao Zedong. *Mao Tse-Tung: Selected Works.* Vols. 1–5. New York: International Publishers, 1954, 1956.

Mar, Gary. "Democratizing the Disciplines: Noam Chomsky and Asian American Studies." *Philosophy Today,* special issue, "Asian America and American Philosophy," ed. David H. Kim and Ronald Sundstrom, forthcoming.

———. "New Media and New Pedagogy in Asian American Studies: Strategies for Transforming Knowledge into a Pedagogy of Empowerment." *American Philosophical Association Newsletter on Asian and Asian-American Philosophers and Philosophies* 3, no. 1 (Fall 2003): 19–32.

———. "What Does Asian American Studies Have to Do with Philosophy?" *American Philosophical Association Newsletter on Asian and Asian American Philosophers and Philosophies* 2, no. 2 (Spring 2003): 27–30.

Martín Alcoff, Linda. *Visible Identities: Race, Gender, and the Self.* New York: Oxford University Press, 2006.

Martin, Bill. "Still Maoist after All These Years." In *Politics in the Impasse: Explorations in Postsecular Social Theory,* by Bill Martin. Albany: State University of New York Press, 1996.

McHale, Shawn. "Vietnamese Marxism, Dissent, and the Politics of Postcolonial Memory: Tran Duc Thao, 1946–1993." *Journal of Asian Studies* 61, no. 1 (February 2002): 7–31.

Mendieta, Eduardo, ed. "Is There a Latin American Philosophy?" *Philosophy Today,* SPEP Supplement, 43 (1999): 50–61.

———. *Latin American Philosophy.* Bloomington: University of Indiana Press, 1999.

Mignolo, Walter. "The Larger Picture: Hispanics/Latinos (and Latino Studies) in the Colonial Horizon of Modernity." In *Hispanics/Latinos in the United States: Ethnicity, Race, and Rights,* ed. Jorge Gracia and Pablo De Greif. New York: Routledge, 2000.

———. *Local Histories/Global Designs: Coloniality, Subaltern Knowledges, and Border Thinking.* Princeton: Princeton University Press, 2000.

Mills, Charles. *Blackness Visible: Essays on Philosophy and Race.* Ithaca, NY: Cornell University Press, 1997.

Miyoshi, Masao, and Harry Harootunian, eds. *Learning Places: The Afterlives of Area Studies.* Durham, NC: Duke University Press, 2002.

Mohanty, J. N. *Essays on Indian Philosophy Traditional and Modern*. Ed. Purushottama Bilimoria. Delhi, India: Oxford University Press, 1993.

Moore, Darrell. "Edward Said and Asian American Philosophical Practice." Unpublished ms.

Mullin, Bill. *Afro-Orientalism*. Minneapolis: University of Minnesota Press, 2004.

Mullin, Bill, and Cathryn Watson, eds. *W. E. B. DuBois on Asia: Crossing the World Color Line*. Jackson: University of Mississippi, 2005.

Nandy, Ashis. *The Intimate Enemy: Loss and Recovery of Self under Colonialism*. New York: Oxford University Press, 1988.

Narayan, Uma. *Dislocating Cultures: Identities, Traditions, and Third World Feminism*. New York: Routledge, 1997.

Ngai, Mae. *Impossible Subjects: Illegal Aliens and the Making of Modern America*. Princeton: Princeton University Press, 2004.

Noh, Jong-Sun. *Religion and Just Revolution: Third World Perspective*. Seoul, Korea: Voice Publishing House, 1987.

Nussbaum, Martha. *Women and Human Development: The Capabilities Approach*. New York: Cambridge University Press, 2000.

Nussbaum, Martha, and Jonathan Glover, eds. *Women, Culture, and Development: A Study of Human Capabilities*. New York: Oxford University Press, 1995.

Ocampo, Ambeth. *Rizal without the Overcoat*. Pasig City, Philippines: Anvil, 2000.

Okihiro, Gary. *Margins and Mainstreams: Asians in American History and Culture*. Seattle: University of Washington Press, 1994.

———. "Safeguarding Democracy: Asian Americans and War." *American Philosophical Association Newsletter on Asian and Asian-American Philosophers and Philosophies* 2, no. 2 (Spring 2003): 24–25.

Omatsu, Glenn. "The 'Four Prisons' and the Movements of Liberation: Asian American Activism from the 1960s to the 1990s." In *The State of Asian America: Activism and Resistance in the 1990s*, ed. Karin Aguilar San Juan. Boston: South End Press, 1994.

Ortega, Mariana. "Homogeneity, Heterogeneity, and Self: William James and New Asian and Latina Voices in the 'U.S. American' Intellectual Landscape." *Philosophy Today*, special issue, "Asian America and American Philosophy," ed. David H. Kim and Ronald Sundstrom, forthcoming.

Outlaw, Lucius, Jr. *On Race and Philosophy*. New York: Routledge, 1996.

Palumbo-Liu, David. *Asian/American: Historical Crossings of a Racial Frontier*. Stanford: Stanford University Press, 1999.

Patterson, Orlando. *Slavery and Social Death: A Comparative Study*. Cambridge: Harvard University Press, 1982.

Quijano, Aníbal. "Coloniality of Power, Eurocentrism, and Latin America." *Nepantla: Views from the South* 1, no. 3 (2000): 533–80.

Quijano, Aníbal, and Immanuel Wallerstein. "Americaneity as a Concept, or the Americas in the Modern World-System." *International Social Science Journal* 44, no. 134 (1992): 549–59.

Rizal, José. *Noli Me Tangere*. Trans. Ma. Soledad Lacson-Locsin. Honolulu: University of Hawaii Press, 1997.

Ryusaku, Tsunoda, Wm. Theodore de Bary, and Donald Keene, eds. *Sourcebook of Japanese Tradition*. Vol. 2. New York: Columbia University Press, 1961.

Said, Edward. *Orientalism*. New York: Vintage, 1978.

San Juan, Epifanio, Jr. *Racism and Cultural Studies: Critiques of Multicultural Ideology and the Politics of Difference*. Durham, NC: Duke University Press, 2002.

Sartre, Jean Paul. "Vietnam: Imperialism and Genocide." In *Between Existentialism and Marxism*, by Jean Paul Sartre, 67–83. New York: William Morrow, 1976.

Selden, Mark, ed. *Remaking Asia: Essays on the Uses of American Power*. New York: Pantheon Books, 1974.

Sheth, Falguni. "The Eclipse of Early Twentieth Century Asian Indian Immigration in American Racial and Postcolonial Discourses." *Philosophy Today*, special issue, "Asian America and American Philosophy," ed. David H. Kim and Ronald Sundstrom, forthcoming.

———. "The Technology of Race: Enframing, Violence, and Taming the Unruly." *Radical Philosophy Review* 7, no. 1 (2004).

Shih, Shu-Mei. *The Lure of the Modern: Writing Modernism in Semicolonial China, 1917–1937*. Berkeley: University of California Press, 2001.

Shrage, Lauri. *Moral Dilemmas of Feminism*. New York: Routledge, 1994.

Sibnarayan, Ray, ed., *Selected Works of M. N. Roy*. Vol. 1–4. Oxford: Oxford University Press, 1987–2000.

Sisson, José. *The Philippine Revolution: The Leader's View*. New York: Taylor & Francis, 1989.

Smith, Janet Farrell. "Multiplicity within Identity: Asian American Cultural Experience in the Plural." *American Philosophical Association Newsletter on Asian and Asian-American Philosophers and Philosophies* 4, no. 1 (Fall 2004).

Spivak, Gayatri. *The Post-Colonial Critic: Interviews, Strategies, Dialogues*. Ed. Sarah Harasym. New York: Routledge, 1990.

Sun Yat-Sen. *China and Japan: Natural Friends—Unnatural Enemies: A Guide for China's Foreign Policy*. Shanghai: China United Press, 1941.

San Min Chu I: The Three Principles of the People. 2nd ed. Taipei, Taiwan: China Publishing Co., 1990.

Sundstrom, Ronald. *The Browning of America and the Evasion of Social Justice*. Albany: State University of New York Press, forthcoming.

———. "Falling into the Olangopo River." *APA Newsletter on Asian and Asian American Philosophers and Philosophies* 2, no. 2 (Spring 2003): 25–27.

Tadiar, Neferti X. M. *Fantasy-Production: Sexual Economies and Other Philippine Consequences for the New World Order*. Hong Kong: Hong Kong University Press, 2004.

Tanaka, Stephan. *Japan's Orient: Rendering Pasts into History*. Berkeley: University of California Press, 1993.

Tran Duc Thao. *Phenomenology and Dialectical Materialism*. Trans. Daniel J. Herman and Donald V. Morano. Boston: D. Reidel, 1986.

Trask, Haunani-Kay. *Native Daughter: Colonialism and Sovereignty in Hawaii*. Honolulu: University of Hawai'i, 1999.

Trinh Minh Ha. *Woman, Native, Other: Writing Postcoloniality and Feminism*. Bloomington: Indiana University Press, 1989.

Velasco Shaw, Angelo, and Luis Francia, eds. *Vestiges of War: The Philippine-American War and the Aftermath of an Imperial Dream, 1899–1999*. New York: New York University Press, 2002.

Wilson, Robert, and Arif Dirlik, eds. *Asia/Pacific as Space of Cultural Production*. Durham, NC: Duke University Press, 1995.

Wilson, Thomas. *Genealogy of the Way: The Construction and Uses of the Confucian Tradition in Late Imperial China*. Stanford: Stanford University Press, 1995.

Wright, Richard. *The Color Curtain: A Report on the Bandung Conference*. Jackson: University of Mississippi Press, 1994.

Yang Xiao. "Liang Qichao's Political and Social Philosophy." In *Contemporary Chinese Philosophy*, ed. Chung-Ying Cheng and Nicholas Bunnin.

Young, Marilyn. *The Vietnam Wars, 1945–1990*. New York: Harper Perennial, 1991.

Young, Robert. *Postcolonialism: A Historical Introduction*. Malden, MA: Blackwell, 2001.

Yu, Henry. *Thinking Orientals: Migration, Contact, and Exoticism in Modern America*. New York: Oxford University Press, 2001.

Yun, Lisa. *The Coolie Speaks: Chinese Indentured Laborers and African Slaves in Cuba*. Philadelphia: Temple University Press, 2007.

Zia, Helen. *Asian American Dreams: The Emergence of an American People*. New York: Farrar, Straus, and Giroux, 2000.

About the Contributors

Lewis R. Gordon is Laura H. Carnell Professor of Philosophy and director of the Institute for the Study of Race and Social Thought and the Center for Afro-Jewish Studies at Temple University. He also is president of the Caribbean Philosophical Association. He is the author and editor of many books, and most recently coeditor, with Jane Anna Gordon, of *Not Only the Master's Tools: African-American Studies in Theory and Practice* (Paradigm Publishers) and *A Companion to African-American Studies* (Blackwell Publishers).

Jorge J. E. Gracia holds the Samuel P. Capen Chair in Philosophy and is State University of New York Distinguished Professor. He has written more than a dozen books and two hundred articles and has edited more than two dozen books. Among the books he has authored are *Individuality: An Essay on the Foundations of Metaphysics* (1988, Findlay Prize 1992), *Philosophy and Its History: Issues in Philosophical Historiography* (1992), *A Theory of Textuality: The Logic and Epistemology* (1995), *Texts: Ontological Status, Identity, Author, Audience* (1996), *Metaphysics and Its Task: The Search for the Categorial Foundation of Knowledge* (1999), *Hispanic/Latino Identity: A Philosophical Approach* (2000), *How Can We Know What God Means? The Interpretation of Revelation* (2001), and *Old Wine in New Skins: The Role of Tradition in Communication, Knowledge, and Group Identity* (2003). He is the first philosopher in North America to publish an anthology of Latin American philosophy, the newest edition with Elizabeth Millan-Zaibert: *Latin American Philosophy for the Twenty-First Century* (2004). He works in metaphysics, hermeneutics, philosophical historiography, and the history of medieval and Hispanic philosophy. He is currently working on a book entitled *Surviving Race, Ethnicity, and Nationality: A Challenge for the Twenty-First Century*.

Randall Halle is Klaus W. Jonas Chair of German Film and Cultural Studies in the Department of Germanic Languages and Literatures at the University of Pittsburgh. He received his PhD in 1995 from the University of Wisconsin–Madison. In addition to numerous articles, Professor Halle is the coeditor with Sharon Willis of the double special issue of *Camera Obscura* on Marginality and Alterity in Contemporary European Cinema (nos. 44 and 46). He is author of *Queer Social Philosophy: Critical Readings from Kant to Adorno* (University of Illinois Press, 2004). His research interests include queer theory, social philosophy, cultural studies, film theory, critical theory, and transnational studies. He has received an NEH fellowship for study at the University of Chicago and a DAAD fellowship for study at Cornell University. For the academic year 2004–2005 he was a senior fellow in the Berlin Program for Advanced German and European Studies at the Free University.

Sarah Lucia Hoagland is professor of philosophy and women's studies at Northeastern Illinois University in Chicago. She specializes in lesbian philosophy. She is author of *Lesbian Ethics: Toward New Values*. This book's thesis is that the values from Anglo-European ethical philosophy undermine rather than promote lesbian connection. The book develops an ethics relevant to lesbians under oppression, one that avoids both blaming the victim and "victimism," embraces the spirit of lesbian resistance, and encourages plurality. She is also coeditor of *For Lesbians Only* with Julia Penelope, and *Re-reading the Canon: Feminist Interpretations of Mary Daly* with Marilyn Frye. Sarah is a collective member of the Institute of Lesbian Studies in Chicago, a staff member of the Escuela Popular Norteña, and a research associate of the Philosophy Interpretation and Culture Center, Binghamton University in Binghamton, New York.

David Haekwon Kim is associate professor of philosophy at the University of San Francisco. Previously, he was director of Asian American Studies at the University of San Francisco and chair of the American Philosophical Association Committee on the Status of Asian and Asian American Philosophers and Philosophies. His research and teaching interests include ethics, political philosophy, philosophical psychology, and non-Western or hybrid philosophies (e.g. African American philosophy, modern Asian philosophy, and Asian American philosophy). He is editor of *Passions of the Color Line* (SUNY, forthcoming), and coeditor (with Ronald Sundstrom) of a forthcoming special edition of *Philosophy Today* on

Asian America and American philosophy. His current work focuses on black and Asian conceptions of race and imperialism.

Lucius T. Outlaw Jr. is presently professor of philosophy, director of the African American Studies Program, and associate provost for undergraduate education at Vanderbilt University. Foci of undergraduate and graduate teaching include W. E. B. DuBois, Ralph Ellison, Alexis De Tocqueville, and matters of race in the founding and development of the United States of America. His areas of specialization are African philosophy, African American philosophy, continental philosophy (phenomenology and hermeneutics), and social and political philosophy. Recent publications include "On Courage and Democratic Pluralism," in Barbara Darling-Smith, ed., *Courage* (University of Notre Dame Press, 2002), and "'Afrocentricity': Critical Considerations," in Tommy Lott et al., eds., *Companion to African American Philosophy* (Blackwell Publishers, 2003). He is also the author of *On Philosophy and Race* (Routledge). He is presently working on *In Search of Critical Social Theory in the Interests of Black Folks* to be published by Rowman & Littlefield.

Nancy Tuana is the Dupont/Class of 1949 Professor of Philosophy and Women's Studies at The Pennsylvania State University and director of the Rock Ethics Institute. Her research and teaching specialties include feminist philosophy and feminist theory, with expertise in the areas of feminist philosophies of science and feminist epistemologies, feminist philosophy of history, and philosophy and sexuality. Her publications include *Engendering Rationalities* (SUNY Press), *Feminism and Science* (Indiana University Press), *The Less Noble Sex: Scientific, Religious, and Philosophical Conceptions of Woman's Nature* (Indiana University Press), *Revealing Male Bodies* (Indiana University Press), *Feminist Interpretations of Plato* (Penn State Press), and *Women and the History of Philosophy* (Paragon House). She is series editor of the Penn State Press series *Re-Reading the Canon*, and coeditor of the *Stanford Encyclopedia of Philosophy* entries on feminist philosophy.

Dale Turner, who teaches philosophy at Dartmouth College, is a Teme-Augama Anishnabai from Northern Ontario. His courses cover indigenous philosophy, contemporary Native American issues, and governmental issues. His PhD is in philosophy from McGill University and his area of study is political theory. Turner's community has been involved in a century-old land dispute with the provincial and federal governments, which has recently resulted in an unfavorable Supreme Court decision. This experience has led Turner to study philosophy in an attempt to better understand the meaning of "sovereignty," and especially the meaning of indigenous or "tribal" sovereignty, in both theory and practice. Turner's courses reflect the importance of asserting and protecting tribal sovereignty in Indian Country. At the same time, students are encouraged to develop their critical thinking skills, especially when thinking about contemporary Native American issues. His manuscript *This Is Not a Peace Pipe: Towards a Critical Indigenous Philosophy* is forthcoming with University of Toronto Press.

George Yancy teaches philosophy at Duquesne University. His articles and reviews have appeared in the *Journal of Speculative Philosophy, Review of Metaphysics, Journal of Social Philosophy, Philosophy and Social Criticism, Radical Philosophy Review, Hypatia: A Journal of Feminist Philosophy, Encyclopedia of Feminist Theories, Western Journal of Black Studies, AME Church Review, APA Newsletter on Feminism and Philosophy, CLA Journal, Black Arts Quarterly, Social Science Quarterly, Popular Music and Society*, and more. Yancy's book publications include *African-American Philosophers: 17 Conversations* (Routledge, 1998), which was named an Outstanding Academic Book by *Choice* for 1999, *Cornel West: A Critical Reader* (Blackwell Publishers, 2001), *The Philosophical i: Personal Reflections on Life in Philosophy* (Rowman & Littlefield, 2002), *What White Looks Like: African-American Philosophers on the Whiteness Question* (Routledge, 2004), *White on White/Black on Black* (Rowman & Littlefield, 2005), which was also named an Outstanding Academic Book by *Choice* for 2005, and *Narrative Identities: Psychologists Engaged in Self-Construction*, coedited with Susan Hadley (Jessica Kingsley Publishers, 2005). Yancy is the recipient of the McAnulty Fellowship (Duquesne University) and the prestigious McCracken Fellowship (New York University). He is coeditor of the *APA Newsletter on Philosophy and the Black Experience.*